Mastering

Shakespeare

04

04

05

Macmillan Master Series

Accounting
Advanced English Language
Advanced Pure Mathematics
Arabic
Banking
Basic Management
Biology
British Politics
Business Administration
Business Communication
Business Law
C Programming
C++ Programming
Catering Theory
Chemistry
COBOL Programming
Communication
Databases
Economic and Social History
Economics
Electrical Engineering
Electronic and Electrical Calculations
Electronics
English as a Foreign Language
English Grammar
English Language
English Literature
French
French 2
German
German 2
Global Information Systems

Human Biology
Internet
Italian
Italian 2
Java
Manufacturing
Marketing
Mathematics
Mathematics for Electrical
    and Electronic Engineering
Microsoft Office
Modern British History
Modern European History
Modern World History
Pascal and Delphi Programming
Philosophy
Photography
Physics
Psychology
Science
Shakespeare
Social Welfare
Sociology
Spanish
Spanish 2
Spreadsheets
Statistics
Study Skills
Visual Basic
World Religions

Macmillan Master Series
Series Standing Order ISBN 0–333–69343–4

You can receive future titles in this series as they are published by placing a standing order.
Please contact your bookseller or, in case of difficulty, write to us at the address below with
your name and address, the title of the series and the ISBN quoted above.

Customer Services Department, Macmillan Distribution Ltd
Houndmills, Basingstoke, Hampshire RG21 6XS, England

Mastering
Shakespeare

Richard Gill

Illustrations by Stephen Cranham

MACMILLAN

For Jane Clarkson

© Richard Gill 1998
Text illustrations © Stephen Cranham 1998

First published 1998 by
MACMILLAN PRESS LTD
Houndmills, Basingstoke, Hampshire RG21 6XS
and London
Companies and representatives throughout the world

ISBN 0–333–69873–8

A catalogue record for this book is available from the British Library.

This book is printed on paper suitable for recycling and made from
fully managed and sustained forest sources.

10   9   8   7   6   5   4   3   2   1
07 06 05 04 03 02 01 00 99 98

Typeset by EXPO Holdings, Malaysia

Printed and bound in Great Britain by
Biddles Ltd
Guildford and King's Lynn

Contents

Preface

I wonder if you've opened this book because you have to 'do' Shakespeare. Perhaps that makes you feel gloomy. If it does, rest assured you're not the only one. I've met many students who ask, with a frown: 'Do we have to do Shakespeare?'

Shakespeare's picked up a reputation for being irrelevant, old-fashioned, heavy, intellectual and establishment. Once you know the plays, these seem strange complaints. The more you read him, the more you see that he's writing about *your* life – its loves, hopes, problems and trials. We can see ourselves in Shakespeare. In one sense, he's old-fashioned, but we spend our lives coming to terms with people who aren't like us and we find that we've a lot in common. Just how much we've got in common with Shakespeare can be seen in the popularity of films. I recently heard a student say that *Romeo and Juliet* was the best film she'd ever seen.

A film such as that shows us that Shakespeare's work isn't heavy. It's wonderful art but it's not earnest and heavy. There's always something light, familiar, effortless and even chummy about this work. Certainly he makes you think, but this is because he shows us that living forces thoughts out of people.

I can understand why students don't like the establishment feel of Shakespeare. Because he's compulsory from the age of 14, he might feel like algebra. The only way to cope with this is to remember that the *plays* aren't establishment works; the comedies are all about how to outwit the older generation, and histories and tragedies show that kings are ordinary human beings.

But there's often another problem. A friend of mine was once teaching *The Tempest* to a lively group. He thought things were going swimmingly until one day three students approached him and said: 'We don't understand a word of what's going on in this play.'

If you have this feeling, you're not alone. When I did my A-levels I had the uneasy feeling that I might be misunderstanding whole sections. You won't be surprised to hear a teacher tell you that the best way to cope with this is: get to know the play. The more you get to know Shakespeare, the clearer he becomes. For a start, you can get the story clear. Of course, there's more to getting to know Shakespeare than this, but important points emerge in the moment by moment unfolding of the plot.

As you get to know the plot, you'll become familiar with the characters. In the early stages you'll have to keep reminding yourself who they are, what they want, what they've done and what they know. And remember, some characters are in disguise, so keep track of what the character knows and what the others think they know. If you're in doubt, mark your script 'D' for disguise.

Some people have problems with the words. In fact, once you've got used to him, the gist of what Shakespeare's saying comes easily. In long speeches, begin with the general sense, and piece together how they work out bit by bit. Always remember that what matters as far as meaning is concerned are the sentences, not the lines of verse. If individual words bother you, look them up in a critical edition. Some words have changed their meaning since Shakespeare's day. And remember, some bits still puzzle the experts!

We should always remember the positive things about our experience of Shakespeare.

- **He's memorable** My mother never claimed to like Shakespeare, but I can remember as a child her gripping account of seeing *The Merchant of Venice*. Her memory was of the excitement of the story and the drama of the play's main scene.

- **He's enjoyable** It's my experience that of all the works students study at A-level, Shakespeare is the author they most enjoy. Furthermore, examiner's reports frequently show that students do better on him than anyone else.

- **He's adaptable** You can perform him in all sorts of ways. I once heard a professor of English say she saw a production of *The Merchant of Venice* done by a Chinese company in Hong Kong. They played it as pure farce, and the audience loved it.

- **He's part of our world** There's a sense in which he's not so much an author as a whole way of thinking and feeling. It's not only the pithy phrases, scraps of speeches and characters that have become part of the language, it's the stories themselves: *Romeo and Juliet* as the tale of love in a divided society or *The Merchant of Venice* as the story of love and prejudice in a commercial world.

- **He's varied** He never quite does the same thing again. Although we talked about comedies, tragedies and histories, each play is a distinct world of characters, language, mood and atmosphere.

- **He's haunting** Shakespeare is a powerful presence in our imaginations. Recently, someone said to me that events in the royal family reminded her of Shakespeare's histories. One of the strange facts about being alive is that when we experience something important – a struggle for power, a disappointment, a new love – we often discover that Shakespeare has already been there. As another friend of mine once said: 'The trouble with dying is that one hasn't finished with Shakespeare.'

This book is designed to do two things: give you some lines of thought about the *kind* of plays he wrote and provide ideas on individual plays. If you look at the Index, you'll find that there are discussions of your set plays in the general sections and, occasionally, as part of the discussion of other plays. In the sections on individual plays I've dealt with them in the order in which they were probably written; the exception is in the sections on the Roman tragedies and the English histories, where the order is historical.

A note on the text I've tried to provide a textual location for all the quotations. I've used the *Oxford Shakespeare* (general editors: Stanley Wells and Gary Taylor), though the fact of resetting extracts means in some cases that the number of lines per extract in this book may differ from the Wells/Taylor edition lines cited. If you're using another edition, you may find that some references, particularly those to passages in prose, are slightly different.

Acknowledgements

I'd like to record my thanks to Julia Bullock and Suzannah Tipple for their help and advice in the writing of this book. I'm very grateful to Stephen Cranham for the vivid illustrations. I'm not sure how many ideas in this book are 'mine'. Probably not many. Working on Shakespeare has always been something I've done with other people, so I'm aware that there are a lot of people (teachers, pupils and friends) whom I should thank. To all those who've helped me in ways of which I'm now unaware, I extend my apologies. Those I do recall are: Joan Allen, John Atkins, Tania Benedictus, John Booth, the late Raymond Brett, Rachel Burkitt, Alan Caine, Rachel Card, Simon Carter, Fiona Chamberlain, Jane Clarkson, Professor Philip Collins, Richard Cooper, James Essinger, Emma Fawcett, Margaret Finch, John Florance, Richard Ford, Miriam Gill, Naomi Gill, Andor Gomme, Sue Gregory, Catherine Groves, David Hopkins, the late Arthur Humphreys, Monica Jones, Jenny Kinton, Tom McAlindon, Patricia Maclachlan, Nicholas Montague, Tony Moore, the late David Palmer, Adam Pokorny, Keith Povey, Roger Rees, Bernard Richards, Neil Roberts, David Roe, Ian Robinson, Marion Shaw, George Spaul, Michael Sweeney, Eric Swift, Jan Todd, David Towsey and Joan Ward.

RICHARD GILL

Part I
The World of Shakespeare

What's it all about?

1.1 Themes in Shakespeare

▶ **'what a question's that'** (*The Merchant of Venice*, 3.4.80)

Readers of Shakespeare often ask:

'What's it all about?'

One thing needs to be said about this question: it's not very carefully worded.

Shakespeare's plays aren't (and can't be reduced to) a set of 'messages'. If Shakespeare had wanted the point of, say, *Julius Caesar* to be – don't kill leaders, because somebody else will kill you – he could have scrawled it on London Bridge. He didn't do this; he wrote a play.

A play is not chiefly a way of getting ideas over. It does something else:

- **a play dramatises human situations**.

Through dramatisation things emerge which in the classroom we call:

- themes
- ideas
- issues
- preoccupations or
- concerns.

These emerge in such a way that they're not separable from the life of the drama; for instance, *Julius Caesar* is 'about' friendship, because on stage Brutus, kills his friend, Julius Caesar.

One of the things readers and audiences have to get used to is:

- **in Shakespeare's plays there are lots of themes**.

Shakespeare is our most imaginative writer; his language is rich, and his plays teem with ideas. For instance, *Julius Caesar* is, among other things, about the following:

- the fluctuation of popularity (The crowds that shout for Caesar once shouted for Pompey.)
- the danger of placing too much power in the hands of one man (The conspirators fear this will happen with Caesar.)

- the blurring of public and private motivation (Is Cassius against Caesar because he may become a tyrant or does he also envy him?)
- the difference between confidence and foolish pride (Caesar is warned about a plot but dismisses it.)
- the morality of taking drastic decisions because of what might happen in the future (Those who kill Caesar don't know that he'll be a tyrant.)
- the nature of honour and the danger that upright people face when their opponents are prepared to use any means to win.

In answer to the question 'what's it all about?', the best answer is: 'lots of things'.

1.2 Themes in individual plays

▶ 'so singular in each particular' (*The Winter's Tale*, 4.4.144)

Those themes from *Julius Caesar* might be called political. This isn't surprising: *Julius Caesar* is a play about power. Its story concerns people who think it's better to kill their friend than run the risk that he'll become a tyrant. Political stories produce political themes.

Stories generate the themes, so

- **themes depend upon the nature of the story.**

This means that:

- **each play has its own themes.**

This is what we should expect. If a theme is the importance of an action, then different actions are going to produce different themes.

We can see this in *King Lear*. The plot arises in part from Lear's very difficult relations with his children. Consequently, we think about such issues as:

- what it is to be a parent and a child
- the differences between children
- the duty children owe to parents
- the pains of ingratitude
- the folly of trusting those whom you don't understand
- the need for forgiveness.

Because each play is its own special world:

- **many of the themes in an individual play are related to each other.**

1.3 Shakespeare's main themes

▶ 'greater themes' (*Coriolanus*, 1.1.218)

Although each play has its themes, there are some that run through several like a thread woven into a piece of cloth. These common themes are often very broad. Here are some of them.

The contrast between appearance and reality

Drama emerges when characters are not what they seem. This is often the case in comedies, when a character's real identity is concealed by disguise. In *Twelfth Night*, the disguised Viola says: 'I am not that I play' (1.5.177).

Deception

Sometimes one character fails to understand another, because he or she has been deceived. In *The Taming of the Shrew*, Baptista is deceived by Lucentio and Hortensio, when he accepts them as teachers of his daughters.

Change

Some of the central moments in the plays are when characters change their minds. Brutus agrees to join the conspiracy; Coriolanus decides not to attack Rome; Macbeth decides to pursue the murder of Duncan. What we see is a world based on the idea that change is the stuff of life.

Knowing yourself

One of the most important changes is the one in which a character wakes up to something in him or herself, which was previously hidden. When he first sees Juliet, Romeo discovers that he wasn't really in love with Rosaline.

Human nature

Shakespeare's characters often reflect on what it is to be a human being. Sometimes they use the word 'nature', at other times they play on the word 'kind', meaning type, as in humankind, as well as considerate and helpful. Hamlet does this in his riddling conversation with Claudius: 'A little more than kin and less than kind' (1.2.65). Hamlet is hinting that what is 'kind' in the former sense is not 'kind' in the latter.

Belonging and not belonging

Shakespeare always shows us characters as members of groups; those we see on stage are brothers, sisters, daughters, sons, mothers, fathers, lords, servants, friends, kings and subjects. Because that's what people are like, it matters that we belong. Therefore divisions in families and nations, as in *King Lear* and *Hamlet* are often the topics of drama.

Losing and finding

One of the most important forms of not belonging is being lost. In Shakespeare there are a number of ways in which a character can be lost: the lovers in *A Midsummer Night's Dream* are physically, emotionally and, in so far as they fear for their sanity, mentally lost. Finding also comes in different forms: characters can find themselves through self-knowledge, discover a long-lost member of the family and come to see someone else in a better light.

Freedom

One of the questions that haunts a character in a dramatic crisis is the extent to which he or she is free to act or not to act. There's the uneasy feeling that the stars are what really govern us. Hence, as a part of his persuasion of Brutus, Cassius has to assert that the reason why things are as they are lies 'not in our stars/But in ourselves' (*Julius Caesar*, 1.2.141–2).

Death

In many plays the characters know that they are going to die. Even if a character doesn't realise this, the audience often does. King Lear claims at the beginning of the play that he is preparing for death, yet the audience sees that for much of the action he is wilful, inconsiderate, thoughtless and reckless – qualities which suggest that he's not someone trying to live out what is left to him in the certainty that he's mortal.

Renewal

As well as a sense of mortality, Shakespeare's characters often seek and find renewal. Renewal can be finding the lost (*The Winter's Tale*), marrying the right person (the comedies), restoring a broken relationship (*The Tempest*) or bringing peace after war (*Henry V*).

1.4 The themes of love and war

▶ 'double business' (*Hamlet*, 3.3.41)

But what about our original question:

- What's it all about?

The themes briefly outlined above are general. When we ask what something is about we often want a more specific answer. Are there themes of a more specific kind in Shakespeare?

Of course, this is a dangerous question. We might end up simplifying Shakespeare so much that nothing of his richness, breadth and variety remains. But there are two reasons why we should try:

(1) we won't be overwhelmed
(2) we'll have something to build on.

What answer, then, can be given? Shakespeare can be viewed as being about a 'double business':

- **love and war.**

This is a big but not a surprising claim. It's big because it says that many areas of Shakespeare can be illuminated by those two ideas. It's not surprising because almost from the very beginnings of civilisation love and war have been the themes of literature. The plot of Homer's *The Iliad* is how the love of Paris for Helen led to the Trojan war. Shakespeare (who wrote about the Trojan war in *Troilus and Cressida*) also sees these two mighty themes entwined in human affairs. Not every play is about love and war, but the feelings and ideas associated with them are present in very many of the plays. At this point a few facts might help.

The words 'love' and 'war'

Thirty-eight plays by (or in part by) Shakespeare have survived. The word 'love' appears in all of them. In some it's very frequent; here are some figures:

The Two Gentlemen of Verona	162
Romeo and Juliet	120—
As You Like It	104
A Midsummer Night's Dream	103
Much Ado About Nothing	89

That list, of course, doesn't include words that are grammatically related to 'love' such as 'loved', 'lover', 'lovest' and 'loving'.

There are fewer mentions of 'war' in Shakespeare, but they are, nevertheless, numerous. Of the 38 plays, it appears in 33 of them. But of the five plays in which it doesn't appear, one is *Romeo and Juliet*, a play based in a city in which the two leading families are virtually in a state of civil war, and another is *The Merchant of Venice*, which can be read as being about a religious and cultural war between Christians and Jews. Plays in which the word 'war' frequently appears are:

Coriolanus	40
Antony and Cleopatra	35
Henry V	30
King John	22
Troilus and Cressida	20

It would be a mistake to decide simply on the basis of those figures, that Shakespeare is three or four times more interested in love than he is in war!

It's clear that of the two love *is* the more important theme, but that's not something that can be simply established by counting words. Counting words is useful, but it overlooks the visual impact of the theatre. It's important to remember:

• **in the theatre war is very visible**.

Anyone who has seen productions of *Macbeth* will be aware of how many scenes there are with armed soldiers, often smeared in sticky stage blood. This is also the case with *King Lear*. Reading it in class, it's easy to overlook the fact that most of the second half of the play is set in a war, and that on stage we'd see uniforms, banners and weapons. The actual word is only mentioned four times in *King Lear* (and only four times in *Macbeth*, too!) yet the theatrical experience is of camps and battlefields.

War, in the shape of division and conflict, is found in Shakespeare in stories about divided cities (*Romeo and Juliet*), split families (*As You Like It*), friends who've turned cool (*Julius Caesar*), children who turn against parents (*King Lear*), tensions between classes (*Coriolanus*) as well as between factions within a nation (the *Henry IV* plays), within an empire (*Antony and Cleopatra*) and between nations (*Henry V*).

1.5 The best thing and the worst thing

▶ 'What is love?' (*Twelfth Night*, 2.3.46)

Shakespeare shows us what most people have always known:

- **love is the best thing and the worst thing that can happen to anybody**.

Love is usually the driving force behind the comedies but it's not confined to them. One of the painful things about the tragedies is that love is sometimes the cause of suffering. If Othello were not in love with Desdemona, there would be no tragedy. Love isn't always refreshing and renewing.

When then is it like to experience this overwhelming feeling?

1.6 Young love

▶ 'this man and maid' (*The Tempest*, 4.1.95)

Love in Shakespeare is usually between the young. The energy and drive of *Romeo and Juliet* is the joy, exuberance and passion of young love. It's pointless to complain that the characters are foolish. That's what love does to you. The schemes, dodges, bursts of fanciful poetry and even the fights are all expressions of how heady the passions of love are.

Young love can strike suddenly

It's up to the actor how he plays Romeo's first sight of Juliet. Since his first words express wonder, it's clear that something has happened to him. Whatever the actor does, it must be consistent with the words Shakespeare gives him:

> What lady's that which doth enrich the hand
> Of yonder knight?

> (1.5.41–2)

He doesn't know who she is, but he says she enriches the one whose hand she's holding (probably in a dance). What he says in his next speech shows that he has, in a moment, undergone a very drastic change:

> Did my heart love till now?...

> (1.5.51)

When love strikes, the whole of your life (including your idea of your past) changes.

1.7 The value of love

▶ 'to love, to wealth' (*Love's Labours Lost*, 1.1.31)

Love and value

When Claudio in *Much Ado About Nothing* has fallen in love with Hero, the possibility of having her for himself is so wonderfully unlikely that he puts it in terms of the purchase of an exquisite jewel:

> Can the world buy such a jewel? (1.1.171)

Love *is* the best thing that can happen to you, so it's valued above everything else. This is why in Shakespeare images of wealth, treasure and money are often used.

Shakespeare, even in the charmingly improbable plots of the comedies, is realistic about money. He shows that one of the reasons for courting a girl is that she's rich. The buccaneering Petruchio in *The Taming of the Shrew* says he's not put off by Kate's reputation for being argumentative, because 'wealth is burden of my wooing dance' (1.2.67).

In a far more romantic vein, the wonder of waking up to love after the disorientating nightmare of confused feelings is expressed in *A Midsummer Night's Dream* in the image of finding a jewel:

> And I have found Demetrius like a jewel
>
> (4.1.190)

Nor should it be forgotten that there are bits of stage business in Shakespeare that depend upon the visible presence of wealth. In *The Merchant of Venice*, Portia is associated (particularly in the early part of the play) with money. She is 'a lady richly left' (1.1.161), whose hair is likened to 'a golden fleece' (1.1.170), and her father has decided that her husband will be the one who chooses which of the golden, silver and lead caskets contains her picture. This stress on wealth is in keeping with the play as a whole; Venice exists by trade, so all areas of its life are measured in terms of money (see 6.15 and 6.16).

We can sum up the position in this way:

- **Love is like wealth – and it's good to have it**.

1.8 Sudden love

▶ 'a plague/That Cupid will impose' (*Love's Labours Lost*, 3.1.197)

The point about those words is that love can be as fierce as the plague. When, in *Twelfth Night*, Olivia falls in love, she says:

> Even so quickly may one catch the plague?
>
> (1.5.285)

Love can strike as quickly as the plague, and its effects can be as devastating. We have to remember that, unlike us, Shakespeare's audience were familiar with the plague's ravages.

It might also enable us to see another way in which the metaphor works. Both love and the plague have symptoms; there are signs that a person has the plague and also signs that someone is in love. This is frequently a topic of conversation in the plays.

1.9 The signs of love

▶ 'old signs' (*Much Ado About Nothing*, 3.2.38)

The 'old signs' referred to here are the signs of love. When Benedick falls in love with Beatrice, Claudio says:

If he be not in love with some woman there is no believing old signs. (3.2.37–8)

Claudio concludes that Benedick's in love, because

● **he's displaying the symptoms.**

Though Shakespeare never uses that word, it's what he means; those in love are like those suffering from an illness: we know from signs that someone is ill and when someone is in love. The 'old signs' seen in Benedick are: he brushes his hat, shaves, uses scent, is melancholy, washes his face, puts on make-up and plays music (3.2.38–55).

1.10 How lovers behave

▶ 'here come the lovers' (*A Midsummer Night's Dream*, 5.1.28)

Love is *public*; if you know what the signs are, you can tell whether or not someone's in love. This, of course, is important for drama. If there is an agreed set of signs that a person's in love, a player can use these on stage to indicate his or her state of mind. In Shakespeare's day (as in ours) there was a recognition that love made a person behave in a particular way. Shakespeare eagerly fixed on the link between playing a part in everyday life and playing on the stage (see 2.3).

When Theseus, the Prince, says 'here come the lovers', he knows they are lovers because they behave like lovers:

● **to be in love is to play the role of the lover.**

At the beginning of *Much Ado About Nothing*, Don Pedro tells the newly in love Claudio:

> Thou wilt be like a lover presently.
> And tire the hearer with a book of words
>
> (1.1.289–90)

When he says Claudio will 'be like a lover', Don Pedro means that he will be like someone who has bought a book and is following its instructions. As we might say: he's playing it by the book.

Petrarchan love

In Shakespeare's day the most popular picture of what a lover was like was drawn from the Italian poet, Petrarch, who in his poems to Laura, created the role of the lover:

- **the Petrarchan lover** was pale, off his food, wrote poetry, was melancholy, enjoyed being alone, liked sad music, thought his beloved (at times) to be cruel and proud, felt he would die when he parted from her and adored her in religious language.

A way of putting this is to say that there was a *convention* as to what a lover was like.

- **A convention is a kind of agreement between author and audience that a particular set of actions and words will be interpreted in a particular way.**

It's like a code or set of rules. Once the audience recognises the signs, it knows what to think about the character and the action.

The man in Shakespeare who is very clearly acting out the role of the Petrarchan lover is Orsino in *Twelfth Night*. This is established in the opening scene. He is languid, moody, poetically plays with words, listens to music, talks about the nature of love, lavishly praises his beloved (though in later scenes he, conventionally, calls her cruel) and exits to enjoy the pleasures of solitude and melancholy musing. (See Illustration 1.)

1.11 How lovers talk

▶ **'if you speak love'** (*Much Ado About Nothing*, 2.1.90)

When it happens to them

- **lovers respond by being inventive with words.**

Shakespeare inherited a tradition of love language that borrowed words from a range of human activities to express the feelings of love.

This is what Romeo says when he first sees Juliet:

> O, she doth teach the torches to burn bright!
> It seems she hangs upon the cheek of night
> As a rich jewel in an Ethiope's ear –
> Beauty too rich for use, for earth too dear.
> So shows a snowy dove trooping with crows

> (1.5.43–7)

In this extract the words cluster together to suggest the value and wonder of Juliet. She is a model for how torches burn; she is like a starry jewel shining in an Ethiopian's ear; her beauty is so exceptional it can't be bought or sold, and she is as radiantly different from others as is a snow-white dove from black crows.

If people feel this is all a bit excessive, they would, in one sense, be right:

- **the language of love is extravagant.**

Because love drives lovers to find intricate ways of praising beloveds, lovers are like poets and dramatists. Shakespeare surely enjoys the lavishness of lover's language. He might even see a parallel between what he does and what they do. This is not to say that he doesn't sometimes keep his distance; he knows those in love can be comical and that excess in language can be absurd.

Illustration 1 A Petrarchan lover

1.12 Laughing at lovers

▶ 'most loving mere folly' (*As You Like It*, 2.7.192)

Audiences laugh at lovers. They might not go as far as these words from a song in *As You Like It*; the impression in Shakespeare is not that most loving is foolish but that some of it can be.

- **The spectacle of someone falling in love at first sight can be comical.**

This is something to do with the extreme character of the feeling, its suddenness, the contrast with the character's previous state of mind, the fact that one person can be hopelessly in love while others feel nothing and, of course, the excessiveness of the language.

In *The Taming of the Shrew*, Lucentio arrives in Padua to study 'virtue and that part of philosophy ... that treats of happiness' (1.1.19–20). But then he sees Bianca. We are surely meant to find his change of heart amusing. In a very short while he's forgotten about 'virtue' and all he seeks is the love of Bianca. Moreover, he has, as he tells us, the classic symptoms: '... I burn, I pine, I perish ...' (1.1.153). He also knows how a lover should behave!

Shakespeare shows us that love is overwhelming, wonderful – and absurd. The audience in a comedy is usually distant enough to see that the characters do extra-ordinary and even ridiculous things for love.

A point that does need to be emphasised is:

- **in Shakespeare it's usually the men that are absurd.**

The girls seem to understand love and know what to do to get their men, but the boys are lost and comical. In *As You Like It*, Rosalind has to sort out the tongue-tied Orlando; without her efforts they'd never get married. The maturity and wisdom of the women is also seen in their patience; they know men are silly and change their minds too quickly.

1.13 Love, action and enterprise

▶ 'and now 'tis plotted' (*The Taming of the Shrew*, 1.1.186)

It's all too easy to think of Shakespeare's young lovers as embarrassingly romantic in their language and spineless in their behaviour. (No character has annoyed my pupils more than Florizel in *The Winter's Tale*.) But in most plays love doesn't have that effect.

- **Love inspires characters to action.**

Would the Romeo who was soppy about Rosaline have killed Tybalt? The energy of that play derives its force from love.

In the passage from which the line above comes, Lucentio, having gone weak at the knees at the sight of Bianca, is soon plotting an ingenious scheme that will enable him to court her. The words 'and now 'tis plotted' are spoken by his wily servant, Tranio, who dresses as Lucentio and plays his part with dazzling skill.

- **This enterprising energy provides the impetus for the plot**.

Comedies are not only about the young falling in love; the young are the ones who through intrigue and trickery make the plot work. The movement of a comic plot is an expression of the energy of young love.

1.14 Cupid and the blindness of love

▶ **'the sign of blind Cupid'** (*Much Ado About Nothing*, 1.1.237)

Cupid is mentioned a lot in Shakespeare; there are over 50 references in 14 plays. Not all of the references are from comedies, but the majority are: he's mentioned most in *A Midsummer Night's Dream*, *Love's Labours Lost* and *Much Ado About Nothing* (but see 9.6).

In Roman mythology Cupid was the son of Venus (goddess of love) who caused people to fall in love by firing arrows through their hearts.

- **The most important thing about Cupid is that he's blind, so he's no idea at whom he's shooting**.

Cupid, therefore, 'accounts' for the aspects of love discussed in this section:

- the flight of the arrow means that love is sudden
- love can be painful
- the fact that Cupid is blind means that he doesn't know at whom he's shooting, so we can fall in love with the most unlikely people.

Cupid's blindness makes sense of the oddity of love; it's a way of saying that love is a strange, chancy and unpredictable business.

1.15 Love and the old

▶ **'Saturn and Venus this year in conjunction'** (*2 Henry IV*, 2.4.265–6)

An example of the breadth of Shakespeare is that he doesn't neglect the old:

- **he knows that Cupid can make the old suffer the pangs and craziness of love**.

There's something crazy about Antony giving up his responsibilities as one of the leaders of the world for Cleopatra. This isn't something we can explain or understand; it's strange and rather frightening. That's why the play opens with one of his soldiers saying that:

> this dotage of our General's
> O'erflows the measure ...

> (*Antony and Cleopatra*, 1.1.1–2)

'Dotage' is the crucial word; in Shakespeare's plays it can mean feebleness of mind and excessively strong feelings. In Antony's case it means both. In him Venus (love) is in conjunction with Saturn (old age).

Antony's followers might have said of him what Falstaff's buddies do in *2 Henry IV*. Falstaff is old and fat, and Doll is a prostitute well past her sleep-by date, but because there's real affection, the scene is mellow. Nevertheless, the words about Venus and Saturn also touch on the folly and the pathos of love in old age.

1.16 Sex

▶ 'When the blood burns' (*Hamlet*, 1.3.116)

There's no getting away from it

- sex is important in Shakespeare.

Many of the words he uses have explicitly sexual connotations (see 4.11). The words above are spoken by Polonius, who warns his daughter Ophelia about being too familiar with Prince Hamlet. The blood he talks of is sexual desire; heat is a common term for being sexually aroused.

Sex in Shakespeare is seen as the natural end of love. Marriage in a Shakespearean comedy is often seen as explicitly involving sex. When Hymen, the presiding deity of marriage, enters at the end of *As You Like It*, he sings of marriage as the 'blessed bond of board and bed' (5.4.140). 'Board' means food and 'bed' means bed.

- Sex may be fun, but Shakespeare is also aware of its danger.

One of his earliest poems was *The Rape of Lucrece*, in which Tarquin, the rapist, wrestles with overwhelming and, in the end, irresistible lust. And sex can offend; Hamlet taunts Ophelia with a vocabulary that some readers still find (and are supposed to find) shocking (*Hamlet*, 3.2.107–11).

A jaundiced recoil against sex can be found in the language of Thersites in *Troilus and Cressida*; having seen the way the world goes, he cynically sums it up as

wars and lechery (5.2.197).

1.17 The pains of love

▶ 'O misery' (*Othello*, 3.3.175)

Thersites' comments are those of the onlooker, who doesn't care about the people he's observing. He's the detached cynic who sees people suffering but feels no pain himself. But with Othello it's different. Because he loves his wife and is jealous of her, he suffers dreadfully. The word 'misery' can stand for the pains of love – the desperation, the hopeless longing, the suspicions, the envy and the bitter feelings of rejection. As was said above, Shakespeare knows that love can be the worst thing that ever happens to you.

Because love must be expressed:

- those who are unable to voice their feelings are particularly miserable.

This is the plight of Viola in *Twelfth Night*. She has disguised herself as a man in order to gain access to the Court of Duke Orsino, but no sooner is she there than she finds she's fallen in love with him. Since there's no way in which she can express her feelings, she has to invent an imaginary sister, whom she both imagines and fears is like herself. This imaginary sister 'never told her love' and so allowed 'conceal-ment, like a worm i'th' bud' to gnaw away at her. Thus 'she pined in thought' (2.4.110–12).

Another character in *Twelfth Night* who suffers the pains of love is Sir Andrew. In all senses of the word, he's a sad figure – old, thin, easily duped, directionless and, for most of the time, lacking in self-knowledge. At one point Toby says that Maria, a lady in waiting, adores him, to which Andrew replied: 'I was adored once, too' (2.3.175). We've no idea who adored him, but somehow the falling cadence (the gradual drop in the pitch of the voice as the sentence unfolds) tells us it was a long time ago. Sir Andrew is wistful but

- **some lovers suffer extreme pain**.

One of the most wretched is Troilus, who has to look on while Diomedes seduces the woman whom he has slept with the night before. Because the audience watches him as he, in secret, watches Diomedes and Cressida, they feel something of the hopeless inaction of Troilus.

Among the most unhappy of Shakespeare's forlorn lovers are the homosexuals. Within the world of the plays, there's no way in which they can find happiness. Antonio in *The Merchant of Venice*, of whom it's said 'I think he only loves the world for him' (2.8.30), generously helps Bassanio (the 'him' of the quotation) but can expect no love in return.

1.18 Love and war

▶ 'slain in Cupid's war' (*Pericles*, sc.1.81)

The trials of love are like the trials of war. Although when he speaks of 'Cupid's wars', Antiochus is not talking about military engagements, the language about love and the language about war often meet.

Love as war

Some characters talk about love in terms of war. *Much Ado About Nothing* opens with soldiers returning from a war. No sooner has the news arrived, than Beatrice begins to joke about a soldier called Benedick. Leonarto, the head of the house, explains:

There is a kind of merry war betwixt signor Benedick and her. (1.1.58–9)

The war, of course, is a war of words, but the image of warfare is appropriate in a play, which works by showing that Beatrice and Benedick always aroused strong feel-ings in each other.

Love in the time of war

In some plays love occurs in wartime. It's already been noted that *Romeo and Juliet* is a love story that takes place in a virtual state of warfare between the two leading families of Verona. Even more explicit is *Troilus and Cressida*, a play in which the love of the two central characters has the Trojan war as its setting.

Plays about both

In *Henry V* the action moves from war to love, when Henry, victorious from the battle of Agincourt, woos the French princess. In *Troilus and Cressida* the two themes are interwoven. In the first scene Troilus asks:

> Why should I war without the walls of Troy
> That find such cruel battle here within?

(1.1.2–3)

Shakespeare's audience would recognise that what is happening outside is the most famous war of all time – that between Greece and Troy – and what is going to happen within (both within the walls and the hearts of the lovers) is one of the world's most famous love stories.

1.19 The ambiguity of war

▶ 'pride, pomp, and circumstance of glorious war' (*Othello*, 3.3.359)

Most societies have mixed feelings about war; heroes are praised, victories celebrated, the dead commemorated, but equally, those who have experienced it think that virtually any price is worth paying if it can be avoided.

When (not too long ago) British forces went to the Falklands, the campaign produced mixed reactions. There was joy at the victory, admiration for the heroism of the troops, and the people welcomed home those troops with bunting and bands. But it was war; many were killed, many disfigured, and the reality of some of the fighting – some of the Argentine troops in the final battle died of bayonet wounds – brought home what a bloody business war is.

We shouldn't expect the past to be any different:

• **Shakespeare is aware of the ambiguity of war.**

Just think of that word 'pride' in the quotation from *Othello*. There is a proper pride in serving a cause in war, but pride can also be selfish. In other words, Shakespeare knows both sides:

> That magical word of war ...

(*Antony and Cleopatra*, 3.1.31)

and the

> 'rough frown of war'

(*King John*, 3.1.30)

1.20 Leaving for war

▶ 'Yours in the ranks of death' (*King Lear*, 4.2.25)

One of the reasons writers turn to the subject of war is that it creates opportunities to write about a very wide range of feelings.

Take, for example, going to war. The spectacle of troops leaving for battle was a feature of British life. The scene has been painted, written and sung about. It's a heady occasion – bands, streamers, hope in the air, the assurance of victory. And there is fear: some won't come back; the parting of some warriors from their beloveds will be a final one.

Shakespeare devotes a whole scene of *Henry V* to soldiers leaving for war. Pistol, Nim, Bardolph and the boy are to go to France. They leave quietly. Pistol gives some practical advice (what else can you say when you know you might not come back?), kisses his wife and goes – 'Touch her soft mouth, and march' (2.3.53). Most don't come back.

In *King Lear*, Edmund leaves in a very different style. He bids farewell not to a wife but to Goneril, the woman with whom he's having an adulterous affair. Their parting is a kind of lovemaking (the language is charged with sexual meanings), and after their final kiss, he signs off with an irresistibly seductive gesture that even Errol Flynn would have been proud of:

Yours in the ranks of death.

(4.2.25)

1.21 Staying behind

▶ 'a moth of peace' (*Othello*, 1.3.256)

These are Desdemona's words in her plea to be allowed to accompany Othello to Cyprus. The contrast she draws is between her husband fully engaged in the business of the world and his wife left behind like a moth in the fusty room of peace.

A very difficult case of the difference between those who actually do the fighting and those left at home appears in *Coriolanus*. The most strenuous (and simple-minded?) defender of the glories of war in that play is Coriolanus's mother, Volumnia. The audience can't be blind to the difference between the way she takes pleasure in the wounds of her son and the modest way in which he is reluctant to show the people his wounds in the public ritual in which he asks them to accept him as consul (the chief governor of the city).

Looking at war from the point of view of those who remain is an example of how Shakespeare allows the audience to see a situation from different viewpoints.

1.22 The Professionals

▶ 'of great expedition and knowledge in the ancient wars' (*Henry V*, 3.3.22–3)

This is the description of Captain Jamy by Fluellen. He goes on to say that Jamy will 'maintain his argument as well as any military man in the world' (3.3.24–5). Fluellen praises Jamy but has harsh words for another soldier – Captain McMorris. A crucial factor in this conversation is that Fluellen, Jamy and McMorris are all professional soldiers, so their praise or criticism comes from a shared code of military practice.

In the discussion of one professional by another, a point emerges about what people are like in war:

- **war brings out differences**.

We see that officers such as Jamy and Fluellen are different from common soldiers such as Bates and Williams, to whom Henry talks on the night before Agincourt. Both those groups are different from Bardolph, Nim and Pistol, who are only in the war to steal, and all are different from the king. (See Illustration 2.)

War separates men

At the siege of Harfleur, Fluellen has to drive the reluctant Bardolph, Nim and Pistol into battle. Before Agincourt the splendid Williams brings out in conversation with the disguised king that Henry, as commander, is not in the same position as Williams is as an ordinary soldier. Williams argues (4.1.133–44) that if the king's cause is not a moral one, then the deaths of his soldiers will be 'a black matter for the King'. In Henry's prayer that follows, he reflects on the differences between his and a common man's responsibilities. The king, he says, 'must bear all' (4.1.230), and then despondently asks what kings have that the common people don't. He concludes that it's 'ceremony' and then asks:

> And what art thou, thou idol ceremony?

> (4.1.237)

The success of the scene rests in Shakespeare showing that the moment when Henry is closest to his soldiers is the one that forces on him how different he is from them.

War brings men together

But come the battle, and the tone is quite different. War here is seen as uniting men. Perhaps Henry's words are what any good commander would say to steel the nerves of his troops on the eve of a battle they are unlikely to win. Nevertheless, those who have fought affirm that the imminence of battle creates a sense of brotherhood in all classes:

> For he today that sheds his blood with me
> Shall be my brother; be he ne'er so vile.

> (4.3.61–2)

The 'brotherhood' he speaks of is not just a class matter. 'Vile' probably means wicked. Henry is probably appealing to those such as Pistol who have not been good soldiers. If in this battle they fight well, they will be the brothers of a king. The sense of brotherhood – 'we band of brothers' (4.3.60) – that unites them is one based on what it is to be a soldier. No wonder people watching this play have compared the soldiers to those who held the line at Waterloo or who, amid a barrage of enemy fire, continued to walk steadily towards the German lines on the first day of the Battle of the Somme.

1.23 The spectacle of war

▶ *'Enter Martius, bleeding, assaulted by the enemy' (Coriolanus, 1.6.3)*

The quote above is a stage direction. Caius Martius (later called Coriolanus) has entered the enemy city of Corioli alone, the gates have shut upon him and he is

Illustration 2   An Elizabethan soldier

presumed to be dead. Then they open, and he appears, bloody, under attack but still valiantly fighting (see Illustration 3). Under his inspiration, the Roman army attacks, and the town is taken.

No words can do justice to the impact of that scene on stage. This is true of every fight in Shakespeare.

As was said above, the impact of battles, wars, fights and the emotional conflicts between characters can only be appreciated by a reader of the plays if he or she imagines what it would look like on stage. We have to imagine the:

violent action
staring eyes
sweat
clash of weapons
movement of large numbers
yells and screams
thumps of falling bodies
dramatic exits
rising pitch of voices
confused clang of noises off stage
blood.

This is a point, above all, about the theatre:

- **one of the reasons that Shakespeare is interested in war is that it provides some stunning visual moments**.

The following moments impress through the sheer physical impact of the actions:

- the bleeding Captain in *Macbeth* who gives a report of Macbeth's exploits in the battle
- the sight in *King Lear* of the blind Gloucester alone on stage, while the noise of battle rages offstage
- the massacre of the French prisoners in *Henry V*
- Coriolanus proclaimed as a hero by his troops
- Brutus carried off the stage at the end of *Julius Caesar*.

1.24 War's victims

▶ 'We would have all such offenders so cut off' (*Henry V*, 3.6.108)

If anyone wants to play the not very sensible game of enlisting Shakespeare to support one's beliefs, pacifists are up against it. Shakespeare doesn't preach against war.

But he doesn't preach in favour of it either. He knows that war, even victorious war, can be a very nasty business.

This is painfully evident in *Henry V*. Bardolph, Nim and Pistol go to war to loot. In the siege of Harfleur, after Fluellen has beaten them into fighting, Bardolph ('Nim and Bardolph are sworn brothers in filching', 3.2.42–3) steals a pax from a church. A pax is not a particularly sacred object – it's a small tablet handed round during mass for the attenders to kiss – but sentence of death is passed on him. The king is begged for mercy, but his cold answer is: 'We would have all such offenders so cut off' (3.6.108). So Bardolph hangs – in some productions on stage.

It's always painful to see deaths in war in personal terms, and in the case of Bardolph the personal element goes as far as the king himself, for Bardolph was a mate of his in his unreformed days when he liked to pass his time with the riff-raff of London. In an earlier play, Bardolph even jokes with Henry about hanging; they are talking about Falstaff's page:

> An you do not make him hanged among you,
> the gallows shall be wronged.

> (2 Henry IV, 2.2.89–90)

The idea is that the gallows will be wronged (cheated) if they don't get the page. Most audiences feel that Bardolph is wronged because he goes to them. Furthermore, most feel that Henry is wrong for not showing mercy to one of his old sidekicks. Yet that's Shakespeare's point:

- **in war there can't be special allowances made for individuals.**

Military discipline must be impersonal; Bardolph is not to be treated as the likeable drunkard and thief we've got to know in 2 Henry IV, but as someone who's stepped out of line and must pay the penalty.

1.25 Honour

▶ **'when honour's at the stake'** (*Hamlet*, **4.4.56**)

In spite of the ambiguity of war, the image of the soldier is, for many of his characters, an honourable one. The distraught Ophelia, desperately puzzling over the change in Hamlet, thinks about his virtuous qualities. These include the life of the soldier:

> O what a noble mind is here o'erthrown!
> The courtier's, soldier's, scholar's, eye, tongue, sword,

> (3.1.153–4)

This idea is important at the end of the play, when Fortinbras gives an order:

> Let four captains
> Bear Hamlet like a soldier to the stage,

> (5.2.349–50)

Hamlet admires the enterprising Fortinbras. They never meet, but Hamlet sees his army marching, almost to certain death, to the Polish wars. In his soliloquy, he reflects upon the nature of honour:

> Rightly to be great
> Is not to stir without great argument,
> But greatly to find quarrel in a straw
> When honour's at the stake.

> (4.4.53–6)

Such is honour, says Hamlet, that even if the issue is a minor one, you should take action when honour is 'at the stake'. This isn't necessarily Shakespeare's view, but it's what a lot of his characters think.

1.26 Conflict in Shakespeare's plays

▶ 'conflicting elements' (*Timon of Athens*, 4.3.231)

As has been stressed, there can be conflict without there being war. The conflict between Antonio and Shylock in *The Merchant of Venice* is the tension behind that interesting yet disturbing play.

We can give a new twist to a phrase from *Timon of Athens* and say that

• many of Shakespeare's plays depend upon 'conflicting elements'.

Conflicts between political ideas

In *Julius Caesar*, Cassius wants to prevent Caesar gaining complete power in Rome. What he and his fellow conspirators fear is that Caesar will become a king. Cassius recruits a group of citizens, who assassinate Caesar. This leads to war.

Conflicts brought about by envy

Shakespeare presents envy as a powerful yet ugly element in human life. Its nastiest manifestation is in Iago, who destroys Othello and nearly gets Cassio killed. It's not clear whether envy is the main motive for his actions; what's uncomfortably true is that Iago is a victim of a corrupting and belittling envy.

The conflicts of ambition

'Ambition' is often used of an attempt to seize power illegally. Lady Macbeth says her husband is 'not without ambition' (1.5.18), and when he is winding himself up to kill Duncan he rather desperately clings on to 'vaulting ambition' (1.7.27) as the one spur he has left.

Conflicts between groups

Shakespeare shows that some of the most turbulent conflicts arise when two groups compete. In *Romeo and Juliet* it's two families – the Montagues and the Capulets; in *Julius Caesar* the friends and enemies of Caesar; and in *The Merchant of Venice* the Christians and the Jews.

Conflicts between the generations

Quite often comedies have as their starting point the attempt by the older generation to control the young, and the action gets stared when the young find ways of getting their own way. The clash of generations, however, is not only a comic topic. One of the leading conflicts in *King Lear* (a play that ends with a war) is between parents and children.

1.1 Read carefully and closely a passage from a play you are studying (say, about 20 lines) and see how the themes emerge. If you do this with four or five passages, you may be able to see what ideas are important in the play as a whole.

1.2 Trace through the text the words that embody the play's themes. You might see that in some cases the words grow in meaning as the play unfolds.

1.3 Try to identify the stages in which a theme develops: are there crucial scenes in which the themes become clear, are embodied in actions or change?

1.4 Try to imagine how the visual impact of a performance might bring home to you what the play is concerned with. If you have seen a production of a play you are studying, think about the aspects of the play that the performance brought home to you.

1.5 Whatever the theme is, try to express clearly exactly what aspect is brought out by the action of the play. If, for instance, the play is concerned with love, what aspects of it are particularly prominent?

2 Who's who

2.1 Shakespeare's varied characters

▶ 'which oft our stage hath shown' (*Henry V*, Epilogue, 13)

What we see on stage are not ideas but people. We see people arguing, wooing, pleading, praying, denouncing, meditating and judging. It's out of these activities that themes emerge.

But *whom* do we see? What kind of characters pass before us in Shakespeare's theatre? The simple answer is:

- **In Shakespeare we see all sorts of people.**

There are, to name but a few: carpenters, constables, executioners, fairies, haberdashers, joiners, merchants, prisoners, priests, prostitutes, nuns, rogues, sailors, shepherds, singers, soldiers, stewards, tailors, tinkers, wrestlers as well as kings, queens, lords, ladies and young lovers.

The discussion below can only concentrate on a few. But before starting, we have to make some important points about what interests Shakespeare.

2.2 Common humanity

▶ 'the common people' (*Coriolanus*, 2.2.6)

This phrase usually means anyone who isn't nobility, but in an important sense it refers to *all* the characters we encounter in Shakespeare. They are common in the sense that no matter how important they are:

- **Shakespeare presents them as ordinarily, and sometimes vulnerably, human.**

Most of the time we're more aware of feelings and thoughts than their robes and crowns. Above all,

- **Shakespeare's characters are people.**

2.3 Playing a role

▶ 'A stage where every man must play a part' (*The Merchant of Venice*, 1.1.78)

Shakespeare saw that a lot of the time we act because we're living according to an image of what we think someone in our position ought to do:

● a lot of the characters are aware that they are playing a role.

This link between life and the stage (see 4.2) is something a lot of theatre-goers have noticed. Sometimes people assume that Shakespeare is criticising his characters playing roles.

Most of the time he's not. Shakespeare is an observer of society and he knows how fashions, habits, social expectations and living up to images are present in our behaviour.

This is particularly important in the case of characters who live according to what their role requires. All the world *is* a stage. So when it comes to characters who stick very closely to set roles we should remember:

● Shakespeare doesn't quarrel.

By that I mean that Shakespeare doesn't criticise a character because he or she plays a role. If that makes good drama, then Shakespeare doesn't complain.

● His first duty is towards his art; if something works on stage, he'll use it.

For instance, he likes lovers who go weak at the knees because he can do a lot of things with them on stage – make them active in the pursuit of a beloved, make them objects of laughter, contrast them with other types of lovers. All too often, students studying *Twelfth Night* are told that Orsino isn't really in love but only in love with love. This misses the point; certainly, he acts out the part of an unrequited lover, but that doesn't mean either that he's insincere or that Shakespeare's sniffy about him. Shakespeare doesn't quarrel with Orsino.

2.4 Class divisions

▶ 'high birth' (*Troilus and Cressida*, 3.3.172)

Shakespeare recognises that people divide themselves into groups. There are classes, ranks, orders and divisions in society.

The characters are conscious of the divisions. In *Twelfth Night*, Malvolio, who must be of humble birth, dreams of being married to the Lady Olivia, and her uncle, Sir Toby, insults him in one scene by asking: 'Art any more than a steward?' (2.3.106–7).

● Shakespeare seems able to accept that that is the way the world goes without either openly supporting a system based on rank or preaching against it.

Much of the drama of his plays depends upon a hierarchical social system, because without it he couldn't write about rebellion, the rise and fall of ambitious people and the vulnerability of even a king.

On the other hand, one of the things he wants to insist on is that people share a common humanity. Henry V's meeting with the common soldiers on the eve of the battle is seen by the audience as an event that unites them rather than exposing their social differences.

2.5 Kings in Shakespeare

▶ 'here comes the king' (*All's Well That Ends Well*, 2.3.40)

What kind of a figure does the audience see when a king enters?

The king and the land

The first point to make is:

- **a king is king of somewhere.**

There's no king who doesn't have a land to rule over. In fact, so strong is the bond between kings and their lands that they are often called by the names of their countries – the King of France is often called France. This isn't playing with words. The king represents his country, and its health and wellbeing is intimately tied up with him.

The king and the nation

So close is this bond that

- **the life of the king moulds the life of the nation.**

Richard II shows that John of Gaunt's judgement that Richard's irresponsibility has ruined the nation is true. In the first part of the play Richard is frivolous and wasteful. Shakespeare shows the effects of this in the scene in which two gardeners compare the order they maintain with the neglected state of the nation. They 'Keep law and form and due proportion' (3.4.42), while England is 'full of weeds' (3.4.45) and 'swarming with caterpillars' (3.4.48).

The king and God

An idea that we frequently meet in Shakespeare is the belief that:

- **kings ruled because they have been specially appointed by God.**

This is called the Divine Right of Kings.

Since Shakespeare is aware of how people in authority use high-sounding language to bolster their positions, he shows that this idea is very popular with kings and their supporters.

In a crisis they often resort to it. When Richard II hears of the success his banished cousin, Bolingbroke, is having, he comforts himself with the belief that since he's been chosen by God, he can't be defeated:

> Not all the water in the rough rude sea
> Can wash the balm from an anointed King
>
> (3.2.50–1)

The idea is that the holy oil used in anointing a king at the coronation ceremony will protect him from final misfortune. He's appealing to the idea that there's something sacred about a king.

The king and power

We should never forget the power of the king:

- **the word of a king is law.**

This is recognised in *Richard II* by Bolingbroke, when Richard reduces his sentence of banishment by four years:

> Four lagging winters and four wanton springs
> End in a word: such is the breath of Kings.

> (1.3.207–8)

Something of the almost magical power of a king emerges in those words. Although he doesn't actually say it, Bolingbroke gives us the picture of the seasons and time obeying the words of a king.

The humanity of kings

Because the king is such a powerful figure, Shakespeare can show his audiences what is perhaps the most memorable aspect of his presentation of royalty:

- **kings are human.**

Their humanity is most evident when they are threatened. In a crisis a king shows that he has hopes, fears, longings, uncertainties and anxieties. It's as if Shakespeare strips away the robes and takes away the power of kingly words and reveals the struggles of our common humanity.

In one play we see this happen on stage; King Lear meets a beggar in a storm and so moved is he by the plight of the poor that he strips off his clothes.

- **Kings are often at their most vulnerable – and therefore most human – when their troubles are a combination of political and family problems.**

King Lear suffers in this way, and so does Henry IV. In the case of Henry, he faces rebellions from the families who had helped him to the throne, while his son (the future Henry V) seems to him utterly irresponsible and so unsuitable as a future king.

- **The final devastating proof that kings are only human is that they fall from power.**

When Richard II realises that support for him as king is crumbling, he movingly associates his loss of power with a recognition that he's not essentially different from any other human being:

> I live with bread, like you; feel want,
> Taste grief, need friends. Subjected thus,
> How can you say to me I am a king?

> (3.2.171–3)

Here, 'bread' defines one of the most basic things about our humanity; we all need food to stay alive.

In English history, three kings fell from power and were killed – Richard II, Henry VI, Richard III. Shakespeare wrote plays about all of them.

Killing the king

Shakespeare shows us what a terrible thing this is.

- **Unless we can feel the defiling power of regicide (killing a king) we can't experience the full terrors of some of his histories and tragedies.**

Even the one who kills the king has to understand what an abominable thing it is that he's done.

This is brought home to Macbeth in two ways. The most obvious one is the guilt, the fear and the nightmares. The second is seen in the vivid tribute he pays to the man he's killed. When asked why he killed the servants who slept outside King Duncan's room, he gives a symbolically rich picture of the body of the king whom he's murdered:

> Here lay Duncan,
> His silver skin laced with his golden blood,

(2.3.121–2)

The golden blood suggests Duncan was no ordinary mortal and that everything about him was rich and precious. His silver skin likewise gives the feeling that here was an almost mythical figure – a living king who yet was made of the richest metals. All this is what Macbeth has created. Even the murderer knows what a horrific thing it is to kill the king.

When a king is killed in Shakespeare, it's sometimes possible to feel the echoes of those strange and terrible rituals we read about in the past, when either symbolically or in actuality the king was killed.

We might feel this in *Hamlet*. The killing of Claudius at the end has the feel about it of a ritual that will cleanse the foul and corrupted world of Denmark. Hence Hamlet issues this eerily impressive command when he learns that the king has tried to have him killed:

> O villainy! Let the door be locked!
> Treachery, seek it out.

(5.2.264–5)

It's as if the evil that has its source in the corrupt king must be contained within the room, so Hamlet, as a ritual revenger or even a priest officiating at a sacrifice, has the door closed while he performs the terrible but necessary deed of killing the king.

2.6 Queens in Shakespeare

▶ 'poor Queen' (*Richard II*, 3.4.103)

Shakespeare is less interested in the dramatic possibilities of queens than of kings. In many plays they have two minor but emotionally powerful roles.

Victims of history

One of the features of the history plays is that there are women who are, so to speak, 'leftovers' from the political conflicts of the past. Their husbands and even their sons are dead, and they are left to mourn the awful changes they have seen.

In *Richard III* they form a chorus, which wails over the past and bitterly curses the one who's done the killing. In particular, old Queen Margaret is like a ghost or banshee shrieking against the wickedness of Richard. But there's nothing that she can do. She's a victim of history.

Queens and sympathy

It's not always easy to have sympathy for Shakespeare's kings; they can be arrogant, frivolous, unscrupulous or self-pitying. However, when their queens show them affection we soften towards them. No matter how wayward they are, if they are loved, then there is a warmth in the plays. It's this warmth that the queens supply. One of the reasons why we feel increasingly sympathetic towards Richard II is that the Queen loves him.

One of the signs of this softness and warmth is that the queens often use their husbands' names as well as their titles. This is how the Duchess of Gloucester speaks of her late husband:

> But Thomas, my dear lord, my life, my Gloucester
>
> *(Richard II*, 1.2.16)

To her, he's Thomas before he's Gloucester.

2.7 Unscrupulous characters

▶ 'the murderous Machiavel' (*3 Henry VI*, 3.2.193)

Because he's interested in love and war, Shakespeare, like many authors, recognises that there are two kinds of power:

- sexual and
- political.

One sort of character that he's interested in is the figure who wants power and is prepared to do virtually anything to get it. In Shakespeare's day, the unscrupulous man consumed by political ambition was thought of as a follower of the Italian philosopher, Machiavelli. It was thought that Machiavelli advocated immorality as the way of achieving power. Although this wasn't true of Machiavelli, the name stuck, so any power-seeker was called a Machiavel.

Ambition is a theme of *Julius Caesar*; the conspirators fear that Caesar is bent upon becoming king, but the irony is that Brutus, their effective leader, fails to see that there is a person – Mark Antony – who is much closer to the Machiavellian pattern.

A character who seeks sexual power is Angelo in *Measure for Measure*. He's a strict and apparently unemotional young lawyer who's given complete power in Vienna. When a young nun pleads for the life of her brother, Angelo is suddenly seized with an overwhelming desire for her. When she refuses him, he becomes frankly and brutally demanding. Listen to how exultant he is:

I have begun,
And now I give my sensual race the reign.
Fit thy consent to my sharp appetite.

(2.4.160–2)

There's a disturbing sense in those lines that he's enjoying being the sexual bully. His lust is compared to a headstrong horse, that the rider impels forward with his spurs. The word 'sharp' has a double meaning – the spurs digging into the horse and the keen edge of his sexual appetite.

In the character of Edmund from *King Lear*, both kinds of power-seeking are present. He is the illegitimate son of the Duke of Gloucester who edges his brother out of his inheritance and betrays his father. Once he's become Duke of Gloucester, he begins an affair with the king's daughter while leading another daughter to believe that he's interested in her.

2.8 Families divided

▶ **'between the child and parent'** (*Coriolanus*, 5.3.56)

The scene from which those words come is one of the most powerful in Shakespeare. Coriolanus has been rejected by Rome and has joined his enemies in marching upon the city of his birth. The only thing that can save Rome is an appeal from Volumnia, his mother. The scene might be summed up as what passes between 'the child and parent'.

This theme can also be said to be one of the major preoccupations of Shakespeare.

• **Shakespeare shows us that the feelings that bring chaos to nations have their origin in the lives of families.**

In the relationships between parents and children we see the tensions that make history and cause tragedy. *Hamlet* is as much about a mother and a son and a father and a son as it is about revenging the death of a king.

Hence his plays are full of family relationships: mothers, fathers, daughters and sons.

Families and plots

The plots of many of the plays, particularly the comedies, arise out of tensions between parents and children. A basic comic plot is that of a child who wants to love as she chooses and a parent, usually a father, who wants to prevent her. In the opening of *A Midsummer Night's Dream*, Hermia wants to marry Lysander, while her father insists (with the most horrible threats) that she chooses Demetrius.

The unexpected importance of the family

Parents and children are also important in plays in which their presence is unexpected. It looks as if Shakespeare was so interested in family relationships that he extended the material of his plots so he could include the tensions of family life in the drama of the play.

An example of this is *Hamlet*. The main plot concerns Hamlet revenging the death of his father, but Shakespeare emphasises the anguish and plight of Hamlet by concentrating on the fact that his mother is the new wife of the uncle who has murdered his father. The scenes between mother and son are charged with strong conflicting feelings – nausea, disgust, betrayal, incomprehension, tenderness. Shakespeare shows how the simple outlines of a revenge plot become complex and difficult when meshed with the troubled feelings a son has for his mother.

Daughters and fathers

- **The relationship between father and daughter is the one that most seems to have haunted Shakespeare.**

It's the cause of many comic plots; for instance, Hermia flees into the wood to escape her father. The tragedy of *King Lear* is a tragedy of a man's failure to be what in nature he can't help being – a father. When he banishes Cordelia, he calls her his 'sometime daughter' (1.1.119).

What he doesn't see is that nobody can be a 'sometime daughter'; you are always somebody's son or daughter – even if you're dead.

2.9 Children divided

▶ 'brothers divided' (*King Lear*, 1.2.105)

An aspect of family tension that Shakespeare dwells on is

- **the division between children.**

This is in keeping with the sense we often get in Shakespeare that we are watching the playing out of a folk story. Folk tales and fairy tales often turn upon the troubled relationships of brothers and sisters. In terms of the story, Cinderella needs her ugly sisters so, in the end, she can triumph over them.

The good brother and the bad brother

A folk motif that finds a place in Shakespeare is the contrast between an evil brother and one who is good but easily fooled. This is what we find in *King Lear*; the scheming Edmund is clever, manipulative, ambitious and, given his success with women, very sexy, while Edgar is mild, agreeable, reasonable but too easily deceived (see 22.7).

Trouble between sisters

Sisters are usually milder with each other, but there are some who fight – for instance, Kate and Bianca in *The Taming of the Shrew* and Goneril, Regan and Cordelia in *King Lear*.

Both these plays raise the interesting question of whether we can see similarities between the sisters. This is clearly the case in *The Taming of the Shrew*; both are strong-minded and determined young women. In *King Lear* the symbolic patterning that runs through the whole play might lead an audience to see that Cordelia has nothing in common with the other two. At one point a character says people must be controlled by the stars, because otherwise one father 'could not beget/Such different issues' (4.3.35–6). But this doesn't settle the matter. Cordelia, like her sisters, is single-minded, tough and forthright. It's possible to argue that the horror of the play lies in the fact that although the daughters act differently they are still recognisably sisters.

The centrality of families

The last two points underline what was said above (2.8) about the centrality of families:

- **no matter what the plot is, Shakespeare sets the action in a family context.**

This applies to comedies, histories and tragedies. The effect is to root events in something familiar and ordinary. No matter how unlikely the plot of a comedy is, the relationships we see are familiar. Kings might be almost divine beings, yet they have anxieties about their children.

In tragedy characters suffer as husbands (Othello and Macbeth), fathers (Lear), sons (Hamlet and Romeo) and daughters (Juliet and Desdemona). Perhaps all of Shakespeare's tragedies arise out of conflicts that each of us can see at work in our own families.

2.10 Married couples

▶ 'my husband' (*Macbeth*, 2.2.14)

It's rare that Shakespeare explores married life. Neither the Montagues nor the Capulets make much contribution to *Romeo and Juliet* except to provide the background of family hostility. We don't feel that there's a strong interest in them as characters; they fulfil the needs of the plot, and not much else. But there are exceptions – and very interesting ones.

In two tragedies – *Macbeth* and *Othello* – the main characters are presented as husbands and wives. *Macbeth* is Shakespeare's most searching presentation of a married couple. They are loving (sometimes almost embarrassingly so – 'dearest chuck', 3.2.48); she understands how he thinks and feels and above all what he wants, and when he hears what he takes to be good news – the prophecies of the weird sisters – he immediately writes to her. Part of the tragedy of the play is that we see their marriage crumble away before us – she lapses into sleepwalking, and he broods alone.

We see something of what the Macbeth's marriage was like, but in the case of Othello and Desdemona what is haunting is the feeling of what might have been. The marriage is destroyed almost as soon as it starts, so the theme of the play becomes not only the disintegration of an outstanding figure but the rapid decline and death of marriage that promised so much.

2.11 Lovers and theatrical conventions

▶ 'sweet lovers' (*Love's Labours Lost*, 4.3.216)

Shakespeare's plays are full of lovers; they turn up in the comedies, but they can't be kept out of the other plays. Hotspur in *I Henry IV* is given a loving wife, and one of the factors that makes *Hamlet* so fascinatingly complex is the presence of Ophelia. In the late plays young couples bring new life to a blighted world.

The conventions of love

Shakespeare works with conventions – agreements between authors and audiences that certain actions, characters or plots will be recognised and understood in a particular way. For instance, it's a convention in comedy that fathers want to stop their daughters finding love. It would be a mistake to think that there must be some dark reason why a father is like this; it's simply a matter that the convention requires him to be so.

As we saw in 1.10, the most popular convention about lovers was one that came from the Italian poet, Petrarch. It's not like Shakespeare to borrow a convention without in some way extending or altering it. And this is what he does. In some of his lovers, we can see the 'ghost', as it were, of the Petrarchan convention. But usually it's a knowing ghost. That's to say, lovers often know they are acting out the role of a lover.

When, in *Much Ado About Nothing*, Claudio returns from the wars and promptly falls in love, his commanding officer, Don Pedro, recognises that to be in love means behaving in the way lovers do. He says of Claudio:

> Thou wilt be like a lover presently,
> And tire the hearer with a book of words

(1.1.289–90)

The image of 'a book of words' may be understood to mean either that he will model his behaviour on what it says in a book (Petrarch's poems?) or that, like lovers in books, he will go on and on.

Shakespeare and conventions

It's not so much that Shakespeare works with conventions as that he presents his characters as doing so. It's not that he thinks that a lover has a particular identity as that he shows lovers adopting the conventional ones. He shows us that people deliberately behave in accordance with social and literary conventions.

As we've seen in 1.10, Orsino deliberately models himself on Petrarchan conventions. He says:

> For such as I am, all true lovers are

(2.4.16)

In the first scene he's languid, moody, listens to music, speaks in a poetic manner, lavishes praises on his beloved (though in a later scene he, conventionally, calls her cruel) and exits to brood alone under a canopy of flowers. Orsino knows that there's a particular way of showing everyone that he's in love. There's a role for a lover – and Orsino plays it for all he's worth.

2.12 The beloved

▶ 'O mistress mine' (*Twelfth Night*, 2.3.37)

A lover usually referred to his beloved as his 'lady' or 'mistress'. The word 'mistress' could also carry the implication that it was the woman who was in charge, because the hopes of the lover depended upon her. One of the amusing things about Shakespeare is that:

- **a mistress is very often quite different from how the lover presents her**.

Lovers go in for praise which is so high-sounding that the beloved seems more angel than human being, but when we meet the girls who are the object of this romantic chatter, they are sensible, witty and practical young women who usually know exactly what they want and are not fooled by the poetic rhapsodies spun by their admirers. To put the point another way:

- **Shakespeare's women are usually far more interesting than the men who love them**.

Look at the object of Orsino's love – the lady Olivia. When we first meet her, she's fulfilling a vow to mourn for seven years the deaths of her father and brother. Because there's something indulgent about this, it's easy to imagine that she's really rather like Orsino – brooding, moody and prone to excessive emotional gestures. But when she falls in love, she's decisive. While he languishes at home, she starts plotting. She sends a ring to young Cesario, claiming she's returning one given to her by Orsino. It's one of the delicious ironies of the play that this device would probably work with a man; but Cesario is actually a woman – Viola – and she immediately sees through the trick, realising that Olivia is after her. When Cesario returns, Olivia does her best to persuade 'him', and when he agrees to visit her she's practical and sensible: 'How shall I feast him?' (3.4.2). And she gets on with it. By the time we reach the last scene, Orsino's still playing the part of the Petrarchan lover, while she's got herself a husband.

2.13 Shakespeare's fools

▶ 'to play the fool' (*Twelfth Night*, 3.1.59)

The character of the fool has this in common with lovers:

- **there was in Shakespeare's day a popular idea of what a stage fool was like**.

Having said that, the idea was a pretty broad one. The fool was a bit like the comedian today. It's not enough to say that he or she is a comedian, because people want to know what kind of a comedian is being talked about. In a similar way, the fool came in various forms. Some behaved as half-wits, some were singers, dancers and acrobats, some were mimics, some wise-crackers and some sharp-minded intellectuals who played upon the multiple meanings of words.

Another important aspect of the fools was that they existed outside the theatre. Courts and the households of the rich still employed fools (some of whom were women) as entertainers. They were members of a household with a role and a distinctive dress.

Some professional fools found their way into the theatres. They danced, sang and probably interjected their own lines (see Illustration 3).

A passage in *Twelfth Night* provides a pretty good picture of the stage fool:

> This fellow is wise enough to play the fool,
> And to do that well craves a kind of wit.

This fellow is wise enough
to play the fool,
And to do that well, craves
a kind of wit
He must observe their mood
on whom he jests
The quality of persons
and the time,
And like the haggard
check at every
That comes before his
This is a practice
As full of labour
wise mans
For folly that
shows wan
But wise men
quite taint

Illustration 3 A fool

He must observe their mood on whom he jests,
The quality of persons and the time,

(3.1.59–62)

From that we can build up a picture of how Shakespeare used the fool.

Foolish and clever

The fool is both clever and foolish. He certainly plays the part of the fool; that's to say, he often appears witless. But to be seen as a fool requires a certain intelligence. This is sometimes a useful defence. The fool in *King Lear* is a fierce critic of Lear but when threatened he takes defence in his assumed imbecility.

Fool as commentator

The fool comments on the fashions of the time. In this respect, the fool is like an alternative comedian, who produces laughter by pointing out what is typical (though not usually observed) in contemporary life. Again, the fool in Lear is a good example. He's the most consistently political figure in the play; his shrill chatter frequently returns to the folly of Lear giving up the crown.

Showing up folly

The idea that the fool jests about those around him indicates that though he's the fool, his behaviour aims at showing up their folly. This is central in *Lear*; the task of the fool is to show that the real fool is Lear.

The fool and language

Fools usually expose others through a clever, and sometimes quite bewildering, use of language. In a typical passage the audience is dazzled by a torrent of words. Quite often fools play on their multiple meanings. In *Twelfth Night*, Feste says that he is Olivia's 'corrupter of words' (2.5.35). Sometimes it's complained that Shakespeare's fools aren't funny. This is true. Their jokes are often very complicated and when understood not very amusing. It's best to listen to their piping chatter and enjoy the confusion of words bubbling up.

The privilege of fools

Fools get away with what they say because they are, to quote Olivia, 'allowed' (1.5.90). That's to say, they have permission to say what others aren't allowed to. Even so, there are limits; and in *Twelfth Night*, Feste gets very close to being thrown out.

Fools and conventions

But as with lovers, Shakespeare is not content to stick to conventions. Most of his fools are distinctive individuals with their own ways of talking and, in some cases, their own histories, which come to have a place in the plots of the plays. One of the things that's distinctive about the fool in *Lear* is his very strong affection for Lear. In spite of his bitter criticism of Lear's folly, he calls Lear 'nuncle' and Lear calls him 'boy'.

2.14 Strangers

▶ 'being a stranger in this city here' (*The Taming of the Shrew*, 2.1.88)

Strangers have a vital role in Shakespeare. We may divide them into two classes.

New arrivals

These are new to a city or country. Such characters are not strangers by nature or culture; they can and do fit in. What they provide is the ingredients for a plot in which there's confusion and, in the case of comedy, a happy ending (see 5.4).

Permanent strangers

There are, however, some characters who'll always be strangers. They'll be so for different reasons.

Othello is a stranger because of his culture. It's not just a matter of his being black, but of his thinking and feeling in a way that's quite different from the Venetians among whom he lives.

Shylock in *The Merchant of Venice* is a stranger because of his religion. One of the purposes of the rather odd conversation between Antonio and Shylock about Jacob (1.3) is to underline how their different religions divide them.

Antonio in *Twelfth Night* is a stranger because of his homosexuality. In plays that drive towards marriage as the satisfactory ending, the homosexual is going to be left out. He will always be a stranger.

2.15 Characters and people

▶ 'a kind of character' (*Measure for Measure*, 1.1.27)

In this section the figures in the plays have been called both 'characters' and 'people'. It's time now to make a distinction between them.

When we call a figure in literature a 'character', we're drawing attention to the fact that he or she has been made, devised or created by an author. This is called *characterisation*.

Thinking about the plays requires us to see the figures as characters. We can, for instance, ask questions about the language they are given to speak, the actions they have to perform and the kind of relationship they establish with the audience. What, however, we have to remember is that:

• **to each other, characters are not figures made by an author, but people**.

Lady Macbeth greets Macbeth as 'My husband', not as the central figure in a drama. The whole emotional interplay which gives life to the plays depends upon the characters talking to each other as real people.

2.16 Stock characters

▶ 'I must play the workman' (*Cymbeline*, 4.1.6)

One of the important elements in Shakespeare's characterisation is the way he creates a character out of stock types. 'Stock' means:

- **a figure with clear distinguishing features, who behaves in an expected way and to whom the audience has a predictable response.**

The word 'stock' helps to bring out something very important about such characters – they are familiar; we've seen the type before. They are like goods (stock) in a shop; if we went to buy one, we'd know exactly what we were getting.

Drama has always used stock characters. What's more, the same kind of character turns up over the centuries. In Greek comedies, for instance, there are dim-witted masters helped out of scrapes by clever servants. This is more or less what happens in *The Taming of the Shrew*. Tranio and Biondello are more quick-witted than their master, Lucentio. A twentieth-century version of this is the Jeeves and Wooster stories of P. G. Wodehouse.

The crucial point about Shakespeare is that:

- **stock characters are often his starting point**.

Stock characters can be seen as 'ghosts' behind the figures we meet on stage and page. For instance, in the plays we find the following characters:

The enterprising heroine

Shakespeare has several heroines who go on adventures, usually for the sake of love. They are often the driving force behind the comedies. Were it not for for Viola disguising herself, the plot of *Twelfth Night* would get nowhere. An interesting variant upon the enterprising heroine is Desdemona, who elopes to marry Othello.

The lover

Shakespeare creates lovers who are bashful and tongue-tied (Claudio, Orlando), passive (Orsino), would-be writers of verse (Benedick, Orlando) and, unlike their beloveds, given to romantic gestures (Orlando runs through the forest pinning poems about Rosalind on the trees).

The clever servant

The clever servant usually has to help his master out of difficult situations. Maria in *Twelfth Night* invents and implements the plot that humiliates Malvolio.

The ingenious priest

In some respects, the ingenious priest has the same function as the clever servant – he's there to solve problems. In *Much Ado About Nothing*, it's the priest who helps sort out the difficulties over Hero and Claudio's marriage.

The fool

As indicated above (see 2.13) the role of the fool was to sing, dance, engage in word-play and, in some circumstances, to behave strangely. The fool in *King Lear* combines most of these functions.

The clown

A clown differs from a fool because whereas a fool is clever and witty, a clown is usually slow, unsophisticated and not very bright. He's usually the butt of tricks and jokes. In *The Winter's Tale*, the clown is deceived and robbed by Autolycus.

The humorous character

Any character who was believed to have an excess of a 'humour' (the substances such as choler and bile that gave a person his or her own emotional characteristics) was thought of as funny. Hence, of course, 'humorous'. Of these the melancholy man who broods upon the sadness of life was a familiar stock figure. The melancholy Jaques in *As You Like It* derives from this character.

The malcontent

Jaques also has something in common with the malcontent, a character who exists on the margins of society because either his past or his nature excludes him. The murderers in *Macbeth* have several characteristics of the malcontent; they would like to progress in the court but feel disgruntled because they have been excluded from power.

The revenger

The revenger was a very popular figure in the plays of Shakespeare's time. He was often someone of an upright and even sensitive nature who was so appalled by an act of injustice committed by someone in power that he felt impelled to set things right by taking revenge.

The gull

The gull is any character who is easily deceived (the word 'gullible' is associated with it). Usually a gull is coupled in the play with one who deceives. For instance, Sir Andrew in *Twelfth Night* is gulled by the confident and wily Sir Toby.

The machiavel

As was stressed above, the machiavel is an unscrupulous figure who will stop at nothing to gain power. Edmund in *King Lear* is an obvious example.

The boasting soldier

The soldier who boasts and lies about his exploits is a familiar comic figure. In Shakespeare, Falstaff is a rich development of such a figure – hugely inventive in his boasting and quite unabashed when found out.

Shakespeare's inventiveness

It's important to see that although in a large number of cases Shakespeare's characters derive from stock figures, they don't usually appear on stage as merely familiar dramatic types. Shakespeare is always inventive. One of the signs of his inventiveness is that:

- **where he might just have given us a stock figure he gives us a character with a set of distinguishing characteristics.**

It looks as if he couldn't resist character. By that I mean, he couldn't resist giving a figure a set of distinguishing (and often entertaining, intriguing and likeable) features.

2.17 Character and dramatic function

▶ 'their particular functions' (*Henry V*, 3.7.37)

There is another truth about the way Shakespeare handles character, which is slightly at odds with what has just been said:

- **Shakespeare sometimes moulds his characters according to the dramatic needs of the plot.**

Character can be shaped by dramatic function. Characters do or don't do things because the progress of the plot requires them to.

An example will help. In *Othello* Desdemona is something of a problem if you try to make sense of her behaviour throughout the play. She starts as a bold and adventurous woman who, among other things, recognises the power and importance of human sexuality. Later, however, she becomes passive and naïve (she can't believe that wives deceive their husbands). At the climax of the play she submits to Othello, allowing him to murder her. This is not the determined and forceful woman we met in the opening scenes.

Now it's possible to make sense of her by saying she's in a foreign country (Cyprus), depends too much on her ability to charm and is unused to being a military wife, but it might be that she changes because Shakespeare needs her to do different things at different times. If she remained the tough, worldly and independent woman of the first part, he couldn't have plausibly given us the tragic outcome. The woman who stood up to the Venetian Senate wouldn't have allowed Othello to strangle her.

A useful piece of advice about difficulties in someone's character is to ask whether there might be dramatic needs shaping what is said and done. When puzzled, the reader can look at the immediate scene and think about what characters need to be like for it to be effective.

2.18 Characters explaining themselves

▶ 'Tell me thy mind' (*The Taming of the Shrew* 1.1.21)

Direct self-explanation

When Lucentio asks Tranio to tell him his mind, he means no more than: 'what do you think?' In fact, in the lines that go before, he's told us what he thinks in a theatrically distinctive way. He's said things such as:

> Pisa, renowned for grave citizens,
> Gave me my being, and my father first –
> A merchant of great traffic in the world,
> Vincentio, come of the Bentivolii.

> (1.1.10–13)

When we remember that he's talking to Tranio, all this seems rather odd. Tranio knows it already!

This isn't Shakespeare making a mistake. It's a case of what's been called direct self-explanation or exposition. Drama isn't always like real life. There are moments when the audience needs to know something, so a character tells us things, even if the other people on stage know this already. We have to accept that this is a convention.

A variation upon this is the speech in which a character lets us know what he or she is like. When in Act 3, Sc. 1, Julius Caesar gives his reasons for not lifting the banishment imposed upon Cimber, he talks of how he's 'constant as the Northern Star' (1.60). We shouldn't read this as Caesar bragging but as an insight into the kind of man he is.

Related to direct self-explanation is the expository speech in which a character reveals the circumstances of his or her life that will enable the audience to understand the plot. Egeus's speech in the first scene of *A Midsummer Night's Dream* has this function.

2.19 Understanding Shakespeare's characters

▶ 'the mind's construction' (*Macbeth*, 1.4.12)

One of the problems of understanding Shakespeare's characters is that we come to the plays with our own ideas about what makes people tick. We've built into our language about people assumptions drawn from psychology and sociology, and it's all too easy to apply these uncritically to Shakespeare. When Freudian psychology was popular, it seemed quite natural to interpret Hamlet as suffering from an Oedipus complex; that's to say, someone who wanted to kill his father so he could have his mother all to himself.

Now nobody would want to deny that one of the most powerful relationships in *Hamlet* is that between the prince and his mother. The issue for understanding character is whether the approach through psychology or sociology is always a helpful one.

I want to suggest that it's not necessarily a good way into a character. The issue is this:

- **is Shakespeare interested in explaining the behaviour of his characters?**

Consider another character – Macbeth. When he's murdered the King, Macbeth suffers intense guilt. Does this need explaining? He's killed an old man in his bed. Macbeth's guilt is not at all surprising. Indeed, it would be surprising if he didn't feel guilty.

- **What Shakespeare is keen to explore is not the reason for a feeling but what it's like to have that feeling.**

Most of the time Shakespeare is not interested in explaining why a character feels or does something. Either the reason is obvious or he just doesn't bother to seek reasons. In lots of the plays, characters fall in love. This is a mystery to everybody; Shakespeare has better things to do than give us reasons why, say, Rosalind and Orlando love each other.

In Shakespeare we are presented with the feelings that most people feel at some time or another: anger, disappointment, doubt, fear, jealousy, joy, lust, rage, suspicion, and so on. He shows us what it's like to have these feelings – the feel of feeling them. His characters are not therefore to be looked upon as cases for psychological analysis or sociological theorising.

2.20 Characters and language

▶ 'my language' (*The Tempest*, 1.2.432)

What makes one character different from another is Shakespeare's words:

- **each of his characters is given a distinctive way of speaking.**

This is an aspect of Shakespeare's love of character. Quite often in the plays all that is needed is a stock character, but Shakespeare gives us more – individuality and personality. In *Richard III* two murderers are sent to kill Clarence; all that the plot requires is that they kill him, but Shakespeare makes them very different; one can cope easily with his conscience, while the other is troubled by it.

Individuality is the creation of the words Shakespeare uses. When in *The Tempest* Ferdinand exclaims 'my language', he's actually referring to language in the sense of the English or the French language, but he might well have been talking about the distinctive way in which characters in Shakespeare talks.

These distinctive ways of speaking are created through the following:

- their words
- the shape of their sentences
- the sounds of their words.

Language and character

Examples will help. Listen to Othello talking about how he told stories to Desdemona:

Such was my process,
And of the cannibals that each other eat,
The Anthropophagi, and men whose heads
Do grow beneath their shoulders. These things to hear
Would Desdemona seriously incline

(1.3.141–5)

'Anthropophagi' (cannibals) is a strange, exotic word. Its use places Othello apart from the Venetian society. Such language gives him a quality which is both mysterious and vivid. Yet in the very clear sense of the word, Othello's language is plain. Neither in those lines nor in whole passages in the play does he speak figuratively; words for Othello are weighted with the meanings they have in everyday use rather than with the elaborations of the poet.

It's worth attending to the way in which Othello's sentences are put together. Here there's a departure from the word orders of everyday speech. The obvious way of wording the last sentence would be: Desdemona seriously inclined to hear these things. In Othello's sentence, Desdemona appears in the middle, and the 'climax' is not what she hears but her act of hearing. It might be said that this word order (or syntax) makes her more important and is therefore an expression of his love.

The sound of his words makes his speech distinctive. Whenever Othello speaks, there is a stately rise and fall in the pitch of the words. (These are called cadences.) To my ear the first sentence makes a minor rise and fall on 'each other eat' before reaching its highest point on 'Anthropophagi'. The final sentence has a smooth and almost grave falling cadence on 'seriously incline', the movement of the sounds enacting the seriousness of Desdemona's intent listening.

A character can be distinctive and yet change the way in which he or she speaks. A change in speech can indicate how experience has altered a character or how a character has to adapt to new circumstances. In *Richard II* the king's language in the opening scenes is rhetorical and authoritative, whereas as he loses power he becomes far more elaborate and poetic.

Exercises

2.1 Observe the different ways in which each character is first introduced. You may like to think about what the character says, what he or she does, the stage the plot is at and what other characters say about him or her.

2.2 Trace how the major characters develop. In what scenes do they change the most? What events lead them to change?

2.3 Are there any characters in the plays you are studying that have grown out of stock theatrical figures? In what ways has Shakespeare developed them?

2.4 Try to identify the distinctive ways in which the characters speak. You will have to look at their words, sentences, images and how they respond to what other characters say.

2.5 Look through the plays with which you are familiar and think about the variety of the characters in terms of their status, personality and the detail in which they are presented.

3 What and where: stories, plots and worlds

3.1 Shakespeare's stories

▶ 'there is an old tale goes' (*The Merry Wives of Windsor*, 4.4.27)

In class we sometimes forget just how good Shakespeare's stories are. But not in the theatre; here the action sweeps us along. We should always remember that

● **what we see in the theatre are actions performed by a set of characters.**

Shakespeare's ideas and themes are enthralling, but what makes them so is the fact that they're acted out by characters on a stage. A useful point to remember is this:

● **the story comes first.**

Ideas arise out of the story. *Julius Caesar* is about loyalty and treachery, but those ideas emerge because we see before us a story of how a group of people kill the man who was once their friend.

3.2 The interest of stories

▶ 'your tale, sir, would cure deafness' (*The Tempest*, 1.2.106)

That line is spoken by Miranda in response to her father's rather irritable question: 'Dost thou hear?' Perhaps Prospero sees that her attention is wandering. Though it's pure guesswork, my impression is that Shakespeare is very sure that what he's got to tell us is going to be interesting.

Take, for example, the story of *Measure for Measure*. This is how it gets going.

There was a time when the people of Vienna were sexually wild: prostitution, venereal disease, sleeping around – the lot! The Duke felt he ought to do something, so he devised a plan in which he announced he was going abroad and that a clever and very puritanical young lawyer, Angelo, would be left in charge. The Duke believed Angelo would clear up the moral mess.

This is exactly what Angelo set about doing. He revived an old law which punished sex outside marriage with death. Under this law, a young man called Claudio was arrested, because the girl he had planned to marry was pregnant. Claudio was sentenced to death. He asked his friend, Lucio, to go to his sister and ask for help.

Claudio's sister, Isabella, was about to become a nun. When she heard about her brother she went to Angelo and pleaded for his life. Angelo told her to return later. When she had gone, he admitted to himself that for the first time in his life he was overcome with intense sexual desire. He wanted to sleep with Isabella. When she returned, he put his terms to her: either she slept with him, or her brother would die.

Meanwhile, as in lots of good tales, the Duke had reappeared disguised as a friar – a wandering monk. He's let into the prison, and there he overhears Isabella telling her brother that she's no intention of sleeping with Angelo and that, consequently, he must prepare to die. What is the Duke to do about this?

The complications of the plot multiply from this point onwards, and the end is more or less satisfactory. All we need to notice at this point are the features that make this a good tale. We might single out the following:

- **Rulers**

Like a lot of stories it concerns the problems of rulers; we can see that their lives are full of difficulties.

- **Improbabilities**

It depends upon delightfully unlikely occurrences such as disguise. We know we're in the world of story-telling, where the improbable is taken for granted.

- **Love and desire**

It's concerned with one of the most powerful of human feelings. Sexual desire is sudden and devastating.

- **Families**

Two of the characters are brother and sister – one of the strongest human bonds. Having, therefore, to tell your brother that he must die has a special horror about it.

- **Achieving an ending**

It seems unlikely that the story can have a happy ending. This is particularly teasing because we sense that this is exactly the kind of tale that does end happily.

One thing needs to be stressed about several of these points. It's this:

- **what excites our interest are those things that we are used to finding in stories.**

It's probably because Shakespeare understood people's love of stories that he chose his plots from the famous stories of the past.

3.3 Shakespeare's use of stories

▶ 'like an old tale' (*The Winter's Tale*, 5.2.61)

I think a lot of people who are new to Shakespeare feel a slight twinge of disappointment when they are told that with the exception of *The Tempest* none of Shakespeare's stories are original. We might ask: can he be all he's cracked up to be if he couldn't think up his own tales?

Three points might help us to overcome this feeling.

The world of story-telling

The fact that Shakespeare borrowed his tales shows us what kind of an artist he is:

- **Shakespeare is close to the world of convivial story-telling.**

He happily stands in a tradition where what matters is that a good tale is well told. As long as the tale is enjoyed, nobody bothers about whether or not it's original.

Good stories

- **Shakespeare knew a good tale when he heard one.**

The reason he chose the tales he did is that he knew what people liked to hear and see.

How he tells it

What matters is not the story that Shakespeare heard but the one he tells in his play. Shakespeare alters the order of events, introduces and omits characters and even changes how the story ends.

3.4 Stories and their themes

▶ 'here is every thing' (*The Tempest*, 2.1.54)

When Gonzalo speaks those words, he's talking about how the island they've landed on provides everything for their survival. Those who see Shakespeare find that:

- **virtually everything that matters to people is to be found in these plays.**

In Shakespeare we find the stories that delight people everywhere.

Romeo and Juliet

No story is more haunting than that of lovers drawn together in spite of being divided by class, religion, culture or, in the case of this play, an ancient family feud. In a successful production the audience wants all the impediments to their love to be removed.

The Merchant of Venice

What holds an audience is the old struggle between justice and mercy, a struggle which culminates in a scene that's always popular in literature – the trial. What the audience wants to see is how the victim will escape.

Julius Caesar

Two closely related elements rivet the attention of the audience in *Julius Caesar*. The first is the problem of political assassination. The play poses the questions: will Caesar become a tyrant? is it right to kill him? The second element introduces the issue of the man (Brutus) who is probably better (more thoughtful, more noble) than the cause that he leads.

3.5 Stories and plot

▶ 'the sequent issue' (*All's Well That Ends Well*, 5.3.200)

Plot and story

If we re-arrange that line, we can say the 'issue' in a play is the sequence. What matters in Shakespeare's plays is what happens and the order in which it happens. This is a matter of plot rather than of story:

- **a story** is the order of events in which they happened
- **a plot** is the order of events in which an author chooses to tell the tale.

For instance, in *Measure for Measure* we are about half-way through the play when we are told that the lawyer Angelo had once intended to marry a girl called Mariana but slid out of the agreement. Clearly, this event took place before the opening scene of the play, but it can have no part to play, and therefore can't influence our feelings, until it's mentioned. The point we can learn from this is:

- **always attend to the order of events as they are shown to us on the stage.**

What characters know

This leads to another very important point:

- **when thinking about a play, always remember what each character knows at each stage of the drama.**

The experience of watching a play is one of seeing life as it happens. Characters have memories but they don't know (though they might hope for or fear) the future.

For instance, there's an important scene in *Romeo and Juliet*, in which the eager Juliet is looking forward to her first night with Romeo (Act 3. sc. 2); what she doesn't know is that Romeo has killed her cousin in a street brawl. The audience know this, so see things in a different light from Juliet.

3.6 Aims and expectations

▶ 'I long to hear the story of your life'

(*The Tempest*, 5.1.315–16)

What drives a story is:

- **the aims of the characters.**

Shakespeare presents characters who are driven by a very strong sense of purpose. They want something and they have the energy, the determination and the ingenuity to achieve it.

Expectation and the audience

The drive of the individual characters is inseparable from another factor:

- **the expectations of the audience.**

To expect something is to adopt an attitude of looking forward to what we know is coming. We can't expect the unexpected. In Shakespeare, the audience, if not the characters, knows what's coming. Sometimes (particularly in the comedies) we don't know *how* it's going to come about, but we have a clear idea about *what* the outcome will be. Our attitude, therefore, is either longing or fear, longing in the case of the comedies (we want the girl to get her man) and fear in the case of the tragedies (we can see all too clearly how this is going to end).

Shakespeare arouses our expectation in the following ways:

- we wonder how the characters will achieve their aims (how will the lovers in *A Midsummer Night's Dream* find happiness?)
- we wonder whether characters will change their minds (will Cassius persuade Brutus to join the plot against Caesar?)
- we wonder why a character is in a particular mood (will we find out why Antonio is sad at the start of *The Merchant of Venice*?)

The audience is very rarely surprised. Only in two cases, *The Winter's Tale* and *Cymbeline*, does something occur which we have not been led to expect.

Sequence and significance

When we ask why one scene follows another we often discover that

- **important aspects of a play emerge in the sequence of events.**

In particular, the hopes, fears and problems of the characters are lessened or sharpened by the order and the immediacy of events.

Take, for example, the plight of Viola in *Twelfth Night*. She's disguised herself as a young man and found employment in the court of Duke Orsino as the one who carries messages to the Lady Olivia. Unfortunately for Viola, two things happen: she falls in love with Orsino, and Olivia, believing her to be a man, falls in love with her. Because she's disguised she's trapped. However, as soon as Viola realises that Olivia loves her, Shakespeare reassures us by showing that her twin brother, whom she thought was drowned, is alive. The audience can see that he is a suitable husband for Olivia.

3.7 The movement of plots

▶ 'good plots' (*The Merry Wives of Windsor*, 3.2.34)

Talk about the sequence of scenes brings out what we are sometimes inclined to ignore:

- **a play moves in time.**

This means that though we talk about the design or the structure of a plot, we should remember that this is a structure that *moves*. To talk about plot is to talk about its movement or trajectory; plots have been somewhere and they are always going somewhere.

3.8 The form of Shakespeare's plots

▶ 'half to half' (*Antony and Cleopatra*, 3.13.9)

The twofold movement

When we look at a Shakespeare plot we notice its shape. His plays have a twofold movement:

- the first movement starts with the opening of the play and finishes in the middle scenes
- the second takes us through to the end.

This means that we shouldn't be distracted by the division of Shakespeare into five acts. For a start, we can't be sure that this is what he intended.

A second very important point is that:

- **in the theatre we're not usually aware of divisions between scenes or acts.**

The action is fluid; one set of events leads to another without a break.

This twofold movement tells us three important things about the way Shakespeare's plots develop.

Crisis and resolution

This is the pattern:

- **plots move to a crisis and then on towards a resolution.**

The crisis can be a merry confusion or a dramatic conflict, while the resolution can be joyful or dark and serious. The first kind of plot is comedy, the second kind tragedy.

No formulae

By way of a qualification, we must add:

- **Shakespeare doesn't work to fixed formulae.**

He's got no template which shapes everything he does. In the twofold movement he includes a number of quite different crises and resolutions. For instance, though the crisis in both *Julius Caesar* and *Romeo and Juliet* is a death, each is quite different – Caesar's death is plotted, whereas Tybalt's is a kind of accident.

The pivot

The twofold movement means that:

- the middle of the play is a **pivot** or **fulcrum**.

We see in it the fruition of what started to grow at the beginning and the seeds of the closing action. It's always interesting, therefore, to look at what happens in the third act. For instance, in *Hamlet* the third act shows the game of cat and mouse coming to a crisis; Claudius decides that whatever is troubling Hamlet, it's not madness, and through the play called *The Mousetrap* Hamlet becomes convinced that Claudius is indeed guilty of his father's murder.

3.9 How plots begin

▶ **'the true beginning of our end'** (*A Midsummer Night's Dream*, 5.1.111)

How does Shakespeare get a plot going?

New situations

Shakespeare not only introduces characters to the audience; he does so by showing those characters in new situations. Something has either happened before the play opens or a new event occurs at the start. The characters have to respond.

A Midsummer Night's Dream opens with Theseus looking forward to his marriage, and Hermia faced with an ultimatum from her father.

Tension

Shakespeare shows us tension between Montagues and Capulets at the start of *Romeo and Juliet*, and between Antonio and Shylock at the start of *The Merchant of Venice*.

Plans

Characters respond to tension and new situations with plans. Early on in a play, Shakespeare likes to establish what the characters are up to. Drama might be said to be about the ability of characters to work out schemes in response to the challenges of new situations.

Romeo and Juliet fall in love so they makes plans to marry. Macbeth becomes Thane of Cawdor so he wants to rise higher.

How plays begin

The above points don't actually tell us *how* Shakespeare goes about establishing his plots. Below are some indications, all from the first two scenes of *Twelfth Night*. They consist of 101 lines; Shakespeare is economical in his establishment of the plot and the world in which it happens.

- **Signalling themes**

One of the functions of an opening scene is to signal to the audience what the play is going to be about. This is the first line of the play:

> If music be the food of love, play on …

The play is about love. Even the 'if' is important; love is shown to be a strange and chancy business.

- **Images and action**

Sometimes, Shakespeare uses an image to anticipate later action. In his opening speech, Orsino uses the image of the sea: love, he says, has an endless appetite, which swallows everything (lines 9–14). This image has a bearing on the second scene. Viola emerges from a shipwreck and causes various emotional shipwrecks till the plot reaches calm waters.

- **Links between characters**

We can see that Orsino and Olivia are both wrapped up in their worlds. Orsino wants to so feed on love that his 'appetite may sicken and so die' (line 3) and she to live 'like a cloistress' (1.1.27) – nun. Both Orsino and Olivia need to break out, but neither are likely to do so unless someone intervenes to stir them out of their enclosed lives.

- **New characters**

This is the function of Viola, who appears out of the sea, but unlike the self-absorbed Orsino and Olivia, she's full of enterprising energy. Though fully convinced that her brother is dead (a clear parallel with Olivia), she takes an interest in the Duke (she's heard he is a bachelor) and devises a scheme (disguising herself as a young man) to get her a position in his court.

- **The setting**

In the two scenes we learn something about the setting. Illyria is a place of music, hunting, courteous rituals and, if the sailor is representative, its citizens are kindly and welcoming.

3.10 How plots develop

▶ **'the middle centre'** (*I Henry VI*, 2.2.6)

The middle of a play is the working out of the plot elements. Because there are different kinds of plots, there's a variety of ways in which they work out.

A sequence of actions

The experience of watching some plays is of seeing a swift movement of events. In *Richard II*, the frivolous King seizes John of Gaunt's money. At the end of the scene, we hear that Bolingbroke has set sail, and in the next scene we hear he's landed. Soon Richard has lost power, and Bolingbroke is virtually king.

The planned and the unplanned

One of the preoccupations of the middle scenes is the way chance (often called fortune) frustrates characters' plans. Romeo and Juliet marry but between the ceremony and their first night together, Romeo kills Tybalt. This leads to new plot elements – his banishment and the Friar's fatal scheme.

Plans that go wrong

A plot can progress because plans go astray. In *A Midsummer Night's Dream* Oberon tries to help Helena by ordering Robin to put love drops in Demetrius' eyes. But he gets it wrong. Lysander gets the drops, wakes, sees Helena and instantly loves her.

Move and counter move

In some plays the middle scenes are taken up with the plots and counter plots of two competing characters. For instance, in *Much Ado About Nothing* Don John's plan to wreck the marriage of Hero and Claudio is countered by the Friar's scheme.

Changes in characters

A plot can be developed by a character changing. The plot of *Julius Caesar* moves according to the plans of the conspirators until the entrance, just after the murder, of Antony. In this crisis he ceases to be the reveller and reveals that he's a shrewd and cunning politician.

Confusion of identity

The driving force behind the actions in some middle scenes is the search for identity. The identity in question can be of individuals or of other characters. In *A Midsummer Night's Dream*, the plot shows that the men have to wake up to their real feelings. In the confusions of the wood, both make mistakes; they have to learn what they really feel for the women. Love can be a confusing business.

3.11 How plots end

▶ 'and there an end' (*The Two Gentlemen of Verona*, 1.3.65)

Any ending should resolve what the plot has opened up. All plots raise questions, expectations, hopes and fears. Resolution is what happens when we see how the elements are sorted out. The resolution of a plot should satisfy us in two ways:

- we should be gratified to know what happens to the characters
- we should take pleasure in the formal way in which the author has brought the end about.

There are two aspects of endings which are central to the closing down of any story: the turning point and recognition.

The turning point

Ends are often signalled by a turning point:

- in comedy the action takes an upward turn
- in tragedy it goes in a downward direction.

In *A Midsummer Night's Dream* it occurs when the lovers are found sleeping in the forest; after the hunting party has left, they joyfully recognise that the troubles and confusions of the night are over. In *Hamlet*, it's one of his return from the sea, his fight with Laertes at Ophelia's funeral or his acceptance of the invitation to the duel.

The turning point acts as a signal to the audience that the business of the middle scenes is over, and the action is either returning to normal life or pursuing its inevitable course to a tragic close.

Recognition

Quite often the turning point is inseparable from a moment of recognition. In most cases what's seen is only new to the character; the audience knows it already and has been waiting in expectation for the light to dawn. Recognition takes different forms:

- seeing someone afresh
- finding what has been lost
- discovering something about oneself
- understanding what has really been happening
- emerging from a delusion.

Twelfth Night ends with multiple recognitions:

- when Antonio mistakes Viola for Sebastian, she dares to hope that her brother has survived the shipwreck
- when both Sebastian and Viola meet on stage, they recognise each other for who they are, and the other characters begin to see the mistakes they've made
- Malvolio is made to recognise that he's been gulled, and, what is perhaps more painful, he's told that Feste took a prominent part in ridiculing him.

Shakespeare's plays often end with some or all of the following features.

Death

Tragedies end in death, though we should remember that not all deaths are presented tragically. The death of Richard II has many of the qualities we associate with tragedy – he has fallen from being king to a lonely prisoner, and in his death he gives that essentially tragic impression of being larger than the fate that overtakes him. The same can't be said about the deaths in *Richard III* of Clarence or Hastings.

Inclusion and exclusion

Tragedies and comedies can be distinguished by the way they treat the character who's excluded from his or her society. The exclusion can take a number of forms: lack of recognition, being hunted, disguise, madness, misunderstanding and the threat of death. Tragedy ends in the permanent exclusion of the victim. This isn't just a matter of death. Othello dies, but already he's been stripped of his office, and had he lived all he would have faced was disgrace.

In comedy the victim is readmitted and with that readmittance, as with marriage, society is renewed. In *Twelfth Night*, Viola returns from the strange world of cross-dressing. Of course, Shakespeare is never entirely predictable. Will Malvolio make peace with the people who have humiliated him or will he exclude himself for good?

Wonder

The comedies often end in wonder. The characters are so amazed at what's happened that they utter words of astonishment. Often the joy that accompanies wonder finds expression in songs and dances. The end of *The Winter's Tale* is full of wonder. The scene of recognition and reconciliation is reported by gentlemen of the court, one of whom, Ruggiero, says:

> Such a deal of wonder is broken out within this hour, that ballad-makers cannot be able to express it. (5.2.24–5)

The equivalent to wonder in a tragedy is the sense of the awesome nature of what has happened. In tragedy we come up against what's strange and terrible, sublime and fearful. There's no delight as in comedy, but in all the horror a glimpsed and fleeting sense that we are in the presence of something profound. At the end of *King Lear*, there is this piece of dialogue:

> *Kent*: Is this the promised end?
> *Edgar*: Or image of that horror?

> (5.3.238–9)

The end they speak of is the end of the world, the last judgement, the winding up of history. What happens on stage is so awesome that the language of the end of things is the only one that's adequate.

Telling stories

The desire to explain competes with wonder. At the end of *Much Ado About Nothing* the Friar says of the people's astonishment:

> All this amazement can I qualify
> When after that the holy rites are ended
> I'll tell you largely of fair Hero's death.
> Meantime, let wonder seem familiar

> (5.4.67–70)

The word 'qualify' is particularly interesting; it means something like lessen, diminish or moderate. The Friar, therefore, feels that there's too much 'amazement' and that it's his job to calm things down. He promises to do this by fully ('largely') telling them about how things have worked out so happily.

What we must believe is that after the marriage and the dancing, there'll be stories and explanations that will satisfy everyone. This is the usual pattern in those plots in which some characters have known more than others.

The need to recount and explain tells us two very important things about Shakespeare's plots:

- the audience needs to be reassured that all the characters know what's happened to them

- the audience need to be convinced that what they've seen is, however extra-ordinary, capable of being understood.

The first satisfies our sympathies; the second appeals to our reason and sense of probability.

Ends seen in the beginnings

In terms of literary form, beginnings and ends are the most distinctive aspects of any work. Perhaps because of their importance, Shakespeare sometimes links them.

Othello, for instance, ends, as it began, at night, and Othello and Desdemona are together. *Macbeth* closes, as it started, with the death of the Thane of Cawdor, both are traitors, both have died either after or in a battle.

3.12 The design of Shakespeare's plays

▶ 'like a mirror' (*Pericles*, 1.1.88)

Beginnings and ends are not the only elements in a Shakespeare plot that mirror each other. Occasionally,

- **Shakespeare relies on his audiences recognising that scenes echo and anticipate.**

Words and anticipation

Sometimes a word anticipates a later event. In one of the early scenes of *King Lear*, Edmund in a soliloquy is plotting his advancement when his brother, Edgar, enters. With a characteristic lightness, Edmund jokingly suggests that because Edgar's entrance is like something from an old play he should play the part of the villain:

Pat he comes, like the catastrophe of the old comedy. My cue is villainous melancholy, with a sigh like Tom o' Bedlam. (1.2.131–3)

Tom o' Bedlam was the standard name for a poor, mad beggar. What Edmund can't know is that later, when he's being hunted for his life, Edgar assumes the pose of a mad beggar, calling himself Poor Tom.

Action anticipating action

That scene also anticipates later action: Edmund knows that the word 'catastrophe' means the piece of stage action that brings in the end of a play. (Pretty much what we meant by the turning point.) Edmund intends to make Edgar look ridiculous by comparing him to a figure in a comedy. But the joke rebounds on him. In the catastrophe of the play, Edgar does enter, not as a mad beggar but as a mysterious champion. In the combat that takes place, Edgar kills Edmund.

This effect is often called dramatic irony. Words spoken in an earlier part of the play have a very different meaning when viewed from the perspective of a later event.

Actions anticipating themes

Sometimes in the combination of words and actions, a point about the plot of the play emerges. This happens in *Richard II*, a highly ritualised play with much emphasis on ceremony. Near the beginning, when Richard is proudly acting out the part of the authoritative king, he says he will come down from his throne to greet his cousin, Bolingbroke, who is in dispute with the Duke of Norfolk:

> We will descend and fold him in our arms.

> (1.3.54)

Those on stage should understand his descent as a gracious act. Richard, as king, does not need to descend.

But things are different later on. Bolingbroke, having been banished, returns, and people flock to his cause. He confronts Richard at Flint Castle. Richard is high up on the walls (see illustration 8) but his elevation does not reflect his power; he is king now only in name. He descends to meet Bolingbroke with dramatic flair, his words drawing attention to his actions:

> Down, down I come like glist'ring Phaethon,
> Wanting the manage of unruly jades.
> In the base court: base court where kings grow base

> (3.3.177–9)

Richard's descent enacts the movement of the plot. The image of Phaethon is of one who couldn't manage his horses ('unruly jades') as he drove the chariot of the sun, and, struck by a thunderbolt, plunged to the earth. Richard, often compared to the sun, now plunges to his fate, a fate which is enacted in the forced descent from the walls.

3.13 Plots and sub-plots

▶ 'tell you another tale' (*The Merry Wives of Windsor*, 1.1.71)

Sub-plots

There are plots in which there's a set of actions in addition to the main business of the play. This is usually called the sub-plot.

In *King Lear*, the main business concerns the consequences of Lear giving up the throne and dividing his kingdom. In the sub-plot the Earl of Gloucester is deceived by his illegitimate son, Edmund, into disinheriting his legitimate son, Edgar. Subsequently, Edmund supplants his father.

Three points need to made about the relationship between the main plot and the sub-plot in *King Lear*:

- they have common features; both are concerned with the problems of parents and children
- their themes overlap; both explore the issues of loyalty, treachery, obedience and love
- the themes are more starkly prominent in the sub-plot than in the main one. Both plots are about seeing; in the sub-plot Gloucester is blinded.

3.14 A plot in action

▶ **'what the play treats on'** (*A Midsummer Night's Dream*, 1.2.8)

Talking about various aspects of plots can be confusing, so let's look at the plot of a single play and see how it moves. It's better to choose a comedy, because they are, on the whole, more inventive in plotting. *The Merchant of Venice* displays a number of the elements discussed above.

Act 1, Scene 1 to Act 2, Scene 2

By alternating between Venice and Portia's home, Belmont, Shakespeare establishes the two major plots – the bond plot in which Antonio, for love of his friend, Bassanio, stands as surety for a loan of money, and the casket plot in which Portia's husband will be the one who chooses the casket that contains her picture.

The two plots are united by Bassanio; he needs to borrow money so he can be a suitor to Portia. The most important link is being bound: Portia is bound by her dead father's will, and Antonio accepts from Shylock a bond that if he fails to pay off the loan, Shylock can cut a pound of flesh from him.

The casket plot moves slowly; Portia is passive. The bond plot is busy; by Act 2, Scene 2 Gobbo, Shylock's servant, has joined Bassanio's household.

Act 2, Scene 3 to Act 2, Scene 6

The alternating rhythm of the two plots is now broken by four scenes from a third plot: the elopement of Jessica, Shylock's daughter. She acts out the role of the enterprising heroine, who ventures into danger for love. She passes a letter secretly to Gobbo (that's why he has to leave Shylock's service) for her lover, Lorenzo. She tells him that she'll disguise herself as a page, will steal money and jewels and will wait for Lorenzo to rescue her, when her father leaves the house.

This happens speedily. At the end of this sequence, Bassanio sails to Belmont.

Act 2, Scene 7 to Act 3, Scene 2

The alternating rhythm of bond and casket plot is restored, until the latter is resolved (in Act 3, Scene 2), when Bassanio, the one we hoped would be successful, picks the right one. In keeping with the folk-tale character of the plot, he's the third suitor to choose. There's symmetry established in the working of the casket plot when Gratiano and Nerissa, Portia's lady-in-waiting, agree to marry.

As the casket plot moves upwards, the bond plot descends. We now see the point of the Jessica plot: because Shylock is devastated by the loss of his daughter and his money, he decides, when he hears Antonio can't pay, to have the pound of flesh.

All three plots unite when Lorenzo and Jessica come to Belmont. News also arrives of the danger Antonio's in. Portia, who's been passive for most of the play, now becomes active and enterprising. She proposes that they go through the ceremonies of marriage but postpone the consummations till Antonio is safe. We now see that saving Antonio will be the main business of the second half of the play, and we sense that Portia will have a lot to do with it.

Act 3, Scene 3 to Act 4, Scene 1

Portia now shows herself to be an enterprising heroine. She leaves Lorenzo and Jessica in charge of Belmont, sends a messenger to her cousin, the lawyer Bellario, and exits with the excuse that she and Nerissa will go to a convent. When the men have got nowhere, she arrives in disguise at the trial, saves Antonio and convicts Shylock of a capital offence. Antonio shows mercy, and Shylock's life is spared. Shylock's exit signals the close of the bond plot.

Act 4, Scene 2, to Act 5, Scene 1

What follows is unexpected. Portia, having been subject to the will of her dead father, concocts a plan to put her husband in her power. She and Nerissa ask and are given the rings their husbands gave them, so when the men return to Belmont, they are shocked to hear that the girls have got the rings because they've slept with the lawyers. A letter explains all, and the couples go off to bed. Only Antonio is left without a beloved.

3.15 The 'world' of each play

▶ 'it is a world to see' (*Much Ado About Nothing*, 3.5.34)

If we ask the question where and when do Shakespeare's stories take place, we get two different kinds of answer.

In England

The plays take place in the England that he knew. Hence, in *Julius Caesar*, although the setting is Rome, we hear about chimneys, hats and clocks – all of them features of Elizabethan England.

More important than that, some of the attitudes are those of the England of his day; in particular, the anxieties about the power of the monarch owe a good deal to the shifts in power between the people and their kings and queens.

In its own world

The more important answer to the question about where a play takes place is:

● each Shakespeare play takes place in its own world.

In Shakespeare we get more than a setting; he creates before our eyes a distinctive world of thinking, feeling and seeing. Each of his plays has its own atmosphere.

Talk about worlds can sound a bit strange, so an example is called for.

Example

Macbeth is a quite distinctive world. It has the following features:

- *We are given a strong sense that this is Scotland* The breath melts on the wind, there's fog in the air, the land has its royal sites of burial and enthronement, the nobility live in castles, weird sisters meet travellers upon blasted healths and when conflicts arise, the people resort to bloodshed.

- *The world of the play is a lonely one* Most of the scenes consist of two or three people. Between those few scenes when the stage is peopled, what we see are lonely, tortured souls struggling with their consciences and imagining atrocities.

- *This is a world of fear* Malcolm and Donalbain flee Scotland because they are afraid, and those who are left live in fear of Macbeth. Fear shakes him; he's afraid to take the daggers back to the bedroom in which he's killed Duncan and once he's become king, his fears are focused on Banquo.

- *It's a world of night and darkness* Both Macbeth and Lady Macbeth enjoy imagining the darkness of night collaborating with their wicked deeds. Duncan and Banquo are murdered at night.

- *This is a weird world* The characters are never sure what they see or what is happening: Macbeth and Banquo are not sure what they see when they meet the weird sisters, and Macbeth thinks he sees a dagger which leads him to Duncan.

- *Death is everywhere* The reports of the battle at the beginning are horrific, and if we don't see blood on Macbeth's hands when he encounters the sisters, we certainly see it after he's murdered Duncan.

- *The world is evil* The weird sisters say that 'fair is foul' and the Macbeths, knowing full well what they are doing, murder an old man in his bed.

- *Finally, the poetry has a thickly textured quality* It's as if the world of intense evil finds expression in the clusters of images that are some of the characteristic marks of the play's language.

3.16 Different plays, different worlds

▶ **'countries different'** (*Hamlet*, 3.1.174)

One of the points about Scotland is that it's not England. At one point in *Macbeth*, we see the English court (Act 4, sc. 3) and we hear about the English king – Edward. Edward's court is a place to which people come for healing; Macbeth's Scotland, by contrast, is characterised by disease.

Coming to terms with the different worlds Shakespeare has created, means being aware of what is distinctive about them and appreciating how they differ from each other.

England in the history plays

England is not always the same kind of place in the history plays. The sharpest difference is between the world of *Richard II* and that of *Henry IV*.

Richard II still feels medieval; the play has the finely detailed and stylised quality of late medieval art in which the living flesh of face and hands contrast with gorgeous, highly decorated and patterned clothes. Everyone in *Richard II* speaks in verse; even the gardeners are sober, philosophical characters who sadly meditate in stately verse the fate of England's king. The actions (see 3.12) are also ritualised; the play has the decorum of a state occasion.

In the two *Henry IV* plays, England feels a very different place. We see the taverns of London, we hear earthy prose, we see thieving, trickery, parody and deception. The civil disorder has the quality of a real power struggle rather than the theological debate that it had in *Richard II*. In short, this is a robust, rough and tumble England quite different from the majestic unfolding of the chronicle of Richard's decline.

Rome

The Rome of *Julius Caesar* is different from that of *Coriolanous*. There's a confidence and feeling of security about Caesar's Rome; it's got a long history, so characters can justify their actions by appealing to the example of their ancestors. Rome suffers no real external threats, and the citizens are proud of their republican tradition.

Coriolanus is set in a much earlier phases of the city's history. Rome is just one city state among others, and one of the others – Corioli – is a dangerous enemy. The very existence of Rome depends upon its ability to fight. In such a world, heroes are created. And in early republican Rome the hero must be an outstanding soldier; only such a figure can be the saviour of Rome.

Tragic worlds

Each tragedy occupies a distinct world. We've already looked at the blood-soaked world of Macbeth's Scotland. An element in the dense atmosphere of that play is the commerce the human world has with the supernatural one. This is also true of *Hamlet*, but whereas the world of *Macbeth* is weird and sinister, the supernatural in *Hamlet* is too uncomfortably related to the human. The ghost comes back as a father and a husband, and the tasks he gives young Hamlet – killing his uncle without plotting against his mother – are, because of the family relationships, all but impossible.

Comic worlds

Perhaps the worlds of the comedies are closer to each other than the tragedies. In all the plays there's a feeling of festivity, of games, of playing with words and scheming against others. Many of the comedies have a fool, and his presence gives a common feeling of trickery and playfulness.

Nevertheless, there are differences. In *The Merchant of Venice*, the one thing that links everything in the plot is money: Bassanio is drawn to Portia because she's both beautiful and rich; Antonio shows his love for Bassanio by borrowing money on a ridiculous bond; Jessica not only elopes, she steals from her father, and Shylock's punishment is, in part, an economic one.

This is a very different world from *Much Ado About Nothing*. This is a sophist-icated world of courtesy and wit. Wordplay is highly valued and trickery is practised with gusto and most of the time, with good intentions. This is why the outburst of Claudio at the wedding is so dreadful – it's quite against the spirit of the society Shakespeare has created.

Exercises

3.1 Examine how Shakespeare starts his plots. You may need to think about what problems characters face, what they want and the means they use to achieve their ends. In what ways is the ending of the play evident from the opening?

3.2 Think about how the exact order of events influences the way the audi-ence responds to the play. You will need to be aware of how the audience is led to expect certain events.

3.3 Select three or four characters and look at the place they have in the plot. Are they characters that 'drive' the plot or do they serve the plot's needs by doing things that its successful working requires?

3.4 Try writing an account of the major features of the plots, bringing out as clearly as you can how they are designed and how they move.

3.5 What is distinctive about the 'world' of your play? How is its special atmosphere created? If you are studying two plays, compare the way in which each of them creates a distinctive place and time.

---

4 Words on stage

4.1 Watching plays

▶ **'played upon a stage'** (*Twelfth Night*, 3.4.122)

When Maria and Sir Toby are treating the gulled Malvolio as a lunatic, one of the tricksters says:

If this were played upon a stage now, I could condemn it as an improbable fiction.

A lot is going on in these lines; they raise the issue of just how probable events in drama are and what is the nature of fiction. They also contain a little word that might easily be overlooked – 'now'. The point is: the play (a fiction) is being performed upon a stage now. We are watching it, and the words spoken draw attention to the fact that that is what we are doing:

- **Shakespeare wants us to remember that what we are watching is a play.**

4.2 The stage and life

▶ **'All the world's a stage'** (*As You Like It*, 2.7.139)

A way of thinking about Shakespeare's habit of drawing our attention to the theatricality of his work is to think through those famous words from *As You Like It* quoted above. What lies behind the speech is this idea:

- **we respond to the theatre because it shows us that our lives are like plays.**

We might say that just as what happens on stage reminds us of our lives, so what we do in life is like what happens on a stage:

- **the stage mirrors life and life mirrors the stage.**

The 'All the world's a stage' speech goes on to talk about the parts people play:

> They have their exits and their entrances,
> And one man in his time plays many parts
>
> (2.7.141–2)

Our births and deaths are like players coming on or going off the stage, and in between we have a number of parts to play. The rest of the speech runs through them; significantly, they include the lover and the soldier. This is the idea:

- **life, like the stage, demands that we play different parts or roles**.

It's not surprising, therefore, that in several plays some characters perform a number of distinct functions: Henry V has to be a soldier before he's a lover; Hamlet has to be a madman before he can be the man at peace with himself, and Portia is both a dutiful daughter and an adventurous young woman. Life demands that these roles are played.

Playing a part

The idea that characters on stage play roles produces a number of effects.

(1) They know that what they are playing is a part

Some characters dwell on the differences between their knowledge of themselves and what others make of them. Richard III enjoys being a villain, and this enjoyment is increased when he convinces others that he's entirely concerned about them.

(2) The audience knows what roles characters are playing

One of the enjoyments of the theatre is being on 'the inside' of a character's thoughts and feelings. This means that some of the things they say have meanings for us that they can't have for the other characters. When in *Twelfth Night*, Viola as Cesario talks about her 'sister' to Orsino (Act 2, Scene 4), we know that there's no such person; Viola is her own sister, and the love she talks of, we see, is what she has for Orsino.

(3) Some characters are cast in roles but don't realise it

This is true of those who are deceived and gulled. Poor Malvolio thinks Olivia is asking him to play the role of her lover. In fact, it's a trick that's nothing to do with Olivia.

(4) Unsuitable parts

Some characters are cast in parts for which they are not suited. Here Hamlet stands out. He willingly takes on the role of the revenger, but finds it a part that's very difficult to play. Perhaps an answer to the age-old question about why Hamlet delays is that he's the wrong man for that part.

(5) Watching each other

The fifth link between life and the stage is that in both we watch each other. The Duke in *Measure for Measure* says that though he loves the people he does not 'like to stage me to their eyes' (1.1.68). 'Stage', of course, is significant: being seen is like being on stage.

This gives rise to a piece of stage business, which is remarkable for its capacity to produce widely differing effects:

- **one character watches another in secret**.

The plot of *Hamlet* is one in which Hamlet and the King watch each other. The King sees this as a necessity; at the turning point of the play he says:

Madness in great ones must not unwatched go.

(3.1.191)

(6) The audience watching

Our sixth element is the position of the audience: characters watch each other and audiences watch characters.

Audiences find that watching characters watch other characters can produce effects that are comical and painful. The sight of Malvolio reading the supposed letter from Olivia can be hilarious, but the pain of seeing Othello watch Cassio talking lightly about, as Othello mistakenly thinks, Desdemona is intense.

Life and art

The links between the theatre and life raise an issue that comes to be very important for Shakespeare:

- the relationship between life and art.

Art is about what's been made, formed, shaped, moulded, designed and so on, whereas life is what we find before any shaping or moulding. What Shakespeare and many of his contemporaries were fascinated by was how in life both are present.

In our lives we order, assemble, alter and rearrange our belongings and ourselves.

When Viola goes to see Olivia for the first time (*Twelfth Night*, 1.5.220–37), she rather boldly asks to see the veiled Olivia's face. What follows is a dialogue about art and life. Olivia, also boldly asks: 'Is't well done?' to which Viola wittily replies: 'Excellently done, if God did all.'

The dialogue turns on who's done what; is her beauty something that she's created or is it natural, the work of God? Both characters continue to play with the idea; Viola says in praise:

> 'Tis beauty truly blent, whose red and white
> Nature's own sweet and cunning hand laid on.

The language is all drawn from painting. The colours have been applied – 'laid on' – by the skilful – 'cunning' – hand of the artist nature. The audience might be prompted to wonder what they are seeing – is her face art or life?

4.3 The imagination of the audience

▶ 'Think, when we talk of horses, that you see them' (*Henry V*, Prol. 26)

These words are spoken by the Chorus. He recognises that what the audience see is a big wooden stage, whereas the action of the play concerns a battle between two armies. Later he says:

> And let us, ciphers to this great account,
> On your imaginary forces work.

(Prol., 17–18)

A 'cipher' stands in the place of another; here the players are ciphers standing in the place of the soldiers. Their task is to work upon the imaginations of the audience, so they see what they are told about. The words play upon two meanings of the word 'forces'; its immediate meaning is the imaginative powers of the audience, but if the 'ciphers' work successfully, then they will see the military forces. The Chorus tells us what theatre is about; you must

- **imagine what you do not see**.

Both audiences and readers have to imagine:

- **whenever we read a play we have to act it out in the theatres of our imaginations**.

That's to say, we must imagine a number of the things:

- the age of the characters
- how they are dressed
- at what pace they speak
- what words are given emphasis
- the tones of their voices
- what interpretation they give to the lines
- how they move
- what gestures they make
- how closely they stand to each other
- where they stand on the stage
- the expressions on their faces
- how they enter and exit
- what dances, processions and ceremonies are presented
- what's on the stage
- how the stage is lit
- the sound effects.

You'll be helped to imagine these if you've seen Shakespeare on stage, film or television. Also, some things such as spectacles, music, silence and fights are going to have a physical impact that it's difficult to completely imagine. But remember this:

- **there are some important things that come across very powerfully to the reader**.

An obvious example is the very wide range of meanings words have. Take, for example, the words already quoted from the Prologue of *Henry V*. Would everyone in the audience be able to think over the pun on 'forces'?

4.4 Language and actions

▶ **'the meaning or moral of his signs and tokens'** (*The Taming of the Shrew*, 4.4.78)

At the climax of *The Taming of the Shrew* the clever servant Tranio gestures to his master, Lucentio, that now's his chance to elope with Bianca. Lucentio doesn't understand, so another servant, Biondello, has to tell him 'the meaning' of Tranio's 'signs and tokens'. What Tranio is trying to get over is that there's a meaning in his gestures.

A vital principle of Shakespeare's plays is this:

- **actions are present in the words of the text**.

The difference between any literary language and the language of drama is that in drama the words have to be performed. They are not merely spoken, they are acted out. On stage, words are seen as well as heard. One character in *Cymbeline* talks about:

> ... posture
> That acts my words.

> (3.3.94–5)

What this means in practice is that the words invite the players to act them out. Gesture, movement, grouping, posture and physical states such as crying are indicated in the text. A dramatic text is one that requires to be physically embodied. A player must look for the signs in a text that require to be acted out.

Stage directions in the text

Sometimes a stage direction is built into the text. When *Richard II* says:

> For God's sake, let us sit upon the ground,
> And tell sad stories of the death of kings

> (3.2.151–2)

he must suit the actions to the words. The players might sit in a semi-circle or another arrangement appropriate to the telling of stories.

Gestures and mood

Different kinds of gesture appear in one of the most famous passages in Shakespeare. Here the gestures express mood and theme.

```
Example
```

Macbeth is thinking about killing Duncan.

> Go bid my mistress, when my drink is ready,
> She strike upon the bell. Get thee to bed.
> Is this a dagger which I see before me,
> The handle toward my hand? Come, let me clutch thee.
> I have thee not, and yet I see thee still.

> (2.1.31–5)

The first two sentences are instructions to a servant. It's possible that these are accompanied by light authoritative gestures; 'Get thee to bed' could be an almost casual wave of the hand. But there must be a very different gesture accompanying 'Is this a dagger ...'. He must somehow shape it to himself – 'I see before me' – and when he talks of the handle being towards his hand, what we must see is his hand, perhaps closing round it in a murderous grip.

'Come. let me clutch thee' brings out the tantalising nature of the sight. Is 'Come' spoken cajolingly, as if he's trying to woo the dagger to materialise, or is it more combative, as we might say in a fight 'Come on?' 'Clutch' could be eager or desperate or longing, and the gesture could be stealthy or sudden or violent.

The movement gives us the man and the play; Macbeth is trying to clutch the throne of Scotland, his reaching out enacts his ambition.

The spirit of action

In some scenes a whole set of actions are implied.

Example

After he's married Kate and taken her to his house, Petruchio invites the Tailor to provide clothes. He's no intention of buying anything; all he wants to do is give an outlandish performance of what a discontented person is like.

> *Petruchio*: Thy gown? Why, ay. Come tailor, let us see't.
> O mercy, God, what masquing stuff is here?
> What's this – a sleeve? 'Tis like a demi-cannon.
> What, up and down and carved like an apple-tart? Here's snip, and nip, and cut, and slish and slash,
> Like to a scissor in a barber's shop.
> Why, what o' devil's name, Tailor, call'st thou this?

> (4.3.86–92)

All kinds of hideous expressions of simulated disgust are made possible by 'O mercy, God', and when he criticises the dress he can waggle its offending bits at the tailor. 'Like to a scissor in a barber's shop' might be an invitation to Petruchio to do his own snipping, slishing, slashing and shredding of the dress in front of the luckless tailor.

4.5 The changing life of dramatic language

▶ **'Whilst this play is playing'** (*Hamlet*, 3.2.86)
Something is always happening in Shakespeare's language. This means that:

- successful dramatic language is always on the move, is always changing, adjusting, heightening or playing down an effect and raising or lowering the emotional temperature.

To use a geographical image, we can say:

- **in drama the contours of thought and feeling are always changing**.

Example

In this passage from *Twelfth Night*, Orsino has been giving advice to, as he supposes, young Cesario (Viola in disguise).

> *Orsino*: Then let thy love be younger than thyself,
> Or thy affection cannot hold the bent;
> For women are as roses, whose fair flower
> Being once displayed, doth fall that very hour.
> *Viola*: And so they are. Alas that they are so:
> To die even when they to perfection grow.

Emotionally, this scene is constantly changing. The tone of Orsino's speech shifts from earnest advice to a rather studied kind of regret. (He does the 'time passing, nothing lasts' bit with aplomb.) Viola's speech is both sad and funny. She has to adopt the manner of male nostalgia and regret that female beauty passes, but since that's also her beauty, the regret is more than a show.

Whether it's in a highly charged dialogue in which characters struggle for intellectual and emotional control or a puzzled soliloquy, Shakespeare always keeps the pulse of his plays alive through the ebb and flow of ideas and feeling.

4.6 Prose and verse

▶ 'here follows prose' (*Twelfth Night*, 2.5.133)
▶ 'you talk in blank verse' (*As You Like It*, 4.1 29)

Prose is what we usually write – sentences in which we say what we need to say in appropriate words and in accordance with the rules of grammar. Verse also has to meet those requirements, and in addition verse is written in lines of a given length. If ever you are in doubt in a Shakespeare play as to whether something is written in verse or prose, look at the way it's set out on the page. In particular, look at how the beginnings of lines are printed; if there are capital letters at the beginning of each line, then it's verse, if not, it's prose. For instance, this is verse:

> If music be the food of love, play on,
> Give me excess of it that, surfeiting,
> The appetite may sicken and so die.

> (*Twelfth Night*, 1.1.1–3)

and this is prose:

> What a plague means my neice to take the death of her brother thus? (*Twelfth Night*, 1.2.1–2)

The way lines are set out isn't the only difference between verse and prose, but it's a very useful form of identification.

Verse

Some technical points need to be made first. Shakespeare's lines have two formal features:

- syllables
- stresses.

Shakespeare's lines usually have ten syllables, as in the first three quoted above.

The rhythms of a line are created by stresses or emphases on syllables. In Shakespeare, the lines are formed by five units (traditionally called 'feet'), each of which is formed by an unstressed syllable followed by a stressed one. This 'foot' is called an iamb, and a line of five iambs is called an iambic pentameter. Because the verse doesn't rhyme, it's called blank verse. An unstressed syllable is marked: ´ a stressed one: ˘. The opening line of *Twelfth Night* works in this way:

> If music be the food of love, play on,

Four points need to be made about Shakespeare's verse.

- The verse is close to the rhythms of speech; in 'music' we naturally stress the first and not the second syllable.

- Shakespeare's verse isn't mechanical; it's full of variety. For instance, the second line of the *Twelfth Night* speech starts with an emphatic stress on 'Give'.
- The rhythms of his lines are the rhythms of the thoughts and feelings they express.
- The later the plays, the freer and more flexible the rhythms.

Prose

What both the prose and the verse share is *form*. Shakespeare's prose doesn't just flow in an unthinking way; it's composed.

This is how Hamlet speaks to Rosencrantz and Guildenstern:

> What a piece of work is a man! How noble in reason, how infinite in faculty, in form and moving how express and admirable, in action how like an angel, in apprehension how like a god – the beauty of the world, the paragon of animals! And yet to me what is this quintessence of dust? (2.2.304–9)

This is no outburst. He opens with a short sentence that acts as a terse summary of his subject. What follows are clauses that echo each other in their vocabulary and syntax – 'How noble ... how infinite ... how express ... how like ... how like ...'. He reaches his climax with two balanced, high-sounding claims to significance – 'the beauty of ... the paragon of ...' before deliberately deflating the grand effect with the thump of 'quintessence of dust?'

4.7 The uses of verse and prose

▶ 'words, life, and all' (*Richard II*, 2.115).

Knowing about blank verse or balanced prose doesn't get us very far. What matters is what Shakespeare's verse and prose achieves.

Language and status

Traditionally, characters of high rank speak verse, while those further down the social scale speak in prose. So Theseus in *A Midsummer Night's Dream* speaks verse, while the mechanicals – the workmen – speak in prose.

This is a useful though very rough guide. Some high-born characters speak both; Brutus in *Julius Caesar* is an example.

Language and issues

Another distinction is between tragedy and history on one side and comedy on the other. There's a tendency for the weighty matters of tragedy and history to be presented in verse and the lighter material of comedy in prose. This occurs within plays; the comic scenes in the histories are sometimes in prose, as in the case of the Falstaff scenes in the *Henry IV* plays.

Four things can be said about Shakespeare's use of prose and verse.

(1) Audience expectation

The first is that Shakespeare knew his audience would associate verse and prose with characters of particular social classes. Hence, he can work with their expectations to produce delightful jokes. At the start of *The Taming of the Shrew* Christopher Sly, a drunken tinker, is carried off by a mischievous lord, who has him bathed and clothed and then tries to convince him that he's not a tinker at all but a lord who's lost his memory. As soon as Sly is convinced, he starts speaking in elegant verse!

(2) Prose and states of mind

Prose can indicate a state of mind. The obvious case is madness. Both Lady Macbeth and Ophelia in *Hamlet* speak verse, but descend into fragmentary prose when mad.

(3) Responding to verse and prose

Shakespeare can trust his audience to respond more emotionally to verse than to prose. The most famous example is in *Julius Caesar*, when Brutus reasons with the crowd in cool prose, while Antony rouses them with highly emotional verse.

(4) Verse and heroes

Shakespeare never gives a hero nothing but prose. In all the great tragedies, the central figure has outstanding passages of verse. Verse, it seems, is the only adequate way of conveying the significance of what's happening.

4.8 Shakespeare's verse

▶ 'full of noises/Sounds' (*The Tempest*, 3.2.138–9)

When we read Shakespeare's verse we have to

● **read the sentences and not just the separate lines**.

The ends of lines don't necessarily complete meanings; what completes meaning is the end of the sentence. Hence when Juliet speaks in defence of Romeo, we need to read the whole sentence to get her meaning:

> Ah, poor my lord, what tongue shall smooth thy name
> When I, thy three-hours wife, have mangled it?

> (3.2.98–9)

We have to see that this is a run-on line (the sentence carries on to the next line), so Juliet doesn't just ask who'll speak smoothly (kindly) about Romeo but how any one can be expected to speak well of him if she doesn't.

Sounds and rhythms

Like all poetry we have to allow the sounds and rhythms of the language to work on us. For instance, in *Measure for Measure*, the Duke talks to a Friar about his strong preferences for the quiet life:

> My holy sir, none better knows than you
> How I have ever loved the life removed

> (1.3.7–8)

The fluid quality of the poetry (think about how the 'h' and 'l' sounds smoothly interlace) suggests that the 'life removed' is one of enviable quietness, and the rhythms give the language a sense of longing. The rhythms enact the meaning.

Textures

The textures of the language also contribute to the effects of the verse and prose. By texture I mean the combined effect of all the sounds the words make. Listen to Macbeth:

> Ere the bat hath flown
> His cloistered flight, ere to black Hecate's summons
> The shard-borne beetle with his drowsy hums
> Hath rung night's yawning peal, there shall be done
> A deed of dreadful note.
>
> (3.2.41–5)

The textures here are thick. The abrasive-sounding words are packed so densely that we have to sound them one by one – The shard-borne beetle'. Even the alliterations clog rather than loosen the flow of the line: 'his drowsy hums/Hath rung'.

Cadence

An important aspect of dramatic language is what is called cadence – the rise and fall in pitch a voice makes as it moves towards the end of a line, phrase or sentence. Cadences enact and reinforce the emotional energy of the language. Othello is famous for what has been called the 'music' of his verse. This music is largely a matter of rising and falling cadences. When he's reunited in Cyprus, his language is an expression of his love overcoming his fears:

> It gives me wonder great as my content
> To see you here before me. O my soul's joy
> If after every tempest come such calms.
>
> (2.1.184–6)

The voice swells like the seas he's just crossed. It reaches a high point in 'great' and then subsides with relief into 'content'. Likewise, there's a rising cadence on 'tempest' and a falling yet steady one on 'such calms'.

Variety

A writer might compose lines in which a syllable count is rigidly observed and the patterns of stresses are regular. Nevertheless, language is not even; the natural stresses vary from word to word, and what's being said will control the heaviness of stresses. As a result we might expect that in Shakespeare

- **there will be significant variations in the rhythms of speeches**.

Listen to the confidence of Petruchio. When asked what's brought him to Padua, he says:

> Such wind as scatters young men through the world
> To seek their fortunes farther than at home.
>
> (*The Taming of the Shrew*, 1.2.49–50)

There's a youthful swagger and bounce about the lines, which means that neither the weight of stress nor the rhythm is even. 'Wind' is stressed far more than 'through', and surely both 'young' and 'men' would be stressed by a player, in which case there's a lively irregularity about the line.

Distinctive voices

The variety of Shakespeare's dramatic verse is closely related to the emergence of distinctive voices.

Hamlet has a distinctive voice. This is how his first soliloquy opens:

> O that this too too solid flesh would melt,
> Thaw, and resolve itself into a dew,
> Or that the Everlasting had not fixed
> His canon 'gainst self-slaughter!

(1.2.129–32)

You might hear in the insistent 'too too' and the emphatic monosyllables an intellectual excitement that borders on obsessiveness. His delight in analysis and elaboration appears in the second line; he offers 'thaw' as an alternative to 'melt' and spells out what thawing or melting would involve. And this sounds like a quick mind; no sooner has he explored the melting of flesh but he comes up with another idea: 'Or that the everlasting ...'. The voice of Hamlet is heard in the textures and rhythms of the language.

4.9 Shakespeare's imagery

▶ 'painted imagery' (*Richard II*, 5.2.16)

The word 'imagery' is now used in a far wider sense than this sole example from Shakespeare. In *Richard II* it refers to the painted cloths hung from windows to celebrate a pageant. We now use it to refer to any way in which language makes an imaginative appeal through the senses. Shakespeare's verse and prose appeal to the eye, the ear, the nose with immediate force.

Figurative language

Because imagery is used so widely, it covers imaginative scene painting and figures of speech – simile, metaphor, personification and conceit. What often happens is that a passage of scene-painting is expressed in figurative terms; that's to say, language from one area of life is transferred to a different one, so that one thing is seen in terms of another. In *Much Ado About Nothing*, for instance, there's this line about the 'gentle day' first appearing in the early morning sky:

> Dapples the drowsy east with spots of grey.

(5.3.27)

Here the day is a painter, dappling a picture with tiny spots of grey paint.

Extended images

Images are often highly detailed. In *Richard II*, there are a number of intricately worked out images. For instance, when Richard is assuring his followers that Bolingbroke's rebellion will fail, he elaborates an image of the day and night that lasts for ten lines:

> So when this thief, this traitor, Bolingbroke,
> Who all this while hath revelled in the night
> Whilst we were wandering with the Antipodes,
> Shall see us rising in our throne, the east,
> His treasons will sit blushing in his face,
> Not able to endure the sight of day,
> But, self affrighted, tremble at his sin.

$$(3.2.43-9)$$

The image is applied so closely to the current events that it reads rather like an allegory. Bolingbroke is someone who uses the dark to commit evil; first he's a thief and then one who revels under cover of darkness. Richard, however, is the sun, and as he's the king he imagines that the east, where the sun rises, is his throne. When the sun rises, Bolingbroke will be overcome with shame and blush for his sins.

An image that's capable of extension is sometimes called a conceit. There are several examples in the elaborately poetic *Richard II*. Here Richard compares the prison in which he lies to the world:

> I have been studying how I may compare
> The prison where I live unto the world;
> And for because the world is populous,
> And here is not a creature but myself,
> I cannot do it. Yet I'll hammer it out.

$$(5.5.1-5)$$

The crucial words are 'hammer it out'. That's what a conceit does; once the tie between the two things is established, the poet must squeeze out all the possible links between the two.

The growth of an image

Sometimes an image grows in a line, one word making another appropriate. For instance, in *Twelfth Night* Antonio talks about his love for Sebastian. The image that emerges is of religious devotion:

> Relieved him with such sanctity of love,
> And to his image, which methought did promise
> Most venerable worth, did I devotion.

$$(3.4.352-4)$$

'Sanctity' (holiness) leads on to 'image' (a religious statue), 'venerable' (worthy of religious attention) and 'devotion'.

Compression

This is a feature of middle and late Shakespeare. Images grow in the line and emerge in few words. Shakespeare, apparently without effort, allows a vivid picture to emerge, often from a single idea.

When Macbeth decides to persist in his murderous campaign against all those whom he thinks are a threat to him, he says this:

> I am in blood
> Stepped in so far, that should I wade no more,
> Returning were as tedious as go o'er.

> (3.4.137–9)

When he says he's stepped in blood, it could be a commonplace idiom (a bit like saying: I've got my hands full), but by the time we reach 'wade' the full image emerges – someone wading across a river. How frightening that the rather resigned idea – 'I'm wet already so I may as well carry on' – is applied to a campaign of murder. The ordinary nature of the image magnifies the horror.

Words generating meanings

We must remember that what prompts Shakespeare's imagination to work through images are *words*. Sometimes we find images, or hints of images, in a single word. When Enobarbus, one of Antony's friends, criticises Antony for fleeing from the battle after Cleopatra, he says:

> The itch of his affection should not then
> Have nicked his captainship

> (3.13.7–8)

'Nicked' produces a number of pictures; it could mean a cut (his captaincy is damaged), an end (his career is over), a deception (his love for Cleopatra has deceived his soldier's mind), his being taken by surprise or being beaten in a game of chance.

4.10 Rhetoric in Shakespeare

▶ 'sweet smoke of rhetoric' (*Love's Labours Lost*, 3.1.61)

Rhetoric

In the plays we find passages such as this:

> For happy wife, a most distressed widow;
> For joyful mother, one that wails the name;
> For Queen, a very caitif, crowned with care

> (*Richard III*, 4.4.98–100)

Each of those three lines contrast happy pasts with distressing presents. Each phrase begins with the same word, followed by a lengthier one which acts as a contrast. This is an example of what is called *rhetoric*:

- **the deliberate patterning of language for effect**.

Nowadays the word 'rhetoric' means stylish and high-sounding talk. Sometimes there's the suggestion that rhetoric is done for show, that it's fancy and rather empty.

This wasn't the case in Shakespeare's day. Rhetoric was the art of speaking well; there was no hint of hollowness or insincerity. Rhetoric – the careful patterning of speech – was an accomplishment that educated people were expected to have.

Furthermore, this was an age when people were discovering with delight all the things language could do. Language was felt to be richly enjoyable. It's not surprising that of the six occurrences of the word in Shakespeare, four of them come in *Love's Labours Lost*, the play that revels in the possibilities of language. One character talks of 'a great feast of languages' (5.1.36). Rhetoric, like *cordon bleu* cooking, is meant to be relished.

What to make of rhetoric

The problem for today's reader is what to do about rhetoric. There are so many complicated-sounding names such as 'eustathia' – a promise to be constant in loving – or 'synchoresis' – giving a listener an opportunity to judge a speaker – that the student is likely to get lost in a maze of strange terminology.

But even if we find our way about, what can be done with the terms other than apply them? And where does that get us? The study of English literature isn't like bus-spotting.

Here are three things a reader can do when thinking about rhetoric:

- try to appreciate the pleasure such arrangements give
- think about how meaning is made
- think about effects.

How does this work out? Here are two examples.

Example

Example 1: *anaphora*

When a series of clauses begins with the same word it's called *anaphora*. Listen to Othello, painfully convinced that because his wife is unfaithful, his whole military career is over:

> O now for ever
> Farewell the tranquil mind, farewell content,
> Farewell the plumed troops and the big wars,
> That make ambition virtue! O, farewell,
> Farewell the neighing steed and the shrill trump

(3.3.352–6)

The pleasure of these lines comes from the repetition of 'farewell'. We can hear the awful word invading Othello's mind. Bidding farewell to the life of a soldier as a way of coming to terms with betrayal in marriage shows that for Othello his public life is inseparable from his private one; the meaning of war is bound up with the meaning of love. The effect is a haunting one; it's as if in the repeated farewells all that gave meaning to Othello's is becoming ever more distant from him, like an army marching away from someone who once commanded it.

Example 2: *hendiadys*

Our second example is what is called *hendiadys*: two words linked by 'and' that have very close meanings. It's been pointed out that this rhetorical figure appears very frequently in *Hamlet*. In the 'To be, or not to be' speech (3.1.58–92) there are several:

> The slings and arrows of outrageous fortune

> . . . the whips and scorns of time

> To grunt and sweat under a weary life

The enjoyment here is a matter of recognising the links and differences; slings and arrows are both weapons, though both a whip and a scorn might sting they are not the same sort of thing. The meaning is spelt out pretty much in the same way that an image is; to 'grunt and sweat' fills out the picture of a man or beast staggering under a heavy load. The effect is that of an alert mind, full of ideas, which chase each other under the pressure of expression.

4.11 Wordplay

▶ **'there's a double meaning in that'** (*Much Ado About Nothing*, 2.3.246)

Shakespeare's age was fascinated with the power of words. It's not surprising, therefore, that characters often comment not just on what each other says, but on the actual language they use. When, in *The Winter's Tale*, Hermione is accused of treason and adultery, she replies:

> You speak a language that I understand not

> (3.2.79)

Her way of saying that the accusation is untrue is to talk about the unintelligibility of his words.

Wordplay

The most common manifestation of an interest in language for its own sake is 'wordplay':

- **in wordplay characters talk about actual words rather than themes or issues.**

Words are not used to further the subject matter, the subject matter becomes the words that are used. As a result, the passages of wordplay have a merry, zig-zag quality; we don't follow the straight path of an argument but wind and meander as first one and then another meaning of a word is discovered and exploited. Sometimes, we feel lost in a maze of words.

Example

The cut and thrust of wordplay can be found in *The Taming of the Shrew*. When Petruchio meets Kate for the first time, he discovers (to his delight?) that she joins in the wordplay with gusto. At one point Petruchio says he was 'moved' – emotionally impelled – to woo her; she replies:

> *Katherina*: 'Moved', in good time! Let him that moved you hither Remove you hence. I knew you at the first You were a moveable.
> *Petruchio*: Why, what's a moveable?
> *Katherina*: A joint-stool.
> *Petruchio*: Thou hast hit it. Come sit on me.
> *Katherina*: Asses are made to bear, and so are you.
> *Petruchio*: Women are made to bear, and so are you.

(2.1.194–201)

Katherina plays on two meanings of 'moveable' – a piece of furniture and someone who is unreliable. In response to his question, she says that what she has in mind is 'a joint-stool' – a simple, insignificant piece of furniture that is easily overlooked. This association allows Petruchio to invite her to sit on him. She associates this with bearing a burden, which asses do. Petruchio's response is to engage in puns; to 'bear' can also mean to bear the weight of a lover and bear children.

From the above example, we can see that wordplay works in the following ways.

- **The words do the work**

The dialogue is generated by the words themselves. We can feel Petruchio and Katherina's pleasure as the meanings bubble up.

- **The local effects of wordplay**

Wordplay gives life to local areas of a play. Part of the texture of a Shakespeare play is that there are moments when the plot marks time and the language has a kind of jolly holiday.

- **Wordplay and humour**

It doesn't help if we only think of wordplay as jokes. Shakespeare is not just a comedian. What we should try to do as audiences and readers is enjoy language having a holiday.

- **Wordplay and themes**

In some cases wordplay has more than local importance. A pun or ambiguity can focus what a play's about. For instance, there's a pun in *Macbeth* when, after Duncan's murder, Lady Macbeth says that she'll return the knives in order to implicate the grooms:

If he do bleed
I'll gild the faces of the grooms withal,
For it must seem their guilt.

(2.2.53–5)

By gilding (to gild is to coat with gold) the faces of the grooms, guilt (quite unde-served guilt) will stick to them – stick like the blood. The grooms will be guilty because they've been gilded.

Bawdy wordplay

One of the most frequent areas of wordplay in Shakespeare is that associated with sex. The technical name for this is bawdy. Shakespeare is aware of how words can be given a sexual meaning. He's also aware that people enjoy playing this game; the *double-entente* – the word with an 'innocent' and a sexual meaning – is, for many, a constant source of pleasure.

The Nurse in *Romeo and Juliet* (one of Shakespeare's bawdiest plays) clearly enjoys talking about sex; she recalls an incident in Juliet's childhood when the girl fell over:

> A perilous knock, and it cried bitterly.
> 'Yea,' quoth my husband, 'fall'st upon thy face?
> Thou wilt fall backward when thou com'st to age,
> Wilt thou not Jule?' It stinted and said 'Ay'.

(1.3.56–9)

Here the nurse turns innocent talk about a young girl falling on her face to bawdy talk about how, when she's older, she'll fall on her back, for sexual pleasure.

Bawdy can relate to the play as a whole. *Romeo and Juliet* starts with a con-frontation between the servants of the two opposing families – the Capulets and the Montagues. The talk about 'tool' and 'naked weapon' (1.1.31–2) is clearly bawdy, but it's also part of the pattern of the play – the hostility between the two families.

4.12 Dialogue and soliloquy

▶ "tis time to speak' (*Richard III*, 1.3.117)

Speaking on stage is either in dialogue or soliloquy.

- In dialogue we should attend to the 'dynamics' of the speech.
- In soliloquy what matters is the relationship between the speaker and the audience.

Dialogue

The best way to think of dialogue is as some sort of competition or combat. Characters who talk have aims; they want to fulfil these aims, and this often involves persuading, forcing, deceiving, begging, appealing or pleading with another charac-ter. When aims are different, the conversation crackles with the energy of the com-peting participants. Dialogue can, therefore, be thought of as a kind of war, or, if you find that too forceful a way of putting it, as politics.

Think about how this passage from *The Merchant of Venice* works. Bassanio has just chosen the right casket so has won Portia; then some of his friends from Venice arrive:

[*Enter Lorenzo, Jessica, and Salerio, a messenger from Venice.*]

Bassanio: Lorenzo and Salerio, welcome hither;
   If that the youth of my new int'rest here
   Have power to bid you welcome. By your leave,
   I bid my very friends and countrymen,
   Sweet Portia, welcome.

(3.2.218–222)

There is unease here. Bassanio is in Portia's house but he anticipates his rights as its owner by welcoming his friends. But he doesn't welcome everybody. Jessica, Shylock's daughter, is excluded from the welcome, even though she's now Lorenzo's wife.

Bassanio soon realises that he's overstepped the mark. He retreats to a clause tentatively beginning with 'if' and speaks of himself as new to the 'int'rest here'. This is a delicate matter; 'int'rest' can mean the advantage given by his betrothal to Portia or, more bluntly, a legal right. He has the first, but is assuming the second. He recognises he's been too hasty but saying 'by your leave'.

In the light of that passage, we can see that the following aspects of dialogue are important:

- who speaks to whom
- who isn't spoken to
- the tone and how it changes
- how one character responds to another
- how much a character says.

What all of these have in common is *emotional movement*.

Soliloquy

The word 'soliloquy' means a sole or alone speech which only the audience hears. In Shakespeare there are a number of different kinds.

The chorus

The Chorus can't step out of the drama.

- **The Chorus is always a character in the play.**

Although Shakespeare uses them to further the plot (Time in *The Winter's Tale* takes us over 16 years) they are not like narrators in novels who can know virtually everything. Therefore, although it's always essential to listen to what a Chorus says, we can disagree. For instance, it's not clear whether the high-sounding Chorus in *Troilus and Cressida* should be taken seriously.

The aside

A very important aspect is this:

- **whenever a character turns to speak to an audience, a bond is established between them**.

We feel at the beginning of *King Lear* that Cordelia is honest, trustworthy and good. The reason for this is what she says to us in an aside very early on.

The public soliloquy

This can be very disturbing. Audiences watching *Richard III* or *Othello* are button-holed by the villains – Richard and Iago – and thus they might feel accomplices in evil. Perhaps even more difficult to cope with is the case of Macbeth. As he and Lady Macbeth drift apart, he turns increasingly to the audience as the people with whom he can share his feelings.

The private soliloquy

In *Hamlet* we overhear the Prince communing with himself. The soliloquy is not just an expression of intentions but a revelation of his mind; we witness the turbulent drama of his thoughts and feelings.

4.13 The unity and variety of Shakespeare's plays

▶ 'it is so varied too' (*Love's Labours Lost*, 1.1.283)

In the discussions above, a distinction has been drawn between local effects and the plays considered as wholes. It's time to say a bit more about this.

A local effect is anything that happens in a play which is confined to the moment in which it occurs, whereas anything which draws attention to the entire play is concerned with the work as a whole. For instance, Brutus's kindness in allowing his servant to sleep is essentially local, whereas the appearance soon after of Caesar's ghost is part of the theme of Caesar's power, which is felt throughout the play.

Integrated or varied?

At one time those who wrote about Shakespeare liked to stress how integrated the plays are. They saw in Shakespeare an artist whose works were whole and seamless; everything in them had a place. It was common to show how in *King Lear* virtually any line was related to other ideas, so producing what some have called an organic whole.

Fashions have now changed. Writers are keen to stress not the unity but the variety within plays. What, for instance, is the link between the scene in *Twelfth Night* when Viola talks to Feste (3.1.1–58) and the rest of the play? The answer is: not much.

What's to be made of this debate? Two things are clear.

• Continuities

The first is that unless the various parts of a play have something in common, it doesn't add up to a play. To be a play there must be continuities in the plot and the characters. What also needs saying is that plays have distinctive atmospheres and there should be some consistency in the presentation of society.

● Art and variety

The second point is that perhaps we've been misled by the idea that good art must appear to be a tightly and neatly woven pattern. Art needn't be like that, particularly dramatic art. A dramatist may choose, within the limits of plot and character, to introduce different kinds of theatrical activities.

What happens if we take these two ideas seriously? The short answer is that we can recognise dramatic variety within a plot and appreciate

● the scope players have in performance.

┌─ **Example** ───

We shall look at these ideas with reference to *The Merchant of Venice*.

There's variety in the different kinds of plot. The bond plot is always charged with mistrust and antagonism, whereas the casket plot is closer to fairy tale.

There's variety in language and tone. Gobbo's chatter doesn't have much bearing on the plot. Gratiano speaks 'an infinite deal of nothing' (1.1.114), which, again, doesn't develop the plot. The tone of the play shifts; for instance, the trial scene in which Antonio nearly loses his life ends with the merry business (full of bawdy possibilities) of the ring plot.

└──

We can conclude:

● Shakespeare can be read and performed so as to bring out the liveliness of his theatrical variety.

Mixed style

Perhaps we should look upon the plays as being mixed in style, more akin to a variety show in which there are a number of individual acts. There are, after all, songs and dances in the plays. Why can't the Porter in Macbeth be done as a one-off comic turn and why shouldn't Robin in *A Midsummer Night's Dream* be allowed to clown and dance? I sometimes think that what Shakespeare's original audiences would have seen would have been a zestful and short production in which the major parts were given prominence by the vigour and individuality of their performances.

Balance?

We don't have to believe that the text is balanced; that's to say, Shakespeare has carefully weighed the parts so that certain of them will always be more important than others. Think of the trial scene in *The Merchant of Venice*. Do we have to believe that Shakespeare deliberately shaped the text so that Portia will always be seen as both morally right and the better speaker? Might not Shakespeare have given the two players their parts and said: 'it's up to you to make this convincing.' Something like this must have happened, because some theatre-goers have come out siding with Portia and some feeling sorry for Shylock. And some have felt both.

▶ **'this cock-pit'** (*Henry V*, Prol. 11)

In *Henry V* the Chorus has four expressions for the theatre: 'this unworthy scaffold' (Prol. 10), 'cock-pit' (1.11), 'this wooden O' (l.13) and 'the girdle of these walls' (1.19). The playhouse he's writing for is *The Globe*, an enormous wooden building on the south bank of the Thames. Later, Shakespeare wrote for the smaller *Blackfriars Theatre*, where, unlike *The Globe*, the performances were indoors. In addition, his plays were performed at court, in the halls of the Temple (the London home of layers) and in large houses.

Shakespeare's plays were performed in different places. And so it's gone on. Shakespeare has been done in huge theatres with proscenium arches, in the round, on stages projecting into the audience, on stages with very complex stage machinery, on several levels, indoors and out. (To say nothing of film, television, radio and CD-Rom.) The point about his plays is this:

- **Shakespeare's plays can be adapted to virtually any kind of theatre**.

But he did write most of them with certain conditions in mind, and it's useful to have some idea of what those conditions were. Exactly what Shakespeare's stage was like is still a matter of debate; nevertheless, some things are clear.

Shakespeare's theatre

- **The big building**

The theatres were very large. They could probably hold over 2000 people. A play, therefore, was a potentially spectacular and even gorgeous event. To go to the theatre is to see wonders; in *Cymbeline* a god, Jupiter, appears.

- **The big stage**

The stage was huge, probably far bigger than most modern theatres. A full stage such as at the end of a comedy would give a very strong sense of the community gathering together after a series of puzzling events. Likewise, that tortured couple, Macbeth and Lady Macbeth, would have looked very troubled, threatened and isolated on that huge stage.

- **The projecting stage**

The stage projected out into the body of the theatre (the sides might have been straight or tapering), so the players could get very near their audience. The roughly circular shape of the theatre must have made for both intimacy and intensity, particularly in heart-felt soliloquies.

- **The inner stage and balcony**

There was probably a curtained off area at the back of the stage, which could be used for 'discovery' scenes such as the sudden sight at the end of *The Tempest* of Miranda and Ferdinand (see Illustration 5). In addition, there was almost certainly an upper gallery, which could function as a balcony (*Romeo and Juliet*) or castle walls (*Richard II*).

- **Doors**

Apart from a trapdoor (did the weird sisters vanish into this at the end of their scenes?) and a winch (this is probably how Jupiter descended), players came on through two doors at the back of the stage.

- **Costume and props**

The players were probably appropriately costumed, but with the exception of chairs, swords, letters and blood, there was little in the way of scenery and props. The plays were visually exciting, largely because the enormous stage was unencumbered.

- **Speed**

The performances were probably swift. The Chorus in *Romeo and Juliet* speaks of 'the two hours traffic of our stage' (Prol. 12). This means that what we have in the texts might be expansions of what was performed.

- **Acting style**

The style of acting is difficult to guess at. Certainly there were gestures, and in a large theatre they probably had to be on a dramatic scale in order to be seen. What, however, is doubtful is that they appeared over-done. Hamlet certainly didn't like wooden performances in which players strutted with exaggerated gestures. Would he have been able to make such comments if all acting were like that?

- **The audience**

The engagement of the audience was certainly very important. The theatre would not be what it is if there were nobody to cheer, jeer, cry, applaud and shout advice. At times, characters seem to address directly not just those on stage but all those present. The dying Hamlet says:

> You that look pale and tremble at this chance

> (5.2.286)

Those words surely include us all; in the theatre we see the theatre of life.

┌───┐

Exercises

4.1 Choose a short passage from a play you are studying and look at it from the point of view of the richness of its language. Think about its imagery, wordplay, the changes in tone and the sounds of its words.

4.2 Look closely at a passage of dialogue from the point of view of how each character's aims control the movement of the conversation and its emotional pressure.

4.3 Look at the soliloquies in the plays you are studying:
(a) What kind are they?
(b) What do they reveal about the character?
(c) What do they contribute to the movement of the plot?

4.4 Choose a scene from one of your plays and think about how the way it's written invites players to perform it. You should ponder how the text invites gestures, actions and groupings.

4.5 Try to reconstruct how a scene might have been performed on the stage of Shakespeare's *Globe*. Think about the use that could be made of the entrances, the balcony, the inner stage, the size of the stage and the closeness of the audience.

└───┘

Part II
The Comedies

5 Comedy

5.1 Popular ideas of comedy

▶ 'a pleasant comedy' (*The Taming of the Shrew*, **Ind. 2.126**)

When in *The Taming of the Shrew*, Christopher Sly is duped into believing that he's a lord, he's treated to the kind of entertainment a lord might expect – a private performance of a play. So Sly settles down, as countless millions have done, to enjoy 'a pleasant comedy'.

Comedies are popularly held to have certain features, among which are:

- they make us laugh
- they are light-hearted
- they deal with pleasant or trivial subjects
- the characters are recognisable
- we often laugh at people's peculiarities
- they end happily.

Of course, just because we expect these things, it doesn't follow that Shakespeare will serve them up.

5.2 Shakespeare and the nature of comedy

▶ 'have made our sport a comedy' (*Love's Labours Lost*, **5.2.863**)

The first thing we have to say about the comedies is to repeat the point that:

- **Shakespeare does not write plays to a formula.**

Instead, he playfully experiments with dramatic forms and conventions by extending them, juxtaposing them, parodying them and subverting them. He makes sport with comedy.

His plays sometimes contain the elements set out above, but not always in the way we might expect. Let's look at the list again.

- There is laughter in Shakespearean comedy, but there aren't many jokes.
- The mood isn't always light-hearted; some plays are called 'dark' or 'problem' comedies.

- The subjects aren't always pleasant or trivial; lives are threatened, and, in any case, love, a frequent topic, matters very much to those involved.
- The characters are often recognisable characters, but they are very rarely merely stock characters (see 2.15).
- We laugh at the oddities of characters, but often our response is more than laughter.
- Formally speaking, the comedies do end happily, though lots of audiences have been bothered about just how happy the characters will be.

5.3 Comic plotting

▶ 'ruminated, plotted, and set down' (*1 Henry IV*, **1.3.268**)

Those words might describe what Shakespeare does in comedies because:

- **what makes his comedies distinctive is their plotting**.

In Shakespeare, a comedy isn't chiefly a light-hearted play that makes us laugh; it's one that has *a particular kind of plot*. This is the sort of plot we find in Shakespearean comedy:

- The young fall in love but are initially prevented from fulfilling their wishes and desires, usually because of the opposition of the older generation. In order to find happiness, they employ different kinds of schemes. These schemes produce confusion, in which identities are mistaken or lost and people are fooled. As a result of the confusion, discoveries are made and hearts are changed, so at the end all the opposing groups are reconciled and the young are married.

Of course, this doesn't cover every comedy, but certain important things emerge from it. They are:

- the opposition between the old and the young
- love as the motivating force
- the importance of scheming
- confusion in the middle scenes
- the importance of characters achieving self-knowledge
- the experience of being fooled
- the need to understand and to change
- the overcoming of differences
- marriage and the promise of new life

5.4 How comedies begin

▶ 'I will tell you the beginning' (*As You Like It*, **1.2.105**)

Because what matters in comedy is the plot, the beginning of a comedy is always important. How does Shakespeare open his comedies?

Journeys

Much Ado About Nothing starts with the arrival of soldiers, and *A Midsummer Night's Dream* with the departure of the lovers into the wood. Journeys provide characters with the exciting uncertainty of a new place and new people. Because a character is unknown, he or she is more free to act.

Strangers

On a journey characters meet strangers. Those who live in the new place often seem strange to the travellers, and often the plot gets going when the strangers have an impact upon the settled community (see 3.9). Strangers are often exciting; what's more, they can shake a society out of its lethargy.

5.5 Comedy and love

▶ 'and I begin to love' (*All's Well That Ends Well*, 3.2.15)

In *The Taming of the Shrew*, Lucentio announces that he's come 'To see fair Padua' (1.1.2), but once he's seen the fair Bianca he changes his mind about what he's come to university to do. A journey or the arrival of strangers usually leads to another voyage of discovery – Love.

Love

Love is a familiar theme in Shakespeare (see 1.9–1.14 above) and lovers are familiar characters (see 2.10). The plots of most of the comedies are driven by the desires of the young (see 3.10). Moreover, love strikes early – for Lucentio in the first scene of *The Taming of the Shrew* and for Orlando in the second scene of *As You Like It*.

The pains of love

Because Cupid fires arrows into the heart, love is pain as well as happiness; in fact, in many plots, it's the hope of happiness rather than its possession that drives the characters. For most of *A Midsummer Night's Dream* the lovers are frightened and confused.

Men and women in love

It's usually the men who fall in love in a dramatic and ludicrous way; the girls are far more sensible, controlled and mature. The love drops Robin puts in the eyes of the lovers is an expression of the crazed, unstable nature of men in love; the sensible women wait for them to see sense.

The mystery of love

Because Cupid is blind, love is a mystery; no one can explain why certain characters are drawn to each other. Shakespeare doesn't even try, so why should we?

Sex and marriage

When characters plan to fulfil their love, what they aim at is marriage; in comedies, those who aim solely at sexual gratification (Angelo in *Measure for Measure* is an example) are presented as villains.

Purposefulness

Because the plays often start with falling in love and end with marriage, comic plots (though complex) have a purposeful drive; the audience should always be aware of where the play is going even if they can't see how it's going to get there.

5.6 Bars and impediments

▶ 'if there be any impediment' (*Much Ado About Nothing*, 3.2.83)

It's almost a universal rule of story-telling that:

• there's no tale without an impediment.

An impediment is anything that stands in the way of characters' needs and wants, so:

• the need to overcome an impediment fuels comic plots.

Shakespeare sometimes uses the word 'bar'. In *Twelfth Night*, when Viola finds she loves Orsino but is disguised as a young man, carrying messages to the woman whom Orsino loves, she says:

> ... O barful strife.
>
> (1.4.41)

Love is a struggle ('strife') because there are difficulties and impediments. They can be of different kinds.

The ancient law

Sometimes characters impose on the young an ancient and quite silly law; in *A Midsummer Night's Dream*, fathers have the right to execute disobedient daughters!

Excessive reactions

Some characters make up their own excessive law, and this creates problems for lovers. In *Twelfth Night*, Orsino can't court Olivia, because she's decided to mourn for seven years.

Family rules and traditions

A standard and ancient convention for creating a plot is having a rule about the order in which children may marry. In *The Taming of the Shrew*, the younger daughter shall not marry till the elder is wed.

The bashful lover

When a shy lover can't speak to his beloved, there's little prospect of progress. This is what happens to Orlando in *As You Like It*. Needless to say, it's the beloved who sorts him out.

The significance of impediments

The following points can be made about the significance of the 'bar' in comedy.

- **The spur**

As in the case of love, a 'bar' acts as a spur. Because there are problems, those who are inhibited must be resourceful and enterprising. There's something confident and buoyant about comedy; impediments make the characters energetic and imaginative.

- **The old**

It's often the older generation who impose on the young; comedy usually requires the audience to sympathise with the young;

- **Youthful ingenuity**

Because the old attempt to control the young, the plot usually requires that the young outwit the old; admiring youthful ingenuity and laughing at the ineptitude of the old are responses comedy often requires.

- **The sudden removal of the bar**

It's often the case that the 'bar' is suddenly removed at the end without any explanation; this shows it's essentially a convention used by Shakespeare to create the plot.

5.7 Practices and devices

▶ 'In practice let us put it' (*Much Ado About Nothing*, 1.1.311)

Words for plotting

- **Practice**

This is a trick, stratagem, ruse or ploy. The practice Don Pedro refers to in the quotation above is a scheme to help Claudio to win Hero.

- **Device**

The usual meaning of this is a plan. When in *Twelfth Night* Maria sets about to gull Malvolio, 'device' is used six times.

- **Deceit**

This is used occasionally for a trick, as at the end of *The Merry Wives of Windsor*: 'this deceit loses the name of craft' (5.5.218). Interestingly, the word 'deception', so beloved of examiners and critics, doesn't appear in Shakespeare.

- **Trick**

This has a number of meanings, one of which is a plan that aims at deceiving. When Benedick is tricked into loving Beatrice, he says 'This can be no trick' (*Much Ado About Nothing*, 2.2.209). That's exactly what it is!

Practisers

Practices requires practisers – characters who can think quickly and come up with lots of ideas. In most comedies there's one character whose role it is to be the chief practiser – the one who thinks up and implements schemes and stratagems. In *Much Ado About Nothing* it's the otherwise rather colourless Don Pedro, while in *The Taming of the Shrew*, Tranio, disguised as his master, Lucentio, has to think very quickly to get himself out of some sticky situations. These characters are usually enjoyable because we see them thinking quickly.

5.8 Practisers and practising

▶ 'I will practise' (*The Taming of the Shrew*, Ind. 1.34)

Comic plots can be defined as:

- **the interweaving of a number of practices**.

When we watch a comedy, it's possible to enjoy the ingenuity of Shakespeare as he invents a number of practices, develops them to extract maximum confusion and then brings all to a harmonious conclusion. We should remember:

- **comedy is plot, and plot is practice.**

___ Example ___

Much Ado About Nothing is a good example of a play with a lot of practices. The main ones are:

- the masked Don Pedro pretending to be Claudio in order to woo Hero
- Don John telling Claudio that Don Pedro is wooing for himself
- the plan to make Beatrice and Benedick fall in love by making each overhear how the other is dying to be loved
- Don John's plan to deceive Claudio into believing that Hero is unfaithful by making the waiting woman, Margaret, dress as Hero and behave in a compromising way
- Claudio's plan to denounce Hero at the wedding
- the Friar's device of telling those who have denounced Hero that she has died
- Beatrice persuading Benedick to challenge Claudio to a duel
- the suggestion that Claudio should marry a niece of Leonato
- stealing the poems written by Beatrice and Benedick in praise of each other and reading them in public.

What's remarkable about *Much Ado About Nothing* is that there's a new plot in virtually every other scene, and yet the play doesn't seem confusingly complicated or over ingenious.

There are four important things about practices in Shakespearean comedy.

The pleasure of how it works

One of the pleasures of watching comedy is seeing how the various plots relate to each other. The audience enjoys the way competing practices eventually lead to a satisfying ending.

Women are good practisers

Characters in comedy enjoy scheming. Although it's difficult to generalise, women are more resourceful, more imaginative and more courageous than men.

The love of games

Comedy shows that we delight in games. This delight is something to do with the exciting tension between freedom of action and working within limits. In a game we have to observe the rules, but within those rules we have great freedom to manoeuvre.

Festivity

The delight in play is probably related to the traditional games played by people at festivals. For instance, celebrations such as Twelfth Night were often marked by appointing a Lord and Lady of Misrule, who were permitted to break social conventions. Something of this function is performed by Maria and Sir Toby in *Twelfth Night*. Significantly, they mock Malvolio, who is against the spirit of festivity.

Though it's true that the plots of comedies are largely composed of competing devices, it's not true that only comedies contain them. *Hamlet*, for instance, contains a number of competing devices, and the plot of *Othello* might be understood as consisting of Iago's practices against Othello.

5.9 Common practices

▶ 'This is an old device' (*A Midsummer Night's Dream*, 5.1.50)

The words above are spoken by Theseus when he's selecting a wedding entertainment. He complains that one of the ideas is old. He's right:

- **most of the devices in drama, particularly comedy, are old ones**.

We laugh at situations that the Greeks thought were funny. The point is this:

- **the forms of comedy are traditional**.

Because they are traditional they are enjoyable; audiences respond to comedy when they appreciate its conventions. This is in line with what was said above: we know pretty well what the end will be but not exactly how the playwright will get us there. The pleasure of comedy lies in the way audiences see a playwright using the wide variety of practices to achieve an end that both characters and audience (and playwright) desire.

These are the familiar practices and devices of comedy.

Elopement

Elopement is usually a response to a bar, which, in most cases, is imposed by the older generation. In *A Midsummer Night's Dream*, Hermia is ordered, upon pain of death, to marry Demetrius rather than the man she loves, Lysander. Since there seems no way in which he will change his mind, Lysander makes a proposal:

> If thou lov'st me then,
> Steal forth thy father's house tomorrow night
>
> (1.1.163–4)

Those words reveal three things about elopement in Shakespeare:

- to 'steal forth' is dangerous – that's why they have to elope at night;
- there's an element of excitement involved – nightime, the planning of the event, the stealthy movements
- the motive for stealing forth is love.

Impersonation

In *Much Ado About Nothing*, Borachio boasts that he has deceived Don Pedro and Claudio into believing that the woman they see him wooing (though what went on was probably overtly sexual) was Hero and not Margaret.

This is a case of impersonation – of one person pretending to be another. It's not a device that is used a great deal in Shakespeare, probably because it produces problems of sorting out the blame for what's happened. The business with Margaret is dismissed rather too quickly; all we are told is that it was 'against her will' (5.4.5).

Substitution

In *All's Well That Ends Well* and *Measure for Measure* a man persuades (or thinks he's persuaded) a young woman to sleep with him. Unknown to the man, another woman who loves him (and will do anything to secure him) learns of this and swaps places. The girl who actually does go to bed is the heroine – the one who ventures into danger for love. Like all practices, it's a convenient way of getting over a plot difficulty.

5.10 Disguise

▶ 'assume thy part in some disguise' (*Much Ado About Nothing*, 1.1.304)

Disguise is Shakespeare's most highly developed practice. It's not the same as impersonation or substitution. In both of them one character pretends to be another, whereas in disguise a character hides his or her own identity by inventing another:

- **what matters in disguise is concealment**.

Disguise usually happens when the one adopting the disguise creates a new character. For instance, in *The Taming of the Shrew*, Tranio impersonates Lucentio, whereas Lucentio disguises himself by inventing the character of a schoolmaster. The name he chooses is significant; he calls himself Cambio, which means 'change'.

The following features of disguise are important.

Reasons for adopting a disguise

Something unexpected, problematic, challenging or threatening usually prompts a character to adopt a disguise. Disguise is seen as the best way of coping with a difficult situation.

When, in *The Taming of the Shrew*, Lucentio learns that only tutors will be allowed to visit Bianca – the girl he's fallen in love with – he disguises himself as a teacher.

The manner of adopting a disguise

In *As You Like It*, Rosalind and Celia decide to escape from the court in disguise. This is part of what Rosalind says about disguising herself as a man:

> A gallant curtle-axe upon my thigh,
> A boar-spear in my hand, and in my heart,
> Lie there what hidden woman's fears there will.
> We'll have a swashing and a martial outside

(1.3.116–19)

Celia decides upon a name:

> Something that hath a reference to my state.
> No longer Celia, but Aliena.

(1.3.126–7)

What shines through this planning is playful enjoyment. They might feel it's necessary for them to flee, but they don't treat it as an unpleasant task they have to perform; they are buoyant, perky and already relishing the adventure.

The freedom of disguise

Once adopted, disguise creates advantage. One of the advantages is that the one in disguise can go where he or she would not usually be permitted.

This is the point about the disguises of Hortensio and Lucentio in *The Taming of the Shrew*; because they pretend to be schoolmasters they can be close to Bianca, whom they love but can't visit. Meanwhile, Tranio, impersonating Lucentio, participates in the life of the rich gentry, not as a servant, but as an equal. One of the ironies of the play is that he makes a very good job of it.

Speaking and hearing

A very important advantage that disguise creates is:

- **the freedom the disguised character enjoys of hearing and saying what he or she likes.**

Often the result of a 'bar' in a comedy is that lovers can't meet and can't say what they want to say. Disguise makes this possible.

In *As You Like It* there are two 'bars': Orlando and Rosalind are victims of family persecution, and Orlando is so bashful in the presence of Rosalind that he can't declare his love. Once, however, her identity is concealed, love can flourish.

She approaches him in the forest, and he, thinking that she's a young man, confides in her that he can't speak when he's with her. Her solution is a pretty piece of ingenuity. She tells him that she once 'cured' a young man of his love by pretending to be the lady in question:

> He was to imagine me his love, his mistress;
> and I set him every day to woo me.

> (3.2.387–8)

Although Orlando 'would not be cured' (3.2.404), he agrees to the plan. Rosalind, therefore, hears what she wants to hear – that Orlando doesn't want to be 'cured' – and Orlando has the chance of speaking about his love. (See 10.6 and 10.7.)

5.11 Cross-dressing

▶ **'suit me all points like a man'** (*As You Like It*, 1.3.115)

Boys and girls

- One of the most important forms of disguise is that in which **girls dress up as boys**.

This 'cross-dressing' (literally, a transvestite is one who cross-dresses) has a central place in *The Merchant of Venice*, *As You Like It* and *Twelfth Night*.

In these (and other) plays, Shakespeare weaves together two important elements: identity and theatricality.

Identity

Disguise has the potential of raising the issue: who am I? If you can pass yourself off as somebody else, to what extent are you the person you think you really are? The aspect of identity that's sharpest in Shakespeare is that of gender.

Viola realises this in *Twelfth Night*; she reflects upon her identity and her disguise, playing with gender language:

> As I am a man,
> My state is desperate for my master's love.
> As I am a woman, now alas the day,
> What thriftless sighs shall poor Olivia breathe!

> (2.2.36–9)

The balancing of the words 'As I am a man … As I am a women' points to competing and perhaps even equal identities.

Identity and theatrically

The audience is sometimes expected to remember that in Shakespeare's day boys played girls on stage. And sometimes it's even more complicated; in *As You Like It* a boy would play Rosalind, who dresses up as a boy and then, while still in disguise, pretends to be Rosalind.

In Act 1, Scene 4 of *Twelfth Night*, there's the thrill of Orsino being on the verge of seeing through Viola's disguise:

> thy small pipe
> Is as the maiden's organ, shrill and loud

(1.4.33–4)

The thrill is enriched by the audience's recognition that the 'small pipe' (the high-pitched voice) is that of a boy and not a girl in disguise. Whatever identity Viola has, we are reminded that it's one constituted by the processes of drama.

5.12 The problems of disguise

▶ 'Disguise, I see thou art a wickedness' (*Twelfth Night*, 2.2.27)

There's a very funny moment in the second scene of the Induction of *The Taming of the Shrew*. The Lord has done well in convincing Sly that he's really a lord, who's been afflicted by loss of memory. One of his practices is to tell Sly that he's married, and to back this up he sends along Bartholomew, a page boy, dressed as a woman. But things almost get out of hand:

Sly: 'Tis much. Servants, leave me and her alone.
Madam, undress you and come now to bed.

(Ind.2.113–14)

Bartholomew has played his role rather too well, and he has to play it even more expertly to avoid Sly's advances.

The point is an ironical one. Usually, disguise is an advantage, because the one in disguise knows more than the other; but here it's a case of the 'biter bit'.

There is, then, a potential danger in disguise. No character can foresee what will happen. Hence its 'wickedness'.

5.13 Mistaken identity

▶ 'You throw a strange regard upon me' (*Twelfth Night*, 5.1.209)

Mistaken identity is not a practice but it can be the result of one. The plot of one of Shakespeare's earliest plays – *The Comedy of Errors* – depends upon an increasingly bewildering series of such mistakes arising from two sets of twins.

Mistaken identity raises some of the issues that disguise does. For instance, a character might hear what would usually be kept from him or her, and being a twin raises the question of who one is. In Shakespeare mistaken identity has two functions:

- to promote confusion
- to assist in winding up a plot.

In *Twelfth Night* Act 3, Scene 4 Viola is mistaken for her brother by his friend, Antonio. It's an awkward meeting; Antonio is deeply hurt and put in danger. He's a wanted man in Illyria, and before the play is over he's recognised as a pirate.

But this confusion leads to the winding up of the plot. Viola sees that the mistake may have arisen because her brother is alive. In the next scene the brother meets Olivia, thereby providing the 'solution' to the problem of whom Olivia can marry.

5.14 Overhearing

▶ **'I will hide me'** (*Much Ado About Nothing*, 2.3.35)

Devices and practices usually:

- **create an advantage over another character**.

Advantage is gained by overlooking and overhearing. To overhear what someone else says provides a double advantage:

- a character learns what others don't want him or her to know
- the others don't know that the overhearing character knows.

In the theatre we see every aspect of overlooking and overhearing:

- we can see the one who overhears and the one who is overheard.

The involvement of the audience in comedy is important. The plays work when the audience is aware of how much more it knows than the individual characters. Furthermore, it reminds us that we, too, are onlookers.

Overhearing and advantage

Traditionally, overhearing gives the overhearer an advantage. For instance, in the opening of *The Taming of the Shrew* Lucentio and Tranio overlook the scene in which Baptista proclaims that no one will marry Bianca till Kate finds a husband and that he is looking for schoolmasters to educate Bianca.

Overhearing and experimentation

Later in the play (Act 4, Scene 2) Shakespeare experiments. Hortensio, disguised as Licio, thinks that he's seeing things advantageously when he overlooks Lucentio, disguised as the schoolmaster, Cambio, courting Bianca. What he doesn't know (in addition to the fact that Lucentio isn't really a schoolmaster) is that the the man he's with isn't Lucentio but is, in fact, Lucentio's servant, Tranio. Things are actually more complicated than that; neither Lucentio nor Tranio know that Licio is Hortensio in disguise. What Hortensio sees appals him: if Bianca can carry on with a teacher, he'll have nothing further to do with her.

5.15 Advantage and knowledge

▶ 'And watch our vantage in this business' (*The Taming of the Shrew*, 3.3.143)

Advantage

If we try to summarise what practices do, we can put it in this way:

- **practices give an advantage.**

When, in *The Taming of the Shrew*, Lucentio and Tranio discuss how to secure Bianca for Lucentio, the wily Tranio summarises how they'll gain the advantage over the other characters:

> That by degrees we mean to look into
> And watch our vantage in this business.

> (3.3.142–3)

This is a snapshot of the comic practiser at work; 'watch our vantage' means look out for an opportunity of seizing the advantage.

Knowledge

A second point about comedy emerges from this: comedy is about knowledge. More particularly:

- **comedy is about the differences, or disparities, between the knowledge of competing characters.**

The word 'competing' is vital: in comedy the characters are after something. This means that most of them are either after the same thing or wish to prevent someone from gaining it. The society of comedy is a society based on competition. The crucial point is this:

- **in a society based upon competition, the currency is knowledge, and knowledge is power.**

Knowledge is like money; the more you have, the more you can do with it. If one character knows more than another, then that character has power over the one who knows less. This knowledge consists in knowing what other characters are up to. And there's a further element that strengthens the hand of the one who knows:

- **not only does the knower know but the one whose actions are known doesn't know that the knower knows.**

When, in *The Merchant of Venice*, the disguised Portia persuades her husband to give 'him' the ring he gave her, she has power over him because of what she knows and what he doesn't.

It's important to remember the following point:

- **in Shakespearean comedy, the audience always knows more than any of the characters.**

When, in *Twelfth Night*, Sir Toby deceives both Sir Andrew and Viola (disguised as Cesario) by telling each that the other is an expert swordsman, the audience enjoy the advantage he has over them; but what they know, and he doesn't, is that Cesario is, in fact, a young woman.

5.16 How comedy affects characters

▶ 'I do feel't, and see't' (*Twelfth Night*, 4.3.2)

An important element in comedy is how characters respond to the giddy swirl produced by practices. Their responses can be described in the following ways.

Distraction

In Shakespeare's day the meaning of this word ranged from 'confusion' to 'madness'. The middle scenes of comedies show characters who are perplexed and disorientated. The normal rules and customs of life have lapsed, and characters are in a spin. Feste talks about the 'whirligig of time' (*Twelfth Night*, 5.1.373), comparing the confusion of events with a whipping-top.

Loss of identity

As indicated above, practices erode a character's sense of who he or she is. The quotation at the head of this sub-section comes from a speech in which Sebastian says that he can hardly believe what is happening to him.

Isolation

In comedies some characters are subjected to the ordeal of being isolated from the rest of society. In that isolation, they feel their identities are endangered and that they may be slipping into madness. The most dramatic (and perhaps the most vicious) case of this is Malvolio, who's treated as a madman (*Twelfth Night*, 4.2).

The above three points are the dark side of comic practising. There is, however, another.

Comic release

This is the freedom and hilarity, the sense of festivity and holiday that practising brings. The merry games of Rosalind and Orlando, the sudden glad realization that there's mutual love between Beatrice and Benedick, and the convincing excess of Tranio's bidding for Bianca are all cases where practices release energy. Comic release gives characters confidence; once they start playing the comic game, they've no doubt that they'll win.

Of the four, this is the most important effect. Comedy is like a game in which all sorts of wishes and potentialities are fulfilled. It's exhilarating both for those who participate and those who watch.

5.17 How comedies end

▶ 'a happy evening!' (*The Two Gentlemen of Verona*, 5.1.7)

Comedies must end happily. Even when Shakespeare allows sour and discontented characters to intrude upon a closing scene, we recognise their discontent partly because it's at odds with the prevailing atmosphere of merriment.

The triumph of love

Since love is the driving force behind much comic action, the satisfaction of a happy ending must include the fulfilling of lovers' desires. Robin in *A Midsummer Night's Dream* sums it up:

> And the country proverb known,
> That 'every man should take his own',
> In your waking shall be shown.
> Jack shall have Jill,
> Naught shall go ill.
>
> (3.3.42–6)

His use of a piece of country wisdom both expresses and confirms the truth of what he says. We all know that all is well when the right girl has the right man.

Marriage

The right expression of love is marriage. In marriage there's love-making, and love-making, as well as being immensely enjoyable, leads to children. Therefore with marriage there comes the promise of a new generation. This is the note struck by Oberon at the close of *A Midsummer Night's Dream* when he bids his fairies bless the newly-weds:

> To the best bride bed will we,
> Which by us shall blessed be,
> And the issue there create
> Ever shall be fortunate.
>
> (5.2.33–6)

However intimate the bridal bed is, marriage is a public institution. Hence, the closing scenes of many comedies require a full stage. It's not just the lovers who are having their desires fulfilled but society as a whole that's being renewed.

Finding the lost

From the early play, *The Comedy of Errors*, to the last complete one he wrote, *The Tempest*, Shakespeare was intrigued by the subject of the finding of the lost.

In *Twelfth Night*, for instance, more space and more emotion is devoted to Viola finding her brother than to her marriage to Orsino. It looks as if the idea fascinated Shakespeare even more than romantic love.

Reconciliation

Reconciliation is achieved through the loves of the younger generation. At the beginning of *The Winter's Tale*, two kings who have been boyhood friends, Leontes and Polixenes, are divided; at the end they are brought back together by the love of their children.

Sharing

Comedy reconciles in another way. Those who've been excluded in the middle scenes are brought back into society. The lovers in *A Midsummer Night's Dream* find each other, are forgiven by the Duke and invited to celebrate their weddings with him. This is one of the sources of wonder – the feeling that things have worked out well. It's interesting to note that the plays in which the word 'wonder' most appears are all comedies: *A Midsummer Night's Dream, Much Ado About Nothing, The Winter's Tale* and *The Tempest*.

Another piece of sharing is the exchange of stories (see 3.11). In comedy this has a special function. Since the currency of comedy has been knowledge, the end of a comedy must involve sharing that knowledge. Everyone must know what's happened and why.

The importance of form

An important element in all these ways of ending a comedy is the formal point that their business is to round off the play. Because comedies are dependent upon their plots, the way a plot ends is going to be more important in a comedy than any other type of play. What we enjoy is the skill with which the playwright has achieved a satisfactory close.

Although it's speculation, I can't help but feel that Shakespeare saw a parallel between what he does in writing a comedy and what a heroine does in getting her man. Both must plan and both must anticipate how the people they work with will react. Both, as well, get pleasure from doing it.

5.18 The debate about comedy

▶ 'Look you for any other issue?' (*Much Ado About Nothing*, 2.2.26–7)

The argument of this chapter has been that comedy is a play with a particular kind of plot, and that to enjoy it we need to understand its conventions. One of the problems is that some readers (though not many audiences) are dissatisfied with what they find. Their dissatisfaction usually takes four forms.

Triviality

The tone and manner of many of the comedies is light. But what about the suspicion that their subject matter is slight? Is all comedy much ado about nothing?

Two things can be said here.

- Many comedies are about love, and for most of us love is about the most important thing we are ever involved in. Most of us won't kill kings, but we hope that the boy or girl of our dreams will fall for us.

- The second point is a repetition of an earlier one. What we enjoy in comedy is not just what happens but the *way* it happens. What audiences enjoy is the way the playwright brings a happy ending out of the confusion of the middle scenes.

Credibility

When students study plays, questions begin to arise: can't these characters tell the difference between girls and boys? can't they see that someone's in disguise? A number of points need to be made here.

● Conventions

It's simply a convention that people in disguise are not recognised. To *watch* a play is to accept that that is how things happen. It's helpful to remember that these things don't bother us in the theatre; we just accept them.

● Shakespeare does try to make some unlikely things credible

Take the case of *Much Ado*. Because it happens at night and because they have to be at some distance, Don Pedro is duped into believing that Hero is unfaithful. And because Don Pedro, the commander of the soldiers, believes it, Leonato, Hero's father, also accepts the tale.

● Comedy is an interesting blend of the credible and the incredible

Comedy is sometimes defined as realistic characters in unrealistic situations. Although the situations are strange, we can believe that this is how we would react.

Themes

A very clever pupil of mine once asked: 'But what is *As You Like It* about?' It's a real question. The tragedies are about all the big things – guilt, ambition, jealousy, revenge – but it's rather difficult to formulate the themes of comedies. The difficulty reveals an important feature:

● in comedy the themes are often conterminous with the devices.

That's to say, in comedy what a play is about is often inseparable from how it's written. We say that comedy is about deception and disguise because what we see happening on the stage are characters disguising themselves and deceiving others.

Lesser works?

There's a feeling abroad that the comedies are lesser works than the histories or tragedies. This, I think, was behind a comment a pupil once made to the effect that *Twelfth Night* wasn't really an A-level play. If you're inclined to feel this, the following might help.

Shakespeare wrote comedies all his life. He returned to these plots at all points of his career. Moreover, he wrote more comedies than any other kind of play.

Dr Johnson was the most intelligent and perceptive reader of Shakespeare. He valued the comedies, chiefly for the ease with which they are written. Perhaps we should, too:

● in his comic scenes, he seems to produce without labour, what no labour can improve.

5.1 Read through a comedy, keeping a close check on the different levels of knowledge of each character. What advantages does superior knowledge bring? What does differences in knowledge contribute to the audience's enjoyment?

5.2 Examine the development of a comedy from the point of view of the practices Shakespeare employs. Think about the reasons for their implementation and how they work towards the satisfactory winding up of the plot.

5.3 How exactly does disguise contribute to the workings of the plot? For what purpose are disguises adopted? Are there scenes in which disguise brings an advantage or lands a character in trouble?

5.4 How is confusion caused in the plays you are studying and how is it cleared up?

5.5 How is the plot resolved, what are the reactions of the characters and is the audience convinced and satisfied with the outcome?

6 The Taming of the Shrew

6.1 Two different plots

▶ 'Proceed in practice' (2.1.163)

The play has two major plots:

- the Bianca plot in which a number of characters compete for her
- the Kate plot in which Petruchio marries Kate with the intention of taming her.

The Bianca plot

What's interesting is:

- **most of the comic practices appear in the Bianca plot.**

Tranio impersonates Lucentio; Lucentio disguises himself as a Latin teacher and Hortensio as a music teacher, and a Pedant (schoolmaster) impersonates Lucentio's father. In addition, there's overlooking, misinformation and elopement. They all 'proceed in practice'. One of the amusing aspects of the Bianca plot is that the least successful suitor is the one who uses no devices – the aged Gremio.

The Bianca plot is a traditional one in two other aspects:

- it's launched to get round the 'bar' established by the father, Baptista, that no one shall marry Bianca till Kate is wed.
- the young plot against the old. As Grumio says:

> see, to beguile the old folks, how the young folks lay their heads together!
>
> (1.2.136–7)

The Kate plot

In the Kate plot there's little traditional comic business. Petruchio uses no ruses: he doesn't deceive, he doesn't seek advantage through disguise, and therefore he has no superior knowledge to exploit. His behaviour is deliberately strange, but that's not a traditional comic device. The difference between Petruchio and the practisers of the Bianca plot can be seen in his declaration, practisers delivered to Kate in punchy monosyllables:

For I am he am born to tame you, Kate

(2.1.275)

There's no secrecy or subterfuge; Petruchio states his business, so everything he does can be understood as arising from that intention.

If, as the title suggests, the Kate plot is central, then the design of the play is distinctive:

- **not only is Shakespeare combining two very different kinds of plot, but the main business of the drama is separate from the traditional elements of comedy.**

6.2 Kate and Petruchio

▶ 'what company is this?' (1.1.47)

Many of the characters are those you would expect to find in a comedy: a stern father who imposes a bar on the young, lovers who practice to win a heroine, clever servants who help not-so-clever masters, and the stock figure of the old man who's foolish enough to think he stands a chance in the game of love.

The two figures who don't fit in are the two most important – Kate and Petruchio.

Kate

Kate has links with two sorts of characters. Some talk of her as the stock shrew – the belligerent, scolding and uncontrollable woman. Hortensio says

she is intolerable curst,
And shrewd, and froward, so beyond all measure

(1.2.88–9)

She's also linked with a *humorous* figure; that is, one who behaves peculiarly because of an unbalanced make-up (see p. 40). Petruchio hints at this when he forbids her meat because 'it engenders choler' (4.1.160), choler being the element that makes people angry.

But Kate is more than this. She's clever and witty; her wordplay with Petruchio (see 4.11) crackles with intellectual energy. She doesn't hate men; one of her complaints against her father is that he's only interested in marrying off Bianca (2.1.31–6). She clearly enjoys public debate; her speech at the end is the longest in the play. She's also modest; she doesn't want to kiss Petruchio in public (5.1.132).

What's particularly important is that Shakespeare gives the audience a way of understanding why she's so difficult. This emerges in the design of the opening scene:

- **characters talk of her as shrewish before she speaks.**

Gremio is the first to speak:

To cart her rather. She's too rough for me.

(1.1.55)

Prostitutes were often punished by being tied to a cart and whipped. Kate sees exactly what Gremio is saying; she asks whether her father intends to turn her into a 'stale' – another word for prostitute – by publicly exposing her to such ridicule.

Could Shakespeare be indicating that she behaves the way she does because she's insulted?

Petruchio

Petruchio is a lively, enterprising and fearless extrovert. He's young and adventurous; he talks with relish about war (a preparation for love?); he's educated (he rattles off a list of famous women – 1.2.68–70); he knocks his servants about; his cultured background is seen in his knowledge of falconry and he's quite unabashed by any complaint about his behaviour.

One of the most distinctive things about him is his tone. He speaks with verve and bounce (see 4.8) and confidently launches into any enterprise. But it would be wrong to play him as a bullish male intent on living up to a jaunty, macho image. Petruchio is more subtle and more intimately low-key than that. This comes out in one particular word – 'chat':

O how I long to have some chat with her!

(2.1.161)

And therefore, setting all this chat aside

(2.1.267)

Chat is easy, friendly, relaxed and light-hearted conversation. And all those words are clues to Petruchio's character. He has a buccaneering side, but the full picture is more mellow, genial and companionable.

The other interesting question about him is:

● **What does he feel about Kate?**

He makes his motives for marriage clear in a strongly rhythmical line and a characteristically merry and energetic image:

As wealth is burden of my wooing dance

(1.2.67)

But is that all there is to say? Certainly, he's very strenuous about money:

I come to wive it wealthily in Padua

(1.2.74)

But he's also insistent with Kate about something else:

For by this light whereby I see thy beauty,
Thy beauty that doth make me like thee well

(2.1.272–3)

The plot of the play works by showing a change in Kate (see 6.4). Does it also show one in Petruchio? Is he a character who starts with the intention of marrying a rich woman, whom he can bring to order, but discovers that she's someone he loves?

6.3 The place of the Induction

▶ 'Well, we'll see't' (Ind., 2.139)

There's a third plot element in *The Taming of the Shrew*:

- it starts like no other play of Shakespeare with two Induction scenes of over 270 lines, which form no part of the Katharina or the Bianca plots.

In the Induction a lord tricks a drunken tinker, Christopher Sly, into believing he's actually a lord, who, for seven years, has been under the mistaken impression that he's a drunken tinker.

But although the Sly scenes have a rumbustious earthiness – they start with him being thrown out of an ale-house, and there are vivid Stratford references such as 'Marion Hacket, the fat ale-wife of Wincot' (Ind. 1.20) – we never hear from him after the close of 1.1. This raises a question.

What's the purpose of the Induction?

The answer is that there are links between the Induction and the rest of the play.

- **Identity**

Sly is convinced that he's a lord, and on one reading of the play Kate becomes convinced that she's not a shrew.

- **Dreaming**

Sly is told he's woken up to the truth, and Kate might be said to wake up to the possibility of living life another way. Also, dreaming reinforces the unreality of what we are seeing; those in the theatre are experiencing art, which is a kind of dream.

- **Practising**

The Lord and his attendants have the enterprising relish of comic practisers; their ingenuity anticipates the later practisers – Lucentio, Tranio, Hortensio.

- **Games**

The Lord has been hunting. This might anticipate the 'game' of the last scene when the men wager on the obedience of their wives.

- **Farce**

Both the Induction and the play contain farce – laughter created when characters are knocked about; Sly's thrown out of the ale-house, and in the play several servants are beaten.

6.4 Study and love

▶ 'Aristotle's checks' (1.1.32)

Shakespeare gives Lucentio a distinctive approach to the business of love, that's consistent with what's brought him to Padua. He reveals that he's come to Padua to study Philosophy:

for the time I study,
Virtue and that part of philosophy
Will I apply that treats of happiness
By virtue specially to be achieved.

(1.1.17–20)

What he says is a summary of what the Greek philosopher Aristotle teaches in his *Ethics*: everything we do has an end, and the end of people is to achieve happiness by living according to the virtues; the virtues being such qualities as courage and patience.

Tranio, his servant, has slightly different ideas; they should not, he says,

So devote to Aristotle's checks
As Ovid be an outcast quite abjured.

(1.1.32–3)

Roughly speaking, that means: let's not be so controlled by Aristotle as to forget Ovid. Ovid was a Latin poet who wrote two famous works: the *Metamorphoses* (a poem about changes and transformations) and *The Art to Love*, a daring and sometimes highly erotic account of love-making. Tranio is thinking of the love poem – in other words, he's saying: remember what students go to university to do! Lucentio takes his advice.

When he woos Bianca, it appears that he's forgotten Aristotle and is only thinking of Ovid. In 4.2. Bianca playfully asks him what he reads; his answer is:

I read that I profess, The Art to Love.

(4.2.8)

Not only does he study Ovid on love, he also practises it.

So has Ovid won? The apparent joke against Lucentio is that he comes to an ancient university town with the strict intention of studying Aristotle, but one sight of Bianca transforms him into an ardent lover. *Metamorphoses* is about change! But in one sense he's being very Aristotelian. Aristotle said that every activity had an end or purpose; when he saw Bianca, Lucentio certainly found one!

Ovid provides the terms in which to understand the play to the very end. In 5.1, when Lucentio appears with Bianca, Baptista wants to know if Cambio really is Lucentio. Bianca gives the answer:

Cambio is changed into Lucentio.

(5.1.111)

This is a joke; Cambio means 'change', and the transformation of Lucentio into Cambio and back to Lucentio will remind the audience of Ovid's *Metamorphoses*.

6.5 Is Kate tamed?

▶ 'Tis a wonder, by your leave, to see her tamed so' (5.2.189)

What is to be made of these words – the last in the play? They raise its major issues:

- is Kate a shrew?

- is she tamed?

It might have been possible once to say that what the play shows is that all a husband has to do is starve his wife (4.1.184), deny her sleep (4.1.185), sex (4.1.170) and tear up her clothes (4.3.86–162) and she'll soon see sense. But you can't read the play that way now.

What's happened is that there's a strong social and literary interest in the treatment of women. The 'knock'm about a bit' school doesn't get a hearing.

As far as *The Taming of the Shrew* is concerned, this has been wholly beneficial, because it's made people look harder at the text. One possible case is as follows.

The real Kate?

When, on their journey back to Padua, Kate assents to what her husband says, Petruchio comments:

> thus the bowl should run.
> And not unlikely against the bias.
>
> (4.5.25–6)

The image is drawn from the game of bowls. In bowls each wood is weighted, so its natural movement is a curve in the direction of the weight or 'bias'. Petruchio is claiming that Kate is now behaving naturally, according to the bias of her nature. It follows that her shrewish behaviour was against her nature. Does this make sense?

It's surely not impossible to believe that the Kate of the opening scenes is an unhappy girl who's not herself. Every time we see her, she's quarrelsome or violent. In fact, she doesn't enjoy anyone's company until her wordplay with Petruchio (2.1.180–274), when we see her nimble mind at work, playing off meanings with an intellectual equal. That scene shows what she can be like and what civilized society can offer – a delightful skirmishing with words. It sometimes looks as if the best thing we can do is be witty with words.

It may be significant that it's in that scene that Petruchio first uses the word 'tame':

> For I am he am born to tame you, Kate
>
> (2.1.275)

He has, as he intended, wooed her 'with some spirit' (2.1.168), but having seen what she can be like (or what she's really like), there's a point in taming her. This might be the way to read his long soliloquy on their marriage night (4.1.175–198). He compares her to an untamed falcon. The image might be said to do justice to her native spirit and the swiftness of her wit.

The nature of taming

It's possible to interpret the taming as Petruchio acting out the worst excesses of her behaviour, so she can see what she's like. He, so to speak, is the mirror in which her behaviour is reflected. In short, he plays a part. The theatrical metaphor may be useful: because that's the role she's been given, Kate acts out the part of a shrew. The same unreasonable gusto is present in Petruchio's performance. If she can see it's a performance, she might see that other (more natural) roles can be played.

Running with the bias

The theatrical metaphor is useful in understanding the next stage. What is it for Kate to run with the bias? An answer is:

- **to be witty and playful.**

We've seen her wit in the wordplay. In what immediately follows we see the playful spirit. An old man (Vincentio, father of Lucentio) comes along the road, and Petruchio asks Kate to address him as a young woman. (4.4.27–49). She does so, in the spirit of a game. Vincentio calls her 'my merry mistress' (4.5.53). He would hardly call her that if he thought she was serious.

The final scene

With this in mind, the last scene can be played not as a test in obedience but as a collaboration. It's not explicit in the text that they're co-operating, but the language, accompanied by appropriate gestures, enables players to make it clear that they are. Also, the scene abounds in images of games; for instance:

> The bird you aimed at, though you hit her not
>
> (5.2.50)
>
> O sir, Lucentio slipped me like his greyhound
>
> (5.2.52)

These may be taken as strong hints that the scene itself is a game. It's also significant that it's Petruchio who proposes the wager. Could it be played that the word he uses to Grumio – 'command' – is in a kind of code? He and Kate have both used it before:

> *Katharina:* Go, fool, and whom thou keep'st command.
>
> (2.1.256)
>
> *Petruchio:* They shall go forward, Kate, at thy command.
>
> (3.2.224)

It's possible to read Kate's final speech on wifely obedience in the same spirit. It has a theatrical air to it; she clearly enjoys delivering it (it's meant for the widow rather than Bianca), and its hyperbole (talking in a more elevated manner than the subject matter requires) is surely not meant to be taken literally.

The final game of the play is the game of love. Their marriage is not yet consummated, so both leave eagerly for the marriage bed.

Exaggeration

One more comment is needed. If there's so much emphasis on games, does this lead us back to the theatre as game? The Lord played upon Sly, and in a similar way Shakespeare has played on us – he's made us watch a play. If a play is a kind of game, perhaps we should see in it the elements of exaggeration, make-believe and fantasy that are so often associated with the theatre.

6.6 The role of Bianca

▶ 'maid's mild behaviour and sobriety' (1.1.71)

Bianca gets a bad press. I've only rarely met classes who like her. What she's accused of is deceit; she pretends to be mild and obedient – the ideal wife and daughter – but in fact she's selfish and scheming. It was once popular to say that Kate has become a shrew, but Bianca is a shrew by nature.

Some of this true. Bianca has been successful with both her father and her suitors. She's managed to be daddy's girl and the obscure object of desire for lots of panting men. Should we blame her for that?

Two things might be said. The first is that we are usually asked to applaud those in comedies who get what they want. She's obviously sorted out that Lucentio is the man for her (he showed some spirit in the way he wooed her), and she cleverly deceives her father. Shakespeare doesn't usually make practices a moral matter, so why should Bianca be blamed for doing what every comic heroine does – making sure of her man?

The second point is that she's good at the game of love. When Lucentio woos her, she keeps a delicate balance between aloofness and encouragement – 'presume not ... despair not' (3.1.43). She's a worthy sister of Kate – quick-witted, resourceful and exciting.

Finally, there's the question of her marriage. It may be that one of the jokes of the play is that Tranio proved a better wooer than his master (I've seen it played that way), but Lucentio is a scholar with a certain dash. He'll be a worthy sparring partner for the talented Bianca.

Bianca is not 'mild', but that's not something the play asks us to admire. In fact, it's possible to regard her as a kind of heroine; she's played her game and won without any of the fuss Kate had.

__ Exercises __

6.1   Do both Kate and Petruchio change?

6.2   What interest is there for an audience in the Bianca plot?

A Midsummer Night's Dream

7.1 The elements of the plot

▶ 'write a ballad of this dream' (4.1.206–7)

The plot of *A Midsummer Night's Dream* is different from *The Taming of the Shrew* in this way:

- **all the groups of characters are involved in the same kind of plotting and practising.**

In *A Midsummer Night's Dream*, all the participants contrive or are contrived against. The plot has four elements.

(1) The court of Theseus and Hippolyta

Theseus must uphold the law that requires a daughter to obey her father upon pain of death, and, when all the permutations of mistaken identity have been explored, he overrules the angry father.

(2) The lovers

The lovers start as characters who control the direction of the plot by running away into the forest, but once there they are manipulated by the fairies' practices.

(3) The fairies

The fairies in the person of Oberon are the chief agents of the plot; they cause the merry and bizarre confusions of the middle scenes.

(4) The mechanicals

They start as an independent group until Bottom is transformed by Puck and drawn into Oberon's quarrel with Titania.

Each of these groups have a characteristic way of talking:

- the court characters speak blank verse
- the lovers often speak in rhyming couplets
- the fairies often speak in lyrical, short-lined poetry
- the mechanicals speak prose.

Nothing is ever entirely neat in Shakespeare. Oberon speaks in elegant blank verse to Titania but he also speaks in rhyming couplets similar to those of the lovers.

7.2 Oberon and plotting

▶ 'here comes Oberon' (2.1.58)

If there's a central group, it's the fairies; they are the ones who move the plot along.

The fairies' plotting

In the first scene in which the fairies appear, Robin is recognised as 'that shrewd and knavish sprite' (2.1.33) who frightens village girls, interrupts farm labour and misguides travellers. With such a follower, it's not surprising that the 'Captain of our fairy band' (3.2.110) – Oberon – is the chief practiser of the play. He plots against his Queen, Titania, and tries to help the lovers sort themselves out. At the end of the play there's another intervention; in some of the most delicate lyricism of the whole play, Oberon leads the blessing of the three marriages.

The incompetent practiser

Shakespeare is doing something else here:

● **he takes an interest in the character of the incompetent comic practiser.**

It's as if he's saying two things:

● a way of furthering the plot is to have plans failing rather than working out
● audiences may enjoy seeing someone get it wrong.

The first of these points is seen in the way Helena at one point has both men desperately seeking her. The second is in Oberon's exasperation when he sees his plans have misfired. On two occasions he rounds on Robin in the kind of frustrated rage that audiences always find amusing.

Oberon's aims

Oberon practises against his Queen and the lovers. His motives are mixed. He's angry with Titania, because she won't give up the child that he covets. We might accuse him of being vindictive; he certainly enjoys the practising when it's going well:

> This falls out better than I could devise.

> (3.2.35)

But he knows when to stop:

> Her dotage now I do begin to pity

> (3.3.46)

is what he says when he finds her in the arms of the ass-headed Bottom.

With regard to the lovers, he's well-intentioned. His motive for intervening in the tumult of young love is that he feels sorry for Helena and wants to make Demetrius understand how it feels to be an unrequited lover:

> Ere he do leave this grove
> Thou shalt fly him, and he shall seek thy love.

> (2.1.245–6)

7.3 Shakespeare's fairies

▶ 'and we fairies' (5.2.13)

Shakespeare gives the fairies a distinctive way of speaking, a distinctive stage presence – they often appear as a group – distinctive movement ('I'll put a girdle round about the earth/In forty minutes' [2.1.175–6]) and he links them with the night and the countryside.

The moon

The play is watched over by the moon; it first appears in the third line of the play, and six lines later there's this beautiful image:

> And then the moon, like to a silver bow
> New bent in heaven

> (1.1.9–10)

which is appropriate to both Theseus and Hippolyta, as both hunt.

The moon, which is associated with night, hunting, madness, revelry and femininity, helps to ground the fairies in our imaginations. We glimpse the realm they occupy – a strange, silvery and slightly dangerous world. There are 26 mentions of the moon, far more than in any other Shakespeare play.

The countryside

The fairies seem to emerge from the English countryside as if they were the 'gods' of flowers and trees we read about in Greek and Roman myths. They embody the essence of the natural world – the greenness of green, the life and fragrance of a summer flower, the purposeful liveliness of microscopic creatures.

The effect of this is to make the fairies both familiar and strange. The first fairy we meet beckons us to see a cowslip as a flower and the home of the attendants upon the Fairy Queen:

> The cowslips her tall pensioners be.
> In their gold coats spots you see;
> Those be rubies, fairy favours;

> (2.1.10–12)

The language says: look again and imagine – the cowslips are attendants, and the tiny spots are the jewels given as rewards for good service. We see the fairies by re-imagining the English countryside.

7.4 The trials and joys of love

▶ 'The course of true love never did run smooth' (1.1.134)

As it turns out Lysander's bit of comfort to Hermia is an under statement. Hermia has been threatened with death, a life in a convent or marriage to someone she doesn't like, and later in the play she's scorned by the man with whom she's eloped.

The play shows what endless popular songs have said – love is crazy.

Men in love

And the men are crazier than the women. Look at the plot. Hermia has always loved Lysander, and Helena has, likewise, always favoured Demetrius. They get angry with each other (friendships fare badly when there's rivalry in love) but they don't change their minds about their (silly?) men.

It's the men who change. Lysander turns from Hermia to Helena, and Demetrius from Helena to Hermia and then to Helena again.

Love and sight

What they see is one of the concerns of the play:

• *A Midsummer Night's Dream* **is about seeing**.

The men see superficially. Cupid is blind, but his random arrows work on the eyes – once the beloved is seen, the lover is snared. 'Eye' and its old fashioned plural 'eyne' appear 60 times, more than in any other Shakespeare play. Helena sadly sums up (1.1.226–51) how the fickle Demetrius has changed his affections; he dotes on 'Hermia's eyes' (line 230) and once all his oaths of love were for her until he 'looked on Hermia's eyne' (line 242). Her conclusion is that true love

> looks not with the eyes, but with the mind

> (1.1.234)

Young men are dazzled by appearances; therefore, they are easily distracted. This is the point about the juice that Robin pours into their eyes. It comes from a flower wounded by Cupid's arrows (2.1.155–74), and so represents the wayward, unpredictable and aimless nature of sudden infatuation.

Laughing at lovers

What the lovers get up to is undoubtedly amusing; we are invited to laugh at their hyperbolic language and excessive behaviour.

Hyperbole is talk that's in excess of the subject matter; it's what we mean by 'over the top'. There's an amusing moment when Helena wakes Lysander, who, because Robin has put the love-drops on his eyes, instantly falls for her:

Helena: Lysander, if you live, good sir, awake.
Lysander: And run through fire I will for your sweet sake.
  Transparent Helena, nature shows art
  That through thy bosom makes me see thy heart.

> (2.2.108–11)

The suddenness of love is amusingly caught in the way the waking Lysander feels so in tune with Helena that he completes her rhyming couplet.

Waking up

The lovers undergo the ordeal of frantic uncertainty. The men are young and under the control of what we'd now call raging hormones. The darkness of the night reflects their troubled thinking, and the presence of the moon hints at an element of madness. Their reliance on all the clichés of love indicates that they are caught in and controlled by the standard roles of lovers.

And then they wake up. What they say is evidence that they've come to their senses:

> These things seem small and indistinguishable,
> Like far-off mountains turned into clouds.

> (4.1.186–7)

What exactly did happen to us? Did we feel the frenzy of distracted love? Were those feelings quite as important as we felt they were? Those are the kind of questions that prompt the beautiful image of the state of mind which is uncertain whether the far-off features are clouds or mountains.

It's left to Hippolyta in the next scene to combine the language of sight and of growth to indicate that they are now beyond juvenile fantasy; what their story points to is:

> something of great constancy

> (5.1.26)

'Constancy' here means certainty; in other words, she's inclined to believe what she's been told of the wild dream in the wood. Yet we wouldn't be wrong to detect wordplay; something of 'great constancy' – a lasting and rational love – has emerged out of the night's turmoils.

7.5 Theseus and the plot

▶ 'I will overbear your will' (4.1.178)

Helping the plot

Theseus tells Egeus that he's going to ignore the law concerning the punishment of disobedient daughters, so Hermia can marry Lysander. His role here is to help the plot to work. He is not being a character at this point, he's a function of the plot.

Dreams and the imagination

Shakespeare doesn't go in for philosophy, but he does dramatise the perplexities that lead to it. In a private conversation, Theseus and Hippolyta discuss the truth of what the lovers experienced. Theseus tends to interpret the lovers' story as the product of the imagination:

And as imagination bodies forth
The forms of things unknown, the poet's pen
Turns them to shapes, and gives to airy nothing
A local habitation and a name.

(5.1.14–17)

It's a rather cynical view; but can it be dismissed? As with many moments in Shakespeare, we want to say both 'no' and 'yes'. As we said above, Hippolyta wants to be more generous; she talks of 'constancy'. The tale of the wood can't be dismissed. But it is a work of imagination – Shakespeare's work. He's given the 'airy nothing/A local habitation' by making the whole fairy world. His art has bodied forth what we see on stage. Theseus's speech reminds us that this is a play about imagination.

Theseus the man

Theseus, however, is more than someone whom Shakespeare finds useful to move things along. He's witty, changeable, very male at times (he can't wait for his marriage night!) and tactfully amusing. There's a delicious moment when, out hunting, the party find the lovers asleep in the woods. Now what would you think? Of course, Theseus knows the answer, so with diplomatic delicacy he 'innocently' says:

No doubt they rose early to observe
The rite of May

(4.1.131–2)

If he weren't a Duke, someone might have said: 'A likely story!'

7.6 The mechanicals and the conventions of drama

▶ 'Hard handed men that work in Athens here' (5.1.72)

The simple mechanicals (manual workers) raise some of the most sophisticated and subtle issues in the play.

The conventions of drama

The mechanicals are rehearsing a play in the hope that it will be chosen for performance at the Duke's wedding celebrations. But they have gone hilariously wrong:

● they don't understand theatrical conventions.

However funny their actual performance in 5.1 is, what's really amusing is seeing a group putting on a play when they've no idea of how conventions establish understanding between performers and audience.

For instance, they think the ladies will be frightened by the appearance of a lion; it never occurs to them that 'the Duchess and the ladies' (1.2.71) know they are in a theatre. Hence, it's comically unnecessary for the actor playing the lion to point out that he's an ordinary chap:

Then know that I as Snug the joiner am
A lion fell, nor else no lion's dam.

(5.1.221–2)

He doesn't see that acting means being somebody else.

Yet in laughing at them, we might fail to see that another character, who should know better, is also unaware of theatrical convention – Theseus. Hippolyta and the lovers find the mechanicals amusing, but Theseus is uncertain. He joins in the amusement but he puts up an interesting defence:

The best in this kind are but shadows, and the worst are no worse if imagination amend them.

(5.1.210–11)

What he says is that all plays are unreal – 'shadows' – and if we exercise our imagination even the worst will seem better. But imagination can't be brought in like a magic wand; it only works through the words of the text and the performance of the players. It looks as if Theseus's grasp of art is almost as weak as the mechanicals.

The place of parody

What the mechanicals play is what might have happened to the lovers. The course of true love not only goes over rough ground but sometimes over the cliff.

One of the intriguing issues about the *Dream* is whether it was written before or after *Romeo and Juliet*. What makes it intriguing is the similarity between the play of Pyramus and Thisbe and the end of *Romeo and Juliet* – the lovers commit suicide because they mistakenly believe that their beloveds are already dead.

The difference between the two is crucial – we laugh at one and not at the other. This might be the point. Is Shakespeare parodying (making an art form amusing by exaggerating its form and conventions) in the *Dream* the sort of thing he'd done or was about to do in *Romeo and Juliet*? He might be saying:

● **it lies within the power of art to make a story a tragedy or a farce**.

The argument that he was doing this is that he was already having fun with theatrical conventions. This fun could naturally extend to the substance of the play – whether what we see is tragedy or comedy.

Meeting the Fairy Queen

Bottom spends a night with the Fairy Queen. This is not something that all men can boast of. Titania is often presented on stage as wildly and outstandingly beautiful – lavishly clothed, sexy, sophisticated; in fact, the stuff that male dreams are made of.

What it also makes possible is acting which is difficult but quite wonderful when it comes off. Here is this simple man (not very different from most men) who's been to bed with Madonna or whatever Spice girl is felt to be the most desirable woman alive. The actor playing Bottom has the opportunity of bringing that wonder back into the world of the mechanicals.

Bottom is 'changed' (3.1.109) and 'translated' (3.1.113) when he receives the ass's head. The word 'translated' can mean being taken away to fairyland. Most are never the same again after this journey; but Bottom bounces back with his usual irrepressible bossiness – and perhaps with something else:

...I have had a most rare vision. I have had a dream past the wit of man to say what dream it was. Man is but an ass if he go about t'expound this dream. (4.1.202–3)

'Rare' is a word Shakespeare uses for what is the finest, the most refined, the most exquisite of experiences. He knows that, like religion, what he's seen is inexpressible, and he proves that he's no ass by recognising that those who would try to explain the dream (Sigmund Freud take note) are fools.

Exercises

7.1 In what ways are the fairies the central figures of the play?

7.2 In what ways does the play deal with 'the lunatic, the lover and the poet'?

8 The Merchant of Venice

8.1 Antonio's sadness

▶ 'And mine a sad one' (1.1.79)

If *The Merchant of Venice* were a piece of music, it would open out of key. We pick up a conversation that's already under way; Antonio says that he doesn't know why he's so sad. The tone gives us his character: melancholic, brooding, puzzled, uncertain. It's a state he's resigned to; as he says, the world is:

> A stage where every man must play a part,
> And mine a sad one.

> (1.1.78–9)

Why is Antonio sad?

Antonio says he's yet 'to learn' (1.1.5) what's brought it on. He might be be hedging, because as soon as he's alone with Bassanio he says:

> Well, tell me now what lady is the same
> To whom you swore a secret pilgrimage,
> That you today promised to tell me of.

> (1.1.119–21)

'Well' is the giveaway; it's an awkward way of introducing the topic that's gnawing at him – the man whom he loves has fallen for a woman.

At this point one thing is pretty clear to the audience:

- **Antonio is unhappy because he fears he may lose his beloved.**

8.2 Antonio's love

▶ 'To suffer with a quietness of spirit' (4.1.11)

The Merchant of Venice has a different feel from Shakespeare's previous comedies; it's dark, troubled and emotionally intense. We are introduced to this world in the downbeat opening and in the character of the Merchant himself – Antonio. Three things are important about him; they all concern his love for Bassanio.

(1) The strength of his love

Although Shakespeare's comedies are all to do with love, not everyone loves with the same intensity. In some of the plays there are characters who are haunted by a love they can't control.

And so it is with Antonio. Because no one comments on the intensity of Bassanio's love for Portia, what Solanio says of Antonio's love for Bassanio:

> I think he only loves the world for him

> (2.8.50)

has considerable force.

(2) The extent of his love

We don't see the real extent of his love till the trial scene.

Antonio's behaviour seems curiously passive, until we see that this is his big chance to show Bassanio how much he loves him. There is an almost desperate eagerness in Antonio's anticipation of the knife in his heart:

> I do beseech you,
> Make no more offers, use no farther means,
> But with all brief and plain conveniency
> Let me have judgement and the Jew his will.

> (4.1.79–82)

'Beseech' is strong and 'conveniency' quite extraordinary. The word means 'fitness' or 'appropriateness'; this, he says, is the right thing to do. Right because it will show finally and unambiguously how much Antonio loves Bassanio. In fact, it's not only the Jew's will, it's his as well.

This may make us feel uneasy. He shouldn't be so keen to throw his life away upon a pretty boy, who's the average Venetian yuppie.

But in his willingness to throw away his life he does show himself to be better than the man he loves. Bassanio chooses the lead casket upon which is written:

> Who chooseth me must give and hazard all he has.

> (2.7.16)

It's the right choice; he gets the girl. But did he 'give and hazard (gamble) all he has'? No. His hazard is actually financed by someone else's money – Antonio's! The only one who does risk everything in the game of love is Antonio; and he nearly loses it.

The final irony revealed in this scene is the very close link between Antonio and Shylock. Both are merchants and both lose what they love. Shylock, too, gives and hazards all he has – and he loses. The man who's lost his religion has lost everything.

(3) The hopelessness of his love

What Antonio wants is an unmistakable sign from Bassanio that he feels for him. The nearest he gets to it is the business of the ring; Antonio urges him to give it away (4.1.446), and Bassanio complies.

The irony is that the ring plot lands Bassanio entirely in Portia's power. Furthermore, it brims with bawdy innuendoes of a heterosexual kind. The play closes with overt anticipations of the sexual delight (the marriages are not yet consummated) in which Antonio will have no part. His ships have come home safely, but even for a merchant, some things matter more than money. He remains on stage, while the others go to bed.

8.3 Venice

▶ 'Like signors and rich burghers' (1.1.10)

Antonio is the key character – the Merchant of Venice. And what is Venice like? It is such a strong presence that we might almost call it a character.

Wealth and show

Shakespeare's audience must have heard about this extraordinary city; Venice was wealthy, exotically full of foreigners, almost entirely dependent on trade, the centre of a huge empire and rich in works of art. In some respects it was the Hong Kong or Singapore of its day – tiny island states existing solely on trade. Something of this emerges in Salerio's opening speech:

> Your mind is tossing on the ocean,
> There where your argosies with portly sail,
> Like signors and rich burghers on the flood,
> Or as it were the pageants of the sea,
> Do overpeer the petty traffickers
> That curtsy to them, do them reverence,
> As they fly by them with, their woven wings.

(1.1.8–14)

Salerio develops a lengthy comparison (a conceit) between Antonio's impressive fleet of ships and the leading citizens of Venice, parading through the streets. The sails filled out by the breeze are like the pot-bellies of the proudly strutting gentlemen, and the small ships giving way (or lowering their topsails) are implicitly compared to those who show their respect to the 'signors'.

Venice was a place of pageants, festivals and carnivals, a city given to revelry and rich display. Something of that richness is present in 'woven'. Venice was itself a work of art, woven like the sails and fabrics for which it was so famous. And Salerio's poetry is like that; with sumptuous Venetian showiness, it weaves together the two striking yet complementary images of ships and proud citizens.

All this has an impact on the plot.

8.4 Portia, wealth and wooing

▶ 'a lady richly left' (1.1.161)

Wealth and wooing

- in Venice you have to appear wealthy to woo a pretty girl, and a pretty girl is worth wooing because she's rich.

We have to accept that in Shakespeare's play wealth enters all areas of life. This is Bassanio's first report on Portia:

> In Belmont is a lady richly left,
> And she is fair,
>
> (1.1.161–2)

We can tut-tut all we like about the fact that riches are mentioned first, but it makes no difference; that's what love and marriage are like in Venice.

8.5 The spirit of enterprise

▶ 'had I such venture forth' (1.1.15)

Venture

Trade gives life in Venice a particular texture. In the first scene of the play, we hear two important words: 'venture' and 'hazard': 'Believe me, sir, had I such venture forth' (1.1.15). This is 'merchant-talk'; 'venture' means a commercial enterprise. The word is used three times in the first 45 lines of the play, and, significantly, Antonio uses it when he's talking to Shylock (1.3.88). *The Merchant of Venice* is about characters taking financial risks.

The word also has metaphoric force:

- financial ventures are a metaphor for the adventure of love.

This is surely the case with Antonio; the 'venture' of his fleets is a metaphoric anticipation of the nearly fatal one he makes when, for love of Bassanio, he signs the bond.

Hazard

The word 'hazard' appears in the first scene, where it has overtones of gambling (1.1.151). In Shakespeare it usually means any act which is a matter of risk, chance or danger. It's also, significantly, used to mean a venture. It occurs in *The Merchant of Venice* more times (eight) than in any other Shakespeare play.

The chief use of the word associates the bond plot with the casket plot. Portia says to the Prince of Morocco:

> After dinner
> Your hazard shall be made.
>
> (2.1.44–5)

Given the conditions of choosing (for instance, promising never to court another lady if one chooses wrongly), the casket is a hazard, because a great deal is risked. Love is like a risk undertaken in business.

8.6 Religion and love

▶ 'Become a Christian and thy loving wife' (2.3.21)

Another element that colours all life is the cultural and religious division between Christian and Jew.

Jessica

Jessica is very interesting in this respect. As the quotation above shows, to elope is to change your religion. She deserts both her father and the religion of her fathers. In this sense, no other heroine risks so much. In a city fiercely divided in this way (Christians spit at Jews – 1.3.111), religion is as much an element in love as is money. In the particular weave of this play, an elopement (a standard comic practice – see 5.6) is inseparable from the culture of religious division.

So though elopements are the stuff of comedy, this one doesn't feel blithe and care-free. When Jessica is about to descend in true elopement style from her balcony, she says:

> For I am much ashamed of my exchange
>
> (2.6.35)

The exchange (a financial word) could be her clothes (she's disguised as a page) or her theft, but equally possible is that it's the exchange of religion that troubles her.

8.7 The centrality of Shylock

▶ 'I am a Jew' (3.1.55)

In a play in which the whole of life is dyed by financial deals and religious divisions, Shylock has a central place. This is something the theatre has long recognised; it's the plum part, which every Shakespearean actor must play. It's probably the major prose part in Shakespeare. Like Richard III, it's also one of the great villain roles.

However, unlike Richard, the demands made on the actor are numerous and diverse. It's not clear in the text (and certainly not in our present cultural climate) whether Shylock should be played to arouse hostility or pity or both.

Shylock and the plot

We must remember how the plot of the play works. Act 1, Scene 3 establishes a long-standing mutual hatred between Antonio and Shylock. We hear about this before Shylock offers the terms of the bond.

It's not clear whether he intends to insist on this (he does talk about 'merry sport' – 1.3.142), but when his daughter leaves and Antonio's ships are wrecked, he goes ahead. The trial scene won't work unless we believe that he will plunge his knife into Antonio. The plot, therefore, clearly establishes that Shylock was not prepared to do what Antonio did – show mercy.

Shylock and Antonio

If Shylock is in the wrong about seeking revenge, Shakespeare shows that Antonio is guilty of hatred. Shylock accuses him of spitting; we are surely supposed to be shocked that Antonio doesn't deny this:

> I am as like to call thee so again,
> To spit on thee again, to spurn thee, too.

> (1.3.126–7)

Those lines show that:

- **this is not the sort of play in which the audience can unambiguously prefer one character to another; both Antonio and Shylock have very unattractive sides.**

Shylock's feelings

Shakespeare gives Shylock the most moving speech in the play – 3.1.50–69:

> Hath not a Jew eyes?
> Hath not a Jew hands, organs, dimension, senses,
> healed by the same means, warmed and cooled by the
> same winter and summer, as a Christian is?

> (3.1.55–8)

It's a speech that lays bare the humanity we all share. It dwells on the basics of life – our bodies, senses and our very survival. If we are all brothers and sisters, then prejudice is wrong.

Shylock is a man of feeling. There's a moving moment in the trial scene when everyone (rather pompously?) is saying how much their beloveds mean to them, when Shylock bursts out with:

> I have a daughter:
> Would any of the stock of Barabas
> Have been her husband rather than a Christian!

> (4.1.292–4)

Those words awaken us to the grief for his lost daughter; we see his pursuit of Antonio in that light. His speech might make us balance the mixing of 'My daughter, O my ducats' that caused so much amusement earlier (2.8.15) to the hostile Solanio.

Shylock and religion

Shylock introduces the religious dimension of their quarrel in Act 1, Scene 3. He talks at length about how Jacob thrived by questionable means.

It shouldn't be surprising, therefore, that he plays the trial scene in a religious way. Shakespeare presents Jews as living by the law; and it's the law that Shylock insists on. He won't or can't take notice of Portia's plea for mercy.

Here, however, we may feel that Shakespeare is against him. At one point he says:

My deeds upon my head!

(4.1.203)

Shakespeare's audience would surely recognise that as an echo of the account of the trial of Jesus, when the crowd shouts that punishment can fall upon them and their children (St Matthew 27:25). Is it fair to put him into the position of echoing those words?

His punishment is also religious – he must become a Christian. To many people having to change religion might seem slight, but Shakespeare grew up in a world in which religion was a vital issue. Thirty years before his birth, the Church of England came into being, and adherence to the Church of Rome became, in some cases, a punishable offence. We know that Shakespeare's father was fined for not attending church, so it's possible that they still adhered to the 'old religion', as Roman Catholicism was called. Did Shakespeare make the Christians impose this punishment because he knew from his father's case (and maybe his own) the agonies of being forced to conform to a religion in which one did not believe?

8.8 Portia and the outcome of the plot

▶ 'O sweet Portia' (3.1.248)

From a dramatic point of view, it looks as if Portia is going to be a disappointment: for half the play the most she does is wittily mock her suitors (Act 1, scene 2) and, possibly, lead Bassanio to make the right choice of casket by having a song sung with lots of rhymes in it for 'lead'. Once, however, Antonio's plight becomes known, she emerges as the Shakespearean heroine who's inventive and enterprising.

Portia's speech on mercy

She delivers the speech on mercy that's the necessary contrast to Shylock's insistence on law. We've been prepared for this earlier on. Act 3, Scene 4 opens with Lorenzo praising Portia for her elevated ideas of friendship. It's one of those scenes that opens when its events are already happening. What they've been doing is debating. One of the pastimes of courts was intellectual debate, conducted according to quite strict rules of rhetoric. They have been debating friendship, and Lorenzo has been impressed.

When, therefore she delivers the mercy speech (4.1.181–202), we know she's an accomplished speaker. The interesting issue is:

● to whom is she speaking?

Two audiences we can easily identify – the two groups who are impressed: the court and the audience. But she gets nowhere with Shylock, because the speech is intended for Christians. (See Illustration 4.)

Portia's strategy

Her failure here leads to her next strategy – that of taking Shylock up to the line before defeating him. Some have found her 'playing' here disagreeable: why does she manoeuvre him into a position where he might even lose his life?

Illustration 4   The Merchant of Venice: the trial scene

What's certain is her toughness. 'O sweet Portia'! No longer suffering from the bar of her dead father, she's independent and forceful. It's quite fitting that she ends the play having put her husband in the wrong (the ring plot). This marriage is going to be as interesting as Kate and Petruchio's or Beatrice and Benedick's.

Exercises

8.1 Can you account for the very different reactions audiences have had to Shylock?

8.2 Examine the impact of money upon the plot and characters of *The Merchant of Venice*.

Much Ado About Nothing

9.1 Plot, amazement and comedy

▶ **'All this amazement'** (5.4.67)

'Amazement' has as its root meaning 'being lost in a maze'; hence it means bewilderment, distraction and perplexity. Those words are spoken by the Friar who, as a typical comic contriver, has sorted out the plot by producing something quite astonishing – a girl who's apparently come back from the dead.

Of course, this amazement is felt by the characters and not the audience; we've followed the practices, and while what we've seen is complex, it's not confusing.

- **The plot is so carefully constructed that we can see exactly where it's going.**

As soon as something difficult occurs, Shakespeare produces the means of getting round it; for instance, no sooner has Don John put his second deceiving practice into action, than the culprits are arrested. A happy ending is always possible.

This means it's quite wrong to talk about the play, as many have done, as a comedy that might have been a tragedy.

9.2 The doubling of characters

▶ **'a double heart'** (2.1.261)

The heart of the play is a set of doubles.

Doubles

Characters in the play are paralleled and contrasted. For instance, there are two sets of brothers: Leonato and Antonio, and Don Pedro and Don John.

On the female side we have cousins instead of sisters, but we see that the love and loyalty Beatrice has for Hero is the same as a sisterly devotion.

Both the Pedro brothers are practisers: Don Pedro tries to establish marriages, Don John to destroy them. Pedro is assisted by his followers – the residents of and visitors to Messina – and Don John has his henchmen.

These henchmen, along with Margaret, provide a parallel to and grim parody of Claudio and Hero, who are experiencing love for the first time.

Not only are Hero and Claudio contrasted with Borachio and Margaret but they are also contrasted with Beatrice and Benedick. Claudio falls in love, while Beatrice and Benedick have to be tricked into declaring (or even admitting?) their love.

9.3 Characterisation

▶ 'So you walk softly, and look sweetly, and say nothing' (2.1.80)

Complaints of that kind are sometimes made about the play. It's said the characters are neither vivid nor memorable. What is Leonato like? Is Hero of sufficient interest? Isn't Claudio are rather colourless young man?

What is to be made of these worries?

Restrictions

In the case of some characters it looks as if Shakespeare has deliberately restricted their range. Some might have been developed further, but Shakespeare decided against it. For instance, Don John has the makings of an interesting character. He's moody and melancholy, but that's about it.

Dramatic function

In a very complex plot it's not surprising that a number of characters don't do much more than fulfil their plot function. This might be the answer to the Don Pedro problem. In a world of comic practising, there needs to be a chief practiser, and this is the role Don Pedro is given. He gets both the major plots going. He has the status and authority to do this, but apart from a delight in playing tricks, it's not necessary that he has much more about him.

Characters with one scene

Minimal characterisation doesn't, of course, mean characters who are blanks. What it does involve are characters who have a few, though important characteristics. Claudio is an interesting example: the plot requires him to be young, uncertain, dependent upon those in authority and new to the world of love.

Yet Shakespeare makes it worth while for someone to play him. The scene in the church when he mistakenly denounces Hero is his scene. Played well, he can be moving, in spite of the appalling things he dreams up about her; he's essentially an innocent, who's been disappointed in love for the first time and he's no way of coping with it but anger. And we must remember, he weeps in the scene (4.1.155).

Character parts

Some of the juiciest parts are actually those of minor characters. Dogberry, with his attempts to talk in an official language that he imagines is fitting for a man in his high office, is a delightful character. He has a range of moods: respectful to Leonato, angry with the villains and considerate about Verges. Acted well, it's a rewarding and amusing part.

Although very minor, the watch have some delightful lines. The first Watchman says:

let us go sit upon the church bench till two, and then all to bed. (3.3.86)

9.4 The distinctiveness of Beatrice and Benedick

▶ 'Beatrice and Benedick' (2.3.135)

The exception to everything said above is Beatrice and Benedick. They are richly detailed characters. For instance, Benedick keeps up the pose of being the woman-hater but, left to himself, he begins to wonder whether he, too, will fall in love. He imagines an ideal wife in an engagingly speculative tone, ending with this blithe throwaway:

and her hair shall be of what colour it please God (2.3.33)

Most of the other characters don't have that light, musing, meditative side.

One of the most careful bits of characterisation in both of them is the difference between their mutual criticism: hers is personal, his general. She constantly makes fun of Benedick; he talks about women in disparaging tones. Perhaps Shakespeare is observing a difference here between men and women. Men think of women in general:

'That a woman conceived me, I thank her.' (1.1.223)

Benedick doesn't talk about his *mother* but of *a woman*. But though Beatrice talks about men, she very frequently focuses on individuals, in particular on Benedick.

Beatrice and the women

Beatrice is the outstanding character; she's always carefully individualised, and so there's a constant and exciting sense that her speech and actions are unpredictable. When in love, Benedick starts to behave a bit like a stage lover, but Beatrice never takes on the role of the beloved.

Furthermore, her interesting independence as a character is related to her insistence upon a female view of things. For instance, one of her reasons for not marrying is that she doesn't want to be dominated by a man. She puts it with characteristic lightness:

...Would it not grieve a woman to be overmastered with a piece of valiant dust? – to make an account of her life to a clod of wayward marl? (2.1.54–6)

Of course, Beatrice knows we are all, according to the Bible, made out of the dust, and in this no woman is different from a man. And that's her argument – both men and women are mortal creatures, so why should women be controlled by men?

Some have thought that this is a play about girl power. Their wit, their enterprise, their patience, their good sense, their control of situations are evident throughout. Some have felt that Benedick loves Beatrice more than she does him.

Margaret

In some respects Margaret is a bit unsatisfactory in that she has to be both helpful and dangerous to Hero. However, there's one moment when she has to be more than a plot device. What we see in Act 3, Scene 4 is a scene of all the girls together. They are being girls; that is, they are looking at events from their point of view rather than the men's. They talk of marriage, clothes, the colour of hair, and Margaret talks about sex. When Beatrice, who has a cold, says she's 'stuffed', Margaret remarks: 'A maid, and stuffed!' (3.4.60)

This is a play that delights in the separate world of female conversation.

9.5 Wooing, art and the plot

▶ 'so fine a story' (1.1.294)

Wooing and the plot

In the first scene of *Much Ado About Nothing* we see a group of characters who think they know exactly how the plot of the play will work out. Don Pedro puts it with confident neatness:

> 'Tis once: thou lovest,
> And I will fit thee with the remedy.
> I know we shall have revelling tonight.
> I will assume thy part in some disguise,
> And tell fair Hero I am Claudio.
> And in her bosom I'll unclasp my heart
> And take her hearing prisoner with the force
> And strong encounter of my amorous tale.

(1.1.301–8)

In Don Pedro's world, events follow as a matter of course: Claudio loves, so Don Pedro will produce the 'remedy'; it's as easy as that. The remedy comes in the form of art – that is, in the form of what's organised and shaped. Art thrives in courts, because courts exist by turning life into ritual and ceremony; courts are living art. The 'revelry' takes the form of a masked ball; that is, a dance in which the participants disguise themselves by wearing masks. Other words in the speech pick up the theme of art: 'part' and 'disguise' from drama, 'unclasp' means to open a book, and the aim is the telling of an 'amorous tale'.

Life and art

This confidence in the ability to order life, to turn the rough and uneven course of nature into the smooth lines of art, is found throughout the play:

- in *Much Ado About Nothing* **the characters transform bitty and unpredictable life into the harmonious symmetries of art.**

We see this in three ways.

(1) Wit and courtesy

The characters make life elegant and smoothly finished through the wit and courtesy of their language.

- 'Wit' had a number of meanings in Shakespeare's day: imagination, intelligence, wisdom and thought leading to plans.
- 'Courtesy' is obviously associated with the court; as such it came to mean good and appropriate manners.

Both wit and courtesy are expressed in wordplay. Wordplay is the ordinary and necessary business of talk turned into art.

After the marriage between Hero and Claudio has been arranged, there's some joking about finding a husband for Beatrice. Don Pedro makes an offer (it could be played as a gallant jest or as the prelude to a proposal), to which Beatrice replies:

No, my lord, unless I might have another for working days. Your grace is too costly to wear every day. But I beseech your grace, pardon me. I was born to speak all mirth and no matter. (2.1.306–9)

Beatrice is light and tactful. She compliments him by comparing his high status to wearing costly clothes – not something to be done everyday. She then excuses herself by playing on the familiar distinction between what's said and how it's said, decorating the point with a happy alliteration on the contrast between 'mirth' and 'matter'.

One of the charming aspects of the play is that virtually everyone tries to speak elegantly. Dogberry, the Constable, is aware that courtesy in speech is required, so he peppers his talk with what he thinks is suitable language. His amusing mistakes are often in the form of malapropisms – using a word which is wrong, but close in sound:

Marry, sir, I would have some confidence with you that decerns you nearly. (3.5.2–3)

He means 'conference', not 'confidence', and 'decerns you nearly' is his attempt at 'concerns you closely'.

(2) Knowing your role

When in the first scene Benedick is asked for his opinion of Hero, he says:

Do you question me as an honest man should do, for my simple true judgement, or would you have me speak after my custom, as being a professed tyrant to their sex? (1.1.159–61)

Benedick is effectively saying: do you want me to tell you what I really think, or do you want one of my usual performances? In other words, he knows that a lot of the time he's playing a part.

One of the ways in which the civilized nature of this society emerges is in the conscious living out of roles: Benedick is the woman-hater, Beatrice the one who merrily mocks Benedick, Hero the quiet, dutiful daughter, Claudio the man who's been a soldier and now wants to be a lover.

And one more thing: there's sometimes the awareness (or near-awareness) that the characters are in a play. This emerges in the imagery drawn from art (including drama), the sense of the public nature of what they are doing (Claudio shames Hero in public) and in the intimacy characters have with the audience. When Benedick hears that Beatrice loves him, his soliloquy is easy, open and friendly. I see him as sharing with us the role he should now play:

... They say too that she will rather die than give any sign of affection. I never did think to marry. I must not seem proud. Happy are those who hear their detractions and put them to mending. (2.3.216–18)

Benedick tells the audience that Beatrice won't give 'any sign of affection'. The theatre is about signs. If she won't give the signs of love, Benedick must by playing the role of the lover.

(3) Enjoying the practising

No characters in Shakespeare take to practising so easily or do it with such relish and gusto.

This is amusingly evident in Act 2, Scene 1, when Claudio's marriage has been arranged, and the characters are left with nothing to do. Since practising is their chief delight, they fix on a scheme to fill the time. This is the proposal of the arch-practiser, Don Pedro:

> ... I will in the interim undertake one of Hercules' labours, which is to bring Signor Benedick and the Lady Beatrice into a mountain of affection th'one with th' other. (2.1.341–3)

Notice the element of role-playing; Don Pedro delights in the hyperbole of comparing his task with the legendary labours of Hercules. And you can hear his enjoyment as his voice rises to the triumphant cadence of 'a mountain of affection'.

9.6 Cupid and practising

▶ 'for we are the only love-gods' (2.1.361)

The most astonishing form of the desire to raise ordinary life to the level of art comes at the close of Act 2, Scene 1. Don Pedro has outlined his plan to make Beatrice and Benedick fall in love, and then he winds up the scene with an amazing (even outrageous) claim:

> ... If we can do this, Cupid is no longer an archer; his glory shall be ours, for we are the only love-gods.

They even want to control Cupid! Cupid stands for the unpredictable and inexplicable nature of love. Blind Cupid twangs off his arrows, which fall he knows not where. And Don Pedro wants to pension him off, so that the practisers of Messina will be the only ones who discharge arrows. As the only gods of love they'll be in sole charge of all affection, and because they can see they'll be quite specific about their targets. Even love will become part of the finely woven artistic fabric of living.

9.7 The limits of practising

▶ 'if peradventure this be true' (2.1.21)

Nature and art

Shakespeare finds the Messinian world he's created both interesting and useful. He's an artist and he finds the impulse to turn life into art entirely understandable. What the characters do is similar to what he does.

In a number of his plays, the theme of the relationship between nature and art is important. Anyone who wants to make nature as smooth and ordered as art will have to accept that it's possible that nature isn't quite as controllable as the 'artists' hope.

And so it turns out. There's an interesting occurrence in the second scene. Leonato's brother, Antonio, reports that a servant of his overheard Claudio and Don Pedro talking and deduced from this that Don Pedro was going to propose to Hero.

This is significant: overhearing is a comic practice – and it turns out to be wrong. Leonato is aware of this – the quotation above shows that the news might not be true. The scene is carefully placed. In the opening scene, we see the attempt to sort out life neatly and conveniently; in the second scene we see the means of making life neat – the comic practice – going wrong.

This is not to say that Shakespeare is saying that the characters are wrong. He's not asking us to take sides; still less is it his intention to judge them as wrong. Shakespeare doesn't quarrel; he's as interested in those who want to turn life into art as he is in the way life resists such a transformation.

9.8 Making mistakes

▶ 'some strange misprison in the princes' (4.1.187)

This is the judgement of the Friar on the accusations made against Hero. 'Misprison' means mistake; what he's saying is they've got it wrong.

They are not the only ones. Throughout the play, the characters make mistakes; for instance, Antonio thinks Don Pedro is wooing Hero and Beatrice and Benedick are misled into thinking that each loves the other.

Making mistakes shows that comedy is about disparities (different levels) of knowledge. Only in plays in which knowledge is crucial can mistakes be important.

- *Much Ado About Nothing* **might therefore be said to be about how mistakes are made, the consequences of mistakes, how they are detected and how put right.**

Shakespeare is very careful to show that it's understandable, as well as easy, to make mistakes. For instance, Benedick says he would be inclined to believe that the story that Beatrice loves him is a trick, were it not for the presence of Leonato:

... I should think this a gull, but that the white-bearded fellow speaks it. Knavery cannot, sure, hide himself in such reverence. (2.3.117–19)

The crucial thing here is that Benedick knows he lives in a world in which we can get things wrong, but he's inclined to believe what's been said because of the reliability of the 'white-bearded fellow'. Benedick is mistaken – Leonato is deceiving him. But does that mean Beatrice doesn't love him? In one sense, they've no evidence that she does, but the play shows that they are unerringly right in what they say, even though they think they are gulling Benedick.

The play is about being right and wrong, but in the world of *Much Ado* a character *can* be both right and wrong.

9.9 Art in the service of nature

▶ 'kind of merry war' (1.1.38)

Art helping nature

The points where the desire to make life into art comes most unstuck are the episodes including Beatrice and Benedick. Though here Shakespeare teases us. When Don Pedro plays the love-god, Beatrice and Benedick do what the Don's script tells them – they immediately discover that they love each other. Furthermore, Benedick does something about it by declaring his love. In a fraught conversation about the ghastly events in the church, he says, suddenly but quite naturally:

I do love nothing in the world so well as you. (4.1.269)

She answers with equal ease:

… It were as possible for me to say I loved nothing so well as you. (4.1.271–2)

It's worth asking why. The answer might be something to do with natural inclination. *Much Ado* can be played as Beatrice and Benedick having strong feelings for each other, that have become submerged. From Beatrice's words in the opening scene about Benedick challenging Cupid (1.1.37–40, 62–8), we might guess that he made advances to Beatrice but was rejected. It's also notable that she talks about him a great deal, and that he was very angry (too angry?) when, in the masked ball, she was wittily rude about him (2.1.224–4).

The plot of the play is that the practice – the art – of Don Pedro releases the natural affection. In this sense, it can be played to show that art allows and encourages nature to be fully itself.

Art failing to control nature

But, as with most of Shakespeare, it can be read another way. Shakespeare might be interested in what's beyond control. Don Pedro performs the labour of a Hercules by bringing the two into a mountain of affection, but where that affection leads to is something quite beyond his power to order.

Beatrice and Benedick discovering love and stepping beyond the roles set down for them works through a rediscovery of one of the plot elements – war. In Leonato's speech at the start (1.1.8–11) and Claudio's significant description 'this ended action' (1.1.280), the war is sealed up and forgotten about. We might think that Beatrice is being surprisingly tactless when she reminds everyone that war involves killing – 'how many hath he killed?' (1.1.40). She knows that it does, and when necessary she reminds Benedick in chilling terms. After he's declared himself, he offers to do anything for her; her answer is as swift as a sword-thrust: 'Kill Claudio' (4.1.290).

At that moment Beatrice knows the plot is about love and war. It's a different plot from the one Don Pedro planned.

9.10 The mood of the play

▶ 'Why, it must be requited' (2.3.212)

In spite of the horrible things that are said in Act 4, Scene 1, *Much Ado* is a happy play. One of the reasons for this is an easy lilting cadence that slips naturally from the tongue. In scene after scene, this little tune ripples through the flow of language. It's a verbal gesture that in the form of a casual throwaway invites the listener to make a silent acknowledgement (or a gentle nod of the head) to what has been said. Here are some:

Well, we are all mortal (1.1.57)

Amen, if you love her (1.1.207)

and God give you joy (2.1.282)

Well, God's a good man (3.5.35)

These lilting turns of phrase have an unstrained confidence that requires no affirmation.

If our ears are atuned to the cadences of the play we'll never be worried about the outcome. Moreover, we'll know that they are spoken to us – the audience. One of the charming aspects of *Much Ado* is that sense of trust, of easy give and take, that exists between players and watchers. They know they are performing a play; and they have the confidence to know that we'll enjoy it, perhaps especially because its much ado is really about nothing.

Exercises

9.1 Some audiences have found the atmosphere of *Much Ado About Nothing* playful, while others think it is sinister. What arguments would you use in explaining what you think the play's prevailing mood is?

9.2 'Apart from Beatrice and Benedick the play offers an audience very little.' What is your view of this statement?

---

10 As You Like It

10.1 The pastoral element

▶ 'Why, whither shall we go?' (1.3.105)

Court and countryside

As You Like It works within what is known as the pastoral tradition. This depicts an imaginative world in which, by convention, life thrives in a near-perfect landscape, where shepherds and shepherdesses tend their flocks beside quietly murmuring streams in a perpetual Maytime. The shepherds, sometimes called swains, are lovers and poets, and shepherdesses sometimes welcome and sometimes resist their attentions. Such a life is free from anxiety, largely because it's nothing to do with the court.

The world of the Forest of Arden has close links with the pastoral tradition: we meet shepherds; it's a place where love can thrive, and we hear in Duke Senior's speech the conventional distinction between court and country:

> Are not these woods
> More free from peril than the envious court?
>
> (2.1.3–4)

A forest

The Forest of Arden is not a paradise, and not every lover in it is happy (Phoebe is the disdainful mistress, and Silvius her unrequited lover) but it's never a place of mad distraction. Instead, for the central characters – Rosalind and Orlando – it's a place of blithe merriment. Only in the forest can their love find expression.

Journeying into the forest is an adventure. There's a gleeful tone about the planning in Act 1, Scene 3. Rosalind and Celia discuss disguises and invent names, and when Rosalind proposes stealing the clown, Touchstone, there's just a hint that he'll go because he's in love with Celia:

> He'll go along o'er the wide world with me.
> Leave me alone to woo him. Let's away.
>
> (1.3.131–2)

10.2 Father and daughter

▶ 'a banished father' (1.2.4)

Rosalind says to Celia she could show 'mirth' if:

> you could teach me to forget a banished father (1.2.4)

Rosalind, like Portia, is unhappy, but whereas Portia's unhappiness is caused by her father's casket lottery, Rosalind's results from being parted from her father.

Even more surprising is that Rosalind's love for Orlando is related to her father. Usually a daughter faces trouble from her father when she falls in love, but Rosalind is encouraged when she learns that Orlando's father was Sir Rowland de Boys:

> My father loved Sir Rowland as his soul
>
> (1.2.224)

10.3 Love

▶ 'what think you of falling in love?' (1.2.24)

As You Like It opens with a scene of division: Oliver has treated his brother Orlando like a servant, so Orlando says he will leave. In the second scene we learn that another pair of brothers – Duke Senior and Duke Frederick – are at odds.

Into this symmetry comes Rosalind, daughter of Duke Senior, and Celia, daughter of Duke Frederick. Celia tries to cheer up her cousin, and Rosalind responds to 'be merry' (1.2.22) with:

> From henceforth I will, coz, and devise sports. Let me see, what think you of falling in love? (1.2.23–4)

Those words assure the audience that they are watching a comedy; however deep the divisions are (see 10.4), love will find a way of sorting things out. Moreover, the business of unravelling the knots caused by suspicion and hatred will be a merry one, because to fall in love is a sport. That's not to diminish love; it's to bring out the elements of game, play, holiday and make-believe:

- **love has the transforming effect of a holiday in that the lovers feel they are living in a new world.**

10.4 The importance of Rosalind

▶ 'But heavenly Rosalind!' (1.2.279)

We said that in *Much Ado* we saw the world of women on their own and the power of women. This now becomes a central feature of *As You Like It*; there are long passages in Act 1, Scenes 2 and 3 where the two women talk about their feelings, so the separate world of girl-talk is established early on.

Female power is seen in the rest of the play:

- **no character equals Rosalind.**

She's the chief practiser, arranging for Orlando to court her in a way that will allow him to say what he wants and needs. She's also the cause of some of the complications (believing her to be a young man, Phoebe falls in love with her) and at the close she winds up the business by managing the marriages. She even partly steps out of her role to deliver the Epilogue, aware that this is unusual:

> It is not the fashion to see the lady the epilogue (Epilogue, 1).

Love

If an audience has doubts about just how deeply Beatrice is in love, there's no doubt about Rosalind. She talks of love, in Act 1, Scene 2 and falls in love in Scene 3, no doubt partly impressed by Orlando's success in the wrestling bout. When she hears he's in the forest, she's excited (Act 3, Scene 2) and when he's late (Act 4, Scene 1) she suffers all the agonies of the person who's desperately in love. Her moods change; when he's there, she's cross because he's late, rumbustious in her mockery of conventional attitudes and delightfully encouraging. If we have any doubts about her feelings, we should remember that she faints when she hears he's been attacked by a lion.

Rosalind's enterprise

Many heroines adventure for love, but none do it with such high spirits. Listen to the way she relishes adopting a male disguise:

> We'll have a swashing and a martial outside.
> As many other mannish cowards have

> (1.3.119–20)

She obviously enjoys the dressing-up business and she amuses herself to think that she'll be as cowardly as the men who also strut in the way she will.

Her wit

Rosalind's mind is keen in its detection of double meanings. When she's disguised as a young man and pretending to be Rosalind, Orlando asks who could be 'out' – unhappy, out of key – in the presence of a beloved. She mischievously seizes on the word, playing upon another meaning of 'out' – out of one's clothes, naked. Orlando blunders on, using the word 'suit', meaning, for him, a plea for love. Rosalind merrily plays with the bawdy implications:

Not out of your apparel, and yet out of your suit (4.1.82).

Orlando, she's saying, has not stripped for love, but he is making a mistake in his pursuit of love.

Her confidence

Rosalind is buoyantly confident in her wit. She verbally fences with anyone, ticking off Phoebe and putting Touchstone in his place.

Her confidence comes out in the slightly cynical way in which she dismisses some ideas of love. Orlando, getting a bit close to the Petrarchan lover, says he'll die if his beloved won't have him. She's not going to put up with such conventional posturing, so mocks a list of famous lovers, pointing out, with splendid commonsense, that whatever they died of, it wasn't love:

> ...Troilus had his brains dashed with a Grecian club ... Leander, he would have lived many a fair year though Hero had turned nun if it had not been for a hot midsummer night, for, good youth, he went but forth to wash him in the Hellespont and, being taken with the cramp, was drowned. (4.1.91–7)

Her kindness

Yet Rosalind is considerate and sensitive. As someone in love herself, she knows it matters, so at the close of the play she does her best to sort everything out. She makes sure that if Phoebe can't have 'her', she'll have Silvius, and that Silvius will take the girl who has so far rejected him. Then she says:

> I have promised to make all this matter even.

> (5.4.18)

'Even' means smooth; Rosalind wants the end to be as harmonious as possible. She embodies the spirit of comedy – the desire to bring a happy ending out of confusion and uncertainty.

10.5 Orlando and speech

▶ 'What passion hangs these weights upon my tongue?' (1.2.247)

Though *As You Like It* is the happiest and most care-free of all the comedies, there's an impediment to the lovers' happiness: Orlando is tongue-tied.

There's a subtle point here; love is inseparable from expression. Wit – the proper use of language – isn't a luxury, it's the stuff of life. If we can talk about our feelings and, as Rosalind shows, laugh at them, then we can fully enjoy the riches of life. In Orlando's case, it's not merely a matter of etiquette – women can't speak unless they're spoken to – but of his need to say what he thinks and feels.

10.6 Courtship and games

▶ 'Nay, you must call me Rosalind' (3.2.418)

Rosalind discovers another impediment – her male disguise:

> what shall I do with my doublet and hose! (3.2.214)

She therefore has to be particularly bold and enterprising. Her device seems a curious one:

> I would cure you if you would but call me Rosalind and come every day to my cot, and woo me. (3.2.410–11)

She says she'll do for him what she did for another young man in love – pretend to be a disdainful mistress. Surely the actress must enjoy the hyperbole of her description:

grieve, be effeminate, changeable, longing and liking, proud, fantastical, apish, shallow, inconstant, full of tears, full of smiles (3.2.395–6).

She needs to know how serious Orlando is. Orlando is behaving pretty much like a standard lover (we hear he's been stretched out beneath a tree – 3.2.229); is his love just a pose or is it his way of expressing what he feels? (See Illustration 1.)

The actress playing Rosalind must find a way of showing her pleasure when Orlando replies:

I would not be cured, youth. (3.2.409)

10.7 Love and disguise

▶ 'You a lover?' (4.1.38)

Act 4, Scene 1 is Shakespeare's most sustained treatment of the possibilities of disguise.

The situation is pleasingly complex: Rosalind, in love with Orlando, is disguised as a boy, who, to help Orlando court her, is pretending to be Rosalind. Add to that the boy-being-a-girl-being-a-boy business, and we have that characteristically Shakespearean relish for playing multiple roles.

In this situation, Orlando can speak and she can answer:

Orlando: Then love me Rosalind.
Rosalind: Yes, faith will I, Friday and Saturdays and all.
Orlando: And wilt thou have me?
Rosalind: Ay, and twenty such.

(94.1.107–10)

The language here is free from the artificiality of so much love talk; it's colloquial, easy, light and certainly more convincing than the verses he pinned on trees.

The dialogue raises the issue of the relationship between the natural and the artificial (nature and art) in human life. It seems natural, yet, because it's a game, it reminds us of the elements of play in 'ordinary life'. They are playing, but in life and love we *all* play.

In this game, disguise makes it possible for the characters to say and hear what in normal circumstances they would not be able to. Orlando is able to say that he would like to be talking to Rosalind, and Rosalind can hear him saying it:

Rosalind: Am not I your Rosalind?
Orlando: I take some joy to say you are because I would be talking of her. (4.1.83–4)

The joy is not only his; she too must 'take joy' to hear this being said.

10.8 The holiday mood

▶ 'for I am now in a holiday humour' (4.1.64)

The most memorable thing about the play is its mood. Love is a kind of holiday, so Rosalind encourages Orlando to woo. This breezy, relaxed feel is present in a number of the play's aspects.

No scheming

Unlike *Much Ado*, the characters of ill-will – Oliver and Duke Frederick – don't consistently scheme; both are quite open in their treatment of Orlando and Rosalind in that there's no attempt to hide hostility.

Change

Not only are the ill-willed characters open but they undergo dramatic changes – Oliver is saved by Orlando from the lion and falls in love with Celia, and Duke Frederick has a religious conversion and so gives up the court.

Variety

As You Like It comes closest to the idea of a plot as diverting variety rather than strict unity. One of the pleasures of the play is its different kinds of language and stage business.

For instance, Silvius and Phoebe offer a contrast to Rosalind and Orlando; both fall in love at first sight, but the latter pair avoid the amusing excesses of the Petrarchan lovers. Touchstone performs the role of parodist, making fun of a number of ways of speaking. His individual 'performances' stand on their own as feats of linguistic agility.

The 'litany' of repeated phrases in Act 5, Scene 2 has its own restrained and quiet beauty and acts as a foil to the merry banter of the wooing in Act 4, Scene 1.

Finally, the songs are a delight in themselves.

What happens?

The answer is: not much. This is a pleasingly relaxed play with little going on. Shakespeare is content to weave together the paths of several lovers, leaving the variety and the brilliance of the language to entertain the audience.

Ritual ending

It has the grandest ending of any of the comedies until the final plays – the promise of magic, the puzzlement of the characters and then the entrance of the two girls as themselves and, finally, Hymen's almost mystical celebration of marriage.

10.9 The character who doesn't fit in

▶ 'The melancholy Jaques' (1.2.26)

Sometimes the leading actor in a production will play Jaques rather than, say, Orlando or Duke Senior. Certainly, this decision brings out the variety of the play, for Jaques is an operatic role with one or two good scenes and the most famous speech in the play. He has virtually no effect on the plot; in fact, no sooner has he ended the 'seven ages' speech with its portrait of senility, than the characters busy themselves with feeding old Adam.

His most important role is his refusal to participate in the happy close. Jaques has no quarrel; it's just that he decides the seclusion and remoteness of the woodland is preferable. He thus passes an interesting judgement upon comic endings – Shakespeare is aware that in spite of the pressures of plot and convention there are some characters who, because of who they are, can't join in.

Exercises

10.1 Can you explain why Rosalind is such a popular character in the theatre?

10.2 Is the lack of action a positive or negative feature of *As You Like It*?

Twelfth Night

11.1 How the plot starts

▶ **'What country, friends, is this?' (1.2.1)**

Illyria

Twelfth Night has one of the most memorable openings in Shakespeare:

> If music be the food of love, play on,
> Give me excess of it, that surfeiting,
> The appetite may sicken and so die.

Listening to these smooth and lyrical lines, it's easy to miss what Orsino is saying. He asks for more music so that he'll have too much – 'surfeiting' – and his 'appetite' for love will die.

What's to be made of this? Perhaps Shakespeare is not only giving us an idea of what Orsino is like but starting to form a picture of Illyria.

- **Illyria is a world of art, rigid social order ('play on' is the order given by a master to a servant) and self-indulgence.**

Somehow life has gone wrong. There's discontent and even nausea. (The word 'sick' did mean to vomit in Shakespeare's day.)

This is how the third scene starts:

> What a plague means my niece to take the death of her brother thus? I am sure care's an enemy to life.

That rumbustious line is spoken by someone who's fed up with the stifling life of Olivia's household. In its stagnation, the household is not much different from Orsino' court.

The newcomer

But the second scene is different. Viola steps out of the sea rather like a figure from Greek mythology and asks:

> What country, friends, is this?

There's a sadness in that scene (she thinks her brother has been drowned), but it feels buoyant. Life in Illyria is stale; Viola is like a fresh and much-needed sea breeze.

11.2 Music, harmony and discord

▶ 'for I can sing' (1.2.53)

Harmony

Orsino is charmed by the harmony of music but, like a typical Petrarchan lover, he's not at ease with himself – he's out of tune.

Twelfth Night is notable for its music. It has songs and snatches of songs (eight in all), talk about songs and the image of music is important. It could be that what Shakespeare is giving us is a way of understanding the change Viola brings. In the second scene she says she can sing, and although she never does, singing can work as an image for what she brings to Illyria – harmony.

In the play there's a desire to keep in time and in tune. When Malvolio tries to break up late night drinking and singing, he accuses them of having 'no respect of place, persons, nor time'. Toby's reply is:

> We did keep time, sir, in our catches.

> (2.3.90)

The implication is that if their singing was in time, then there was respect for place and persons. If the singing is fine, all else is well.

Discord

The opposite to harmony is the discord of self-absorbed characters. It's as if they are so self-enclosed they don't see that they are out of harmony with the world around them.

The character that wakes them up from this state is Viola. Orsino takes a liking to her/him, and in the two scenes they have together, his language borders on the embarrassingly intimate. (I once saw a production in which he kissed Cesario.)

As Cesario, Viola certainly wakes Olivia out of her obsession with the role of the mourning daughter and sister. Significantly, what wakes Olivia up is Viola's passionate portrait of herself as a lover who would

> Write loyal cantons of contemned love
> And sing them loud even in the dead of night

> (1.5.259–60)

Olivia responds to that; the prospect of Viola singing 'cantons' turns her from a dedicated mourner into an enterprising wooer.

In a sense Viola does sing 'cantons … in the dead of night', only the night is the metaphoric one of the narcissistic love that blights Illyria.

In their own way the three drinkers do the same; they 'sing them loud even in the dead of night' (and keep time as they do) as a protest against Olivia's unnatural mourning and the discord of Malvolio's ambition, self-satisfaction and pride.

▶ 'good Cesario' (2.4.2)

It's not easy writing about Viola and Cesario; do you use 'him' or 'her'?

That's a problem that Viola had. When she realizes that Olivia has fallen in love with her/him, she recognises in a soliloquy that this is due to her being both male and female (see 5.11).

Three points can be made about this very strong awareness of being both male and female.

Identity

One of the important things about *Twelfth Night* is that Shakespeare goes a long way beyond plot and the workings of stock characters. In the characters he gives us much more – more emotions, more personal characteristics, more complicating needs and desires – than the workings of the plot actually require.

Invention and satisfaction

What Shakespeare gives us is someone who invents another character. This is not in any of the sources of the story; in those the Viola figure simply impersonates her brother. It may be that because she creates a distinct character she not only learns what it's like to be a man but also arouses in others very powerful feelings.

What happens to these feelings? If we have feelings for someone, those feelings can be satisfied by marrying him or her. But nobody can marry Cesario, because he's not there to be married. This play can't end with neat pairings. Olivia marries Sebastian and Orsino marries Viola, but those strong, sometimes aching, feelings for Cesario are left unsatisfied. This is why at the end of the play we sometimes feel that the plot hasn't dealt with the feelings it's aroused; there are still aches and longings that can't be resolved.

Male and female

Shakespeare is clearly interested in hermaphrodite figures; that is, in figures who are both male and female.

This interest surfaces in the twins. They both invent characters – Viola invents Cesario and Sebastian invents Roderigo (2.1.15) – and there might be the hint that together they'd form the ideal figure with male and female characteristics.

▶ 'The madly-used Malvolio' (5.1.308)

A puritan?

Malvolio is the male star role in a play with lots of good parts. The characters think he is important; they find him, variously, infuriating, reliable, unpleasant and ridiculous but they talk about him a lot!

We must be careful not to simplify what's said about him. Maria says:

sometimes he is a kind of puritan. (2.3.134)

The puritans were a religious and political group noted for their seriousness, the way they saw success in life as divine reward, their sober dress, their disapproval of merry-making, and the theatre, their hard work, their support of parliament and their membership of non-conformist churches such as the Presbyterians. Perhaps the most important point about them was their success; they were going places.

Fun-loving gentry such as Sir Andrew and Sir Toby couldn't be expected to trust such figures, but their suspicion of Malvolio is deeper than that.

Maria doesn't actually say that he's a puritan but something more suspicious, namely that sometimes he's 'a kind' of one. She follows this up with the accusation that he's a fraud:

The dev'l a puritan that he is, or anything constantly but a time-pleaser (2.3.141–2).

Certainly he is ambitious: his fantasies overheard by those in the 'box-tree' (Act 2, Scene 5) include lording it over Sir Toby. His ambitions seem entirely worldly – 'to be Count Malvolio!' Perhaps Maria is right – he's merely someone on the make.

Yet his response to the letter is typical of puritans:

Well, Jove, not I, is the doer of this, and he is to be thanked (3.4.81–2).

Our reactions

Sometimes we feel he's being justly ridiculed. Anyone who can ignore all the ambiguities in the letter and assume it comes from Olivia is so lacking in self-knowledge that all we can do is laugh.

But when he's treated as a madman, we may think not only that the baiting has gone too far, but also that Malvolio has some dignity. He says in Act 4, Scene 2 'I think nobly of the soul'; and perhaps we do of him.

A point not often made about him is something that he doesn't do. When Cesario refuses Olivia's ring, Malvolio leaves it on the ground; an utterly unscrupulous man would have pocketed it.

11.5 Madness, revelry and folly

▶ 'sad and merry madness' (3.4.15)

Malvolio's humiliation takes the form of being treated as a madman. This is appropriate:

- *Twelfth Night* **contains more references to madness than any other of the plays.**

Love

There's the madness of love. Orsino is mad in the sense that he's withdrawn into a world of his own romantic making, and Olivia speaks of her own state as madness.

Revelry

Another kind is the madness of revelry. In Act 2, Scene 3 Malvolio bursts in on a scene of marry-making with the words:

My masters, are you mad? (2.3.83)

Folly

Feste occasionally plays on the idea that as a fool he is touched in his wits, and in his opening scene he defends himself by proving that Olivia is really the fool because she mourns her brother, whom she believes is in Heaven.

Delusion

In one sense Malvolio *is* mad; he has swollen fantasies about marrying Olivia and is unable to see that she's not interested. Such a bloated imagination (hardly a puritan feature) marks him out as someone whose mind is already a dark room; his self-absorption shows that he's shut away in darkness from the light of human company.

11.6 Class

▶ 'she'll not match above her degree' (1.3.105)

Class

'Degree' here means class. Sir Toby is talking about whom Olivia will marry. The meaning is that she'll marry someone of her own class. If he's right, Malvolio's fantasies were always hopeless (2.5.37–8). It's true he's not *above* her, but he is almost certainly below.

Considerations of class are very common in English literature, particularly comedy, but *Twelfth Night* is of particular interest because its preoccupation with class is more far-reaching than in any other of the comedies.

Much of this comes from Sir Toby. He's clearly a member of the landed gentry but appears to be financially dependent upon his niece. This might explain why he's difficult; for instance, he stridently insists on his status; 'am I not consanguineous?' (related by blood) (2.3.74). When faced with the authoritarian Malvolio, Sir Toby resorts to a class insult: 'Art more than a steward?' (2.3.109).

An unstable world

The significance of this emphasis on class may lie in what Shakespeare is attempting to do. He's working with many of the conventions of comedy – separated twins, the girl disguised as a boy – but he's chosen to root his play in a world which isn't stable. That's to say, one in which gentry are losing their power, and people such as Malvolio are climbing the social ladder.

Perhaps this makes revelry more important; the characters enjoy themselves while they can. It also means that their practices are against a social upstart.

11.7 The character of Feste

▶ 'Feste the jester' (2.4.11)

The observer

Feste bears out an important point about *Twelfth Night*: where we might have had mere dramatic function, there is moral and psychological complexity. There's much more in the characters than the plot requires.

In her explanatory soliloquy in Act 3, Scene 1, Viola says that to play the fool you have to be observant.

Feste certainly is observant. He sees that Orsino is a self-indulgent melancholic, that there's a strong element of performance in Olivia's mourning, and he might even see through Viola's disguise:

Who you are and what you would are out of my welkin (3.1.56).

His witty learning

Moreover, he's clever or, as the text has it, witty.

Classical references are very much his style. His fantasies have a Greek or Roman ring to them. Sir Andrew recalls Feste's 'very gracious fooling last night':

thou spok'st of Pigrogromitus, of the Vapians passing the equinoctial of Queubus. (2.3.22–3)

That's nonsense, of course; but it sounds like the kind of Greek epic you might meet in a dream. Feste is a learned, even an academic fool.

His situation

In Act 2, Scene 4 Curio says that Feste is 'a fool that the Lady Olivia's father took much delight in'. He's now dead, and Feste has become a leftover, a survivor from a different world. A more stable world certainly, and one in which there was no Malvolio. It's not surprising, therefore, that he sometimes wanders off to Orsino's; he has to curry favour in case he loses his place in Olivia's household.

His style

It may be that because he goes back to Olivia's father's time, he's becoming out of date. Olivia tells him 'your fooling grows old, and people dislike it'. Possibly the witty parodies of the epic style appealed only to the previous generation.

His style certainly suits a sophisticated audience. One of his learned parodies is the clergyman; he puts Olivia through her catechism (a set of questions and answers designed to test an understanding of religion), he gives Orsino a mock benediction (a blessing) when he leaves him, and as part of the baiting of Malvolio he plays Sir Topaz, the curate.

Verbal wit

Feste's verbal ingenuity is something he draws attention to; it is, so to speak, written on his calling card. He says to Cesario that he is the lady Olivia's 'corrupter of words'

(3.1.35) The phrase is a fruitful one; like all fools he plays with the multiple meanings of words but he does so in order to corrupt them.

Temperament

A standard theatrical convention is the clown who appears cheerful and carefree but who, beneath the grease paint, is unhappy. In the case of Feste, we sometimes glimpse a difference between the man and the role.

He can be bitter. In the otherwise merry exchange with Viola he comes out with:

> but in my conscience, sir, I do not care for you. (3.1.27–8)

What may be behind that bitter remark is an envious fear that Cesario is becoming too popular with Olivia.

The need to protect his position might be seen in his vindictive treatment of Malvolio. Feste was in danger of losing his job when, in Act 1, Scene 4, Malvolio insulted him in front of Olivia. When the baiting of Malvolio is explained in the last scene, Feste drags up the incident:

> but do you remember, 'Madam, why laugh you at such a barren rascal, an you smile not, he's gagged' – and thus the whirligig of time brings in his revenges. (5.1.369–72)

The significant thing about his words is that they come at the end of the play, when, by convention, there's peace and reconciliation between those characters who have been at loggerheads.

Songs

There's a note of world-weary melancholy in many of the songs. Even the sprightly 'O mistress mine' plays upon the *carpe diem* theme that 'youth's a stuff will not endure' (2.3.51). The refrain of Feste's final song is suggestive of a life that's become accustomed to disappointment:

> For the rain it raineth every day.
>
> (5.1.388)

11.8 The passing of time

▶ 'We did keep time, sir, in our catches.' (2.3.90)

The passing of time is very important in *Twelfth Night*. It makes itself felt in many ways.

Trust

Viola closes Act 1, Scene 2 with trust in what time will bring. She's little reason to trust but with quiet confidence she hands herself over to whatever may come to pass:

> What else may hap, to time I will commit
>
> (1.2.56)

Her attitude is refreshingly different from Orsino's obsessive dwelling on the moment when he first saw Olivia. Perhaps Shakespeare is indicating that women are better at looking forward, while men can get bogged down in nostalgia.

The past in the present

The past is very much present in this play. In the opening scenes we hear of the devastating first sight Orsino had of Olivia, the effect of her father's and brother's death on her, the apparent drowning of Sebastian and the annoyance created by Feste's wanderings. Early events, such as Malvolio's insulting of Feste, come to have an effect on the course of the play. In *Twelfth Night* we feel the weight of what's gone before.

Something of the burden of the past is felt in the pointed use of the past tense. When Viola expresses her feelings for Orsino, she invents the character of her sister, who hopelessly loved a man:

> My father had a daughter loved a man

> (2.4.107)

The two past tenses – 'had' and 'loved' – make remote not only the unrequited love of the fictional sister, but also her own hopes of securing Orsino's affection.

Getting old

The passing of time is more painful for those who are no longer young. The song the (ageing?) Feste sings to the (ageing?) Sir Andrew and Sir Toby says that youth won't endure.

It won't for any of them. Perhaps that explains the excesses of their revelry; if they were easy about it, would they talk so much about their jesting, dancing and drinking? Perhaps that's also true of Orsino and Olivia. If they too are getting old, then the need to find a suitable spouse might be felt more keenly. And it's harder to get over love when you are old.

In Act 2, Scene 4 Viola, imagining her pining sister, says she sat in 'a green and yellow melancholy' (Line 113); those are the colours of the play – the green of flourishing spring and the autumnal yellow of the fading leaf.

Passing the time

The play toys with the issue of how we should spend our time. In particular, it mulls over the relationship between everyday life and the special seasons of festivity and merry-making.

It's not easy to get this relationship right. Malvolio is surely wrong; we need 'cakes and ale' (2.3.108). But 'cakes and ale' – the festivals when we can make merry – are by their very nature occasional pleasures. Life needs a rhythm; we can't party everyday; but that's what Sir Toby wants:

> My very walk should be a jig. (1.3.124)

In other words, there would be no life lived at a normal walking pace; each step would be danced. That's just as foolish as the restraint Malvolio wishes to impose. When life is a dance, there's no place for dancing.

Change

In *Twelfth Night* there is an awareness of change. This comes out in expressions of uncertainty; 'perchance', meaning both perhaps and what might happen, echoes through the early lines of the second scene. No sooner has Viola established herself in Orsino's court as Cesario than she asks whether he's 'inconstant' (1.4.7), and in the intimate exchanges of Act 2, Scene 4 Orsino himself says that men's affections are 'more giddy and unfirm' than are women's.

The one thing that we're told doesn't change is art. This insight is significantly placed at the end of the play. The very last line of Feste's closing song is:

> And we'll strive to please you every day.

> (5.1.398)

The 'we' can be read as the company of players, who, in presenting the changes and chances of this mortal life, are constant in their desire to please. But not even that lasted; within 40 years the Malvolios of England (the parliamentary party who defeated the king and the gentry in the Civil War) closed the theatres.

Exercises

11.1 'For all the fun and merry-making, there is a note of sadness in this play.' Examine why someone should want to make this statement about *Twelfth Night*.

11.2 In what ways might Viola be said to be the central character of *Twelfth Night*?

Part III
The Problem Plays

Shakespeare experimenting

12.1 The problems of the problem plays

▶ 'all difficulties' (*Measure for Measure*, 4.2.204)

It's customary to call some of the plays Shakespeare wrote after *Twelfth Night* 'problem plays', 'problem comedies' or the 'dark comedies'. This isn't a category invented either by Shakespeare (he never uses the word 'problem' or by his early editors. It was only at the end of the nineteenth century when playwrights tackled social problems that the term was applied.

It's probably stuck because the plays it refers to are distinctive. Having said that, there's no agreement as to which the plays are: everyone agrees that *All's Well That Ends Well* and *Measure for Measure* are 'problem plays', but some add *Troilus and Cressida*, and others want to include *Hamlet* and *Cymbeline*.

Categories

Here a note on categories might be useful. We are often taught that all the objects in a category must have one, or a number, of features in common. Categories needn't be like that. They can be loose groupings in which each object has something in common with some of the others but not necessarily all of them.

12.2 The problem plays as comedies

▶ 'All is well ended' (*All's Well That Ends Well*, Epilogue, 2)

In the cases of *All's Well That Ends Well* and *Measure for Measure*, there's no problem in calling them comedies. They have comic characters, plots based on practices and they end with a scene in which the issues are resolved more or less happily. Here are some comic features.

Comic characters

Both plays have adventurous and courageous heroines. In *All's Well* Helena follows her beloved to the wars, while in *Measure for Measure* Isabella steps out of her convent to plead for her brother, and Mariana willingly participates in the bed-trick.

Bars

In *Measure for Measure* the bar is the revival of an old law that punishes sex outside marriage with death. Helena's bar in *All's Well* is a more traditional one: she loves a man who's her social superior. When she marries him, another bar arises – he won't sleep with her. In addition, he establishes what seems to be an impossible condition: he will not recognise her as his wife till she bears his son and wears a ring he never removes from his finger.

Practices

The central practice of both plays is the bed-trick. In both a man makes advances to a young woman for sexual gratification. The woman who loves him arranges to take her place in bed. The trick works, so the man is deceived into believing he's having sex with the woman he desires when in fact it's the one he wants to forget.

Practising figures

In *Measure for Measure* the Duke adopts a disguise to see how his plan of leaving Angelo in charge of Vienna is going. When he tries to help, he finds himself thinking up a series of ruses in order to bring about a happy ending.

The ends

Both plays end with the heroine's desires fulfilled. They get their men. Each play closes on an upbeat; whatever ghastly events they've been through, the characters can look forward with hope and a renewed zest for life.

12.3 The dark mood

▶ 'muddied in fortune's mood' (*All's Well That Ends Well*, 5.2.4)

But even though *All's Well* and *Measure for Measure* are comedies, there's something that makes audiences think of them as slightly different from the other comic plays.

Their moods are darker and more troubled, 'muddied' in fact.

Love and war

In *All's Well* the 'hero' Bertram leaves for the war rather then sleep with his wife. He underlines this by turning his dismissal of her into bravado:

> Go thou toward home, where I will never come
> Whilst I can shake my sword or hear the drum.

(2.5.89–90)

He seems rather proud of himself, even perhaps because of the bawdy suggestions in 'come' and 'shake'.

Love and sex

There's a lot of sex in the language of Shakespearean comedy. It's not always related to love, but that's the common linkage. What's also clear is that sex is regarded as fun; marriage is good because there's lots of love-making.

Most of the fun has gone in *All's Well* and *Measure for Measure*. For most of the time, love is unfulfilled, as in Bertram's refusal to sleep with his wife; or, as in the case of Claudio, its fulfilment leads to the executioner's block. For much of the time love and sex have got separated. Angelo has no love for Isabella; he just wants to have sex with her. The sexual act itself is often made to seem furtive, guilt-ridden, brutal and manipulative.

Death

People do die in comedies, but it would still be true to say that Death doesn't brood over the plots. It turns up quite a bit in the problem plays.

War has an important part in the plot of *All's Well*, but it's *Measure for Measure* that really confronts audiences with the presence of death. It's felt to be uncomfortably close in Mistress Overdone's complaint that the brothel business is in decline:

> Thus what with the war, what with the sweat, what with the gallows, and what with poverty, I am custom shrunk. (1.2.80–2)

'Sweat' means plague; its nasty, moist, clinging quality brings out the physical closeness of death.

12.4 Experimenting with comedy

▶ 'give me leave to try success' (*All's Well That Ends Well*, 1.3.245)

These words are said by Helena when she's asking permission to go to the court to try to heal the king. We're going to give them a much wider meaning.

The problem plays are Shakespeare's attempt to test or try out the conventions of comedy. In short:

- **the problem plays are experimental.**

Two conventions are played with. In both cases Shakespeare is seeing how far he can go with them.

The unworthy husband

All's Well explores the possibilities of:

- **a marked mismatch between the woman and the man.**

Shakespeare tackles this problem: Bertram is such an awful man, can audiences be happy when they see Helena making considerable efforts to get him? Just how dreadful he is emerges in the scene when he tries to refuse the King's order to marry Helena. One of the things he says is:

A poor physician's daughter, my wife? Disdain
Rather corrupt me for ever.

(2.3.116–17)

So abhorrent is the idea of being married to a poor woman that he says he would rather suffer the king's disapproval for the rest of his life. And she's present when he says this!

This is a problem about comic conventions. A comedy is usually about the desires of the young and the plot leads, after much confusion, to their sexual union. For such a plot to work, the audience have to approve of the youthful desires and want what the young want. As a result, the audience will feel happy when the plot is resolved and the young go to bed.

If, as in this case, the man is deplorable – brutal, snobbish, unfeeling, egocentric – and the woman a quite wonderful Shakespearean heroine – bold, clear-sighted, purposeful, loyal, loving – can we be happy with their union?

This is not something that can be solved. That's one reason we call this a *problem* play! Some things soften the hardness of his character. For instance, he doesn't conceal from Diana, whom he's trying to seduce, that he's married, and he's aware of the dishonour to his family if he gives away the ring – even though he does so pretty smartly. It's true that at the end he promises to love Helena dearly, but by the time he says this he's lied so much, we're not likely to take him very seriously. This is the kind of problem you get when you make an unworthy man the centre of a comedy.

The incompetent practiser

For most of the second half of the play, Vincentio, the Duke, is the chief practiser of *Measure for Measure*. Shakespeare plays with the role by making him less than successful. This is a bold experiment with comic form. Comedies need practices and the practices, consequently, need characters to think them up and carry them out. Will they still work as comedies, Shakespeare implicitly asks, if the practiser is incompetent?

Things go well at first. His first 'solution' is the bed-trick; if Angelo thinks he's had sex with Isabella, Claudio will be pardoned. In some respects things go too well; should someone intending to be a nun be so eager to get Mariana into bed with Angelo? But it happens. There's a very funny scene following the midnight assignation, when the Duke smugly hints at and then talks openly of a reprieve for Claudio. When the letter arrives, Shakespeare gives the Duke a soliloquy in cosy little rhyming couplets in which he moralises upon the irony of Angelo forgiving Claudio because they are both guilty of the same sin:

This is his pardon, purchased by such sin
For which the pardoner himself is in.

(4.2.110–11)

But corrupt nature momentarily outwits the stratagems of art. Comic plotting doesn't work. The letter says that Claudio must die before four o'clock.

There follows a frenzied series of practices, all designed to save Claudio. They are increasingly grotesque, and the Duke is exposed to derision. First, he urges them to execute Barnadine (a rogue who's been awaiting execution for longer than most unfortunates on an American death row), but Barnadine will have none of this. The Duke of Vienna can't persuade the least of his subjects to do the decent thing and agree to have his head chopped off. Eventually, they cut off the head of a man who's died of the plague! An irritant in this long scene is Lucio, who insists on telling the disguised Duke that the Duke would have dealt leniently with cases of sexual impropriety, because he was an old lecher himself. The Duke calls it a day and announces his return.

12.5 Drama and thought

▶ 'fine issues' (*Measure for Measure*, 1.1.36)

Social issues

Measure for Measure is a problem play because it deals with problems. The first half is rich in intellectual explorations of moral and social issues. For instance, running through the play, there's the problem of the extent to which the law should deal with private matters such as sexual relations.

Realistic treatment

Coupled with this interest in issues is a presentation of life which is more realistic than some of the other comedies. The play is set in Vienna (though they all have Italian names!), but it feels like a contemporary picture of London's South Bank – taverns, brothels, prisons. The fact that it deals with the nature of the law, the relationship between justice and mercy, the art of government and nature of sexual morality all give it a rooted, concrete feeling.

This is not to say that this play is a 'study' of contemporary morality (no Shakespeare play is ever a 'study' of anything) but that part of its experimental character is due to the attempt to marry these issues with comic form. It's doubtful whether it entirely works. There's a feeling at the end that Shakespeare brings about his happy ending simply by ignoring many of the problems that have passed across the stage.

Exercises

12.1 In what ways does it make sense to talk about 'problem plays'?

12.2 The problem plays are sometimes called the 'dark comedies'. What features have led people to give them this title?

Troilus and Cressida

13.1 No beginning, no end

▶ **'Beginning in the middle' (Prologue, 28)**

This is Shakespeare's oddest play. The Prologue talks about:

> …what may be digested in a play

> (line 29)

meaning the material that's selected and organised. This has puzzled people for generations:

- **what kind of a play has been 'digested'?**

Shakespeare's audience would regard the Trojan War as fact, so is it a history? On the other hand, since it ends with the death of Hector, the greatest warrior in the play, is it tragedy? But then it's about young love – the material of comedy. No wonder people have been happy to call it a problem play.

Most outrageous from a formal point of view is that this is a play that begins in the middle. What the Prologue (and Shakespeare) is doing is relying upon the audience knowing the story of the Trojan War, so the 'firstlings of those broils' (line 27) – Helen's abduction, the Greek's decision to send forces – are passed over. The action of the play begins in the middle of the war, when there's virtually no action. Formally speaking, something even odder is to come; the play doesn't end, it merely stops.

13.2 Cultural icons

▶ **'Let all constant men be Troiluses' (3.2.198–9)**

The Trojan war

The Trojan War was part of Elizabethan culture. It was the greatest of all wars. The great poets of the past – Homer and Virgil – had written about it, and those writings came to embody what people felt was the tragedy and the glory of all war. The combination of high deeds on the battlefield and the blighted love of Troilus and Cressida brings together Shakespeare's two great themes.

Shakespeare assumed that his audiences knew the story. Cressida is mentioned in four other Shakespeare plays, Troilus in five and Pandarus, directly and indirectly, in eight. In culture they represented the unfaithful woman, the true lover and the procurer – one who finds partners for another's sexual pleasure.

Cultural icons

At one point the status of the story as an established part of the way people thought and felt about human life becomes one of the play's themes. In Act 3, Scene 2, the lovers nervously confess their feelings. The language rises from prose through verse to a ritualised climax which, because it ends with 'amens', has a religious quality. Troilus, Cressida and Pandarus speak of what future generations will make of them. Troilus says that lovers, when discontented with over-used 'similes, truth tired with iteration' (3.2.172) will say:

> 'As true as Troilus' shall crown up the verse
> And sanctify the numbers.

> (3.2.178–9)

Cressida is more uncertain: 'If I be false', she says, although time will have obliterated everything about Troy, nevertheless

> let memory
> From false to false among false maids in love
> Upbraid my falsehood.

> (3.2.185–7)

Pandarus has less to say; in his bustling prose he gives permission to the future to call procurers a pandar:

> Let all pitiful goers-between be called to the world's end after my name: call them all pandars. (3.2.196–7)

Shakespeare knows his audience knows that all of this has come true. The characters are easing themselves into the roles they will perform in Western culture. They change before our eyes from characters in history into cultural icons.

13.3 The most interesting character

▶ 'O Cressida' (3.2.60)

A playwright who likes playing with theatrical conventions can't be expected to leave cultural icons alone, so what does Shakespeare do with Cressida?

One reading of the play is to see her unfaithfulness as the fulfilment of her prophetic doubts in Act 3, Scene 2. We can be pretty certain that that is how Shakespeare assumed his audience would see her. But did *he* see her this way?

There are four crucial scenes.

The soliloquy

In her soliloquy Cressida shows herself to be prudent and even cynical. She declares she loves Troilus, but the game of love is not a blithe *As You Like It*-type holiday but much closer to what's going on outside the walls – war. She makes her point bluntly: once you sleep with them, men are less interested.

> Yet hold I off. Women are angels, wooing;
> Things won are done.

> (1.2.282–3)

It's safer to remain an angel in a young man's eyes; once he's won, you're done. Yielding, therefore, would be defeat.

The morning after

Yet she yields. When she wakes up with him the following morning, she clearly wonders whether she's been wise. She feels he's too keen to go:

> Prithee, tarry. You men will never tarry.
> O foolish Cressid! I might have still held off,
> And then you would have tarried

> (4.2.18–20)

The parting

Cressida's problem is that she's a woman in a society in which men must make the moves. She doesn't have the freedom that most comic heroines have. Her father has deserted to the Greek camp; he wants her with him, so she becomes a pawn in the game of war. In Act 4, Scene 5 they come to take her. All she can do is put pressure on Troilus to continue the affair. She's subtle:

> *Cressida*: I must then to the Grecians.
> *Troilus*: No remedy.
> *Cressida*: A woeful Cressid 'mongst the merry Greeks!
> When shall we see again?

> (4.5.54–6)

The crucial word is 'merry'. She used it before when talking about Helen (1.2.105). There it meant sexually inclined. It must mean the same here. She's pointing out that she'll be in a camp of lecherous soldiers; her implicit question is: and what are you going to do about it?

Significantly, he expresses doubts about her faithfulness. She's angry, and he ends by promising to visit her every night. There's something romantically boyish about his talk of bribing the guards. They exchange tokens.

Overlooking

The overlooking scene is difficult. What is Cressida up to? She's overcome with guilt at giving away Troilus's token, but then she almost casually says:

> But now you have it, take it.

> (5.2.93)

Perhaps the clue is the lack of feeling. It would be good if she lived in a world in which love and faithfulness thrived, but she doesn't. *Troilus and Cressida* is a play in which a girl can't be a comic heroine, so she may as well act prudently and accept a Greek lover. She knows she's not in a conventional comedy so she's got to look after herself.

13.4 Love and the language of war

▶ 'In that I'll war with you' (3.2.167)

Love and war

In *Troilus and Cressida* Shakespeare is interested in:

• **love in a time of war**.

What Shakespeare presents is something that all countries at war have discovered – the war enters all areas of life, so that even love is coloured by it: time might be short; the contrast between pain and pleasure is heightened and partings might turn out to be final.

There's a good case to made out that this is the main theme of the play. The first piece of action is Troilus deciding to unarm:

> Why should I war without the walls of Troy
> That find such cruel battle here within?

> (1.1.2–3)

Outside Troy he fights the Greeks, but it feels pointless when his real battles are within.

Love games and war games

It was pointed out above (13.3) that the love games of the pair are war games. This appears in their language. When they finally confess their loves as a prelude to the first (and only) night together, the scene is full of military images. Troilus talks of 'hostages' (line 104) and of Cressid being 'hard to win' (line 113). In reply to his 'I'll war with you', she says 'O virtuous fight' (line 167). The war lends a dark seriousness to the language.

The play closes on a savage note. There are lots of deaths reported, and Troilus, says Ulysses

> hath done today
> Mad and savage execution,
> Engaging and redeeming of himself
> With such a careless force and forceless care.

> (5.5.37–40)

That last line means he fought with a natural (we might say unforced) energy. We know why; his bitter disappointment in love expresses itself in 'savage execution'. There may be a hint of this in the language. 'Force' was used when writing about rape; in killing the Greeks, is he enacting his desired revenge upon the woman who's betrayed him?

13.5 Where are the heroes?

▶ 'proud of an heroical cudgelling' (3.3.241)

No heroes

Traditionally, the battle for Troy is the most epic expression of love and war. The characters are heroes, the issues the most profound in literature.

But it doesn't *feel* like that in Shakespeare. One of the most distinctive voices in the play is the amusing yet appalling Thersites, a man whose language deflates and diminishes everything he talks about. When he uses an elevated word such as 'heroical' – in the manner of a hero – he follows it with something suggesting blunt and bloody battling – 'cudgelling'.

Apart from *Much Ado*, where it's a character's name, 'hero' only occurs in five of Shakespeare's plays. 'Heroic' is used in two and 'heroical' in three. This chimes in with what Dr Johnson said:

> Shakespeare has no heroes; his scenes are occupied only by men, who act and speak as the reader thinks that he should himself have acted or spoken on the same occasion.

This ties in with what was said about kings (2.5) – they are presented as human beings with the hopes and fears we all have.

Nevertheless, the levelling down of the hero to the ordinary man is uncomfortably thorough in *Troilus and Cressida*. The great men of the epic stories – Agamemnon, Achilles, Hector, Ajax – are sometimes embarrassingly ordinary in their squabbles, inconsistencies and schemings.

No action

It's fitting that in a play in which the heroes aren't heroes, there's very little happening. *Troilus and Cressida* is the least action-packed of any Shakespeare play. There isn't much ado, but what does happen seems to be about nothing.

The inaction deflates the characters. In the absence of heroic deeds, they seem small and insignificant. Even when they do act, they seem as much driven as choosing their course of action.

Appetite

What does drive them is appetite – appetite for love in the case of Troilus, for fame in the case of Achilles or honour in the case of Hector.

'Appetite' appears four times in the play (along with *Othello*, the most times it occurs in Shakespeare). It's also in the imagery. Ulysses has a philosophical passage about appetite's self-destructive power:

> Power into will, will into appetite;
> And appetite, an universal wolf,
> Must make perforce an universal prey,
> And last eat up himself.

(1.3.120–3)

Will becomes appetite, and because appetite needs an object, it creates something to prey on.

The characters seem driven by their passions, so they aren't fully in control. In this sense they're all victims. Some people have seen the play as cynically dismissing the characters as stupid or corrupt; but it can be read as a tough moral reflection upon the weakness of the will and the human tendency to fail and fall short.

Identity

When characters are ruled by appetite, it becomes unclear as to who they are. This is Troilus's experience with Cressida. His sense of her changes so much that he ends not knowing who she is. The last time he sees her he's so confused that he has a long passage about her identity (5.2.117–91), in which, at one point, he says:

> This is and is not Cressid.

> (5.2.149)

Comedy is frequently about the loss and regaining or renewing of identity. If that preoccupation is present here, it's given another dimension. The puzzle is as much about what Troilus sees or can't see as it is about any actual change in Cressida. When we are governed by appetite, the problem becomes the reliability of our seeing rather than the things that are seen.

Unfaithfulness

The air of disappointment and disillusion that many have found in the play is there in its central theme. Characters driven by passion tend to act in the same way. Paris eloped with Helen. As a result, there's a war. The causes of the war – desire leading to unfaithfulness – are repeated in the story of Troilus and Cressida. In them we see acted out the causes of the Trojan War.

And it happens on the battlefield. The play works by the audience believing that Hector is the greatest warrior; not even the mighty Achilles is his match. The only way Hector can be defeated is by deceit and trickery. Betrayal of the laws of war – the laws of chivalry – is the military counterpart of the unfaithfulness of the lovers.

13.6 Relativism, viewpoints and framing

▶ 'What's aught but as 'tis valued?' (2.2.51)

Relativism

This line, said by Troilus, has become the most discussed in the play. He's saying that the worth of anything is nothing more than the value *we* place upon it. We don't recognise value, we *create* it. This view is a relativistic one; the idea that value is value only in relation to something else and not an absolute quality that inalienably belongs to the object. If people change their minds, values change.

This is what you might expect people driven by appetite to think. We know Troilus desires Cressida, and so he values her. In the same way, the passion of Paris for Helen has led her to be the cause of the Trojan War.

We can see this as a symptom of people ruled by the passions. We needn't see it as Shakespeare's view. In fact, it's rather odd that people who see it as central treat this piece of relativism as an absolute principle of the play.

Viewpoints

What is true about this play is that it's one in which a lot of the characters tell us what they think. The word 'opinion' occurs ten times, more than in any other play. Cressida tells us what she thinks about men wooing (1.2.178–91) and Ulysses talks at great length about 'degree' (1.2.74–137). There's also debate; in response to Troilus's remark on value, Hector says:

> But value dwells not in particular will.
> It holds his estimate and dignity
> As well wherein 'tis precious of itself
> As in the prizer.

> (2.2.52–5)

In other words, Hector regards value as a quality of the thing itself, not something given it by the person who prizes it.

There's something very modern about a play which makes viewpoint a central feature, but, of course, viewpoint is the nature of drama. Just because a character takes a particular view of value, it doesn't mean that we should.

Frames

The preoccupation with different ways of looking at things is present in the way one crucial scene is written. The climax – the recognition and turning point – of the play comes when Cressida accepts Diomed as her lover. We see the games both of them play; she's uncertain, he's moody. But we aren't the only ones who see. Shakespeare provides two sets of comments: one from Troilus and Ulysses and the other from Thersites. These characters provide the frame or window through which the main action is seen.

Ulysses is aware of the strong feelings the scene arouses; he's concerned for Troilus and wants to take him away from the painful sight of his beloved prostituting herself:

> You shake, my lord, at something. Will you go?

> (5.2.50)

Thersites is bawdy, scornful and full of derision. In his view this is a grim farce, in which the worst aspects of humanity emerge:

> Lechery, lechery, still wars and lechery!
> Nothing else holds fashion.

> (5.2.196–7)

We don't have to accept either as being the view of the play. The actors should try to make their comments convincing. Is this a play in which important things are at stake or is it merely grotesque?

13.1 Argue for or against the view that Cressida is the most interesting character in *Troilus and Cressida*.

13.2 *Troilus and Cressida* has been described as a cynical play. Why have people come to this judgement, and is it your view of the play?

Measure for Measure

14.1 Governing a nation and governing oneself

▶ 'Of government' (1.1.1)

One of the things that distinguishes *Measure for Measure* from the other comedies is that it is concerned with social, political and moral issues. One of these

• **the nature of government**

is telegraphed to us in the first line of the play. The Duke says it would be pointless for him to debate the business of government, because his deputy, Escalus, has a firm grasp of the subject.

Escalus, however, does not substitute for the Duke in his absence; that privilege goes to Angelo, of whom the Duke says he has

> Lent him our terror, dressed him with our love.

> (1.1.20)

The Duke makes a neat rhetorical balance, by playing off the ability to punish ('terror') against the power to act out of love; that is, reward and show mercy. A few lines later he says:

> Mortality and mercy in Vienna
> Live in thy tongue and heart.

> (1.1.45–6)

'Mortality' means imposing the death penalty, and 'mercy' means sparing the guilty. Again, the language insists that this is what the play is going to be about.

The tact of government

Although the Duke recognises that he's failed to govern Vienna as he would have wished, he does recognise that governing is not a matter of merely following rules. To govern is to exercise 'terror' *and* 'love', 'mortality *and* mercy'. Angelo fails because he can't exercise 'mercy'.

Self-government

Angelo is a lawyer who's at ease when administering justice. What he's not comfortable with is personal feelings and the stormy relationships they give rise to.

- **Angelo thinks he can govern Vienna; but we see that he can't govern himself**.

This is evident in the language he uses to Isabella:

> I have begun,
> And now I give my sensual race the rein.

(2.4.159–60)

Angelo's image is that of giving the horse its head; if his passions are racing, he's not going to restrain himself.

14.2 The character and role of Angelo

▶ 'Lord Angelo' (1.1.25)

Depth of character

In comedy characters are often functions of the plot and therefore lack depth; in particular, what we would call psychological depth. Angelo, however, almost asks to be read in psychological terms:

- **the discipline and cold reserve of the early part of the play give way to an unrestrained sexual indulgence in the second half**.

Angelo looks like the classic Freudian case of someone who's repressed his feelings, until they burst out with uncontrollable fury.

Intelligence

Angelo has one of the sharpest minds in Shakespeare. His language shows that he's aware of important intellectual distinctions. When he's arguing, no one can keep up.

There's a very funny conversation between Angelo and Escalus in which the latter tries to persuade Angelo to be merciful to Claudio. He tries the 'I knew his dad line'. It's up to the actor to show Angelo's (justified?) scorn for that sort of pleading. He then turns to the 'well, you might have been in this position' argument. This is important for the ironic working of the plot, but hopeless as argument. Angelo crushes it with ease:

> 'Tis one thing to be tempted, Escalus,
> Another thing to fall.

(2.1.17–18)

There's no reply possible within the terms of the law to that remark; laws are about what we do, not what we think of doing.

Law: theory and practice

As soon as Angelo has floored Escalus with his argument about the nature of the law, we have a grimly farcical scene in which Escalus has to administer the law.

The case concerns the wife of Elbow, the Constable. The problem is that nobody has a clear idea of what actually went on. And that's the point; it's all very well intellectualising about the nature of evidence, but that doesn't help you identify it!

Law and human feeling

The drama of Angelo is the meeting in one character of a razor-sharp mind and a turbulent heart. The play seems to show that however neatly we sort out the intellectual issues, human life is messier and far more difficult to handle. Angelo can work out what the law demands but he can't control the wild passions of the human heart. We don't know whether he learns that lesson; but we do.

Youth

Angelo makes a mess of his life; he's given the opportunity to restore Vienna and he ends up doing what the rest of the population does – indulging his sexual appetite. He's actually worse than they are, because he abuses power as well as attempting to have sex with a woman who doesn't welcome his advances.

But we must remember that he's young. Knowing that a character is inexperienced can make us soften our otherwise hard judgement. The significance of this is something a performance might exploit. Angelo can be presented as a moving figure if he's shown as struggling with himself as well as the moral wilderness of Vienna.

Fear and guilt

When Angelo learns that the Duke is returning, he's aghast at what he's done; appropriately, his troubled soliloquy (4.3.19–33) reviews his actions in the manner of a judge summing up the main features of a case:

> A deflowered maid,
> And by an eminent body that enforced
> The law against it.

(4.3.20–2)

He's the 'eminent body'; his use of the third person is both lawyer's talk and an attempt to see clearly what it is he's done.

Because he's inexperienced he's likely to feel the guilt and the fear more actuely. Those who are older get used to their failings. This may lead us to feel for him. We may also pity him precisely because his speech is so undignified – regret over what he's done is inseparable from his desire to get away with it.

Tragedy?

Some people have seen *Measure for Measure* as a comedy that might have been a tragedy. This doesn't help. The conventions of the plot are akin to comedies.

But there's one moment when Angelo sees the tragic possibilities of his situation. When he confronts Isabella with his demand, he plays his role with tragic bravado:

> I have begun,
> And now I give my sensual race the rein.
> Fit thy consent to my sharp appetite.
> Lay aside all nicety and prolixious blushes
> That banish what they sue for.

> (2.4.159–63)

This is appalling; he's saying that her blushes actually mean that she wants it. What increases the horror is the relish he shows for the role of the sexual tyrant. Two images combine – the horse as a symbol of passion and mounting a horse as an image of sexual intercourse. His desire is as sharp as the spurs with which he encourages the horse in its headlong charge.

Tragedy is an attitude to experience. The tragic figure knows that the act is wrong but gleefully pursues it with a flamboyance that makes him a public spectacle. Angelo wants to be seen as the sexual conqueror. This is his one moment of tragic bravado; after this he becomes devious and secretive – someone who might be pitied but certainly not an awesome spectacle.

14.3 The character and role of Isabella

▶ 'Heaven give thee moving graces' (2.2.36)

Isabella is the other very interesting character in the play. Her interest is twofold:

- she's a complex character who's tested very severely
- she's central to the issue of justice and mercy.

Not surprisingly, there's disagreement about her. I've taught students who don't see why she shouldn't sleep with Angelo. Other students have been appalled by the harshness of her language to Claudio and the willingness with which she persuades Mariana to do what she wouldn't. (If there is the equivalent of Pandarus in this play, it's Isabella rather than Mistress Overdone!)

Her responses

Not only is Isabella interesting, but she's rather like Angelo. Both of them can be read as characters trying to come to terms with their own feelings.

When we first see her, she inquires whether there are any stricter rules. Is this her repression of adult feelings or an immature and romantic longing for a rigid life?

She's naïve in thinking that her brother will accept that *her* virginity must be preserved, even at the cost of *his* life. Her anger at him suggests not only her youth but an ignorance of the passions of the human heart.

But Isabella grows in a way that nobody else does. Because it's so carefully contrived, it's easy to forget the circumstances of her pleading for Angelo. When she falls to her knees to beg for his life she has to contend with the fact that Angelo attempted to force her into his bed *and* still executed Claudio. Nevertheless, she speaks generously:

> I partly think
> A due sincerity governed his deeds,
> Till he did look on me.

> (5.1.442–4)

The words are delicate; in saying he was sincere in his pursuit of her brother's life, she implies that, by contrast, he was not governed in his pursuit of her. He didn't control his feelings, but in pleading for him she must be in control of hers.

Marriage

At this point it's useful to ponder the issue of the end. The Duke proposes marriage to her in the closing lines of the play. It's often pointed out these days that she doesn't actually accept him. There have been performances in which she storms off. Of course, the play can be performed that way, but the last two lines shouldn't be forgotten:

> So bring us to our palace, where we'll show
> What's yet behind that's meet you all should know.

> (5.1.537–8)

That invitation to hear all the explanations is addressed to everyone, and everyone must include a consenting Isabella. The convent is no place for her.

The themes

The two scenes in which she pleads with Angelo are among the most intense in the play. The rhythms of the language change in response to the drama, and the imagery dazzles with its pictures of the court of heaven (2.2.120–6).

Her language gives a religious radiance to her thought:

> How would you be
> If He which is the top of judgement should
> But judge you as you are? O, think on that,
> And mercy then will breathe within your lips,
> Like man new made.

> (2.2.77–81)

Her language weaves together the theological themes of mercy and judgement in terms of creation and redemption. The granting of mercy saves the one who's guilty, but the chief meaning here is that it redeems the one who grants it. This redemption is seen as a second creation; to breathe words of mercy makes a new man.

It's characteristic of the way the play works that these luminous words work ironically. Angelo does become a new man, but it's as a man of lust that he breathes, and what he breathes isn't mercy.

The effect of such an irony is to diminish Angelo and Isabella. Something far beneath mercy is generated by her words. But there's another irony at work here. Angelo can't speak words of mercy and so can't demand it for himself. In the final scene, all he asks for is instant death. But there is someone who does plead for him – Isabella. He can't show to Claudio the mercy he later desperately needs for himself, so, in keeping with the religious idea that we can't save ourselves, he's dependent upon another.

14.4 The play's title

▶ 'measure still for measure' (5.1.408)

Many people have recognised the echo in the title of the words from the *New Testament* about the measure which we give and receive (St. Matthew 7.2). This echo has led to several interpretations of the play as a religious allegory in which the Duke represents Christ and Angelo fallen humanity.

The difficulty with this view is that it doesn't feel like that because some of the characters are fully developed. Watching *Measure for Measure* makes us wonder about mercy, redemption, and the need for grace, but it does this because we watch characters trying to cope with the trials of their lives.

What then does the title mean? It's possible that

• **Shakespeare is drawing attention to the movement of the plot.**

It can be described as one measure after another: Angelo revives an old law, so Isabella pleads with him. He offers her a way of saving her brother, which prompts the Duke to stage the bed-trick. The play has this to-and-fro quality.

14.5 Different attitudes to death

▶ 'Be absolute for death' (3.1.5)

The atmosphere of the play is dominated by the smell of prison and the nearness of death. What's remarkable is that the attitudes to death are so varied.

The duke

In Act 3, Scene 1 the Duke, disguised as a Friar, prepares Claudio for the headsman's axe. The speech is highly polished and quite unchristian. There's something pretty distasteful about the way the Duke juggles with words:

> what thou hast not, still thou striv'st to get,
> And what thou hast, forget'st.
>
> (3.1.22–3)

When we face death, cleverness about what we do and don't have is close to being obscene. Some have admired the lofty and philosophical tone of the speech; but imagine facing death with this as your only comfort!

Claudio

When Claudio talks to Isabella the language is bracingly different from the Duke's:

> Ay, but to die, and go we know not where;
> To lie in cold obstruction and to rot;
>
> (3.1.118–19)

He spells it out in words of single syllables until the word 'obstruction' sticks in the fear-dried throat. This is real fear, and because it's real, it's alive.

Claudio understands death in terms of extreme sensations:

> To bathe in fiery floods, or to reside
> In thrilling region of thick-ribbed ice

$$(3.1.122–3)$$

The crucial word is 'thrilling'; the capacity of the senses to respond enforces our sense of being alive. This gives death meaning; if life is something that can thrill, then death that takes it away has significance.

Barnadine

Barnardine brings an invigorating honesty to the play.

His execution is the Duke's new device after the failure of the bed-trick. They need a head, and the Duke takes it upon himself to persuade Barnadine to contribute his. Before he appears, there's the funniest line in the play:

He is coming, sir, he is coming. I hear his straw rustle. (4.3.32)

Barnadine greets Abhorson, the executioner, with a matey familiarity:

How now, Abhorson, what's the news with you? (4.3.36)

When he's shown the warrant, he's ready with his objection:

You rogue, I've been drinking all night. I am not fitted for't. (4.3.40)

Technically, he's right; no one should be sent to divine judgement when they are drunk and incapable of confessing. But we can see that this isn't his real 'reason'; in fact, he doesn't have a 'reason', he just wants to be himself. In the end, the Duke sees that people such as he can't be brought round, so he lets him go.

Like the other 'low-life' characters, Barnadine has a gritty integrity that the flummoxed Duke lacks. They know themselves, and they survive because they insist on being who they are. There's something strangely admirable about the reply Pompey gives to Escalus's accusation that he's a bawd (pimp):

Truly, sir, I am a poor fellow that would live. (2.1.213)

14.6 The bed-trick

▶ 'And perform an old contracting' (3.1.538)

How the bed-trick works

In *Measure for Measure* its functions is:

• **to establish a parallel between Angelo and Claudio.**

The judge and the one who's condemned are both equal: both have slept with a woman outside marriage, and in both cases the woman was someone to whom the man was betrothed. Betrothal was not a marriage, but it had the virtual force of one. Once a couple had promised themselves to each other (this could be done either for the present or with a future intention), they could live together, and the existence of this agreement invalidated any marriage either might make with someone else.

Angelo can't, therefore, object at the end of the play to the formality of a marriage service.

Exercises

14.1 Why shouldn't people simply call *Measure for Measure* a comedy?

14.2 'The success of the play rests upon the fact that what we see is not only the severe testing of the central characters but a picture of a whole and very corrupt society.' Explore this statement.

Part IV
The Late Comedies

The worlds of the late comedies

15.1 The last plays

▶ 'to hear an old man sing' (*Pericles*, Prologue, 13)

Towards the end of his theatrical life, Shakespeare wrote four comedies: *Pericles*, *The Winter's Tale*, *Cymbeline* and *The Tempest*. These are usually treated as a separate group and called: 'the late plays' or 'the romances' or the 'late comedies'. They are sometimes felt to be Shakespeare's last words on the theatre and life, and audiences have found in them a mature wisdom and a philosophical acceptance of the course of life.

When Gower, a medieval poet who performs the Prologue to *Pericles*, asks the audience 'to hear an old man sing', it's tempting to think of him as the old sage-like Shakespeare. In fact, he was 44 when it was first performed. This isn't to say that there's not something distinctive about these late comedies:

- **they deal with those issues that increasingly engage people as they grow old**.

15.2 Features of the late comedies

▶ 'a song that old was sung' (*Pericles*, 1.1)

Gower starts his Prologue in this way:

> To sing a song that old was sung

In other words: Shakespeare is telling us that this is an old story.

Time-scale

Like fairy stories and folk tales, the plots cover a long time. In *The Winter's Tale*, a figure, Time, enters with an hour-glass, which he turns to show the passing of 16 years. *The Tempest* sticks to three hours, but the story in the fullest sense, told in graphic detail in the opening scenes, starts at least 12 years before. These plots stretch over time, and in so doing are long enough to interest a family gathered for several nights round the fire on a cold winter's evening. I once told the story of *The*

Winter's Tale to a friend, only to be informed that my listener had lost track of the events somewhere in the middle.

Distance

The Winter's Tale starts in Sicilia, moves to Bohemia and back to Sicilia. *The Tempest* happens on an island, but Prospero recounts the story of his perilous journey from Milan.

Coincidence

Many stories require coincidence, but in the late plays it's essential to the working of the plot. *The Winter's Tale* won't work unless, of all the girls in Bohemia, Florizel falls in love with a shepherd's daughter called Perdita.

Magic

Things work out in these play because characters other than human ones have an influence. In *The Tempest* spirits lead, warn, trick and condemn.

15.3 The elements of the plots

▶ **'Like an old tale still'** (*The Winter's Tale*, 5.2.61)

The plots

The plots of these plays differ from those of the earlier comedies in their design and movement. One way of understanding this difference is in terms of the words 'comedy' and 'romance'. To put it simply:

- **comedy is like a detective story, romance a soap-opera.**

A comic plot, like a detective story, is always going somewhere; the end matters because everything in the story is designed to make sense only at the close.

In soap-operas there's no 'end' to which all characters work. Soap-operas take the characters through a number of crises; but once they've achieved something, the episodes don't stop, though characters might die, marry or just leave the street.

Late comedies and soap-operas

The late comedies are closer to soap-operas than detective stories. In *The Winter's Tale*, for instance, none of the major characters has an aim. Leontes lapses into madness, is woken from it by the crisis of the middle scenes and then takes no active part in the progress of the plot. Paulina is active, but all she can really do is wait for things to turn out as the Oracle said they would. The plot moves almost independently of their doings.

Few practices

One very obvious difference between a romance plot and a comic plot is that romance makes little use of practices. There's disguise in *The Winter's Tale*, but it's hardly central. In *The Tempest* Antonio and Sebastian plot against the King of Naples, but it's not a sophisticated comic practice, merely a case of killing a man while he's asleep.

A positive point can be made out of this:

- **in the late comedies the plot has a measure of independence from the doings of the characters.**

15.4 Reconciliation

▶ 'look upon my brother' (*The Winter's Tale*, 5.3.147)

With the exception of *The Tempest*, the plots of the late comedies are loose and meandering. Perhaps because these narratives are relaxed and expansive, themes emerge more prominently. Those who write about Shakespeare have found more to say about the 'meaning' of the late comedies than they have about the earlier ones.

Reconciliation and restoration

A common pattern in these plays is the division of friends and families and how, through the mysteries of time's working, they are once more united.

These divisions might have led to tragic endings. *King Lear*, for instance, is about division in a family, in a nation and in nature. In the late plays, however, there's a comic impulse at work, which brings characters back together. In *The Winter's Tale* we have the words of the Oracle to give us the assurance that there can be a happy ending.

As was stressed in 15.2, the actual work of reconciliation is not an aim of the characters, but the consequence of how events, not necessarily planned ones, work out. Leontes is reconciled with Polixenes only when their children run away from Bohemia to Sicilia, and Polixenes follows them.

15.5 Young girls

▶ 'The fairest I have yet beheld' (*The Winter's Tale*, 5.1.87)

The late comedies have scenes with a haunting, iconic quality, which vibrate with the great themes that the simple folklore conventions mediate to us: the goodness of the natural order, the hope brought by young love.

Among these scenes are those involving a young woman and an old man. They've been compared to the drawings of William Blake – age and innocence, wisdom and hope. *The Tempest* opens with such a scene: Miranda is tenderly concerned about the fate of those in the storm-tossed ship, while Prospero, who assures her that all is well, wants to unfold the story of their lives to her.

The old and the young

In these plays the younger generation start to heal the wounds left by the older one. Children rescue parents from their despair and provide the means of bringing together those whom divisions have severed. It's like the comedies in reverse: comedies begin with the older generation persecuting the younger; the late plays end with the younger restoring the broken lives of their parents.

The young girl

The focus of this restoration is the girl rather than the boy. They are frequently praised for their outstanding beauty. When Ferdinand first sees Miranda he utters the kind of gasp that we usually hear only at the *end* of a comedy:

O you wonder!

(1.2.430)

Moreover, the scenes in which the young girls appear give a fullness and richness to their significance. When Perdita gives the revellers flowers, there's more than a hint that the whole bounty of nature, what Dryden called 'God's plenty', is present in her.

The lost found

In the late comedies, the finding of the lost is given a special quality, because it focuses on the bond between father and daughter.

It's difficult in the case of *The Winter's Tale* not to see the name of the daughter as meaning 'lost one', from the French 'perdue' – or the Latin 'perditus' – abandoned. Antigonus recounts his dream that Hermione, the mother, said the child should be called Perdita because it is 'counted lost for ever' (3.3.33).

15.6 Natural imagery

▶ 'Welcome hither/As is the spring to th 'earth!' (*The Winter's Tale*, 5.1.150–1)

The seasons

These words are spoken by Leontes when he meets Florizel and Perdita, although at this point he doesn't know that she's his daughter. Their arrival brings a kind of spring to the dark court of Sicilia. Soon there are discoveries, recognitions, reconciliations and the most amazing finding of the lost in the whole of Shakespeare.

Describing these changes in natural images is something that's already happened in the play. When the Shepherd finds the abandoned Perdita, he says, after hearing his son's account of the sinking ship and the man torn apart by a bear:

...thou metst with things dying, I with things new-born. (3.3.110)

The line works like a pivot. From the suspicion and strangled feelings of Sicilia, the play moves into the spring of Bohemia, where there's innocent revelry and a celebration of the goodness of the earth.

The sea

The other great natural force that sounds throughout these plays is the sea. It works in three ways.

(1) Its rhythms

The incoming tide cleans the dirty shore. Shakespeare uses this image in Prospero's speech about those whom he's confused, returning to consciousness:

> Their understanding
> Begins to swell, and the approaching tide
> Will shortly fill the reasonable shores
> That now lie foul and muddy.

> (5.1.79–82)

Returning to our senses is a familiar image in comedy; the confusion is over, and once more the light is clear. In these lines Shakespeare not only uses the cleansing motion of the tide but works on a sense most of us dimly have that the mind is like the sea.

(2) The unpredictable

The sea is often an image of what's untamed and therefore unpredictable. Sometimes Shakespeare has been seen as moving between the two poles of chaos (storms) and harmony (music). The aim of his comedies, on that reading, is to move from the former to the latter, from the uncertainty of storms to the harmony in which everyone and everything finds a place.

The Tempest bears out this pattern. It starts with the threatening combination of a storm and the unpredictable sea and proceeds to the tableau of the lovers, which promises new beginnings. Even a tempest can lead to a happy ending.

Again, we might be in the presence of something religious. The word 'providence' (used six times in Shakespeare and twice in *The Tempest*) means the way things work out for good. Comedy, particularly in the late plays, is providential.

(3) The mythical element

In these late plays, it's hard to avoid thinking about the sea in mythical terms. The sea can be looked upon as the one who brings those who've wronged Prospero to the island. It casts them up on the shore, while keeping the sailors safe till they are required. It is therefore an agent of discovery, recognition and reversal.

15.7 Art and thought

▶ 'mine art' (*The Tempest*, 1.2.28)

Shakespeare, as so often, reminds us that what we are watching is *art*. When the gentlemen say the discoveries at the end of *The Winter's Tale* are 'like an old tale' (5.2.61), we see that what we are watching *is* a tale.

The issue of art is impressed upon us in a number of ways.

The language of art

As with many of his plays, Shakespeare chooses to express ideas in terms drawn from art. In *The Tempest*. Prospero describes his brother's ambitions to become Duke of Milan in theatrical terms; his brother wanted:

> To have no screen between this part he played
> And him he played it for

> (1.2.107–8)

Prospero presents his brother as a man who wants to play the part of Duke for himself and not as a sort of understudy. By extension, we may conclude that Prospero's ambition is to play the part of the Duke again.

Theatrical situations

There are moments in these plays when what happens reminds us of the theatre in which we are sitting. Perdita's welcome to the guests at the sheep-shearing and her giving of flowers is a piece of theatre in itself. This is something that she draws attention to:

> Methinks I play as I have seen them do
> In Whitsun pastorals. Sure this robe of mine
> Does change my disposition.

> (4.4.122–4)

In these words, Shakespeare makes a simple ceremony close to sophisticated art.

Intellectual issues

There are other moments in these plays when the nature of art is raised. One such moment is Ariel's song about the father whom Ferdinand believes is drowned:

> Full fathom five thy father lies,
> Of his bones are corals made;
> Those are pearls that were his eyes;
> Nothing of him that doth change
> But doth suffer a sea-change
> Into something rich and strange.

> (1.2.400–5)

This isn't a piece of philosophy, nor is it a debate or argument. What the lyrics point to is a process of change in which nature becomes art without ceasing to be natural. Pearls were art in one sense – they could be strung on necklaces or worn in the ear – but they are the produce of a natural transformation. In art ordinary things do change, and they often become rich and strange. But their strangeness as art often draws our attention to the wonder of them as natural objects, a wonder we didn't see until art changed them.

15.1 Do you agree that what interests Shakespeare in the late plays is the way characters who suffer appalling experiences and are overcome by very strong passions nevertheless survive and grow in wisdom and personal qualities?

15.2 Trace how Shakespeare uses images drawn from nature to embody the themes of the late comedies.

16 The Winter's Tale

16.1 The shape of the plot

▶ 'Thou metst with things dying, I with things new-born' (3.3.110)

Because of its kinship with 'an old tale' (5.2.61), the play has been spoken of as simple and shapeless. Is it?

Two halves

The quotation at the head of this section is the pivot of the play. Once the Old Shepherd has found the baby, the character of the play alters:

- **the first half is dark and serious, whereas the second is mostly playful and distinctly comic**.

The two halves have been described as winter and spring; the former dominated by suspicion and leading to death, the latter controlled by love and leading to reconciliation.

Language

Two things happen to the language in the second half of the play.

- *There's more prose*: the passages in verse (for example, the love dialogue between Florizel and Perdita) are given importance because many of the surrounding passages are in prose.
- *The language ceases to be knotty and congested*: in the first half of the play, Leontes' clotted verse sets the tone, but in the second half the racy talk of Autolycus and the courtship of Florizel is lyrical and fluent.

Linking elements

Shakespeare gives his play a continuity by including elements that are common to both halves.

- Camillo advises Leontes in the first and Polixenes in the second.
- The words of the oracle provide a link between the two halves.

- Hermione plays the hostess in Sicilia, and her daughter plays hostess at the sheep-shearing in Bohemia.
- When persuading Polixenes to stay, Hermione takes his hand; in Bohemia, Florizel and Perdita join hands in a betrothal ceremony.
- Both Leontes and Polixenes cause upheavals by their manic outbursts.

The Winter's Tale feels like an old story – meandering with many diverse elements. Nevertheless, it's still an organised work of art.

16.2 Understanding Leontes' madness

▶ **'It is a bawdy planet, that will strike' (1.2.202)**

The plot gets going with what can only be called an eruption; Leontes is seized with the crazy idea that his wife has been having an adulterous affair with his boyhood friend, Polixenes. He thinks that the child in her womb is not his but Polixenes'. Because this eruption has such a devastating event, it's been much discussed.

Is there a cause?

It's been pointed out that Polixenes has been visiting them for nine months and that Hermione is heavily pregnant. Some readers have also felt that there's the suggestion in the text that Hermione is flirtatious.

Boyhood

One factor in the scene is the men's sentimental nostalgia about their childhoods. When Hermione is questioning Polixenes about how the two lads grew up, he answers with a romantic image of innocent lambs (1.2.69). Given that he's talking to the wife of his boyhood friend, what he goes on to say is extraordinary:

> Had we pursued that life,
> And our weak spirits ne'er been higher reared
> With stronger blood, we should have answered heaven
> Boldly, 'Not guilty'

(1.2.73–6)

Guilt comes with 'stronger blood'; in other words, with sex. When she jokingly says she gathers from what they've said that they've 'tripped since' (1.2.78), he says that they have faced 'temptations', which he identifies in the form of 'my wife ... and your precious self' (1.2.80–1).

It's worth asking whether Shakespeare is showing us two men who haven't grown up.

Plot

One 'explanation' for his outburst is that the plot requires it. This is a play about a division between two men that takes 16 years to heal. The jealousy of Leontes is the cause of this division.

This is a sufficient reason for his madness, but it's not totally satisfactory, because what it doesn't do justice to is the intensity of the madness and the space Shakespeare devotes to it.

No reason

The best reason for the outburst is that there's no reason for it. The opening of the play is disorientating and frightening precisely because we can't see why it's happening.

In so far as any one on stage understands it, they understand it as something that *can't* be explained. Camillo tells Polixenes it's a sickness and adds:

> but
> I cannot name th' disease…
>
> (1.2.385–6)

Shakespeare shows us something inexplicable, so the best way to feel its force is to leave it as that.

16.3 The functions of Camillo and Paulina

▶ 'good Camillo' (1.2.411)

Camillo and Paulina play a role that's relatively rare in Shakespeare.

- **They act as guides and guardians.**

Camillo and the plot

Camillo has an important function in the plot. He engineers Polixenes' escape from Sicilia, and he brings the major characters back to Sicilia, where, unknown to him, the plot can be resolved.

Paulina and the Oracle

Paulina is a more difficult figure to understand because she's quite complex.

There's something of the angry woman about her; she walks into the gaol to demand the new-born baby and immediately takes it to the court, where, because the king won't listen to sense, she leaves it. She thus provides a comical moment – men left in charge of a baby.

A production must do justice to her faithfulness to the Oracle. The crucial scene is Act 5, Scene 1. Cleomenes and Dion press Leontes to marry again. This is against what the Oracle has said. What makes this scene remarkable is that it was Cleomenes and Dion who went to Delphi to receive the Oracle. Their awe-struck dialogue in Act 3, Scene 1 shows the overwhelming impact it had on them, yet here they advise Leontes to ignore it.

Only Paulina remains faithful. We have to remember that she doesn't know that Perdita is alive; she only has her faith in the Oracle to rely on. If Camillo 'manages' the plot; she makes its resolution possible. Their marriage at the close of the play is symbolically right.

16.4 Hermione's character

▶ **'Hermione, queen to the worthy Leontes' (3.2.12)**

Hermione is not an easy character to play, because she's not immediately attractive in the way that, say, Beatrice and Rosalind are. But she's a character whom Shakespeare has worked on carefully.

Her wit

When invited to persuade Polixenes to stay, she behaves with a charming lightness and vivacity, teasing and cajoling the reluctant King till he, fairly quickly, gives in.

Her reserve

The only thing that momentarily disturbs her is her husband's remarks about his courtship of her. She clearly took some time ('three crabbed months' – 1.2.104) before saying yes. When he reminds her of this, there's an element of uncertainty in her hurried reply:

> But once before I spoke to th' purpose? When?
> Nay, let me have't. I long.

> (1.2.102–3)

Is there a reserved side to her, which he resented? Is his prosecution of her something to do with the pain she put him through, when he was awaiting her answer?

Her control

The scene in which Hermione is arrested opens with a charming family episode. Her son starts a story about 'sprites and goblins'. It's the most famous unfinished tale in Shakespeare. Leontes bursts in like a figure from a ghost story, and Hermione is taken off to gaol.

Her parting words give us a new aspect of her character:

>   Good my lords,
> I am not prone to weeping, as our sex
> Commonly are; the want of which vain dew
> Perchance shall dry your pities. But I have
> That honourable grief lodged here which burns
> Worse than tears drown.

> (2.1.109–14)

Hermione is controlled and aware. She knows she's not like some other women, and she knows, too, that that might count against her. What she also indicates is that her grief is inexpressible.

16.5 Hermione's trial and death

▶ **'accused and arraigned of high treason' (3.2.13)**

We don't see Hermione again until the trial. 'Trial' is hardly the word, since Leontes', as accuser, jury and judge, is determined that she'll be found guilty. Her defence, therefore, is more a case of preparing herself for what's to come.

Her trust

In her first speech she shows that she believes that innocence will be vindicated:

> But thus: if powers divine
> Behold our human actions – as they do –
> I doubt not then that innocence shall make
> False accusations blush, and tyranny
> Tremble at patience.

(3.2.27–31)

One of the things that's embodied in her language is an easy and natural trust in the ways of the gods. Her 'as they do' expresses a belief which is as natural to her as breathing. Given that trust, she can live in patience.

Hermione's trust in 'powers divine' and Paulina's faith in the Oracle show us that the women sustain the plot at its thematic level as well as providing its basic constituents. Interestingly, the other guardian figure also speaks with this easy confidence; he says to the hasty Florizel 'Besides, you know/Prosperity's the very bond of love' (4.4.572–3) as if this is a piece of wisdom everyone will consent to.

Honour

Hermione has no concern for her own safety:

> For honour,
> 'Tis derivative from me to mine,
> And only that I stand for.

(3.2.42–4)

Honour only matters for the sake of her children. Had he the sense to see it, the same goes for Leontes. If none of her children are his, then Sicilia has no heir.

Her death

Shakespeare does two things to make us believe that when she collapses at the news of her son's death, she is indeed dead.

- **Her death is announced by Paulina, whom we trust as reliable and upright.**

- **Hermione appears in Antigonus' dream (3.3.15–45) clothed in white as if she were a departed spirit.**

These look like strong directions, leading us to feel that the close of the first half of the play is dark and awesome.

16.6 How not to repent

▶ 'Apollo, pardon' (3.2.152)

When he hears news of his son's death, Leontes repents:

Apollo, pardon
My great profaneness 'gainst thine oracle.
I'll reconcile me to Polixenes,
New woo my queen, recall the good Camillo,...

(3.2.152–5)

And so on. Shakespeare doesn't intend us to be convinced. Leontes speaks in a neat and fluent manner quite different from the ramblings of his jealous period. His language is too neat; the wrongs against the gods, his friend and his wife can't be dealt with so swiftly and so lightly. Reconciliation can't be achieved merely by saying he will do it.

16.7 The pivotal scene

▶ 'if thou'lt see a thing to talk on when thou art dead and rotten' (3.3.78)

Antigonus represents the world of the court and the Old Shepherd and Clown the world of the countryside. When he's chased off stage by the bear (it's been frightened by the young men out hunting – 3.3.62–7), the suspicions of Sicilia give way to the blithe innocence of Bohemia.

The point about the Old Shepherd is that he has the same doubts that Leontes had; the baby he says is 'behind-door-work' – illegitimate. But instead of having it burnt, he takes it home to look after it.

16.8 Autolycus and Bohemia

▶ 'When daffodils begin to peer' (4.3.1)

Autolycus embodies the Spring, Bohemia and the new spirit of the play when he enters with the freshness of a breeze in Maytime. His song is about thieving and tumbling in the hay with the girls.

• The court

It's important that he's been at court. Like Perdita, he's one that's been thrown out and survived. His association with the court provides a thematic link between the two halves of the play.

• Practices

He's the closest the play comes to a comic practiser; Autolycus steals, adopts a disguise, plays roles and deceives.

• Ballads

The ballads he sells at the sheep-shearing festival characterise the world of Bohemia. This is a folk-culture of festivals and fabulous tales. The interesting thing is that Autolycus the deceiver doesn't seem the deceiver here. The world of tall stories is as much a part of him as it is of his customers.

- **The tables turned**

Audiences usually like Autolycus. Nevertheless, they also enjoy the scene (Act 5, Scene 2) in which the Old Shepherd and the Clown, rewarded by the kings for what they've done for Perdita, lord it over him. We are pleased for them and feel, also, that knavery has been put in its place.

16.9 The significance of the sheep-shearing scene

▶ This your sheep-shearing' (4.4.3)

The scene and the play

The scene has a special shape. It consists of courtship and wooing, merry-making, a potentially destructive disruption created by the older generation, and then plotting to bring a happy ending out of the chaos Polixenes has caused. We've seen this pattern before:

- **the scene follows the pattern of comedy.**

Perdita

This is her scene. She dominates it in three ways.

(1) What she says

She's in the mould of a comic heroine. When Camillo, utterly captivated by her, says were he a sheep he would stop grazing and only gaze (perhaps the silliest compliment paid in the whole of Shakespeare), she replies:

> Out, alas,
> You'd be so lean that blasts of January
> Would blow you through and through.

> (4.4.110–12)

She's also, like a heroine, sexually alert. Her love-talk with Florizel is pretty frank. When she says she'd like to strew him with flowers, he replies: 'like a corpse?' Her answer is openly erotic:

> No, like a bank, for love to lie and play on

> (4.4.130)

'Play' means sexual play. By using the word, she's rescuing it from the associations of furtive infidelity it was given by Leontes in Act 1, Scene 2.

(2) What others say of her

As well as Camillo's silliness, Florizel praises her by comparing her to mythical figures from classical mythology. She's 'Flora' (goddess of flowers), the queen of the lesser gods and the epitome of those legendary beauties that made the gods assume animal forms to possess them (4.4.1–35).

The point about this is that although nobody knows it, her royal nature *is* recognised. She speaks highly sophisticated verse and behaves with grace, wit and boldness. She's no ordinary girl.

(3) Her place in the scene

Perdita is the hostess and also the embodiment of the festival. When she gives out the flowers and bids the strangers welcome she's acting out the part of Spring itself. When she says she would have told the angry King that the sun shines on her as well as on him (4.4.441–6), she stands for the superiority of nature over the artificial distinctions of the court. Her appearance anticipates Hermione's emergence from the shadows.

16.10 Nature, art and Perdita

▶ 'great creating nature' (4.4.88)

The debate about grafting

In the sheep-shearing scene there's a conversation which attracts our attention because it's long and apparently unrelated to the festivities.

Perdita, in handing out her flowers, gives the disguised Polixenes and Camillo 'rosemary and rue', and when they say they are appropriate for older men, she replies that the most suitable flowers would have been 'our carnations and streaked gillyvors', only their rustic garden has none of them. When questioned why this is so, her answer is firm:

> For I have heard it said
> There is an art which in their piedness shares
> With great creating nature.

> (94.4.86–8)

Perdita believes in natural plants rather than ones specially grafted to produce striped flowers. She believes in nature rather than art.

Polixenes believes in art:

> So over that art
> Which you say adds to nature is an art
> That nature makes. You see, sweet maid, we marry
> A gentler scion to the wildest stock,
> And make conceive a bark of baser kind
> By bud of nobler race.

> (4.3.90–5)

In short, grafting is an art but it uses natural means. Perdita will have none of it:

> I'll not put
> The dibble in the earth to set one slip of them

> (4.3.99–100)

Who wins the argument?

Polixenes appears to be the victor. But two things in the scene need stressing:

- his language is too slick: the way he juggles cleverly with the words is cheap and superficial
- within a few lines he shows that his argument was only clever talk, because when faced with the prospect of a shepherd's daughter marrying his son, he refuses to allow the human grafting of the 'gentler scion' and the 'baser stock'.

In the light of this the issue is still open.

Recognition and reconciliation

The strange thing about the return to Sicilia is that Shakespeare doesn't give us the scene we expect and want – the moment when Leontes recognises his daughter and is reconciled to Polixenes. It looked as if the whole plot was working towards this, and Shakespeare merely reports it. We might conclude:

- **if he doesn't deal on stage with the events that we've been expecting, then he must have a good reason; this reason emerges when we hear about the statue.**

The statue

The statue, we are told, is a remarkable work of art:

The Princess, hearing of her mother's statue, which is in the keeping of Paulina, a piece many years in doing, and now newly performed by that rare Italian master Giulio Romano, who, had he himself eternity and could put breath into his work, would beguile nature of her custom, so perfectly is he her ape. He so near to Hermione hath done Hermione that they say one would speak to her and stand in hope of answer. (5.2.93–101)

That makes it clear how near and yet how far art is from nature. It's so 'near to Hermione' that one would think it was her, but, for all the closeness, the artist hasn't got eternity to work in (who has?) and he can't put breath into a statue. For a moment we might wonder if anyone can.

The final scene

Throughout the final scene in which they gaze in wonder at the statue, Shakespeare teases us with words about art. For example, it's the 'carver's excellence' (5.3.30) that there are wrinkles in the face, and 'the colours/Not dry' (5.3.47–8). The most crucial question about the power of art is asked by Leontes:

What fine chisel
Could ever yet cut breath?

(5.3.78–9)

We know the answer to that; not even Giulio Romano's could give breath. Hermione is not a work of art; she's the daughter of 'great creating nature'.

Perdita again

So Perdita was right. Nothing art can do can be compared to the warm (even if wrinkled!) flesh of the living Hermione. We might venture two comments.

- **Shakespeare is still teasing us; art can't rival nature, but we need art to see the wonders of nature.**

- **Did he change his mind?** Was he working towards a big reconciliation scene when he realized that what was more important was the issue of art and nature? Did he write the dialogue about the carnations and then realize that Perdita is so central to the play that the real ending must be one that vindicates her?

Exercises

16.1 Discuss the several ways in which Perdita is central to *The Winter's Tale*.

16.2 'In spite of its apparently rambling structure, *The Winter's Tale* is a very carefully constructed work of art.' What can be said to make sense of both parts of this statement?

The Tempest

17.1 The Tempest and interpretation

▶ 'know thine own meaning' (1.2.359)

Classical form

The Tempest is a play that seems to welcome interpretation. Perhaps the oddest thing about the 'welcome' the play gives to very different readings is that it might have been the least rather than the most accommodating of Shakespeare's works. It very nearly observes the 'classical unities' – one basic action in one place at one time – and such tightness of design might have held the ideas in. As it is, the play has been thought to be about some of the following: government, art and nature, the role of the imagination, the state of the human mind (the idea it all happens in Prospero's head), revenge, the discovery of America and the nature of colonialism, good and evil, magic, the nature of theatrical illusion.

It's worth while asking how this comes about. Here are four suggestions.

(1) Design

The careful patterning of events leads readers to think there must be a significance in the way they are shaped.

(2) Characters

Because one character–Ariel–is not human, we ask what 'he' stands for.

(3) Prospero

Prospero's strong guiding presence leads readers to see symbolic meanings in what he says and does.

(4) The words

There are carefully placed words – 'art', 'nature', 'virtue', 'vengeance' – which invite readers to ponder their meanings.

17.2 Politics in The Tempest

▶ 'You did supplant your brother Prospero' (2.1.276)

Politics

The Tempest is certainly a political play; the plot grows from and consists of a series of usurpations and attempted usurpations.

- Prospero tells (1.2.33–167) the story of Antonio supplanting him.
- in Act 2, Scene 1 Antonio and Sebastian plot the deaths of Alonso and Gonzalo.
- In Act 2, Scene 2 Caliban abandons serving Prospero and in Act 3, Scene 2 he and Stephano and Trinculo plan Prospero's murder.

Families

Politics is a family matter. The three states – Milan, Naples, the island – are ruled by families that are threatened from within and attempt to stabilise themselves through political marriages.

17.3 Colonialism

▶ 'Which first was mine own king' (1.2.345)

Colonialism

The Tempest is concerned with colonialism. Caliban was a native of the island, but when Prospero came he was reduced to being a servant. Once he was 'mine own king'. He ruled nobody, but he was free, and the island was his:

> This island's mine by Sycorax my mother
>
> (1.2.334)

He had more right to it than Prospero.

As with many (all?) colonial powers, Prospero held it by right of conquest. We may be able to accept this more easily had Prospero not been seething with anger against his usurping brother!

The usefulness of the native

Caliban is useful, in spite of the fact that he attempted to rape Miranda:

> But as 'tis,
> We cannot miss him. He does make our fire,
> Fetch in our wood, and serves in offices
> That profit us.
>
> (1.2.313–16)

That is the attitude colonialism induces in rulers. What matters is the profit the colonialists gain; the fact that Caliban performs everyday chores matters more than any anguish his daughter might feel.

Education

Caliban's retaliation is also a colonial response:

> You taught me language, and my profit on't
> Is I know how to curse.

(1.2.362–3)

Education is used by Caliban against Prospero and Miranda. Who is to say that this isn't a proper use of language? The only liberty that often remains for oppressed people is that of voicing defiance. Cursing has its uses.

17.4 The importance of Caliban

▶ 'some monster of the isle' (2.2.65)

What kind of creature?

One of the problems with Caliban is that a lot of what is said about him comes from Prospero; and it's not in Prospero's interest to present him attractively. For instance, he calls him 'tortoise' (1.2.316), presumably because he's slow in obeying orders. Stephano calls him a 'monster'.

Caliban's humanity

But what matters about him is that he's human. When Miranda talks of the men whom she's met (1.2.445–7), she must count him as one of the three. Furthermore, only a human being could say at the end that he will 'seek for grace' (5.1.295).

Caliban's roles

His roles emerge in the links he has with some of the other characters: like Prospero, he's a usurped king and like Antonio, Sebastian, Stephano and Trinculo he wants to supplant authority. Like Miranda he's been brought up on the island and educated by Prospero. The parental pattern is very neat; she has a father but no mother, whereas he only knew his mother. He contrasts with Ariel – he is of the earth, Ariel of the sky; he has little moral sense, whereas Ariel appears to know right and wrong.

How should he be interpreted and judged?

Caliban is bare, unimproved nature; Prospero practises the art that raises life above the brutish level of nature. An art/nature reading emphasises all Caliban's base qualities: his attempted rape of Miranda, his violence, his ingratitude, his folly and his stupidity. He is, therefore, a contrast to Miranda, who has responded to Prospero's art and Ariel, who, although not human, is sensitive to the feelings of others.

But, of course, it's not as simple as that. Is Caliban any worse than Antonio and Sebastian? Both try to kill their political masters, and both want to carry out the assassination while the victim is asleep. Caliban can at least claim to be the rightful ruler of the island.

Caliban's language

No one has a good word to say of him. He's called 'a devil' (2.2.97) and 'this thing of darkness' (5.1.278). And there's the issue of whether he's a natural slave; when he thinks he's free from Prospero, all he says is that he's got a 'new master' (2.2.184).

On the other hand, one of the most magical moments in the entire play is his speech about the isle being 'full of noises' (3.2.138–46). He searches uncertainly for the right words:

> Be not afeard, the isle is full of noises,
> Sounds, and sweet airs, that give delight and hurt not.

It's worth noting his concern; they are strangers and he seeks to console them. Sadly it shows he doesn't learn; he'd done the same for Prospero.

However Caliban is to be judged, the innocence and the wonder of his language must be given weight. Can we call someone who talks like that 'an abominable monster'?

17.5 Prospero's island

▶ 'the isle' (3.2.138)

Shakespeare's isle is a special place. We learn a lot about its natural history: it has a cove ('the deep nook' – 1.2.228), pine trees (1.2.279), oaks (1.2.468), wolves (1.2.290), hedgehogs ('urchins' – 1.2.329), 'berries' (1.2.337), 'mussels' (1.2.467), 'fresh springs, brine pits' (1.2.341), rocks (1.2.346) and a bank (1.2.393).

Our picture of the island mainly comes from Caliban. When he speaks of it, there's a feeling of wonder; even when he's lamenting that he showed Prospero the isle, his bitterness doesn't diminish his awe:

> and then I loved thee,
> And showed thee all the qualities o'th' isle,
> The fresh springs, brine pits, barren place and fertile –
> Cursed be I that did so!
>
> (1.2.339–42)

That passage is typical of another feature of the isle: it exists as isolated spots. Listen, for instance, to Caliban talking to Stephano and Trinculo:

> I prithee let me bring thee where crabs grow,
> And I with my long nails will dig thee pig-nuts,
> Show thee a jay's nest, and instruct thee how
> To snare the nimble marmoset. I'll bring thee
> To clust'ring filberts, and sometimes I'll get thee
> Young scamels from the rock.
>
> (2.2.166–71)

There's a separate place for each wonderful, living thing.

What is to be made of this? Perhaps Shakespeare is suggesting an important difference between Prospero and the isle?

Prospero's word for what he's doing in the play is 'project' (5.1.1). He has an end at which he aims, and all that he does contributes to its achievement. In Prospero's 'project' everything has a place, and all things work together in a unity.

It's not so with the isle. There things are important not because they contribute to an overall scheme, but because they are fascinating and beautiful in themselves. They don't need to be related, because there's no plan they have to fit into.

It's interesting to speculate that in Prospero we have Western man, who organises all things into a unified project, whereas the isle is more Eastern – marvellous places that are significant because each has its own wonder and mystery.

17.6 Issues about Ariel

▶ 'my industrious servant Ariel' (4.1.33)

Lots of examination questions ask candidates to think about Ariel and Caliban. They have a lot in common. They:

- are 'natives' of the isle
- serve Prospero
- want freedom
- create or respond to music.

Some of their differences are clearly contrasted.

- Caliban is associated with the earth, Ariel with the air.
- Ariel assists Prospero's 'project', Caliban attempts rebellion.
- Caliban represents unadorned nature; Ariel is the one who performs Prospero's art.

Ariel isn't human

There is, however, one very important difference: Ariel isn't human. Shakespeare establishes Ariel's other than human nature in his first speech:

> All hail, great master, grave sir, hail! I come
> To answer thy best pleasure, be't to fly,
> To swim, to dive into the fire, to ride
> On the curled clouds

> (1.2.189–92)

In four lines there are five infinitives (verbs in the form of 'to answer' or 'to fly'). The point about infinitives is that they don't have subjects; that's to say, the verb just gives the action and not the person who does it. And in the case of Ariel, this is right; Ariel doesn't have a personality, so the initial establishment of his character is done through the actions of infinitives.

Ariel's gender

It's clear that Caliban is male, but what is Ariel? The answer is not so much that we don't know, but that the conventional distinctions don't easily apply.

The stage direction for Ariel's entrance in Act 3, Scene 3 is:

> *Enter Ariel, like a harpy, claps his wings …*

Ariel is said to be male (*his wings*), but is compared to a harpy – a female revenging spirit. Elsewhere, Prospero tells Ariel 'make thyself like a nymph o'th'sea' (1.2.301), a role that is unambiguously female. Also female is the role Ariel plays in the masque. In 4.1.167 Ariel says: 'When I presented Ceres'. Here 'presented' means played; in other words, Ariel plays Ceres in the masque. Ceres is about as female as you can get; she's both an archetypal mother figure and a symbol of the fruitfulness of harvest.

Ariel's gender isn't something that we can 'solve'; Ariel is referred to as male but plays female roles. This is only a problem if we think of Ariel as human; and that's the point – Ariel isn't.

Ariel and Prospero

Though Ariel isn't human, he has a close relationship with Prospero. This relationship is based on something very extraordinary about the play: only Prospero knows that Ariel exists.

When they first meet, there's a tension we might associate with an intimate or even passionate friendship; Ariel seems glad to have done what Prospero has asked, and Prospero is delighted with what's been achieved. But with the prospect of more work, Ariel becomes what Prospero calls 'moody' (1.2.244).

One intriguing moment calls for a decision as to how it's to be performed. In Act 5, Scene 1 Prospero robes for his encounter with those whom he's shipwrecked. As he dresses, Ariel merrily sings his song of freedom when he will suck like the bee and snugly lie in a cowslip; Prospero almost dotingly says:

> Why, that's my dainty Ariel! I shall miss thee,
> But yet thou shalt have freedom. So, so, so.

> (5.1.97–8)

He doesn't speak so lovingly even to Miranda. The admission that 'I shall miss thee' is poignant. With that degree of intimacy established, it's intriguing to as what 'so, so, so' means. It's often explained as the accompaniment to his dressing; he could smooth out a crease. But there's another possibility: Prospero is kissing farewell to the one to whom he's been closest.

17.7 Understanding Prospero

▶ 'Prospero, master of a full poor cell' (1.2.20)

Character

Because of his plot significance, Prospero is often spoken of as majestic and powerful. In Act 3, Scene 3, when the banquet vanishes and Ariel delivers Prospero's denunciation of the 'three men of sin' (3.3.52), the stage direction for line 17 reads:

Solemn and strange music, and Prospero on top, invisible.

Prospero remains 'on top' (in Shakespeare's day the gallery above the stage) till near the end of the scene. Those that haven't seen a performance must try to picture the power of his controlling and magisterial presence.

But Shakespeare also gives us, as in so many of his plays, a recognisable, complex and not altogether admirable human being.

Prospero has at least three very human failings: he's bad tempered, authoritarian and broodingly revengeful. That Shakespeare intended his audiences to take these features seriously, may be inferred from the fact they are all evident in the second scene of the play: he gruffly complains that Miranda isn't listening; in a bad-tempered ritual he forces Ariel to recall how he suffered before Prospero came to the island, and his revengeful side breaks through when he shifts into the present tense – 'the very rats/Instinctively have quit it' (lines 147–8). He pursues revenge because he still feels pain.

Dramatic perspective

Because Prospero tells us a lot about his past, it's tempting to see him as a narrator with an authoritative view of the action rather than as a figure who speaks only for himself.

As a result of this, readers often find themselves judging things the way Prospero does. In such cases, we should ask:

- **is there evidence for this other than that supplied by Prospero?**

Take what he says about Caliban being fathered by the devil:

> got by the devil himself
> Upon thy wicked dam

(1.2.322–3)

Only Prospero says this; Caliban only ever speaks of his mother. If Prospero is right, then we can expect little good from Caliban, but if he's not speaking the truth, we might form a different view of this perplexing creature.

17.8 The masque

▶ **'such another trick' (4.1.37)**

The masque has a shimmering, magical quality. It's what you might expect at Court – elaborate, civilised, formal and spectacular. This is Prospero's aim; he's celebrating an important political alliance.

Art

The masque is Prospero's art in its purest form. What we see here is a clue to how his art works elsewhere. The trim lines show that he values control. One of the themes of the masque is that squabbles between the gods are over. Prospero tries to do this with the other characters.

Restraint

The message of the masque is that sexual desire should be restrained, so it's a very powerful reinforcement of Prospero's insistence that Miranda and Ferdinand should not have sexual intercourse before marriage.

The reality of the theatre

The masque is a play-within-a-play, but the audience know that Prospero and all the other characters are also in a play. When the play is suddenly brought to a stop, the play-within-a-play vanishes, and within about 40 minutes so will the play we are watching. But Shakespeare has a further surprise. In his speech to Ferdinand, Prospero blurs some very important distinctions:

> These our actors,
> As I foretold you, were all spirits, and
> Are melted into air, into thin air,
> And, like the baseless fabric of this vision,
> The cloud-capped towers, the gorgeous palaces,
> The solemn temples, the great globe itself,
> Yea, all which it inherit, shall dissolve,
> And, like this insubstantial pageant faded,
> Leave not a rack behind.

> (4.1.148–56)

If the punctuation is correct, what this passage says is that in the same way in which the masque vanished, so everything in the world – even those things such as 'cloud-capped towers' that are the products of the imagination – will likewise fade out to nothing. There is no basis for either artistic vision or the substantial things of the material world. All will go. The masque apparently dissolves those differences between art and nature that Shakespeare has made the subject of his plays.

17.9 Wonder in The Tempest

▶ 'O you wonder' (1.2.430)

'Wonder' is one of the most important words in the play. Ferdinand feels it when he meets Miranda. He's trying to ask her whether she's 'married', but as he's framing his thoughts, he catches his breath in amazement, and 'O you wonder!' bursts out.

Miranda and Ferdinand playing chess in the last scene is wonderful. Miranda's cry of amazement as she sees the company echoes Ferdinand's, when he saw her:

> O wonder!
> How many goodly creatures are there here!
> How beauteous mankind is! O brave new world
> That has such people in't!

> (5.1.184–7)

There is so much vigour and innocent delight in those lines that it seems unfair to bring to the scene what we know of the 'goodly creatures' she's gazing at. Perhaps Prospero is as tactful as he can be when he (rather sadly?) says: 'Tis new to thee'. (See Illustration 5.)

17.10 Revenge or reconciliation

▶ 'the rarer action' (5.1.27)

The dialogue with Ariel at the beginning of the last scene shows what Prospero has been up to.

Ariel tells him about the plight of the King and his followers:

Illustration 5 The Tempest: Miranda and Ferdinand playing chess

Your charm so strongly works 'em
That if you now beheld them, your affections
Would become tender.

(5.1.17–19)

We must infer from this that Ariel doesn't think that Prospero's 'affections' (feelings) are tender.

We now see that from Prospero's viewpoint we have been watching a revenge play. Having secured a marriage, he'll punish those who've hurt him.

What happens next is the turning point of the play:

Prospero: Dost thou think so, spirit?
Ariel: Mine would, sir, were I human.
Prospero: And mine shall. (5.1.18–20)

In simple words – all but two are monosyllables – we hear the momentous change from bitter revenge to compassion.

It's at this point that we see what the theme of the play is:

Though with their high wrongs I am struck to th' quick,
Yet with my nobler reason 'gainst my fury
Do I take part. The rarer action is
In virtue than in vengeance.

(5.1.25–8)

This is unusually clear. Though he's still 'struck to the quick', 'virtue' is 'rarer' than 'vengeance'. Shakespeare seems to indicate that Prospero didn't know that this is how it would end.

17.11 How The Tempest ends

▶ 'Please you, draw near' (5.1.322)

Reconciliation?

Apart from the Epilogue, those are the last words spoken in the play. Prospero's 'project' (5.1.1) appears to be complete. Has it worked?

The simplest way of answering that question is to say: 'not exactly'. Prospero brings off all he's planned, but we can't be sure that it has the meaning or significance that he hoped for.

Consider the cases of Caliban and Antonio. Prospero has never expected anything good from Caliban, so when 'this thing of darkness' (5.1.278) says:

I'll be wise hereafter,
And seek for grace.

(5.1.298–9)

the response is more than he planned. Caliban has consistently resisted any kind of improvement; he now freely chooses to seek for 'grace'.

If Caliban yields more than Prospero expected, Antonio probably yields less. Prospero forgives Antonio (5.1.78), but Antonio has nothing to say to Prospero. His only lines are about the market value of Caliban (5.1.268–9)!

Prospero's final invitation to 'draw near' (5.1.318) is charged with meaning. He wants Antonio to draw near to him as a brother as well as entering his house. If Antonio did, for example, embrace him with brotherly affection, then Prospero's invitation to 'draw near' would have achieved the significance he wants it to have. But it looks as if there's a gap; if Antonio doesn't draw near, then there's a disparity between what Prospero set out to do and what he has achieved.

Shakespeare and the audience

Some readers have felt that the play is about Shakespeare as a playwright. Because Shakespeare is interested in the difference between what Prospero aims for and what he achieves, he might see this in terms of his own writing. A playwright doesn't have complete control over the reactions of his audiences; like Prospero at the end of the play, all that he can do is beg for the audience's approval.

Exercises

17.1 How do you understand Prospero, and how does your understanding of his character influence your reading of the play as a whole?

17.2 'The chief theme of the play is power.' To what extent do you agree with this view?

Part V
The Tragedies

(18) Tragedy

18.1 The problems of definition

▶ 'define, define' (*Love's Labours Lost*, 1.2.90)

Tragedy is best treated as a 'group' word – plays with links one to another but not necessarily with an element or elements common to all of them.

There was a time when people had very strict ideas about what made tragedy tragedy and comedy comedy. Dr Johnson saw that Shakespeare's plays were different:

Shakespeare's plays are not in the rigorous or critical sense either tragedies or comedies, but compositions of a distinct kind.

This distinct kind he described as a reflection of the mixed nature of human life in which 'evil, joy and sorrow' are mingled together.

18.2 The vast world of tragedy

▶ 'for the world is broad and wide' (*Romeo and Juliet*, 3.3.16)

- In comedies the plots are very complex and the ideas relatively few.
- In tragedies the plots are often simple and the ideas numerous.

Tragedy, like the world described by Friar Lawrence, is 'broad and wide'.

Many ideas

In tragedies, the pressure of events makes characters think. In their soliloquies and their dialogues they try to make sense of what's happening to them. Consequently, ideas well up. For instance, the main business of *Hamlet*, 1.4 is the appearance of the ghost and Hamlet rushing after it. This prompts the characters to talk about the following issues: traditions, national reputation, the nature of fear, madness, destiny, the imagination, the moral state of the nation and providence.

The sense of the vast

Tragedy is the world of life and death, of love and war, of the whole range of the human passions. As a result

- **the world of tragedy feels vast and huge**.

In moments of crisis, vast images are invoked; for instance, when Hamlet is thinking about his duel with Laertes, his mind is full of thoughts of death and the mysterious providence of God (5.2.165–70).

18.3 Unavoidable death

▶ **'Keeps death his court'** (*Richard II*, 3.2.158)

What matters in comedy is the promise of the new life that's present in marriage. The plot takes an upward movement into a bright future. In tragedy the plot turns downwards, and we are made aware of the passing of time and the certainty of death. Richard II says that death keeps his court – that is, exercises power and authority – in the crown of a king. In saying this of kings, he says it for all people:

- **in tragedy we are always aware we are mortal**.

Meaning?

If life ends in death, what meaning can there be in life?

That's a question that leads people to write tragedies. One of the things tragedy does is show that in spite of death, human life has significance. The patience, the defiance, the need to understand ourselves and the recognition of the needs of others are qualities born out of tragedy, and because these are valuable, then, in spite of suffering and death, life is affirmed.

Failure to recognise limits

Tragedy works with the fact that human life is limited. We are not immortal and we are not all-powerful. The idea of a superman is nonsense. We are limited, and the limits are absolute; we can't get round them.

However, an impulse in tragic figures is to ignore the limit of death. When the tragic figure is pursuing his or her goals, the natural limits of life get in the way:

- **the tragic impulse tries to overstep human limits; tragedy emerges in the discovery that this is impossible**.

Human equality

Death is a leveller in the sense that we all have to die. The tragic impulse is to overcome our natural limitations; wisdom begins when we see that this is foolish.

When Richard II wakes up to his own ordinary mortality, he recognises his kinship with everyone else:

> I live with bread like you; feel want,
> Taste grief, need friends.

(3.2.171–2)

In those simple monosyllables, we hear a king recognising in himself what he shares with all people. One of the triumphs of tragic figures is their recognition that they can't overcome human limitation.

18.4 Division and tragedy

▶ 'these divisions' (*King Lear*, 1.2.134)

The world of tragedy is one of disorder and division. There are quarrels, disputes and characters are at war with each other because of greed, envy, hatred, lust and selfish ambition.

Tragedy happens because this is what the world is like. Conflict lies at its heart.

Divided within

Characters in tragedies often find they are divided against themselves. Othello discovers that it's possible to love and hate the same person.

Divided minds

Madness plays a large part in Shakespeare: Hamlet might be mad and in the middle of his play Lear descends into a frenzied and zany madness.

Divided families

Shakespeare's plays are intensely domestic in the sense that he shows that kings are also husbands and fathers. No matter how outstanding a figure is, we are shown him or her in the context of a family. Hence the tensions that are part of human life show themselves in families.

Divided nations

A nation divided against itself is the theme of some of the plays. Characters want power, and once they've got it they want to make themselves absolutely safe, so the bloodshed continues.

Nature divided

The vastness of tragedy is seen in the way in which in some plays, the conflict lies at the very heart of nature. The storm in *King Lear* is perhaps symbolic of the universal tensions upon which everything rests.

18.5 Order and tragedy

▶ 'by degree stand in authentic place' (*Troilus and Cressida*, 1.3.108)

Order

Shakespeare's vision of the tragic world is of order breaking down.

There are different kinds of order in Shakespeare. Some of them have been touched on in the previous section – order in the mind and order in nature, for instance. The most important point in the tragedies is that:

- **order is regarded by many of the characters as a moral matter.**

Order is thought of as good.

Degree

In one of Shakespeare's most philosophical plays, *Troilus and Cressida*, Ulysses delivers a very long speech about the nature of what he calls 'degree'. This word means a number of things: the proper place and function of something; the grading of everything in an order of importance, and the harmony established when everything works together. Degree is treated as the universal principle that makes order possible. Natural disasters occur when it breaks down:

> The bounded waters
> Should lift their bosoms higher than the shores
>
> (1.3.111–12)

And moral confusion follows the breakdown of order:

> And the rude son should strike his father dead.
>
> (1.3.115)

Moral order is embedded in natural order. To go against the order of nature is to bring about an immoral world.

Social status

Tragedy recognises the importance of social status, but the recognition is not a simple one. Tragedy keeps two things in view:

- differences in social status
- our common humanity.

If we didn't recognise differences in social position, we couldn't understand the spectacle of a king becoming a beggar. This is virtually what happens to King Lear when he wanders on the heath in the storm and arrives at the hovel of Poor Tom. The sight of the pitiful shelter brings home to him the plight of the poor (3.2.28–36). He kneels and, prays, not so much to the gods as to the 'poor naked wretches'. His recognition of common humanity emerges as a result of a social fall.

Choosing to do wrong

Many tragedies wouldn't have their unusual force unless the central figure *chose* to do something which was wrong. One of the eerily fascinating things about Macbeth is that he knows he's doing wrong. He knows that Duncan is a good man and that all that is good in him will cry out:

> his virtues
> Will plead like angels
>
> (1.7.18–19)

Yet he goes ahead.

▶ 'the rack of this tough world' (*King Lear*, 5.3.290)

In tragedies the consequence of going against what one knows to be right is suffering. Macbeth's suffering – his nightmares, his gradual loss of sensitivity, his drifting apart from Lady Macbeth – is the consequence of what he's chosen to do.

But some suffering is not clearly related to what a character has done. It can't be understood simply as a punishment.

- **In tragedy suffering can be horrible because it's excessive or undeserved.**

It's pointless trying to understand *Romeo and Juliet* in terms of deserved suffering. The lovers have done nothing wrong; they've fallen in love and acted upon their feelings. They might be foolish and impulsive, but they're not wicked. Lear has certainly caused havoc, but he might be right in saying that he's 'more sinned against than sinning' (3.2.60).

The irrationality of suffering

Tragedy shows that the world is neither rational nor fair. Some people suffer appallingly, and there seems either no reason for it or the 'reason' is inadequate. Tragedy forces on us the recognition that terrible things happen for which there's no explanation.

The one play that not only contains suffering but actually seems to be about it is *King Lear*. Throughout the play a number of characters say things about the evil that people do and the kind of suffering that follows.

- The first thing to notice is that a lot of what's said is contradictory. The Duke of Gloucester blames the stars, whilst his son, Edmund, thinks evil comes from ourselves.
- The second point is that what's said doesn't really add up. Can we be content with a picture of the gods that either 'kill us for their sport' (4.1.38) or that death and suffering of the wicked shows that the gods exist (4.2.46–8)? We often feel it's cheap if we offer slick answers like that.

▶ 'outstretched heroes' (*Hamlet*, 2.2.265)

It's become customary to talk about the central characters in Shakespeare's tragedies as heroes. In fact, Shakespeare very rarely uses the word. None of the 'tragic heroes' is called a hero.

Common people

Listen again to what Dr Johnson said:

Shakespeare has no heroes; his scenes are occupied only by men, who act and speak as the reader thinks that he should himself have spoken or acted on the same occasion.

A hero in Johnson's view is someone who doesn't respond to life's difficulties in the same way as we do. In Shakespeare, characters are like us: we might not be murderers but if we were, we'd think and feel as Macbeth does.

This is not to say that there's no difference between the central tragic characters and ourselves. Many of them feel things with an intensity that we don't. Not everyone is ever as wildly and intoxicatingly in love as Romeo. But most of us do fall in love. And that's the point: there are no feelings tragic characters have which we don't, even though we might not feel them to the same depth.

Although the word needs careful handling, there is something refreshingly ordinary about many of Shakespeare's tragic figures. He gives Lear speeches in his madness that show him concerned with the everyday business of life – archery practice, magistrate's courts and dogs.

Elevated positions and personal qualities

These plays should be presented in such a way that we feel the awe of a king or a great soldier. What the production should do is give us the feeling that what's awesome is something to do with the *position* they occupy. But position alone isn't enough. A tragic figure must have outstanding personal qualities. That's to say, he or she must have qualities that are not due to social status: Hamlet's quick thinking, Othello's imagination and Antony's daring.

18.8 Tragedy, morality and ambivalence

▶ 'I was born to set it right' (*Hamlet*, 1.5.190)

One of the qualities a tragic figure has is purposefulness: Hamlet has been given a task, which he willingly embraces with relish and energy.

Tragedy won't work unless we find this difficult. The difficulty lies in the impossibility of either fully endorsing or completely condemning what a tragic figure says. We can put the point in this way:

- **our response to tragedy is ambivalent.**

Tragedy pulls us in contrary directions.

We must admire Hamlet's purposefulness, vigour, energy and resolution. We must feel that here's someone who's really alive. What's more, because he's so dedicated we must want him to succeed. We will what he wills.

We feel close to Hamlet and perhaps even closer to Macbeth. We should be able to think that this is strange. Perhaps we don't think about it in when watching the intense unfolding of the action, but after a performance we might recognise that we've been close to someone who's bent on evil.

In addition to our feelings of admiration and closeness we have to say that

- **the tragic figure is *wrong*.**

Because this is an ambivalent response, our feelings of admiration and closeness don't go away. We still have those feelings but we feel them about someone whom we know to be doing wrong.

18.9 Hubris and bravado

▶ 'This is I' (*Hamlet*, 5.1.254)

We need to be more precise about what's wrong with the tragic hero. It's certainly something to do with the fact that he's chosen to do what's evil, but it's more than that.

- **Tragedy is an attitude to one's own experience.**

What makes a tragic figure so attractive and so blameworthy is the way he views his own actions.

Look at how Hamlet responds to the ghost's demand that he becomes a revenger. He doesn't know what's happened but he eagerly says:

> Haste, haste me to know it, that with wings as swift
> As meditation or the thoughts of love
> May sweep to my revenge.

(1.5.29–31)

We can certainly thrill to the urgency of those words, but shouldn't we also be appalled by someone who so outlandishly draws attention to *himself*. This isn't impulsiveness; it's done with full knowledge, and it's said in such a way as to draw attention to the speaker. Hamlet, like a hawk, will cut through the air and fall upon his prey. And like the hawk, people will see him do it. There is in those words great pride in the deed and in the fierceness with which it's done.

Hubris

The Greeks spoke of the tragic figure as exhibiting **hubris**.

This is sometimes translated as excessive pride. Someone who exhibits hubris is often said to be arrogant or presumptuous. The arrogance is seen in breaking moral laws; because of this the Greeks saw hubris as an affront to the gods.

We have to very careful when using the word of Shakespeare because he doesn't use it at all. Perhaps it's useful if we confine it to the conscious display of knowing defiance that marks some characters' actions. When Hamlet jumps into Ophelia's grave to fight with Laertes, his cry 'This is I/Hamlet the Dane', might be called hubris; it's defiant and it calls attention to the speaker.

Bravado

Bravado is another useful word. Again, this isn't in Shakespeare. It means a display, usually of courage or daring, which is boastful and smugly self-assured. To do something outrageous so as to court public astonishment and even approval requires an almost unquestioning confidence in oneself.

Nemesis

The Greeks saw the affront to the gods as deserving punishment; so the tragic figure was brought down. This was called **nemesis**. Shakespeare doesn't use the term, but we might feel that those who are appalled by the public glorification of tragic action might use the term to express their feeling that this is where such outlandish behaviour ends.

Not being one's own judge

It's an ancient principle that

- **no one should be his or her own judge**.

When the worth of what you've done is in question, the responsibility of judgement should be given to others.

The tragic figure wants to judge himself. He wants to persuade those who see him that what he's doing has a grandeur and greatness about it.

18.10 Tragic self-presentation

▶ 'actions that a man might play' (*Hamlet*, 1.2.84)

Tragedy as theatrical presentation

Tragic actions force upon us the extraordinary courage and purposefulness of the characters, but the way they force us to see them may, upon reflection, make us recoil.

We need to ask how exactly Shakespeare sees this self-conscious display working. The answer is

- **Shakespeare sees tragic characterers as acting out roles in a theatrical manner.**

Hamlet talks of the parts that someone grieving might play; in doing so, he's giving us an insight into Shakespeare's essentially theatrical idea of tragedy. The tragic figure plays out his role like the player on stage, so all can see what an awesome thing he's doing.

Playing the tragic role

This is most clearly seen in *Hamlet*, the most theatrical of all the plays. Hamlet is a player of roles – the melancholy man, the revenger, the jilted lover, the madman, the critic, the friend, the son, the thinker, the Prince. To that list we can add the tragic figure, the one who acts out his own terrible fall.

Enjoying the role

As they act out their fall

- **the tragic figures enjoy what they are doing.**

This idea seems strange, but it's an essential part of the bravado. They relish their own performances and find a strange but heady pleasure in their enactment of the tragic role. It's there in Hamlet's words to his mother:

> But heaven hath pleased it so
> To punish me with this, and this with me,
> That I must be their scourge and minister.

(3.4.157–9)

The pleasure (meaning the will and authority to act) is not just heaven's (if it is at all); it's Hamlet's. It's a kind of punishment, but listen how the words swell with pride as the role of 'scourge and minister' rolls off the tongue.

One of the reasons tragedy is a terrifying thing is that we are keenly aware of their pleasure: we know they are wrong, and we sense the depth of their error as we thrill to their courageous energy and joy.

18.11 Fortune and tragedy

▶ 'O, I am fortune's fool' (*Romeo and Juliet*, 3.1.136)

In Shakespeare we always have to make qualifications; he isn't writing plays according to a single formula called 'Tragedy'.

Not every tragic figure can be defined as someone pursuing an end. Some give the impression that they are being pursued, that, to use a word that doesn't appear in Shakespeare, they are victims. Romeo pursues Juliet, but once Tybalt is dead he becomes, as he proclaims, the fool of fortune.

Fortune

Fortune was the idea that uncertainty was built into the way things are. Fortune stands for what is unexpected. Perhaps rather oddly it was imagined to work like a wheel; once you were on it you were carried round. If you started at the top, you might end at the bottom.

The pattern of a play can be read in these terms. In *Julius Caesar*, Caesar starts near the top but plunges with the turn of the wheel to his death (see 26.1).

Villains

Another way in which a tragic figure becomes a victim is through the malice of a villain. Someone in a high position can be brought low through plotting. This is the case in *Othello*. The plot requires someone who coldly hates and ingeniously plans to bring down the central figure.

Opposition

Sometimes a tragic figure is brought down by open opposition. This is the case in the Roman plays (perhaps better called the Roman tragedies). Brutus, Antony and Coriolanus all fall, suffer and die because in Antony, Augustus and the people of Rome and Corioli they meet implacable enemies.

Whose fault?

It makes sense to ask whether in any way they've contributed to what's happened. Did Romeo like the idea of being 'fortune's fool' and did Richard's own folly make him vulnerable? The case of Brutus is very interesting; each time there's a crisis, he overrules Cassius, and the consequences are disastrous. Why does he do this? Is it naïvety, is it pride, is it a kind of death wish?

▶ 'fall to the base earth' (*Richard II*, 2.4.20)

The fall

The fall of the tragic figure has been mentioned a number of times. According to one view of tragedy, it's the essential element. Writers in the middle ages looked upon tragedy in terms of a movement from prosperity to adversity. What mattered was the movement, not the state of mind of the one who fell.

The closest Shakespeare gets to such a plot is *King Lear*; Lear starts as king, but by the crisis of the play he's housed with someone who appears to be nothing but a mad beggar. Lear has fallen (almost literally to the base earth), and the fall is both visible and social.

Character and fall

Shakespeare's characters don't just fall 'externally'. What audiences are usually aware of is a change in their characters. Macbeth knows that he's a mere husk of the man he was. The autumnal imagery expresses his sense that the best of his life has passed away:

> My way of life
> Is fall'n into the sere, the yellow leaf

(5.3.24–5)

'Sere' means dry and withered, and the word 'yellow' here stands for the faded colour of late autumn leaves. That's the state of Macbeth's mind – jaded, worn, life-less, fallen.

The fall and understanding

Audiences usually feel that however important the movement of the fall is, there's more to it than that. Something usually happens to the tragic figure. The point can be put in this way:

- **as the tragic figure falls, there's a rise in understanding.**

It's possible to see patterns at work here: the rise in understanding corresponds to the fall, an outer disaster is matched by an inner learning, as worldly influence declines, the inner person is strengthened.

Richard II loses his kingdom but gains himself. In the first part of the play, he's frivolous and irresponsible; in the second half he becomes aware of his vulnerable humanity and sheds the illusions he had about himself. The actor playing the part must achieve this in a single scene; in Act 3, Scene 2 he must present a man who loses a kingdom and starts to find himself.

The failure to understand

But Shakespeare doesn't always work in this way. Shakespeare knows he can draw all sorts of patterns in his art, but he knows as well that the neat patterns of art don't always correspond with the messiness of life. Suffering can enoble people, but it doesn't always. The painful thing about watching tragedy is:

- **we want the central character to learn and grow but have to recognise that either the learning is fitful or that there's neither growth nor learning.**

Does Othello learn? His final speech can be read as no different from the boasting he's done throughout the play. And nor does tragic suffering always bring a reward. Lear has a strong sense that there might be compensation for his sufferings. At the end he puts the point with painful clarity. Bending over Cordelia's body he says:

> She lives. If it be so,
> It is a chance that does redeem all sorrows
> That ever I have felt.
>
> (5.3.240–2)

We are prepared to believe that this is true, but Cordelia is dead.

18.13 Isolation and inevitability

▶ **'The way to dusty death'** (*Macbeth*, 5.5.22)

The twofold movement

Shakespeare's tragedies clearly demonstrate what was said in 3.8 about the movement of plots:

- **there is a double movement, the first to the crisis the second to the resolution.**

The crisis is reached when the effects of the defiant act are realized. The act might bring power and glory, but the audience will usually see in it the beginning of the figure's destruction.

The resolution is often reached with an accelerating movement accompanied by suffering. When death comes it's both expected and, in terms of the plot movement, satisfying.

Isolation

- **The tragedies work to isolate the central figure from the rest of the characters.**

The particular kind of isolation the plots bring out is usually related to the central figure's stepping beyond the limits of order and morality. By doing this, the figure is exposed as being different from the rest of the people, who either keep within the bounds of what is permitted or don't flaunt their violation of the moral law with theatrical hubris. Once Hamlet decides to be a revenger, he's cut himself off from most of the other characters.

Isolation and the audience

A consequence of this isolation is that the central figure moves closer to the audience. As a general rule, the following is true:

- **audiences are closer to characters in tragedies than they are to those in comedies.**

In comedies, a certain distance is necessary because we need to keep up with the complexity of the plot and to keep track of the large number of characters. In tragedies the plot is simpler and the focus is on the central figure. As the figure is cut off from others, the audience is the body to whom he increasingly turns. Hence, the importance of soliloquies.

Inevitability and responsibility

In tragedy, the impression is sometimes created that events are, in different ways, independent of the will of the characters. The issue of how responsible we are is debated in *Julius Caesar*; Cassius takes the view that we are in charge of our destinies, while Brutus holds to the image of 'a tide in the affairs of men', which, if we take at the fullest swell, 'leads on to fortune' (4.2.272–3).

18.14 Horror and pity

▶ 'Howl, howl, howl, howl!' (*King Lear*, 5.3.232)

To talk about the closeness of the audience and the feeling that events might be inevitable is to recognise the very special place the audience has in tragedies.

Passivity

Although in many ways audiences are active (they certainly do a lot of thinking), the point about them is that they watch and applaud. This can be painful in tragedy, particularly when we become close to the central character. We can listen, we can sigh, we can shed tears, but there's nothing that we can *do* about the events that are unfolding before us.

Pity

This is why:

• **the response of pity is important in tragedy.**

Pity is that feeling of concern which recognises someone's unhappy state. It might lead us to do something, but it would still be pity if we were unable to act. Pity arises because the audience is close to the characters. We pity the characters because they matter to us. I once heard someone criticise a production of *Romeo and Juliet*, because it didn't make the audience care enough.

Horror

Lear's 'howls' speak for us. Tragedy is about what we can't say and what we'd rather not think. The immensity of the universe and the littleness though importance of what people feel wrings out of us that feeling of horror that's so often associated with tragedy.

The horror is seen as much as it's said. The impact of the stage is vital here. To witness the anguish of the characters and see their deaths has an impact it's difficult (but not impossible) to get from the words on the page.

Questions

The horror we experience gives rise to those questions we associate with tragedies – the big questions of why people suffer (*Lear*), why wills are evil (*Othello*), and why people have responsibilities they can't bear (*Hamlet*). People often leave the theatre with lots of questions in their minds.

Serenity

But it's also the experience of audiences that there's serenity at the end. In spite of the horrors, they feel that their minds have been enlarged and stilled. The Greek philosopher, Aristotle, called this '**catharsis**', and the name has stuck. There are three elements to this stilling of the mind.

- Audiences feel calmer because they've followed through the plot to its close. The fact of seeing a work of art unfold satisfies the expectations it has aroused. The form of the play brings consolation.
- The passions that we've seen aroused have followed their natural course, and witnessing the entire course of the feeling brings satisfaction.
- If tragedy is about finding a significance in mortal life, then the emergence of a meaning or an importance in what happens to us has a healing effect.

Tragedy is always painful, is always about unanswerable questions. Nevertheless, the experience of audiences is that while it might be devastating – it's not depressing.

Exercises

18.1 Think about Shakespeare's tragic plays in the light of the view that tragedy is our most serious attempt to come to terms with death.

18.2 What are the different kinds of division and disorder in Shakespeare's tragedies?

18.3 Try to account for why audiences find tragic figures both admirable and deplorable.

18.4 In what ways does Shakespeare present his central figures as theatrically acting out their own tragic falls?

18.5 'The horror of tragic plots is their simplicity.' Is this a helpful way of talking about how audiences respond to tragic plays?

18.6 'The audience feels that tragic figures are towering and outstanding individuals and yet they feel very close to them.' How does Shakespeare make it possible for audiences to feel this way?

Romeo and Juliet

19.1 Youth and passion

▶ **'never was a story of more woe' (5.3.308)**

As the Prince says at the end of the play, there's no sadder story than Romeo and Juliet. Here are two young lives cut short; moreover, the two lovers did no obvious wrong. Even though we are led into seeing the events from the viewpoint of the lovers (we want what they want), it's possible to imagine it all from the perspective of the parents and the Prince. This is the function of the final scene; this was a tragedy for two families as well as two people, and a whole city as well as the two families.

Youthfulness

Romeo and Juliet is full of young people. There's Romeo and his friends – young men with money, status, the freedom to wander, to fight, to dream about girls and to take risks by visiting the enemy camp. They have about them the chic of youth – its impudence, its daring, its confidence and its swagger.

There are fewer young women, and one of them – the dream woman, Rosaline – never appears; but Juliet is alive enough – passionate, energetic and sensual.

Passion

Feelings run high throughout the play. There's a lightness and energy about the merry camaraderie of the young men. Listen to Benvolio and Mercutio looking for Romeo:

> *Benvolio:* He ran this way, and leapt this orchard wall.
>   Call, good Mercutio.
> *Mercutio*: Nay, I'll conjure too.
>   Romeo! Humours! Madman! Passion! Lover!

> (2.1.5–7)

Benvolio evokes Romeo's passion in saying that he leapt the wall, and in a mockery which is never unkind Mercutio ransacks popular beliefs about the strangeness of love and merrily turns them into alternative names for Romeo. We can see in the language that life is a game.

Perhaps though the fiercest feelings come not in the great love duets (for instance, 2.1.91–180) but in the moments when they are alone. Before the duet of Act 2,

Scene 1 Juliet has the speech that contains the famous words about the name of a rose not affecting its scent. That speech begins:

'Tis but thy name that is my enemy.
Thou art thyself, though not a Montague.

(2.1.80–1)

There's no deliberate forcing of passion, no sense of trying out an emotion (something we all have to do); what's there is the sense of someone passionately working out an important meaning for the first time.

19.2 The comic elements

▶ 'And if thou dar'st, I'll give thee remedy' (4.1.76)

Those words could have come from a comedy. This is not surprising:

- **the plot of *Romeo and Juliet* has a lot in common with comedy.**

The role of Friar Lawrence is that of a comic practiser; he devises a clever scheme to bring about the happy ending that the audience wants.

Another comic element is the ball. Romeo's decision to risk going because Rosaline is there is again the kind of stratagem that the young use in comedies to further their aims.

The plot is chiefly comic in its presentation of a bar, imposed by the older generation on the young. The energy of the young, as in most comedies, is directed at getting round restrictions laid down by the older generation.

If the play had ended happily, the audience wouldn't have been surprised.

19.3 Verona divided

▶ 'The quarrel is between our masters and us their men' (1.1.18)

After the solemn and elevated rhetoric of the Prologue, the play explodes in civil strife – the followers of the Capulets and the Montagues brawl in the street. The words of Gregory above show us that the antagonism is long-established. It has no cause; they quarrel because they quarrel!

There's nothing tired, however, about the brawl. Shakespeare makes the insults bawdy, and this gives a lively, youthful quality to the dialogue. When Sampson say: 'Draw, if you be men' (1.1.59), we know that street fighting is a test of manhood; the aggressive wordplay blends sex and violence. The two great themes of Shakespeare – love and war – are acted out before us. We see war and we hear it spoken about in terms of sexuality.

19.4 Tybalt and hatred

▶ 'the fiery Tybalt' (1.1.106)

It's difficult to imagine Tybalt existing outside the civil strife of Verona. The conflict makes him what he is. He unquestionably accepts that war between the Houses is the right way of life and he hates the alternative. He enters the play when the sensible Benvolio is trying to bring the brawl to an end. His first words are a scornful and snobbish challenge:

> What, drawn and talk of peace? I hate the word
> As I hate hell, all Montagues, and thee.

(1.1.87–8)

He can't think there's any other purpose to drawing a sword than fighting.

It's worth while asking why Tybalt is given such prominence. The reason is that it's Shakespeare's way of showing that, among other things,

- **this is a social tragedy.**

Tybalt is locked into a way of life that brings about his own death. The lovers are locked into the same world.

19.5 The Nurse

▶ **'these sorrows make me old' (3.2.89)**

The Nurse is the most enjoyable character in the play. Her frequent remarks about how tired she is provide a welcome relief from the helter-skelter of youthful passion. She acts as a reminder that all passion is eventually spent.

The characterisation of the Nurse is very detailed. She talks a lot; using prose and a very easy, conversational verse. Her talk is colloquial, anecdotal, bawdy, teasing and marked by repetitions. These repetitions give the impression that she's old and well established in the household.

Her love for Juliet seems entirely genuine, and maybe because she's a servant she doesn't press Juliet overmuch with family responsibilities. When she sees Juliet is obviously in love with Romeo, she simply says 'hie you hence to Friar Lawrence' cell' (2.4.68).

The Nurse's role

Within the design of the play, she has a number of important functions. She's the confidante of Juliet, and so is parallel to Friar Lawrence. She's a woman who's seen how passion drives the young, so she raises the question of whether she should have exercised a restraining influence on the lovers. One of the difficulties with the play is that the 'guardian' figures – herself and Friar Lawrence – don't control the lovers or, in her case, lets them down. When she advises Juliet to marry Paris, she not only shows she's not much sense of what marriage is, but also she's no idea how deep Juliet's love for Romeo goes.

19.6 Mercutio and language

▶ **'thou talk'st of nothing' (1.4.96)**

Mercutio

If the Nurse is the most down to earth character in the play, Mercutio is the most dazzling. He's a very confident, clever young man, who expresses his masculinity in glittering language.

He can be scornful and bawdy (what else can we expect from a clever young man?). He enjoys the racy language of the streets; he calls Tybalt 'Prince of cats' (2.3.18), he mocks the Petrarchan conventions that he sees Romeo following (2.3.35–43) and he bawdily jokes about 'a great natural that runs lolling up and down to hide his bauble in a hole' (2.3.84–5).

The Queen Mab speech

But in the Queen Mab speech he does something else – paints in words with the delicacy and impudent skill of an Elizabethan miniaturist. As with so much Shakespeare, we have to *hear* the flood of words:

> Her wagon spokes made of long spinner's legs;
> The cover, of the wings of grasshoppers;
> Her traces, of the moonshine's watery beams;
> Her collars, of the smallest spider web

> (1.4.60–3)

He spins the words with an awareness of how important the succession of sounds is; think how satisfying 'long spinner's legs' is to the ear.

Mercutio is an observer, a commentator and an artist who steps back from the rush of life to produce art which is cool and slightly impersonal. In this he's a living comment on the impetuous Romeo. And he's needed. Romeo in both of his lover's guises is sometimes difficult to take.

Mercutio's death

The irony is that Mercutio dies when he gets involved. Shakespeare ensures that Mercutio is unaware of how the plot has developed. This leads to the ghastly mistake of Mercutio's death. Romeo is married, but no one knows. Because he's married to Juliet he's related to Tybalt, so isn't going to be provoked by senseless insults. Mercutio thinks this is 'vile submission' (3.1.72), so fights and is killed. What is to be made of his dying words?

> A plague o' both your houses.
> They have made worms' meat of me.

> (3.1.106–7)

Is this one of those things that the audience feel needs to be said? From his slightly distanced perspective, Mercutio can say that the dispute is absurd. Is he right to protest or is it wrong of him to make his last words to his friend a curse?

19.7 The love scenes

▶ 'my heart's dear love' (2.2.57)

Rosaline

Rosaline is the most prominent example of that very interesting group of the characters – the ones we never meet. She's Romeo's Petrarchan mistress: a great beauty who's vowed not to love (1.1.205–21). Rosaline is significant because of what Romeo feels, not because of what she's like. Some have wondered whether they've even met.

Because nothing is known of her character, Mercutio enjoys joking about her. The point of his bawdy joking is that whatever she is, she's certainly a woman, hence his merry jests about her beautiful body:

> By her fine foot, straight leg, and quivering thigh,
> And the demesnes that there adjacent lie

> (2.1.19–20)

Three further things need to be said about her:

- Romeo feels leaden ('I have a soul of lead' – 1.4.15) with his love for her; when he meets Juliet, he leaps over the orchard wall.
- She anticipates Juliet not only as an object of love but as a Capulet (1.2.69–70).
- If Juliet had lived, might she too have been a passing phase in Romeo's love-history?

We want to say 'No' to the last question, but this might only show the very strong hold that love ending in death has upon audiences.

The love sonnet

Shakespeare stages the meeting of Romeo and Juliet to bring out the themes of love and war; their words of love immediately follow Tybalt's of hate. The presence of the two men on the crowded stage also anticipates the crisis of the play – Romeo killing Tybalt.

The merriment of the dance and the hatred of Tybalt contrast with the finely turned love sonnet (1.5.92–104), which forms their first dialogue. Sonnets (poems of 14 lines and an intricate rhyme scheme) were Italian in origin and were often about love.

Petrarch wrote sonnets, and what's exchanged in dialogue between them is pretty Petrarchan – lovers are pilgrims, and beloveds the saints whose shrines they travel to worship at. (See 1.10 and 2.11.)

What's the effect of this? Poetry (art) expresses love (nature). Most people begin with raw feeling and try to raise it the level of art. *Romeo and Juliet* starts with what most have to struggle for. Shakespeare might be suggesting two things:

- **although their love is brief they reach a perfect balance of form and feeling**;
- **love that is so finely turned can only exist in the form of isolated moments; this means it couldn't exist in the everyday world**.

The orchard

In Shakespeare's day the orchard scene (Act 2, Scene 1) would have been performed with Romeo on the stage and the boy playing Juliet on the balcony. There is, therefore, no physical contact.

Shakespeare is depending on the audience recognising the convention that whatever is spoken by a character who is unaware that anybody else is on stage must be true. We must also assume that Romeo believes that, and so hears that she thinks he has in himself 'that dear perfection' (2.1.88). She says what she feels, and he hears what he wants to hear.

What troubles Juliet is the social and political nature of love. In this she's different from Romeo. He's only said one thing about love across the Montague–Capulet divide (1.5.117); it's left to her to work out that social divisions need not prevent love, because the beloved's name – a social indicator – 'is no part of thee' (2.1.90).

Juliet takes the lead. She asks: 'dost thou love me?' (2.1.132). She also proposes marriage (2.1.184–90). She's very like the comic heroine who ventures into danger for love. Throughout the play she's determined and decisive. Romeo, by contrast, is still playing the role of the lover. When he insists on swearing to confirm his love, Juliet is much more sensible: 'Do not swear at all' (2.1.154).

While he poses, she's aware that what she's doing isn't an act. She says she knows she ought to 'frown, and be perverse, and say thee nay' (2.1.138), because that's what beloveds do. But since he's heard her 'true-love passion' (2.1.146), all she can say is that he won't think her yielding is due to 'light love' (2.1.147).

Shakespeare seems keen to bring out that this love is deeply felt. He does this through a dialogue towards the end in which she admits that 'I have forgot why I did call there back' (2.1.215). This is what we want to see; the artless admission that her heart and head are so full, she can't control her thoughts:

> I shall forget, to have thee still stand there,
> Rememb'ring how I love thy company.

> (2.1.217–18)

That's real, natural and even embarrassingly common.

Juliet's passion

Shakespeare chooses to show sexual desire more fully present in Juliet than Romeo. This is most evident in her soliloquy, anticipating her wedding night (3.2.1–31). It opens with a conventional symbol of desire – galloping horses – and openly talks of the act of love as a game played 'for a pair of stainless maidenhoods' (3.2.13). She coaxingly says 'Come night, come Romeo' (3.2.17), and gives the elevated Petrarchan language of light and love as a religion a distinctly sexual twist:

> Lovers can see to do their amorous rites
> By their own beauties

> (3.2.8–9)

What Shakespeare gives Juliet is the intense sexual longing of a young girl in love and a maturity concerning the place of love in life. Juliet knows that sex is right. She has an an extraordinary image of the dark night as a matron, who will conceal her in darkness till what she does in darkness will become what befits a married lady:

> till strange love grown bold
> Think true love acted simple modesty.

> (3.2.15–16)

She wants the act of love to be a natural part of her life, not something that has to be hidden.

In her exploration of the language of love she plays upon the word 'die'. In Shakespeare's day, this had the additional meaning of sexual consummation. This sense is behind

> Give me my Romeo, and when I shall die
> Take him and cut him out in little stars

> (3.2.21–2)

The meaning must be that dying is her orgasm. What we may also note is the eerie juxtaposition of love and death (see 19.9).

The parting

The parting scene is brief; Romeo exits at line 59. They are together again only in the tomb.

This is the most convincing of all their scenes, because it's rather trivial, they spend most of it playing a game about whether the bird they can hear is a nightingale or a lark. This triviality makes the scene convincing. At the end of the orchard scene Juliet says 'parting is such sweet sorrow' (2.1.229), and so it is to those who know they'll meet again. But Romeo is going into banishment. It's not surprising that at such moments – the last goodbyes – there's nothing much to say. It's like going to war; the thought that they may never meet again so fills the mind that the tongue can only speak trivia.

19.8 Coping with banishment

▶ 'I must be gone and live, or stay and die' (3.5.11)

Banishment and elopement

That is how Romeo sums up his dilemma. He's been banished from Verona and must go to Mantua.

What's interesting is that neither of the lovers think of doing what everyone in a comedy would immediately do – elope. When they plan their marriage, she says:

> And follow thee, my lord, throughout the world.

> (2.1.190)

But neither of them thinks of eloping. It might be because of family pressure, or that because Friar Lawrence hasn't suggested it, Romeo wouldn't do it. More convincing is that elopement is not in keeping with Romeo's chosen role. He decides he's 'fortune's fool' (3.1.136), and that's the part he's going to play with energetic relish.

19.9 Love and death

▶ 'Here in the dark to be his paramour' (5.3.105)

Like opera and much literature, *Romeo and Juliet* is

● **a story of love and death**.

This note is first struck by the Chorus:

> The fearful passage of their death-marked love

> (Prologue, 9)

'Death-marked' can mean both marked by death and marked out for death. Romeo and Juliet have marked out their passage towards their goal – death.

The inseparability of desire and death surfaces in the first scene. The servants jeer at each other in sexual and military terms. On a symbolic level, this link blights Romeo in the crisis of Act 3, Scene 1; as a married man his libido should be reserved for his wife, but the death of his friend makes him use the weapon of violence.

By the time he comes to part from Juliet, the Petrarchan language of lover's parting as a kind of death is beginning to feel more of a reality than an image. He outlandishly says:

> Come, death, and welcome; Juliet wills it so.

> (3.5.24)

and she has a kind of vision of Romeo 'dead in the bottom of a tomb' (3.5.56).

When they do meet in the tomb, Romeo sees that Juliet is death's bride:

> Shall I believe
> That unsubstantial death is amorous,
> And that the lean abhorred monster keeps
> Thee here in dark to be his paramour.

> (5.3.102–5)

There may be irony here at Romeo's expense; death in this play is anything but 'unsubstantial', it's a very solid presence.

19.10 Their tragedy

▶ 'now at once run on/The dashing rocks' (5.3.117–18)

In the light of the interweaving of love and death, it may be possible to say something about the nature of their tragedy. There are a number of strands to it.

Verona

Romeo is banished to Mantua, but given the situation in Verona, it's hard to see a future for the lovers.

Impetuosity

One of the functions of Friar Lawrence is to signal this in the marriage scene:

> These violent delights have violent ends

> (2.5.9)

In the light of the fact that violent love can turn to violent loathing, he advises 'love moderately' (2.5.14). This is impossible for Romeo.

The death wish

Throughout the play there's the image of a perilous sea journey. In the orchard scene Romeo says that although 'I am no pilot ... I should adventure' (2.1.124–6). His death speech sees him as the 'desperate pilot' steering towards the 'dashing rocks' (5.3.116–18).

Fate

This wilful element, the element of the death-wish, should be balanced by the hints of fate. Friar Lawrence says that Romeo is 'wedded to calamity' (3.3.3).

Youth

We should resist turning the play into a theory about human life, so rather than deciding for one or any of these ideas, we shall merely point to another:

- **Romeo and Juliet are young.**

Their youth might help to make sense of some of the other elements. Romeo is impetuous and Juliet has that decisiveness that goes with a narrow experience of life.

The attraction of death is something that afflicts the young. (That classic number of the teenage death-wish, 'Leader of the Pack' by the Shangri-Las, is still played on the radio.) Fate is present in that things are against them, but in choosing not to elope, it looks as if they too willingly play the role of the 'star-crossed lovers' (Prologue, 6). Their tragedy might simply be that they are young.

Exercises

19.1   Do you agree that Juliet is a far more interesting character than Romeo?

19.2   What exactly should an audience feel at the end of *Romeo and Juliet* and why?

---

20 Hamlet

20.1 Asking questions

▶ 'Who's there?' (1.1.1)

In the opening scene the soldiers do something fundamental to the play:

- **they ask questions.**

Appropriately, the very first line is in this form; one guard hears a noise and makes the customary challenge. By the end of the play one character, Hamlet, believes that all that happens is within the providence of God (5.2.165), so possibly the question is bigger than the guard thinks. Is there anybody there watching this violent human drama with the compassion of a creator?

What chiefly matters is that the play starts with a question. Questions are only asked when people are uncertain. This is the world of *Hamlet*:

- **a world in which there are many unanswered questions.**

Answerable and unanswerable questions

Some of the questions can be answered. The guards ask why they are on patrol, and Horatio is able to provide an answer. Later the King wants to know where Polonius' body is, and he gets an answer from Hamlet.

Other questions can't be answered easily. Is the Ghost to be believed? Hamlet at first expresses no doubt, but later he feels he has to test what the Ghost has said.

Our questions

The characters ask questions; and so do we. In *Hamlet* Shakespeare turns a subject of drama – characters asking questions – into the way in which the drama itself works. The play provokes audiences to ask questions, such as 'is Hamlet really mad?'

The point about this question is that Shakespeare has not given the audience any real advantage over the other characters. We know that Hamlet said he would put on 'an antic disposition' (1.5.173), but we're no better off than the rest of the characters in knowing whether or not he's pretending to be mad or is actually so.

Shakespeare has taken something we all do – ask questions – and turned it into a theme of his play and the very way in which the drama works.

▶ 'this post-haste and rummage in the land' (1.1.106)

The world of politics

The first two scenes sketch out the external threat of Fortinbras. As the play unfolds, we see that he is one of Hamlet's doubles (Laertes is another) – both are nephews and both are seeking to revenge their fathers. One of the unexpected aspects of the play is that Fortinbras eventually inherits Denmark.

We also see the politics of the court: Claudius thanks his courtiers for helping him to the throne (1.2.14–16); he employs Rosencrantz and Guildenstern to find out what Hamlet's up to, and Polonius acts as a spy-master, feeding information back to the King. The atmosphere of the court is close, conspiratorial and secretive. Shakespeare achieves this by showing how its politics are based on suspicion.

Politics and seeing

When Claudius and Polonius overlook Ophelia's arranged encounter with Hamlet, they describe themselves as 'lawful espials' (3.1.34). They assume that what they see will be the truth. But is it? Hamlet has already pointed out to the court that there's a difference between how things seem and how they are (1.2.76–86). Seeing is not believing. If it were, the politics of *Hamlet* would be much easier to cope with.

Politics, seeing and morality

The uncertainty of seeing extends to morality. If a character suspects that another is spying on him or her, there can be no trust. Without trust, relationships are poisoned (an important image in the play). Hamlet poisons whatever feeling existed between himself and Ophelia. We shouldn't forget that after his tirade against her in Act 3, Scene 1 when he accuses her of conventional female faults – vanity, infidelity – and the play scene in which his language to her is openly bawdy, the next time we see her, she's mad. She's been destroyed by the lack of trust that marks the Danish court.

▶ 'hearsed in death' (1.4.28)

Death haunts the play. The word turns up more often than in any other tragedy with the interesting exception of *Romeo and Juliet*. It's visible in the Ghost who's 'hearsed in death' (1.4.28), in Hamlet's mourning clothes, in the mourning the court adopted for Ophelia and the grave in which she's buried and in which Hamlet fights. At the end, there are four bodies on the stage.

Death and uncertainty

Death raises the issue of uncertainty. At one point Hamlet says that no one would suffer the pains of life:

But that the dread of something after death,
The undiscovered country from whose bourn
No traveller returns, puzzles the will

(3.1.80–3)

The language is convincingly imprecise; he can't know what awaits him, so he calls it 'something', and then adds that there are no traveller's tales from that region. The 'will' – the impulse to act or not to act – is 'puzzled'. In Shakespeare's day this meant disorientated and bewildered. Hamlet's point is that our bewilderment about death leads to a bewilderment about life. We can't be certain about either.

Hamlet and death

Because Hamlet is the central character, we tend to regard what he says as the truth about the play. Not only, of course, is this against the nature of drama (characters only represent their own point of view), but it's against the way the play calls into question all we feel sure about.

Given that we don't have to believe Hamlet, we have to ask:

- **is the world of *Hamlet* one of death or is it only the Prince who thinks like that?**

An extreme reading is that the play presents a death-obsessed young man, whose morbid imagination distorts his judgement about everything and everyone. This argument interprets the second scene as showing a merry court celebrating a wedding and engaging in difficult foreign negotiations in marked contrast to Hamlet, who persists in mourning.

But in a play in which the chief problem is perspective, audiences might see the court as callous and frivolous and regard the King and Queen's interest in Hamlet not as concern but arising from either annoyance or suspicion. We might also observe that death is a fact in this play, and that at least Hamlet tries to think about it.

20.4 How the plot works

▶ **'if the King like not the comedy' (3.2.80)**

But on the stage, *Hamlet*, for all its brooding on death, is a play that pulses with life. What we see is a series of exciting incidents – a ghost, spying, the arrival of players, a play that's interrupted, the death of Polonius, a fight in a grave and finally the most exciting swordfight in English theatre. This is a play that buzzes with life.

The plot

Hamlet moves swiftly and easily; we remain in a constant state of eager expectation as one event overlaps with another. A friend of mine once said that in a good production the audience should say: 'perhaps he'll get away with it this time'.

What is it that keeps us on the edge of our seats? One answer is:

- **in *Hamlet* the issues of tragedy are expressed in dramatic forms more associated with comedy.**

Hamlet might have been called *Measure for Measure* or *Much Ado About Everything*. The characters plot against each other with characteristic comic ingenuity, energy and confidence.

Practising

Practising occurs at the beginning and the end. The Ghost would be a comic practiser if it weren't for the fact that he's a ghost. Instead, he employs Hamlet to carry out the revenge for him. If *Hamlet* is a problem play, as has been claimed, then the action subverts the practiser in the way in which it does in *Measure for Measure*. The Ghost picks the wrong man; he'd have had much better results if he'd chosen, say, Laertes!

The final piece of plotting is entirely the King's work, and there's something exhilarating about the way it all goes wrong, even though Hamlet is quite unprepared and therefore can't counter the knavery. Significantly, the word associated with comic plotting – 'practice' – is used twice in the scene. It refers to fencing, but then fencing is a metaphor for what happens in the plot.

Knowledge

A further point about the links between the plot and the comedies depends on the point that the currency of comedy is knowledge, (see 5.15).

- **Knowledge is what all the main characters in *Hamlet* are after.**

Shakespeare has produced a set of plot devices to explore the problem (the tragic problem?) of having to make life-and-death decisions in a world where no one can be certain.

20.5 Hamlet the thinker

▶ 'Now I am alone' (2.2.550)

Hamlet has an intellectual *élan*; that's to say, his thought is swift, light, easy and has a charismatic dash. Listen to the way his mind moves:

> To die, to sleep.
> To sleep, perchance to dream. Ay, there's the rub,
> For in that sleep of death what dreams may come
> When we have shuffled off this mortal coil
> Must give us pause.

(3.1.66–70)

This starts in an exploratory manner. One thought leads by way of poetic association to another. Hamlet knows that in poetry sleep is a metaphor for death. In his thought, sleep leads on to dreams, and then there's that moment so characteristic of Hamlet, the penny drops – 'Ay' – and the conclusion floods his mind in two and a half unimpeded lines. (Illustration 6)

We might not approve of what Hamlet does, we might not agree with what he says, but the way he thinks – its speed, honesty, grittiness, ease and energy – must surely command both our attention and admiration.

Illustration 6   Hamlet in solioquy

20.6 Hamlet and revenge

▶ 'revenge his foul and most unnatural murder' (1.5.25)

Revenge

We must ask:

- is *Hamlet* actually a revenge play?

The best way to approach this question is through looking at what Shakespeare does with the story he's inherited.

Hamlet was an old tale, in which a young prince denied the throne takes revenge upon the man who's killed his father, married his mother and prevented the prince from gaining power. This crucial question is:

- how does Shakespeare present this story of revenge?

We must notice four things:

(1) Hamlet never questions that it's his duty to revenge his father;
(2) Hamlet is such a powerful stage figure that the audience is inclined to think about everything from his point of view;
(3) Hamlet is an intellectual who thinks throughout the play;
(4) Throughout the play there are four other revenger figures – Fortinbras, Laertes, Pyrrhus in the player's speech, and in the play, Lucianus.

Revenge and the audience

We see in the four revengers men of blood who have no moral hesitation about what they are doing. Shakespeare shows us these figures to make us ask:

- can revenge be anything other than thoughtless, cold and bloody?

Think about what they do.

(1) Fortinbras marches thousands of soldiers to what Hamlet thinks is certain death (4.4.6–20).
(2) Laertes is prepared to revenge himself by trickery; he even says he'd 'cut his throat i'th' church' (4.7.99).
(3) In the player's speech, Pyrrhus is 'horribly tricked/With blood of fathers, mother, daughter, sons' (2.2.459–60).
(4) Lucianus in the play poisons a defenceless man with gleeful relish (3.2.243–8)

None of these characters think about what they're doing. Hamlet thinks about everything.

- Had he thought about these figures, would he have wanted to be like them?

The element that Shakespeare brings to the old story is that of Hamlet as thinker. But here he confronts us with an astonishing irony:

- Hamlet never fully sees that these horrific figures are what he would have to be like if he carried out the revenge.

For all his intellectual agility he never sees how dreadful revenge is, nor that he wouldn't be able to do it.

The revenge theme is where Shakespeare locates the tragedy of the play:

- **Hamlet wants to carry out a revenge which is impossible, because of the kind of person he is. We might see that; Hamlet never does.**

20.7 Remembering and forgetting

▶ 'It is, "Adieu, adieu, remember me"' (1.5.112)

Hamlet and memory

'Memory' appears nine times in *Hamlet* (more than in any other play) and there are also eight cases of 'remember' and five of 'remembrance'.

Remembering in a world that forgets

Hamlet remembers in a world that wants to forget. Or rather, in a state in which those in power try to control what people know and therefore what can be remembered.

In such states, people can only retain their dignity by remembering. They may not be able to do anything about what's happened, but as long as 'memory holds a seat/In this distracted globe' (1.5.96–7), they are not entirely slaves of the state. The Czech novelist Milan Kundera wrote a novel called *The Book of Laughter and Forgetting*, which shows that those who remember can laugh.

Shakespeare shows us something similar. One of the reasons why we might admire Hamlet is that he hangs on to what others forget. If anything in the play is heroic, it's Hamlet's refusal to let go a memory of what might be true. To remember is to retain integrity.

20.8 Ophelia's plight

▶ 'The fair Ophelia' (3.1.91)

Sex

Ophelia is introduced in the third scene. Both her brother and father are very concerned about her friendship with Hamlet; they tell her pretty bluntly that all he wants is sex. We can't dismiss this as merely the kind of thing over-protective brothers and fathers say. When they meet for the first time on stage, sex is one of the things that's obsessing Hamlet, and in the play scene he quibbles not very subtly about 'country matters' (3.2.111).

Why it goes wrong

One way of reading Hamlet and Ophelia is to see it as a love that's gone wrong. There are plenty of reasons available as to why it has.

• Gertrude

Those influenced by Freud see Gertrude as the crucial figure. If Hamlet feels deserted by his mother, he might take out his feelings of betrayal on Ophelia. Some of the things he accuses her of in Act 3, Scene 1 (adultery, for instance, lines 139–42) might apply to his mother but couldn't apply to her.

If a man's knowledge of women comes chiefly from his mother, then Hamlet's strong sense of betrayal, strengthened by the Ghost, might make him antagonistic to the other woman in his life. On the other hand, this is usually said of children, and Hamlet is old enough to be at university.

• Polonius

A more immediate cause might be Polonius ordering Ophelia not to receive visits from Hamlet. Hamlet is unhappy at the beginning and then, in the guise of being mad, takes on the role of revenger. We then hear that he burst into her room in a dishevelled state, took her hand, gazed at her and exited in a trance-like manner. If we want to understand Hamlet and Ophelia we might speculate that Hamlet is either distraught because Ophelia has refused to see him or that he realises he can't become further involved with her because that might distract him from his task.

• What might have been

At one point, we have a glimpse of what might have been. At her funeral, Hamlet, lacking all sense of decorum and propriety, interrupts with a protest against Laertes' equally squalid expression of feeling. However appalling their behaviour is, the fact that Hamlet is almost out of control suggests that his feelings are very strong:

> I loved Ophelia. Forty thousand brothers
> Could not, with all their quantity of love,
> Make up my sum

> (5.1.266–8)

There's the glimmering here of another plot. Might Ophelia have brought life into his death-engrossed imagination? Might we have seen, as in a comedy, a marriage which would have renewed the state of Denmark? Not only does Shakespeare give us a play of conflicting perspectives, he even gives us possible alternative plots.

20.9 The passions and Hamlet

▶ 'passion's slave' (3.2.70)

The passions

The passions are feelings such as anger, grief, lust and jealousy. Tragedy often deals with characters who are overcome by a passion, which is so strong that it destroys them.

In *Hamlet* a number of the characters are destroyed. According to the Ghost, it was lust that led to his murder. The passion of hatred consumes and destroys Laertes. Ophelia dies because her mind is deranged by grief.

What are we to make of this? The following argument is based on what Hamlet says. It's only his view; nevertheless, it does make some sense of this issue.

Hamlet and passion

Hamlet experiences a number of the passions: he grieves, is jealous of his mother and hates Claudius:

> Bloody, bawdy villain!
> Remorseless, treacherous, lecherous, kindless villain!

> (2.2.581–2)

When, therefore, Hamlet talks about passion, he does so from experience. The crucial speech is the intimate one he delivers to his friend Horatio.

What he singles out in Horatio is his emotional poise – 'blood and judgement are so well commingled' (3.2.67). This is something that Hamlet – a man afflicted by tempestuous passions – values:

> Give me that man
> That is not passion's slave, and I will wear him
> In my heart's core

> (3.2.69–71)

Too many characters are slaves to passion. Hamlet might have been one of them. The important question is:

- **does Hamlet resist being overwhelmed by passion?**

Act 5 is crucial. When Hamlet returns from the sea, he's more serene, and in the final scene there's a philosophical calm about him. Speaking of the moment of death, he says with a religious detachment:

> If it be now, 'tis not to come.
> If it be not to come, it will be now. If it be not
> now, yet it will come. The readiness is all.

> (5.2.166–8)

If something will happen, but doesn't happen now, it follows that it must happen in the future. That's the simple logic of his argument. But it doesn't feel like a piece of logic-chopping; here is someone who can trust that the logic of language applies to the most fundamental facts of life. He caps his inference with a piece of spiritual wisdom – what matters is not when death comes but whether we are prepared for it. That must include whether one has resisted being 'passion's slave'.

Like everything in this play, it's possible to dispute that Hamlet is ready, but a case can be made out that at the end he's controlled (he sorts out who will succeed him) and prevents Horatio from giving way to sudden passion by stopping him committing suicide. Even the killings have the quality of ritual.

If Hamlet dies free from the passion that has destroyed those dying around him, then he has achieved something central to tragedy – become larger than the death that overtakes him.

Passion and art

Hamlet admires poise in art as well as in people. Before he talks to Horatio he says this to the player about the control of emotions:

> for in the very torrent, tempest, and as I may say the whirlwind of your passion, you must acquire and beget a temperance that may give it smoothness. (3.2.5–8)

The words associated with chaos in nature – torrent, tempest – are aspects of art because we need to feel in art the pressure of raw feelings. But feelings should never take over, so the player in the turmoil of tempestuous feelings must be temperate and smooth. Art should not be the slave of passion.

We might ask whether the play meets this demand. The argument that it does is that its exciting narrative doesn't prevent it from raising issues of considerable importance. In the heat of the story, the mind remains free to think about issues such as the morality of revenge.

20.10 Plays, players and playing

▶ 'Madam, how like you this play?' (3.2.218)

Hamlet is the most theatrical of all Shakespeare's plays. It's theatrical in a number of ways.

Symbolic moments

There are symbolic moments or 'tableaux' when the figures form a group that has a representative force. Three of them are:

- Hamlet killing Polonius through the arras
- Hamlet with drawn sword standing over the praying Claudius
- Hamlet holding Yorick's skull.

Does killing Polonius show us how squalid the passions of revenge are? Hamlet thinks it's the King, while we see the death of an old man. Hamlet standing above the kneeling Claudius is a figure of divine justice; but it's terrible hubris for anyone to think that he or she can carry out God's justice. Holding Yorick's skull is an encounter with what Hamlet has brooded on throughout the play – death.

'Play'

The words 'play' and 'player' in literal and figurative uses appear more in *Hamlet* than any other play. This forces on us the issue of the roles that characters choose to play. It might be clear to us that Hamlet shouldn't play the role of the revenger, but what is the part that a man in his situation should perform? That's something the play doesn't tell us. There's tragedy in this:

- **the only role he can play – the revenger – is one that he shouldn't play.**

The play-within-the-play

The Mousetrap invites us to think about audiences. An audience responds to what it sees. If the playwright is successful, the audience will think and feel as directed by the words and actions they hear and see. But the power of the playwright is not complete; there can't be absolute control of what an audience thinks and feels.

Hamlet imagines that he can control Claudius's reactions. He waits for Claudius's 'occulted guilt' (3.2.78) to show itself. Art can serve life. The theatrical presentation of a ghastly crime can make a real murder 'speak/With most miraculous organ' (2.2.594–5).

We have to ask whether the play does indeed 'catch the conscience of the King' (2.2.606). The King rises in distress, when the murderer does what the Ghost claimed Claudius did. Hamlet is convinced that the play has proved the King's guilt. Further support is that the next time we see Claudius, he's praying about what he's done.

Shakespeare, however, makes it possible for us to believe that Hamlet shouldn't have been so convinced. What Claudius sees is a *nephew* killing a King. Might he see the play as Hamlet threatening him? He doesn't know about messages passed by ghosts. Why should he think that Hamlet might have discovered the truth?

Being an audience is more complicated than Hamlet imagines.

20.11 Deciding about Hamlet

▶ 'Good night, sweet prince' (5.2.311)

- How is the character of Hamlet to be judged?
- How does he compare with the other characters of the play?

These are questions that audiences frequently ask.

Hamlet and the Ghost

The Ghost makes intolerable demands on Hamlet. Had this been a comedy, Hamlet would have found ways of deceiving the Ghost; the tragedy is that he tries to obey him. The play makes it clear that old Hamlet was a warrior king – in the first scene we hear that he challenged old Fortinbras of Norway to personal combat. Neither Hamlet nor the new world of the court is like that – the play ends with a fight, but it's conducted under the gentlemanly rules of fencing.

It's hard to avoid the impression of an authoritarian father out of touch (can ghosts be in touch?) and making demands that are morally hideous. Hamlet is at his worst when he's close to carrying out what the ghost demands.

Hamlet and Claudius

Politics and the treatment of Gertrude invite a comparison between Hamlet and Claudius. Claudius can't be faulted as a politician. Fortinbras wouldn't have behaved with the same confidence (even impudence) if Claudius had survived the final blood-bath. Fortinbras says that had he become king, he would have 'proved most royally' (5.2.352); but is there any evidence for that?

Claudius and Gertrude appear to be very happy with each other. A sign of his love is that he's prepared to shoulder the guilt of killing old Hamlet in order to hold on to his Queen (3.3.55). Hamlet's harshness in Act 3, Scene 4 is an expression of his anguish; can it be that he's not concerned with Gertrude at all?

Hamlet and Polonius

Both Hamlet and Polonius are concerned with Ophelia. It would be easy to say that her father is oppressive and out of sympathy with the young. This is true; what sort of father would use his daughter as bait in a political game? But is he any worse than Hamlet? Hamlet's tirade against her in Act 3, Scene 1 is horrible, more horrible than anything Polonius actually says, but at least Hamlet's not manipulating her. Ophelia is a victim of two men, both of whom treat her with exceptional cruelty.

A judgement?

Hamlet is morally questionable: his obsession with his mother, his imaginations of bloody revenge, his callous treatment of Ophelia, his desire not just to kill but to damn Claudius, his killing of Polonius, his killing of Rosencrantz and Guildenstern, his self-regarding outburst at Ophelia's funeral. He displays the hubris of the man who plays out his tragic role, bragging to his mother that he is heaven's 'scourge and minister' (3.4.159).

But he's a man in an impossible situation – the wrong man for the task of revenge and the man whose situation gives him no other role. He remains faithful; he remembers when everyone else forgets; he doesn't sink to the level of Laertes; he resists being passion's slave and he never stops thinking. He's an ambiguous figure, but what is tragedy without moral ambiguity?

20.12 Stories in the play

▶ 'To tell my story' (5.2.301)

Unfinished stories

The play opens with two unfinished stories – one about the appearance of the Ghost (1.1.33–7) and one about the preparations for war (1.1.69–106). At the end of the play, Hamlet is concerned that his story be told:

> in this harsh world draw thy breath in pain
> To tell my story.

> (5.2.300–1)

The story, like so many in Shakespeare, will be told in that strange twilight when the play is over; but we get a hint of what Horatio will say:

> So shall you hear
> Of carnal, bloody, and unnatural acts,
> Of accidental judgements, casual slaughters,
> Of deaths put on by cunning and forced cause;

> (5.2.334–7)

Horatio reduces the play to a melodramatic tale of blood. Where in that is the Hamlet who strove to remember and who tried to think through the significances of what he was doing?

Perhaps that's why Shakespeare opens the play with unfinished tales – it's a signal to the audience to join in by finishing what's been started. So at the end, the story of Hamlet is handed over to us; we're asked to complete it, to tell Hamlet's story.

20.1 What is it about *Hamlet* that makes audiences and readers ask so many questions about it?

20.2 Do you think that Hamlet is in any sense an admirable character?

20.3 Why is *Hamlet* so popular on the stage?

21 Othello

21.1 The response of the audience

▶ 'The object poisons sight' (5.2.374)

Othello *and the audience*

I once heard a story of a lady who went to see *Othello* and found it so painful that she got up and shouted: 'you stupid fool, can't you see he's having you on!' This reaction is entirely understandable:

- *Othello* **is the most painful tragedy to watch.**

The audience is in the uncomfortable position of feeling that it's being poisoned.

Iago's power

Iago has more soliloquies than Othello. These soliloquies have power partly from how they are placed – at the ends of the third, fourth and sixth scenes. In each he plots the action; whatever happens, Iago is there to guide events.

His soliloquies are public. He tells us openly what he wants to do. For most of the play, everything happens exactly as Iago planned. This is how the poison works:

- **he takes us into his confidence, so we become his passive accomplices.**

We watch the writhings of Othello in the knowledge given to us by Iago. As a result, we not only share his knowledge but are led into sharing his viewpoint. It's not surprising that many students take to Iago; the play is designed to lead us into that trap.

The passive audience

The point is:

- **in *Othello* we are pained by our inability to act.**

There must have been many people who when watching *Othello* wished they weren't in a theatre. The agony of watching *Othello* is that of seeing the plot move with its terrible, inevitable momentum, knowing all the while that we, who know enough to stop it, can't.

Audiences react with frustration and anger against Othello: why can't he see? why is he so trusting of Iago? why can't he believe his wife? Again, I've known students who've been hostile to Othello because they find him so stupid.

What's interesting about this reaction is that Shakespeare knows how to cope with it. Our frustration is given a voice. When Emilia realises what's happened she says what many in the audience might have wanted to say:

> O gull, O dolt,
> As ignorant as dirt!
>
> (5.2.170–1)

Her outburst might be ours; we're relieved that someone has said it.

But we have to reckon with the possibility that Shakespeare allows us this way of airing our frustration only to make us think again. Is Othello just a dolt, just ignorant as dirt? We might also want to give a place to Cassio's judgement: 'for he was great of heart' (5.2.371).

21.2 Gulling

▶ **'Thus do I ever make my fool my purse' (1.3.175)**

We first meet Iago when he's gulling the foolish Roderigo. He's such a dolt that we might feel he deserves it, but the experience of watching him delude Othello is very different; in fact, it's the most painful in the whole of Shakespeare.

One of the dramatic functions of Roderigo is to act as a parallel to Othello. Both love Desdemona, both trust Iago and both are gulled.

Whatever is potentially painful in watching someone gulled is eased in comedies by making the figures involved close to stock types. If the gull is very foolish, it's easier to laugh.

- **It isn't possible to feel detached in Othello, because of the detailed presentation of the central figure.**

We know the depth of his love for Desdemona, so seeing him gulled about this, the most important thing in his life, hurts those who watch.

Iago, the plot and practising

Many of the play's devices are akin to those of comedy. *Othello* was written about four years after *Hamlet*, and in both there are signs of what he learned from devising the marvellously intricate comic plots of *Much Ado* and *Twelfth Night*.

If the plot of *Othello* has links with comedy, then Iago is the chief practiser. One of the play's ironies is that Iago is on stage when Brabantio accuses Othello of being 'a practiser / Of arts inhibited' (1.2.79–80). Brabantio means magic, but standing by is one who uses entirely human means to control and destroy people.

Iago manipulates Othello and directs the plot through misinformation.

- **In the trade of knowledge, Iago deals in lies.**

His stock material is commonplace – stories about sexual infidelity – but he knows how and when to tell them.

What's uncomfortable is that he's so good at practising. This might be why students admire him. He has a project which he carries out with expert control. He'd do well in Quality Assurance; he sets down his aims and he achieves them! As Bradley says, he's an 'artist'. He exercises over everything he does that cool control of form that art requires.

Brabantio

Brabantio might have been in a comedy. He's an angry father, who's deceived by his daughter, when she ventures for love.

The first three scenes present the vital ingredients of a comic plot: lovers elope; they encounter opposition from a father, and the opposition is overcome. In this respect the Senate does what Theseus does in *A Midsummer Night's Dream* – sweep aside the objections of an angry father.

But Shakespeare does one more thing with Brabantio. He dies of a broken heart (5.2.211–13). The man who played a comic role is seen in another light. The hurt and outrage were real and deadly.

Overhearing

One of the ways in which Iago provides the proof that Othello desires is through the essentially comic device of overhearing. In Act 4, Scene 1 Othello overhears Cassio talking about the doting prostitute, Bianca, and sees Bianca with the handkerchief he gave to Desdemona. Iago has led him to believe that the light, sneering remarks of Cassio are about Desdemona.

Othello is in the position of power. The character who overhears what another says, knows what the other knows and knows that the other doesn't know that he knows it. What he doesn't know is what we know – he's mistaken in what he hears. The deception is brilliant. A moment's thought will reveal that Iago's story about Cassio and Desdemona is absurd – when have they had the time to do it? But in his heightened state of confusion and desperation (he's only just come round from his fit, induced by Iago's account of Cassio's dreams of copulating with Desdemona), Cassio's talk and the handkerchief become hard evidence.

21.3 Iago, honesty and trust

▶ 'Honest Iago' (1.3.294)

'Honest' and 'honesty' are used 52 times ('honest' more so than in any other play). The word undergoes a number of changes. It can mean rough and hearty; Iago is thought to be honest because he's open, direct and apparently uncomplicated. It also means virtuous. One of the horrible things about the play is that the word, poisoned by its association with Iago, is used when Othello says that he thinks his wife is innocent:

I do not think but Desdemona's honest

(3.3.230)

In Iago's mouth it also means stupid. Though happy to be thought honest in the bluff, hearty sense, he's dismissive of those who wear themselves out in the service of others (1.1.49).

Iago and honesty

As far as the drama of *Othello* is concerned, Iago's honesty is a problem. The issue is a huge one, but it can be put in plain terms:

- **is what Iago says ever to be trusted?**

When a character lives by lies, how do we know when he's not lying?

Is Shakespeare conducting an experiment: a central character who is the motivating force of the plot but who nevertheless lies so frequently that we begin to question virtually everything he says?

What we can trust

We can rely on enough to see the plot working. We don't doubt that Iago hates Othello and is trying to bring him down. Nor do we doubt that he strings Roderigo along to fleece him of his wealth. It also seems likely that he wants to be Lieutenant. We know he tells Brabantio the truth about Othello eloping with Desdemona. And, of course, in order to arrange the deaths at the end, he must tell the other characters when to arrive. If Iago were not reliable in these matters, there could be no play.

What are Iago's beliefs?

There are some things which we have to say we can't know. For instance, what does Iago think? When Roderigo tells him he can't help loving Desdemona, he says:

'Tis in ourselves that we are thus or thus. Our bodies are our gardens, to the which our wills are gardeners (1.3.319–21).

Whatever we think of this narrow and reductive view of life, it doesn't help us to know whether Iago is showing us what he really thinks.

What we can doubt

Iago tells Roderigo a story that is intended to explain why he hates Othello. The story (1.1.7–32) is that Iago, an experienced soldier, was supported by a 'three great ones of the city' in his bid to become Othello's Lieutenant. Othello, however, took no notice and appointed the inexperienced Cassio.

What evidence is there for this? The answer is: virtually none at all. Nobody else talks about the 'three great ones', and there's no evidence that Cassio is not an experienced soldier. At the end of the play, he's felt suitable to be military governor of Cyprus. Shakespeare catches us unawares. The play has only just started, and we've no reason not to believe what we hear but *we* may have been gulled.

The soliloquies

Although the convention is that **characters tell the truth in soliloquies; we can't depend upon this in the case of Iago.**

We can believe his plans, but what of the rest? Some of the things he says are difficult to take. For instance

I hate the Moor,
And it is thought abroad that 'twixt my sheets
He has done my office.

(1.3.278–80)

The first statement is borne out by virtually everything he does. But what evidence is there that they whisper in the streets that Othello has slept with Emilia? Is there any evidence that it's true at all?

Bradley's principle is a wise one. He says we should believe nothing Iago says unless there's other evidence to support it. This even applies to what he says in the soliloquies.

21.4 Iago and motive

▶ **'Demand me nothing'** (5.2.309)

At the end of the play Othello asks:

demand that demi-devil
Why he hath thus ensnared my soul and body?

(5.2.307–8)

Iago's reply is:

Demand me nothing. What you know, you know.
From this time forth I never will speak word.

(5.2.309–10)

And he doesn't. Not even the threat of torture prompts him to say anything.

Motives

Why Iago does what he does is something that has puzzled many people. Because we can't believe that Othello denied him the Lieutenancy, we can't trust the argument that he does it get his own back. Nor can we believe that he's getting back at Othello because of the Moor's adultery with Emilia.

That accusation might, however, tell us something. What Iago says is that he

hates the Moor
And it is thought abroad...

(1.3.278–9)

not, as we might expect: 'because it is thought …' The word 'and' indicates that there's no connection between the two things.

The most famous remark about Iago's motives was made by Coleridge, who said this about Iago's soliloquy in Act 1, Scene 3:

the motive-hunting of a motiveless malignity.

What Coleridge is saying is that we must recognise that we can't answer the question about Iago's motive, because there isn't one. There's no 'because' about what he does. His malice can't be explained; it's just malice:

● **Iago's evil is not to be explained.**

Part of what it is for something to be evil is that it's beyond comprehension.

21.5 The image of chaos

▶ **'Chaos is come again' (3.3.93)**

Othello is preoccupied by the tension between harmony and chaos:

• **Shakespeare uses the motifs of chaos and harmony to give shape to the play's themes**.

What we see in the first act is the threat of chaos overcome by Othello's magisterial presence. Brabantio comes at night with soldiers; Othello responds with this exquisite line:

> Keep up your bright swords, for the dew will rust 'em.
>
> (1.2.60)

Shakespeare establishes this pattern in order to prepare us for its undoing in the central acts. In Act 2, Scene 1 it seems that even the wild energies of nature respect Othello. He comes through the storm which wrecks the Turkish fleet and is restored to Desdemona:

> O my soul's joy,
> If after every tempest comes such calms
>
> (2.1.185–6)

The rise and fall of the cadence enacts both the storm being stilled and his pleasure at meeting Desdemona.

But in Act 3, Scene 3 passion leads the way. Before Iago begins the 'temptation' scene, Othello says, as Desdemona exits:

> Perdition catch my soul
> But I do love thee, and when I love thee not,
> Chaos is come again.
>
> (3.3.91–3)

And it does. When Iago's doubts have poisoned his mind, he collapses (3.4.43).

21.6 Othello, stories and wonder

▶ **'the story of my life' (1.3.128)**

Before we look at how Iago brings chaos to Othello, we need to appreciate the kind of figure Othello is.

Othello is a figure apart from others. He's a mercenary (Shakespeare must have known that Venice employed mercenaries to lead their troops) so is free to leave the service of Venice when he chooses. We don't know much about his background other than it's not European, and clearly he doesn't know very much about women, which is a bit odd for a soldier.

Stories

Othello comes from a story-shaped culture; he thinks and feels in stories. His is not a world of explanation or argument. When accused of bewitching Desdemona, he tells a story about how he told his stories:

Her father loved me, oft invited me,
Still questioned me the story of my life
From year to year, the battles, sieges, fortunes
That I have passed.

(1.3.127–30)

This is his culture – a world in which people are given their identity through the stories they tell about themselves. Significantly, at the end it's a story that he resorts to. Othello hardly argues anything; to know his story is to know him.

Wonder

Othello arouses wonder and has a gift for wonder. He knows his stories arouse wonder in others:

And of the cannibals that each other eat,
The Anthropophagi, and men whose heads
Do grow beneath their shoulders. These things to hear
Would Desdemona seriously incline

(1.3.142–5)

The swell of the voice on 'Anthropophagi' indicates that the wonder is his as well as hers.

Belief

Othello's natural inclination is to trust and believe. When Brabantio says that Desdemona might deceive him, he replies:

My life upon her faith.

(1.3.294)

One of the astonishing things Shakespeare does in the play is show a man who accepts unquestioningly things that we would find it hard to take. Of the handkerchief, he says:

There's magic in the web of it.
A sibyl that had numbered in the world
The sun to course two hundred compasses
In her prophetic fury sewed the work.

(3.4.69–72)

It would belittle Othello to call this primitive. It has the bracing quality of minds that haven't been taught to doubt. It might seem distant, but his capacity to believe has about it the thrill of an exotic culture marked by a purity of heart and mind.

Innocence

This gives Othello an innocence. Like a good comic heroine, it's Desdemona who has to lead him on in the ways of love (1.3.143–68). In matters of sexual feeling, he's more modest and embarrassed than she is. In front of the court he claims because he's old, his desires are 'defunct' (1.3.264), whereas she makes it quite clear that her sexual longings need to be satisfied (1.3.257).

21.7 The 'temptation' scene

▶ 'My lord, you know I love you' (3.3.121)

The temptation scene is the crisis of the play. After that, Othello can never be the same again.

Questions

Iago subverts Othello through questions. Because Othello comes from a narrative culture, he can't cope with them. The following concern Cassio:

> *Iago:* Indeed?
> *Othello:* Indeed? Ay, indeed. Discern'st thou aught in that? Is he not honest?
> *Iago:* Honest, my lord?
> *Othello:* Honest? Ay, honest. (3.3.103–7)

The questions open up terrible possibilities of uncertainty. Questions exist by drawing attention to what we don't know or can't be sure of. When they come quickly, the mind can be disorientated; we don't know what to rely on.

Othello's culture can't cope with this. The world of stories demands imaginative assent. If we start to question everything, the story collapses. In the relentless, destabilising questions we see two cultures clashing – a traditional folk culture and modern Europe with its scientific need to be certain. But if we need to be certain, we have to start with doubt.

The expression of doubt

Iago's questions enrage Othello. He asks Iago to tell him what he's thinking:

> And didst contract and purse thy brow together
> As if thou then hadst shut in they brain
> Some horrible conceit. If thou dost love me,
> Show thy thought.
>
> (3.3.117–20)

Iago is performing the role of one who doubts. We don't only express doubts in our words, we do it with our bodies. We do what Iago does – knit our brows together.

Friendship

The assumption of the 'temptation' scene is that Othello has no doubts about one thing – that Iago loves him. Trust is natural to Othello; Iago is probably reliable when he says:

> The Moor is of a free and open nature,
> That thinks men honest that but seem to be so
>
> (1.3.391–2)

The scene can't work without that natural trust that Iago exploits and betrays. Othello says that because Iago is honest, these signs of doubt are not 'tricks of custom' (3.3.127).

The desire to know the worst

It takes two for deception to occur. In the case of Othello, it's sometimes hard to suppress the thought that he wants to believe something bad;

> give thy worst of thoughts
> The worst of words.

> (3.3.137–8)

As a storyteller, he wants to know the worst story that can be told about him, so:

- **Iago chooses the story form to poison Othello's mind against Desdemona.**

The role of the jealous man

Iago succeeds because he teaches Othello the role of the jealous man. Othello is probably right when at the end he says he's 'not easily jealous' (5.2.334). He becomes so because Iago shows him how:

> it is my nature's plague
> To spy into abuses, and oft my jealousy
> Shapes faults that are not

> (3.3.151–3)

Iago does teach Othello to imagine 'faults that are not'. The image he uses is significant; jealousy can be caught like the plague. One way of catching it is to see it being acted out.

The desire for certainty

Othello can't live with uncertainty. His narrative mind can't cope with the business of weighing probabilities. Hence, when he's told that he might lapse into jealousy he says:

> No, to be once in doubt
> Is once to be resolved.

> (3.3.183–4)

To those who love deeply and live by faith, uncertainty is either impossible or devastating. He must know.

Love and proof

The tragedy of Othello is that:

- **once he's been shaken by Iago's insinuations, he must have proof.**

His is a culture of stories; Venice is a world of calculation, of commerce and science. He's picked up enough of this culture to know that proof matters.

> I'll see before I doubt; when I doubt, prove;
> And on the proof, there is no more but this;
> Away at once with love or jealousy.

> (3.3.194–6)

This can be done for science, but it doesn't apply to love. There can be no proof for love, because love is not a matter of measurement or the weighing of evidence. All the person in love can say is what Othello says to Desdemona's father when he's warned that she might deceive him: 'My life upon her faith' (1.3.294).

The worst thing he says is:

> Villain, be sure thou prove my love a whore.
> Be sure of it. Give me the ocular proof

(3.3.364–5)

Not only is this horrible – gazing at his wife having sex with another man – but utterly mistaken. Proof by observation is not the kind of test that's appropriate to love. Othello suffers because he gets science wrong. There can be no proof that Desdemona loves him. Love shouldn't and can't be tested. Othello, lost between a folk and a scientific culture, can't see this.

Iago's temptation works because it plays upon the kind of man Othello is. He's trusting, loving, given to wonder and his commitment is total. Someone like that can't cope with doubt.

21.8 Othello's language

▶ **'I think this tale would win my daughter, too' (1.3.170)**

Othello's language is the most beautiful in Shakespeare. To appreciate what has been called his 'music', we have to atune our ears as well as exercise our imaginations:

> Most potent, grave, and reverend signors,
> My very noble and approved good masters,
> That I have ta'en away this old man's daughter,
> It is most true, true I have married her.
> The very head and front of my offending
> Hath this extent, no more.

(1.3.76–81)

The first thing that needs to be observed is:

• **the virtual absence of figurative language.**

In this sense Othello is not poetic. Words are not extended by transplanting them to unaccustomed contexts; they work with the meanings they've acquired from standard usage. Here 'ta'en away' means taken away, 'marriage' means marriage and 'true' means true.

The second feature is:

• **his majestic rising and falling cadences.**

These suggest both control and integrity. The first three lines have sustained and grave falling cadences, which, both in terms of music and syntax, lead to the climax of 'most true'; 'most' rises and 'true' falls. This pattern is repeated in the second half of the line – a rise on 'marriage' and a fall on 'her'.

Othello also has:

• **unusual word order and usage.**

We weren't expecting 'most'. Nor on grounds of meaning alone do we need the repetition of 'true'. The syntax is dramatic rather than rational; most of us would say: 'the extent of my offending ...' rather than work with the carefully delayed verb – 'hath'.

21.9 Othello's tragic status

▶ 'It is the cause' (5.2.1)

- Is Othello a hero or a fool?

The heroism of Othello

Many audiences find Othello heroic. His trade is that most associated with heroes – the soldier – and such is his achievement that the greatest empire of Shakespeare's day entrusts him with the command of her forces in an emergency.

When he's commanding, he's authoritative without being overbearing. People seem happy to serve under him; Iago wants a higher position, but he never complains that Othello is his commander. Perhaps the most important thing about him is that Desdemona loves him. When we first meet her, she's a very remarkable person. There's the impression that she's one of the great women of Venice. Her love for him is an argument for him being outstanding.

Othello's folly

Against this is his folly and his pride. His folly might be accounted for by the difference in culture (see 21.6 and 21.7). His pride can be seen as his desire to play out the tragic role he thinks he's been cast in – the wronged husband.

- He's so eloquent that it looks as if he might enjoy it.

Even when he kills his wife, he makes it into an epic task; the word 'cause' had the meaning of an important matter that had to be resolved. The horrific thing is that he presents himself as someone who's pleased he has a role to perform.

The critics have argued on both sides: F. R. Leavis thought he was self-centred, Helen Gardener regarded him as noble. Can the truth be that tragedy obliges us to see Othello with double vision? We must both warm to and recoil from the heroic in Othello. If our reactions were simply admiration or condemnation, there wouldn't be that ambiguity which is the special feature of tragedy.

21.10 His final speech

▶ 'a word or two before you go' (5.2.347)

One of the significant aspects of the play is the final speech (5.2.347–65). What's to be made of it?

Simplicity

The language is surprisingly casual and low key. 'No more of that' he says at one point; it's a shrug from someone who's not bothered about what he's just said. What's to be made of this? Is his control so sure that he sounds at ease or is it that he's lost touch with how he should behave?

Irony?

Does he intend the words to be ironical? What about:

> I have done the state some service

Some service? The irony could be that he's done them great service or that in behaving as he has, he's done them no service at all.

Judgement

Othello acts as his own judge:

> Set you down this

When we hear that remark, should we refuse? We might say that a man who's just murdered his wife – and done it as a kind of religious sacrifice – hardly deserves to be listened to.

Is it true?

Does Othello know himself? Is he right when he says he's not 'easily jealous', or is our experience of Act 3, Scene 3 that he all too soon takes up the role of the jealous husband? Did he love 'wisely' or not? Othello is very sure of these things. Are we?

The exotic settings

This is perhaps the most exotic of all his speeches; we hear a tale of the Indian who threw away a pearl, of an Arabian tree dropping 'medicinable gum' and a fight in Aleppo. But what's it there for? Is it a pathetic attempt to do the kind of thing that impressed Desdemona? Is it Othello being himself again, returning in imagination to the world he understands?

The final story

In his final story Othello is both the defender of Venice killing an enemy and, because he stabs himself, the enemy. Is this the recognition that he's played an ambiguous role or is he unaware of the irony? If the first, then he dies knowing himself; if the second, he dies in ignorance.

21.11 The question of themes

▶ 'What is the matter?' (5.2.175)

What is *Othello* about? This is a problem because

- unlike *Hamlet* and *King Lear*, *Othello* is not a play that yields 'ideas'.

Its major preoccupations are those that directly arise out of the story – the nature of love, the importance of trust, the dilemma of being uncertain. The action doesn't stimulate the major characters to ponder and reflect. As a result, we don't either.

- **More than any of the other tragedies, *Othello* remains a story.**

It's about the events that happen in it.

One of the reasons for this is that Othello himself is not the kind of character who reflects on his experience. If he was, he'd have seen through the lies of Iago.

The effect of all this is that despite its elegance of form (the best constructed of all the tragedies?) and its lofty tone, the play is raw. We see terrible emotions destroying an exceptional figure. No ideas can protect us from its harrowing story.

Exercises

21.1 'It's easy to feel sorry for Othello but almost impossible to admire him.' What do you make of that view?

21.2 Describe in detail the experience of an audience watching *Othello*. What theatrical resources does Shakespeare employ to lead the audience to feel the way it does?

21.3 What problems of understanding and interpretation are presented by the character of Iago?

King Lear

22.1 Themes, characters and drama

▶ **'This great world' (4.5.130)**

Gloucester might have been talking about the play he's in. The world of *King Lear* is vast. There are a number of big dramatic roles; we see a wide range of social groups and the non-human presences – Nature, the gods – hover on the verge of being characters.

The characters

A production of *King Lear* provides opportunities for a number of rewarding roles. Lear is the major role, but players can make a lot of Goneril, Regan, Cordelia, Kent, Gloucester, Edmund, Edgar, Albany, Cornwall, the Fool and Oswald. We see a king, dukes, servants and a beggar. They embody a wide range of feeling and outlook.

Characters and symbolism

The characters seem to stand for something: Cornwall for cruelty, Kent for loyalty, Edmund for ambition, Lear for wilfulness. The characters form a good group and an evil group, with Lear and Gloucester placed between. The evil group tries to destroy them, while the good group guides and rescues.

Themes

Like *Hamlet*, *King Lear* is thematically rich. Sometimes it feels that this play is about every important issue that has troubled the human heart. Certainly, in its own way it tackles many of the issues that religion deals with.

One of the reasons we think this is that the characters directly voice the play's issues. It's clear, for instance, that one of the themes of the play is gratitude and ingratitude. This is what Lear says when Goneril, his daughter whom he regards as ungrateful, confronts him:

> Ingratitude, thou marble-hearted fiend

> (1.4.237)

The play isn't in this sense a subtle work of art. Shakespeare doesn't leave it up to the audience to work out what its major concerns are; the themes are given prominence, brought to the front of the stage, through their direct expression by the characters.

Plot

Unlike the tightly written *Hamlet* and *Othello*, *Lear* is a huge, rambling and even sprawling piece. For instance, in the middle of the play, while Lear rages in his madness, the story almost seems to mark time; its virtual plotlessness has a feel of the drama of Beckett at this point.

Stage business

What gives the play its drama is the variety of stage business. A lot of different things go on in *Lear*. Important actions include: carrying, kneeling, putting someone in the stocks, binding, physical intimidation, cutting oneself with a knife, holding a mock trial, creeping into a shelter, hiding letters, blinding, leading the blind, rough fighting and a combat.

- **The actions define the characters**.

Cornwall and Regan bind Gloucester to a chair and then blind him. The old Servant and Edgar lead the blind Gloucester and Kent carries Lear.

Varieties of drama

King Lear is a play that mixes styles and conventions. The confrontations in the second act between Lear and Goneril and Regan are written in a high epic style, whereas in the mad scenes much of the writing is in prose, with Tom's insane chattering, Lear's ramblings and the Fool's piping common sense.

The start of the play gives no indication of what's to follow. The story of the opening is close to folklore. There's a traditional tale called 'Cap o' Rushes' in which a father makes the same demands of his daughters that Lear does. One of the fascinating aspects of Lear is that from such a start, a tragedy of universal dimensions follows.

22.2 Different kinds of division

▶ 'the division of the kingdom' (1.1.3–4)

In dividing the kingdom, Lear divides his family, his court, and his nation. Accompanying these human divisions there is the storm, which is expressive of a greater divide – a split in the order of nature.

Links

The link between the human and the natural world is a feature of the play. Because we can see these links, we become aware of the interweaving of themes in the play. One idea leads to another. This gives *Lear* an organic feel; it's as if the elements of the play have grown together.

Images of cracking

The play is full of images of things cracking, breaking or bursting. The universal aspect of division is represented by the word 'crack'. The storm scene opens with Lear saying:

Blow, winds, and crack your cheeks!

(3.2.1)

At the end the anticipation of death is given in similar language. Gloucester's heart 'burst smilingly' (5.3.191) and Kent says of the dying Lear:

Break, heart, I prithee break.

(5.3.288)

Politics

When Kent tries to make Lear change his mind, he says: 'Reserve thy state' (1.1.149).

The word 'reserve' means to keep something for oneself and to keep something safe. Both meanings might be at work here. Kent is telling Lear not to give up his power; he might also be saying that power in the land will only be safe in Lear's hands.

22.3 Cordelia, love and sacrifice

▶ 'Thy youngest daughter does not love thee least' (1.1.152)

The question

The plot starts when Lear puts a question to his daughters:

Which of you shall we say does love us most?

(1.1.51)

We should be uneasy about this. Notice the way the word 'we' interrupts the rhythm of the line. Notice, too, that Lear is the arbiter of who loves him most.

The language of love

One of the difficulties of the opening scene is that all the characters get language wrong. Cordelia (not a girl to mince words) condemns her sisters' speech:

If for I want that glib and oily art
To speak and purpose not

(1.1.223–4)

It's a pretty good description of how Goneril and Regan talk; they play the game Lear wants them to.

But Cordelia herself might have been more careful:

> I love your majesty
> According to my bond, no more nor less.
>
> (1.1.92–3)

There's no justification for 'no more nor less'; and it's not true either.

Lear's mistake is even greater. He says things that are opposed to the most basic meanings of our language. When he casts her off, he says that the 'barbarous Scythian', who eats his own children, will be

> as well neighboured, pitied, and relieved
> As thou my sometime daughter.
>
> (1.1.119–20)

This doesn't make sense; no one can be a 'sometime' daughter. Women are always daughters; men are always sons.

Love is expressed in language. To get the language wrong is to get love wrong.

Loyalty

One of the expressions of love in the play is loyalty. Kent returns to serve Lear, and when his knights desert him, the Fool remains to suffer with Lear in the storm. Gloucester is helped by a tenant, who has served him and his father for 80 years. What these two characters have in common is that they both suffer in order to serve Lear: Kent is put in the stocks and the Fool, we must assume, dies after the storm.

Love

Because Cordelia can be interpreted as representing sacrificial love, the play can be seen as showing the cost of such love.

Sacrificial love is love that's prepared to suffer and perhaps even die; if the one who loves does die, then that doesn't invalidate what she's done, it simply shows the lengths to which love will go. The world of *King Lear* might be terrible, but perhaps it's not bleak.

22.4 Lear and hatred

▶ 'To match you where I hate' (1.1.209)

The play is also about hate. In particular it's about the most horrible kind of hate there is:

- **the hatred of a parent for a child, the hatred, that is, for what one has made**.

Lear, with monstrous hubris, chooses to hate Cordelia, because she disappointed him. Cordelia is said to be 'new adopted to our hate' (1.1.202).

22.5 The two plots

▶ 'there's father against child' (1.2.109)

The plots and the themes

An interesting feature of *King Lear* is that:

- **the themes of the play are more clearly present in the Gloucester sub-plot than in the Lear main plot.**

Take the case of learning from experience. Gloucester, in trying to frame his thoughts about the terrible things that have happened to him, moves from the view that the gods torture us:

> As flies to wanton boys are we to th'gods;
> They kill us for their sport.
>
> (4.1.37–8)

to one that accepts in patience what happens to us. Edgar says that men

> must endure
> Their going hence even as their coming hither.
> Ripeness is all.
>
> (5.2.9–11)

Gloucester responds with touching simplicity: 'And that's true, too.'

In that word 'ripeness' there's a sense that maturity is wholeness. If we wait for life to take its course, no matter how intense our suffering is, there's a harvest, a ripeness and plenty, in our experience. This is clearer in the Gloucester sub-plot than the Lear main plot.

22.6 Seeing and blindness

▶ **'See better, Lear' (1.1.158)**

A theme that the sub-plot makes very prominent is that of seeing. Neither Lear nor Gloucester can see their folly or the malice of their children. That's why Kent demands that Lear sees better. He needs to see what his daughters are really like and the mistake he's making. Because he can't see, he suffers.

Gloucester also suffers for not seeing, but the form of this suffering is horribly appropriate to his failure – he's blinded. In his suffering, he begins to see his errors and to bear his sufferings rather than seeking to end his life (the theme of patience is common to both plots). When the old servant who leads him says that without a guide he can't see where to go, Gloucester says:

> I have no way, and therefore want no eyes.
> I stumbled when I saw.
>
> (4.1.18–19)

Now that he's blind, he can see more than when he had sight. The same can be said of Lear's madness. Does he understand more in his ravings than when he was secure as the pensioner king?

22.7 Edgar and Edmund

▶ **Brother, I say' (2.1.19)**

Edgar

In theatrical terms, Edgar is a far more difficult character to understand than Edmund. The reason for this is that

- **Edgar is more like several characters**.

Edgar has to be a gull, a mad beggar and a champion, in whose hands the future of the state is left. He's all these things because that's what the plot requires: Edmund must have a gullible brother, there must be a naked beggar to bring home to Lear what it is to be human, and Edmund must be defeated. Beyond this there's one other role he performs:

- **Edgar is a thinker**.

Even in his earliest scenes, when his chief function is to be manipulated by Edmund, he shows himself to be a rational man. When Edmund pretends to take astrological predictions seriously, Edgar sceptically inquires:

> Do you busy yourself with that? (1.2.140)

We can hear the 'surely not' in the voice.

His most important scenes are in Act 4. He's the only character who thinks as a way of coping with the horrors of the middle scenes. After the storm he emerges with the philosophy that if he's seen the worst, it follows that whatever comes next must, by definition, be better. He uses the image of the wheel of fortune; if you're at the bottom, the only way is up:

> The lamentable change is from the best;
> The worst returns to laughter.
>
> (4.1.5–6)

Then his blinded father enters. The bravery of Edgar is seen in his honesty; he sees through his own thinking:

> Who is't can say 'I am at the worst'?
> I am worse than e'er I was.
>
> (4.1.25–6)

Edgar is making a point about grammar; in human life we can never use the superlative ('worst') of any human experience. There is no bottom to the world of *King Lear*; events can continue their terrible descent into misery for ever.

Because the logic of working through definitions has let him down, when Edgar first sees his blinded father he resorts to a language which is expressive of his outrage and which concentrates not on categories of thought but the brute reality of life:

> World, world, O world!
> But that thy strange mutations make us hate thee,
> Life would not yield to age.
>
> (4.1.10–12)

In the repetitions of 'world', it's as if he's both trying to get the horrors of life into focus and in so doing protesting against its injustice.

It's brave of Edgar to abandon his attempt to understand and, instead, try to see and protest. It's equally brave of him later to return to thinking again. His sublime 'Ripeness is all' (5.2.11) is an attempt to make sense of life through the image of natural growth.

Edmund

Edmund plays a number of roles but, unlike those played by Edgar, they are closely related; he is a machiavel, deceiver and lover.

If it's performed with an appropriate, knowing and well-executed swagger, Edmund's first entrance is compelling. His speech plays with the popular idea of illegitimacy – that bastards are unreliable and immoral. The common word was 'base' – low, corrupt, self-seeking and deceitful.

It's important to be clear what Shakespeare's doing; he's not presenting Edmund *as* a stock bastard but as someone who knows what other people *think* of bastards and who deliberately adopts a way of life to confirm their worst suspicions.

The result is a very entertaining piece of theatre. He knows he's the victim of prejudice:

> Why brand they us
> With 'base', with 'baseness', bastardy, – base, base–
> Who in the lusty stealth of nature take
> More composition and fierce quality
> Than doth within a dull, stale, tired bed
> Go to th' creating a whole tribe of fops
> Got 'tween a sleep and wake.
>
> (1.2.9–15)

Since the world calls him 'base', Edmund plays the game of being base with words. Coming after a scene about succession, order and authority – about all that's legitimate – the speech has real bite. Legitimacy depends upon children lawfully conceived within marriage, but to Edmund this is a comical business – 'Got 'tween a sleep and wake' – whereas the bastard is energetic because he's been conceived lustfully in the stealth of nature.

Edmund is a soldier and a lover. In fact, he's a gleeful parody of those Elizabethan courtiers who were fierce in war and engaging in love. No doubt if he had time, he'd have written sonnets. Numerically speaking, he's Shakespeare's most successful lover – he has two women fighting over him. Any one who plays the part must shimmer with sexual charisma; he must be so desirable that the two sisters who at the end of the first scene said (in one version of the play) 'let us hit together' (1.1.302) end up struggling to the death against each other for his affection.

This has an effect on him. Throughout the play he's been entirely selfish, but when at his death he sees the bodies of the two women who've died for him, he says: 'Yet Edmund was beloved' (5.3.215).

This can be played as a revelation. He's been pretty cynical about them, but at his death he suddenly sees the cost and depth of love. When he's seen what two women did for him, he attempts to do something for Lear and Cordelia:

> Some good I mean to do,
> Despite of mine own nature.
>
> (5.3.218–19)

At the end Edmund recognises and is impelled to act by the power of love.

22.8 The different meanings of 'nature'

▶ 'Thou, nature, art my goddess' (1.2.1)

'Nature' appears 40 times, 'natural' twice and 'unnatural' 7 times. Here are some of its most important uses.

Human nature

The word has the meaning we expect it to have; it means what people are like, both in their shared humanity and their individual characteristics.

When France sees that Cordelia is being condemned for being no more than stubborn, he asks:

> Is it but this – a tardiness in nature

(1.1.235)

Though a common usage, we should note that this is what this play (and many of the other tragedies) is about. It asks:

- **what are the limits of human nature?**

This question leads on to another issue: what is it to be unnatural?

Nature and goodness

The word 'unnatural' is often used in a moral sense; to behave unnaturally is to behave wickedly. This, of course, means that natural behaviour is good behaviour.

Lear sees that if nature is good, then some things we naturally do are in fact moral duties. When he desperately turns to Regan because he thinks she'll treat him well he says to her:

> Thou better know'st
> The offices of nature, bond of childhood,
> Effects of courtesy, dues of gratitude

(2.2.350–2)

Because she's his child, she will do what children ought to do: be courteous and grateful. To be a child is to be grateful.

This raises a fundamental issue:

- **what's at stake here is whether the natural order is good.**

In other words, if we say of something that it's natural, do we mean by that that it *must* also be good?

Shakespeare shows experience wringing these questions out of people. In the bizarre 'trial' Lear says:

> Then let them anatomise Regan; see what breeds about her heart. Is there any cause in nature that makes these hard-hearts? (3.6.34–5)

He's asking the fundamental question: are we evil by nature? If it's not our nature to be evil, where does it come from?

Nature as Lear's will

One of the ways in which Lear is perversely wrong is in his assumption that what he thinks and wants is natural. With frightening confidence, he summons nature, whom he sees as a sort of goddess figure:

> Hear, nature; hear, dear goddess, hear:
> Suspend thy purpose if thou didst intend
> To make this creature fruitful.

(1.4.254–6)

Lear is unaware of how he's distorting language. If nature means anything, it means the power of reproduction. Lear asks nature to prevent Goneril from having children; in other words, he wants nature to be unnatural. He can't see that nature is not another word for our selfish wants.

Nature as selfish ambition

Lear has no irony when he talks of nature. With Edmund, it's otherwise. He starts his soliloquy with a piece of rhetoric that sounds as if the young man is trying to be like the old one we've just seen ranting:

> Thou, nature, art my goddess. To thy law
> My services are bound.

> (1.2.1–2)

In fact, Edmund believes in no such thing. He doesn't believe in any goddess, and he certainly doesn't believe that he's bound to anything or anyone. Nature in his mouth means nothing more than the self and what the self wants.

The created order

The play is steeped in the teeming world of a thriving natural order. We hear about the wind, the rain, thunder, lightening, whirlwind, hawthorn, bog, quagmire, standing pool, hog, fox, dog, worm, sheep, cat, frog, toad, tadpole, newt, rat, crows, choughs, wheat, samphire, burdocks, hemlock, nettles, cuckoo-flowers and corn.

This thickly textured mesh of natural things is wet, cold, slimy, prickly, rough and hard.

The world of nature is presented in two closely related ways:

- **it feels non-human to the audience**
- **the characters imaginatively include it in their own pictures of the world.**

A hawthorn bush is just a bush – thick, stark in shape and sharp to the touch. The natural world is alien and other. However, Shakespeare also shows us how characters use images drawn from nature in their pictures of the world. Lear sees the thunder and lightening as judges and Tom (or Edgar?) sees the grotesque and slithery side of nature as somehow matching the inhospitable world of people that's made him an outcast.

The natural and the supernatural

A Gentleman says of Lear:

> Thou hast a daughter
> Who redeems nature from the general curse
> Which twain have brought her to.

> (4.5.201–3)

Nature here stands for a sick and sinful world as opposed to a world that has been healed and reconciled. Christian theology tells the story of how all people and the very earth itself were corrupted by the fall of Adam and Eve ('twain') and how God himself rescued them by sending his son, Jesus Christ, to bring people and nature back into a proper relationship with God. This is called redemption. The imagery doubles Adam and Eve with Goneril and Regan; they have, as it were, corrupted nature, and the love of Cordelia (a kind of Christ figure) brings redemption.

22.9 Dover Cliff

▶ 'Come on, sir, here's the place' (4.5.11)

Seeing and hearing

One of the ways Dover Cliff works is by playing off the contradiction between what we see and what we hear. For a start, we don't see Dover Cliff, because the scene doesn't take place at Dover. What we see is a huge flat stage, what we hear about is the dizzying heights of a cliff; we see someone fall flat on his face in the traditions of farce, but what we and Gloucester are told is that he's been miraculously spared after falling from the cliff to the beach.

The issue becomes: which should we believe? Shakespeare seems to be pressing theatrical illusion to the point where audiences might say it no longer works.

The symbolic landscape

Edgar's aim is to get his father to read the scene symbolically. We must come to see that the landscape is symbolic of Gloucester's mind.

The ground over which they walk is 'even', but Edgar insists that it's 'horrible steep' (line 3). Gloucester must make the hard climb towards self-understanding and self-acceptance.

When they reach the 'top', Edgar says:

> You are now within a foot
> Of th' extreme verge.

(4.5.25–6)

In Edgar's understanding, this is true in at least two senses. Gloucester has gazed so deeply into the depths of evil that he's in danger of plunging into despair. But he's also on the verge of understanding, of being able to live with the terrible things that have happened to him.

Dover Cliff

Edgar's spell-binding picture of the great height of Dover Cliff and the terrible feelings of vertigo experienced as one gazes down is one of the most imaginative speeches in the whole of Shakespeare. And yet, within the terms of the play, it isn't true.

The words are about the power of the imagination. How telling, for instance, is the way the words convey the low, background noise of the sea which we don't hear:

> The murmuring surge
> That on th' unnumbered idle pebbles chafes
> Cannot be heard so high.

(4.5.20–2)

The words pattern out the sound of the sea sliding irregularly over the pebbles (the word 'idle' is crucial), but it's illusory – the sounds couldn't be heard so high up, and, in any case, because it isn't Dover, there are no pebbles.

He might be thinking over his own art – the playwright tries to make real what is made up. It might, also, put into perspective what Edgar's doing.

- **He's trying to get his father to re-imagine his life.**

Like the sight and sounds of Dover Cliff, we can ask whether, in symbolic terms, it's true or false.

Miracle

When Edgar, playing yet another character, claims to have found a man who's fallen from the top to the beach, he says: 'Thy life's a miracle' (4.5.55). He knows that the miracle of the fall isn't true, so either he's tricking Gloucester or he's working with another sense of 'miracle'. What this other sense might be can be gleaned from:

> But thou dost breathe
> Hast heavy substance, bleed'st not, speak'st, art sound.

> (4.5.51–2)

That description applies to anybody; and perhaps that's the point. What Edgar is driving at is that even in the face of life's horrors, we can still say that human life as we have it is a matter of wonder and thankfulness. The miracle is in life itself.

22.10 Love, measurement and suffering

▶ 'what can you say to draw/A third more opulent?' (1.1 85–6)

Love and measurement

This is the question Lear puts to Cordelia. In what he says, there's the assumption that love can be measured. If Cordelia believes this is false, she gives the only answer possible: 'Nothing, my lord'(1.1.87). If love can't be measured, nothing can be said. In saying 'nothing', therefore, Cordelia says a lot.

Lear, however, insists on the mathematics of human affection; when faced with Goneril and Regan's suggested reductions in the number of his followers, he says to Goneril:

> I'll go with thee.
> Thy fifty yet doth double five and twenty,
> And thou art twice her love.

> (2.2.432–4)

This is consistent with what he frequently says to Goneril and Regan – they should love him because of what he's given them.

Suffering

King Lear explores the injustice of suffering. Shakespeare makes it clear that there's no relation between doing good and happiness. He achieves this through some stark juxtapositions of words and actions. Gloucester does what he can to help Lear once the old king has walked out into the storm. Kent says to him:

> the gods reward your kindness!
>
> (3.6.5)

In the very next scene, his eyes are gouged out.

An even starker juxtaposition comes at the end; Albany says:

> The gods defend her!
>
> (5.3.231)

What follows is the sight of Lear entering with Cordelia dead in his arms.

This is what people have called the problem of evil; if there's an all-powerful and all-loving God, why is there suffering?

Suffering, the gods and measurement

This is such a harrowing play that it's easy to assume that Shakespeare is presenting a Godless world.

But there is an alternative. Perhaps *King Lear* is a protest against the kind of thinking that seeks to find a neat pattern in things. This is similar to what was said in 22.4 about love. Love can't be measured; if it could be, it wouldn't be love. Is it the same with evil? Suffering can't be explained, it can only be borne.

22.11 Making sense of the end

▶ 'Is this the promised end?' (5.3.238)

Redemption?

Does Lear 'see better'?

Those who want to say', yes', think of the play as a drama of redemption in which Lear moves from blindness to a clear vision of what really matters. It would be dishonest to deny that this is what we'd *like* to happen.

Two moments suggest that it does. The first is the scene in which he recovers from his madness and accepts the love of Cordelia.

The second moment is the speeches he makes before he and Cordelia are taken off to prison; they 'will sing like birds i' th' cage' (5.3.9), and he says:

> Upon such sacrifices, my Cordelia,
> The gods themselves throw incense.
>
> (5.3.20–1)

Whether the sacrifices are what she's done for him or what they're doing in giving up the world, the significance is that Lear has found fulfilment. He can now take upon himself 'the mystery of things' (5.3.16).

Against such a reading of the play is the final scene in which he howls with pain, brags of killing the man who hanged Cordelia and openly says that if she lives, all his sufferings will be redeemed. We should remember two things about this problem.

- Lear is very old. Did Shakespeare deliberately choose a character too old to learn from his suffering?
- We can't expect a play that raised so many questions to end without raising more. Tragedy is ambiguous; part of that ambiguity is that we don't always know what to think.

The final scene

The final scene is ambiguous. There are lines that point to hope, and lines that prompt despair. Shakespeare orchestrates it so that we hear both harmony and dissonance. Kent asks whether this is the 'promised end', and Edgar balances that with 'or image of that horror' (5.3.238). Kent says 'break, heart', while Edgar encourages Lear to 'Look up' (5.3.288). Lear's 'look there' (5.3.287) is mysterious. It's in keeping with a play about seeing, but what is it that Lear wants us to see? Does he think she's alive, or is this Shakespeare's way of pointing to what really matters – sacrificial love?

One thing that's certain is that the play doesn't feel like any other at the end. Time seems to stop. There's no sense that they are going to leave the stage to explain things to each other. They speak their final words and lapse into silence.

Exercises

22.1 Explore the significance of the storm scenes in *King Lear*.

22.2 What is it about *King Lear* that makes people say it is Shakespeare's most profound play?

22.3 What do you feel at the end of *King Lear*?

23.1 The atmosphere of the play

▶ 'As thick as hail/Came post with post' (1.3.95–6)

Macbeth is a short and intense play; to borrow a phrase that's recently become popular, it's the most 'hard-driven' of all Shakespeare's plays. This quality is present in a number of ways.

The plot

The plot is economical; nothing is irrelevant. Each scene furthers the progress of the story, and there's virtually no element in the entire play that's not related to the plot movement.

The plot is clear. *Macbeth* is about the rise and fall of a warrior. We hear about his exploits in the first act; in the second he kills Duncan and in the third he becomes the king himself. The downward movement of the fourth and fifth acts shows him suffering different forms of isolation till his inevitable death in the last-but-one scene.

Pace

The play moves quickly. Until the invasion of the armies from England, Macbeth is the motivating force of the plot; he is, so to speak, both Iago – the plot manipulator – and Othello – the plot victim – because as he drives himself on he moves swiftly towards his own destruction.

Word and deed

A feature of the plot is the close association of word and act and, consequently, of anticipation and fulfilment. At the end of the scene in which the Apparitions warn him of Macduff, Macbeth plans the destruction of Macduff's family. The very next scene is the only one in Shakespeare as terrible as the blinding of Gloucester in *Lear*. Within 90 lines of Macbeth's decision, a child is killed before us.

The scenes

Apart from the long scene in England, every scene in the play is less than 200 lines. Some of the most intense scenes, such as Act 3, Scene 2 (Macbeth and Lady Macbeth alone before the banquet), are less than a 100 lines long.

What gives them their intensity is a combination of emotions at a high pitch and repeated images. Consider Act 3, Scene 2. There are many words about thought and the mind: thoughts should have died with those whom they've killed (lines 12–13); their minds are tortured in 'restless ecstasy' (lines 23–4), and Macbeth's mind is 'full of scorpions' (line 37). References to blood, killing and murder occur in the following words: 'destruction' (line 9), 'died' (line 12), 'killed' (line 15), 'the dead' (line 21), 'grave' (line 24), 'bloody' (line 49), 'cancel' (line 50) and 'tear to pieces' (line 50). As in many scenes in *Macbeth*, night and darkness are prominent: 'seeling night' (line 47), 'light thickens' (line 51) and 'night's black agents' (line 54).

23.2 The weird sisters

▶ **'Fair is foul' (1.1.10)**

Macbeth is a play that deals with evil. What's unclear is the extent to which the weird sisters embody evil. When we see them in Act 1, Scene 3 before Macbeth arrives, they are mischievous and nasty, but hardly wicked. The scene in which they throw revolting things into their cauldron isn't exactly evil either. Macbeth does great evil, but his acts can hardly be blamed on the sisters. They predict, but they don't tell him what to do.

The one moment when it's relevant to talk about evil occurs in the opening scene. Most of this short scene is taken up with the agenda of the next meeting – the date, place, time and purpose – and then at the end, we hear these words:

> Fair is foul, and foul is fair,
> Hover through the fog and filthy air.

(1.1.10–11)

The really frightening word is 'is'. The sisters say that what is fair – good, beautiful, right – *is* foul – ugly, shameful, wicked. The two things are identical. If they are, moral words collapse; if good means evil, then neither word has a meaning at all.

Macbeth and evil

Is this what Macbeth is like? The answer can only be 'yes and no'. It's often observed that he echoes the sisters on his first entry:

> So fair and foul a day I have not seen

(1.3.36)

The day has been fair *and* foul. He knows the difference; but not at every moment in the play.

There are times when Macbeth wants to talk about what we would call his evil actions in words that are robbed of moral significance. Listen to him working himself up to killing Duncan:

> If it were done when 'tis done, then 'twere well
> It were done quickly.

(1.7.1–2)

The words he uses are about as morally neutral as possible. The murder is referred to as 'it', and the act is something that is 'done'; neither of the words carry, as moral words do, the judgement that what is being spoken of is either right or wrong. This moral neutrality comes close to the bluntness of identifying 'fair' with 'foul'.

But at other moments Macbeth uses moral terms openly and freely. He knows he's doing wrong:

> He's here in double trust;
> First, as his kinsman and his subject,
> Strong both against the deed; then, as his host,
> Who should against his murderer shut the door,
> Not bear the knife myself.

(1.7.12–16)

'Trust' and 'murderer' are both moral words, and as soon as he mentions 'host' he knows that he shouldn't be the killer of the man he's protecting. Perhaps the best way to understand the blend of moral and non-moral words is to see the non-moral ones as an attempt to overcome the moral ones.

23.3 Macbeth and death

▶ 'Strange images of death' (1.3.95)

Reports from the battlefield

The second scene opens with a man covered in blood, who gives an account of Macbeth's part in the battle. The style is epic; he wants the king to understand the drama of the event, so he peppers it with unwieldy comparisons such as that of the two tired swimmers. What we, nevertheless, hear is a tale of bloody slaughter:

> he unseamed him from the nave to the chops,
> And fixed his head upon our battlements.

(1.2.22–3)

Shakespeare makes it possible for the audience to see the reality of the battle through the elevating haze of heroic rhetoric.

Ross's words to Macbeth about 'strange images of death' (1.4.95) sum up the account of a man who seems to revel in bloodshed. The audience might pick up the hints of danger, but the court doesn't. Why?

A warrior culture

Macbeth can be understood, as can *Coriolanus*, as a tragedy of culture. In *Macbeth*, Shakespeare presents a warrior culture. Scotland is an unstable country torn by internal divisions and open to attack from hostile neighbours. In a culture that requires warriors, the successful fighter is celebrated in an epic language that praises his courage and his conquests.

Macbeth is such a figure. It's notable that as soon as he's praised and rewarded by Duncan, Macbeth plans to replace him. Some readers have been disturbed by the suddenness of the Macbeths planning to kill the king, but suddenness is the point. In a warrior culture, military success is what everyone admires, so once a soldier embodies the qualities valued in the culture, it's natural for him to want to be the leader.

This happens to Macbeth in the scene in which he's told he's been given the title of Thane of Cawdor. While the other characters talk, his mind is framing the events in terms of a heroic drama of his glittering success:

> Two truths are told
> As happy prologues to the swelling act
> Of the imperial theme.
>
> (1.3.126–8)

It's as if he's framing a saga that will be sung round the fires in draughty halls, when the king and his nobles have supped.

The hero

Macbeth knowingly behaves as the hero. This is probably not surprising in a culture that values success in war. In heroic and epic stories, what the hero does is called a 'deed'. It has an elevated meaning; deeds are noble and require the utmost bravery. Only a man of outstanding qualities can do a heroic deed.

One of the features of Macbeth's language is that he calls his murders 'deeds'. The word occurs twice in the soliloquy at the start of Act 1, Scene 7 and, most significantly, in the scene when he returns from killing Duncan. His words on entering are: 'I have done the deed' (2.2.14). The sentence combines the neutral 'done' with the epic 'deed'. The word is used five times in this scene.

Blood

Blood is one of the many images that run through the play. In Shakespeare, 'blood' meant sexual desires, people to whom one is related, and the royal succession, as well as what runs in our veins.

Macbeth is a man of blood because he sheds blood and broods upon killing. Thoughts of blood invade his thinking. When he talks about the coming night he can't separate it from his planned murder of Banquo:

> Come, seeling night,
> Scarf up the tender eye of pitiful day,
> And with thy bloody and invisible hand
> Cancel and tear to pieces that great bond
> Which keeps me pale.
>
> (3.2.47–51)

The image itself hovers uneasily between that of someone muffling himself against the cold and a berserk murderer who rips apart his victim. To Macbeth night means murder, and murder means blood.

23.4 Horror, poetry and goodness

▶ 'horrible imaginings' (1.3.137)

Intensity of response

The Macbeth we see at the beginning of the play is a man who responds to life intensely. This is part of his first soliloquy:

                    Present fears
Are less than horrible imaginings.
My thought, whose murder yet is but fantastical,
Shakes so my single state of man that function
Is smothered in surmise, and nothing is
But what is not.

$$(1.3.136–41)$$

It's not entirely clear what he's saying here; the words seem to rush out under the compulsive pressure of the terrible thoughts he's having. They have a physical effect on him; he shakes with fear, excitement, and even wonder.

He's certainly a man of strangely intense feelings and sensations. It's difficult to describe such a mind. It would be wrong to go for medical or psychological terms, because there's no invitation implicit in the play to offer a diagnosis. It's better to say that he's a visionary or a poet.

Poetry

Shakespeare chose to give Macbeth some of the most dazzling poetry he ever wrote. The thrill he feels when he contemplates killing Duncan issues in poetry that's vivid and ecstatic:

            And pity, like a naked new-born babe,
            Striding the blast, or heaven's cherubim, horsed
            Upon the sightless couriers of the air,
            Shall blow the horrid deed in every eye
            That tears shall drown the wind.

$$(1.7.21–5)$$

Like much great poetry, these words are hard to understand; why is 'pity' 'like a naked new-born babe'? We might pity a babe in a storm, but that's different from comparing the babe to pity. Moreover, the babe commands terror rather than pity; with the cherubim it blows (as in the wind and a trumpet) the 'deed' everywhere.

Duncan's goodness

Macbeth is talking about killing Duncan. What do we know of the King? A quick answer would be that he's loved because he's good and holy. If we think that, we should ask where we get that picture from. The disturbing answer is: Macbeth.

This is what he says about the old man he wants to kill:

                    Besides this Duncan
            Hath borne his faculties so meek, hath been
            So clear in his great office, that his virtues
            Will plead like angels

$$(1.7.16–19)$$

There's very little in the Duncan we actually see to justify this. Where's the virtue and the holiness? It's not there because it only exists in Macbeth's imagination. Only Macbeth sees the sanctity of his golden blood lacing his silver skin (2.3.112).

Why should Macbeth imagine the goodness of someone he's going to destroy? There's no answer to that other than one that re-arranges what's been asked.

- We have a glimpse into the evil of Macbeth when we see that he creates a goodness so he can destroy it.

Macbeth isn't evil simply so he can become king; he does evil because it's evil.

23.5 The Macbeths' language

▶ 'Come, thick night' (1.5.49)

Lady Macbeth, though in many ways different from her husband, is like him in her love of evil. This love is seen in the language they share.

Lady Macbeth

> Come, thick night,
> And pall thee in the dunnest smoke of hell,
> That my keen knife sees not the wound it makes,
> Nor heaven peep through the blanket of the dark
> To cry 'Hold, hold!'
>
> (1.5.49–53)

Macbeth

> Ere the bat hath flown
> His cloistered flight, ere to black Hecate's summons
> The shard-borne beetle with his drowsy hums
> Hath rung night's yawning peal
>
> (3.2.41–4)

They sound like people singing from the same hymnbook. Both enjoy setting a scene for some act of evil, both talk of the darkness of night, and both relish the evil associated with it. The language of hell and of Hecate (the mistress of witches) is trippingly familiar to them. She is more sensual ('come' is an invitation to love), while he is more poetic (the 'cloistered flight' of the bat is an unexpected detail); but both of them utter words with mesmeric power.

23.6 Why Macbeth kills the king

▶ 'If it were done' (1.7.1)

When Lady Macbeth enters in Act 1, Scene 7, Macbeth says they will 'proceed no further in this business' (line 31); by the end of the scene he prepares himself for 'this terrible feat' (line 80). Many people have asked what happens in between to make him apparently change his mind.

Ambition

The first thing that needs to be said is that he doesn't really change his mind. The soliloquy which opens the scene is about his desire to do it. He can see difficulties, which seem enormous, but the speech ends with an image of ambition:

> I have no spur
> To prick the sides of my intent, but only
> Vaulting ambition

$$(1.7.25–7)$$

The image is of a rider facing a jump. The only thing the rider can do is dig his spurs in the horse; all that Macbeth can use as a spur is his ambition. No matter how dangerous and overwhelmingly wrong the deed is, Macbeth wants to do it.

One way of understanding what he's up to is to see him as needing her encouragement, and getting it by pretending he's no longer interested. What he gets is two very powerful acts of persuasion.

Manhood

Lady Macbeth taunts him with this jibe:

> When you durst do it, then you were a man

$$(1.7.49)$$

Her ambiguities must be quite deliberate; 'do it' means both kill the king and have sexual intercourse. He must prove that he's a man not by making love but by stabbing an old man. She knows him; she probably knows that he loves her; they are both young. Epic deeds have the excitement of sex.

The babe

She also says:

> I have given suck, and know
> How tender 'tis to love the babe that milks me.
> I would, while it was smiling in my face,
> Have plucked my nipple from his boneless gums
> And dashed the brains out, had I so sworn
> As you have done to this.

$$(1.7.54–9)$$

This comes from nowhere. Lady Macbeth appears to produce it as an example of resolution, but it's a curious thing to choose. Most people would respond with disgust. If that's what it means to keep a promise, it's better to break it. Yet it works with Macbeth. Why?

Macbeth isn't disgusted; he's persuaded. He's got what he wanted from her. The dreadful truth is that Macbeth accepts the argument for the same reason that might lead us to reject it.

- **He accepts it because it's evil.**

What she gives him is an image of something overwhelmingly wicked, something as wicked as killing Duncan. When he sees it in all its wickedness, he has the courage to do it. Macbeth wants to kill the king because it's a terrible thing to do.

Macbeth's ambition is not to be king, it's to kill the king. Lady Macbeth never thinks about what it will be like to be queen. To put it in modern terms, neither has a political programme. All they want to do is tyrannise, to bathe Scotland in blood. A dead king, a murdered general, a massacred family – these are their aims.

▶ **'These deeds must not be thought/After these ways' (2.2.31–2)**

The scene in which Macbeth returns from the murder of Duncan is the most tense in the play. The opening exchange – just single words and phrases – evokes the fear and the thrill of what they've done:

Lady Macbeth: Did you not speak?
Macbeth: When?
Lady Macbeth: Now.
Macbeth: As I descended?
Lady Macbeth: Ay.
Macbeth: Hark! – who lies i'th' second chamber?
Lady Macbeth: Donalbain.

(2.2.16–18)

The words might be whispered, but they speak loudly of their states of mind. Macbeth has descended, and though he might not have spoken, the high tension of their words say a great deal. They've been understood in terms of the language she uses in the persuasion scene:

> But screw your courage to the sticking-place
> And we'll not fail.

(1.7.60–1)

The 'sticking-place' is a term either from archery (loading a crossbow) or, more likely, tuning a musical instrument. When the pegs will no longer turn, the sticking-place has been reached. Turn it more, and the strings break. In those one word exchanges we hear the strings snap.

We don't see the 'deed' being done, but we share Lady Macbeth's (perverse?) excitement as she gloats that

> He is about it.
> The doors are open

(2.2.5)

Do we sense both pleasure and fear in her words: the doors are open, so he might be seen killing the old man? Do we hear an unnatural thrill in her words?

Guilt

Macbeth wonders at his guilt. The actor should bring out the astonishment as well as the horror in:

> But wherefore could I not pronounce 'Amen'?
> I had most need of blessing, and 'Amen'
> Stuck in my throat.

(2.2.29–31)

Macbeth isn't tracing the connection between sin, and guilt, he's wondering at why when he needs to say 'Amen', the word sticks in his throat. The crucial word is 'and', not 'but'; 'but' would have accounted for why he couldn't say it, 'and' merely records that it sticks. The physical accompaniment of emotion gives the feelings a vivid immediacy.

Macbeth's guilt is expressed in images, which have, as we'd expect with Macbeth, a poetic intensity. In little over 50 lines Macbeth talks in terms of religious ritual, public execution, sleep, knitting, bathing, feeding and the sea. What comes through is that he feels strongly that he's violated what's holy, everyday and natural.

Sleepwalking

One of the functions of Act 2, Scene 2 is to show the difference in response between Lady Macbeth and Macbeth; she's practical, whereas he explores the nature of what he's done with the imagination of a poet.

At one point she says:

> These deeds must not be thought
> After these ways. So, it will make us mad.

> (2.2.31–2)

This is hubris. We know that 'these deeds' *must* be thought of in this way.

It's easy to see her sleepwalking in psychological terms – she repressed her guilt, so it takes her over in the form of an illness, one symptom of which is sleepwalking. This isn't wrong; it's merely too obvious. Shakespeare uses the scene to remind us of what's happened. It's the nearest we get to seeing the killing of Duncan. What matters about the scene is its horror and terror:

> Yet who would have thought the old man to have had so much blood in him.
> (5.1.37–8)

That's what she saw when she went into the room. What she saw was not a king but an old man, who looks like her father; and rather than the old man being shrivelled, he's full of blood. The terms she uses are those that should have guided them: it's wrong to kill old men in their beds. One of the functions of the sleepwalking scene is to remind us through the horror of her recollections of a goodness they both have violated.

23.8 Discovery and the banquet scene

▶ 'What sights, my lord?' (3.4.115)

Discovering the body

The crucial moment in the discovery scene is when Macbeth is asked why he killed the grooms. This is his reply:

> Who can be wise, amazed, temp'rate and furious,
> Loyal and neutral in a moment? No man.
> Th'expedition of my violent love

Outran the pauser, reason. Here lay Duncan,
His silver skin laced with his golden blood,

(2.3.108–12)

Detached from the scene, we can see through this. Macbeth is too controlled. He produces a beautiful but far too neat image of Duncan's golden blood patterned on his silver skin with the delicacy of lace. This is art, not an outburst of natural passion.

The feast

The feast shows us that Macbeth wants to feel absolutely secure. When the murderer tells him that Fleance escaped, he says:

Then comes my fit again; I had else been perfect,
Whole as the marble, founded as the rock

(3.4.20–1)

The sense of the word 'perfect' here is only found in Shakespeare; it means contented and satisfied. Such contentment comes from knowing he's safe. We can see this in the images that follow.

The play shows that his way of achieving safety results in even greater insecurity. Having killed, he feels insecure, so he kills again. Banquo's ghost appears just after the assurance from the murderers that he's dead.

One question from Ross (a shifty figure who always ends up on the winning side) is very dangerous:

'What sights, my Lord?'

(3.4.115)

This can be seen as a turning point in the political life of the play. Macbeth has become king, but already we know there are suspicions. The next political move we hear about is that Macduff has fled to England. The final movement of the play has begun.

23.9 Macbeth's suffering

▶ 'Tomorrow, and tomorrow, and tomorrow' (5.5.18)

Suffering

Macbeth suffers. The nature of his suffering is an expression of the nature of his sins. Macbeth has violated nature – 'murdered sleep' (2.2.34) – so he's deprived of what's natural.

The most terrible suffering is his inability to feel what everyone feels. He knows exactly why he can no longer feel fear:

I have supped full with horrors.
Direness, familiar to my slaughterous thoughts,
Cannot once start me.

(5.5.13–15)

Those whose diet is horrors no longer find horrors horrific.

At the end he can still speak, even if it shows in what he says that he can't feel:

> Tomorrow, and tomorrow, and tomorrow
> Creeps in this petty pace from day to day
> To the last syllable of recorded time

(5.5.18–20)

The deliberate but lifeless rhythms, the dull alliterations, the flat cadences enact the mind of someone who can no longer feel what it's natural to feel. The only natural thing about it (and this rescues him) is that he can say it.

23.10 A heroic death

▶ 'I will not yield' (5.10.27)

A hero to the end

From Act 5, Scene 3 to the end, Macbeth assumes the role of the reckless hero. He knows that what's coming is a bloody fight that he can't win. He plays the role of the doomed hero with relish; when he's told that all the reports of an invading army have been confirmed, he says:

> I'll fight till from my bones my flesh be hacked.

(5.3.31)

That's grim but it's not mere heroic fantasising; he does know that that's what happens in battle. Perhaps he even relishes the prospect.

Humour

But Macbeth goes onto the battlefield still believing (or half-believing?) that he's safe from anyone born of woman. When he kills Young Siward, he mockingly dispatches him with a blunt epitaph:

> …Thou wast born of woman.

(5.9.13)

It would be appropriate (though difficult) for an actor to play the line with bitter humour.

The final test

The real test of his firmness comes when he's told that

> Macduff was from his mother's womb
> Untimely ripped.

(5.10.15–16)

When he hears Macduff's words he honestly admits he's subdued. This is remarkable from a man who's played the role of the warrior hero with an energy and a commitment unmatched in the whole of Shakespeare.

The one thing that stings him out of resignation is the threat that if he surrenders to Macduff he'll become 'the show and gaze o'th' time' (5.10.24). Macduff imagines him treated like a freak at a fairground:

> We'll have thee as our rarer monsters are
> Painted upon a pole, and underwrit
> 'Here may you see the tyrant.'
>
> (5.10.25–7)

Macbeth responds. He's played out his role of the bloody tyrant with gusto, and the prospect of being an object of curious fascination is incompatible with his strong sense of his heroism. So his heroic manner returns:

> I will not yield
> To kiss the ground before young Malcolm's feet,
> And to be baited with the rabble's curse.
> Though Birnam Wood be come to Dunsinane,
> And thou opposed being of no woman born,
> Yet I will try the last.
>
> (5.10.27–32)

It's difficult not to be heartened by that response. Everything is lost except his pride. There's something bracing about the defiant 'yet'; and the different meanings of 'try' – to test, to prove, to attempt – show him recovering all his heroic courage.

But as with all tragic gestures, it's ambiguous. At the end Macbeth is reckless, self-destructive, proud and swaggering. He must fight, and in fighting he knows that we will be stirred and even invigorated by the spectacle.

The final fate

Shakespeare sways our feelings again in the last scene. One way in which he recruits sympathy for a character is by showing people mutilating the body. The final scene is Malcolm's until Macduff enters with Macbeth's head. At that moment we feel that a wrong, an outrage, has been committed. Macbeth has been a man of blood, but he's the one we feel for in this final degradation.

23.11 More and less than a man

▶ **'I dare do all that may become a man' (1.7.46)**

One of the taunts Lady Macbeth aims at her husband is that he's like the cat in the popular proverb, who let

> 'I dare not' wait upon 'I would'
>
> (1.7.44)

The proverb she's referring to is one about a cat who wanted to eat fish but didn't want to get her feet wet.

Macbeth is aware that she's challenging his heroic status. His reply asserts that he's the fearless man who's afraid of nothing:

> I dare do all that may become a man;
> Who dares do more is none.
>
> (1.7.46–7)

The word 'become' means whatever is proper, fitting or suitable. It's clear that to both of them, killing the king is something that would 'become' a hero.

In this dialogue they stumble over the essence of their tragedy:

- **the horrible irony is that Macbeth *does* dare to do more than becomes a man.**

There's a thrill seeing someone trying to go beyond the limits of humanity. Yet Macbeth becomes less than a man; he almost forgets 'the taste of fears' (5.5.9) and he feels he can't respond appropriately to his wife's death. This is consistent with 'Who dares do more is none'. 'None' can mean either more or less than a man – a superman or a beast. The tragedy of Macbeth is that he aims at the former and comes close to being the latter.

Exercises

23.1 'This is Shakespeare's most sustained presentation of evil and yet audiences feel so close to the central (and most evil) character.' Explore how Shakespeare makes audiences feel this about *Macbeth*.

23.2 What does the marriage of Macbeth and Lady Macbeth contribute to the play?

23.3 'The poetry is both intense and beautiful, but the opportunity for gripping stage action is limited.' Do you agree with this view of *Macbeth*?

Part VI
The Roman Tragedies

Shakespeare's Roman World

24.1 The city of Rome

▶ 'the Roman state' (*Coriolanus*, 1.1.67)

Rome

The Roman tragedies – *Coriolanus*, *Julius Caesar*, *Antony and Cleopatra* – are about a state. Rome was the greatest empire that Shakespeare's world knew of. It stood for splendour and success. It was both history and myth; history because there were numerous writings about it, and myth because it represented in a full and vivid way certain human qualities.

In his Roman plays, Shakespeare almost makes the city a character. Things are done for Rome. Brutus justifies killing his friend by saying:

> I slew my best lover for the good of Rome
>
> (3.2.44)

A state being formed

Shakespeare is interested in a state that is being formed. *Coriolanus* shows a small city state struggling against war-like neighbours; *Julius Caesar* is about the last days of the Roman Republic and the first of the Empire, and *Antony and Cleopatra* is about how that Empire stabilises itself.

24.2 Politics and the individual

▶ 'our great competitor' (*Antony and Cleopatra*, 1.4.3)

The state and the individual

In a state that's acquiring its identity, there's likely to be an uneasy relationship between its outstanding individuals and the people's sense of their nation. They'll admire those who embody the ideals of the nation – the orators, soldiers and statesmen – but will fear that the outstanding figure might become a tyrant.

The theme of the Roman tragedies is:

- **the conflicts between the state of Rome and its outstanding figures.**

In this sense the plays are social. The central subject is the state, and the leading characters are defined by their relationships to it. Three figures emerge.

The authority figure

There's usually a character who embodies the state. Julius Caesar is the figure to whom all the people look. The opening scene shows people crowding the streets to welcome the man who comes to his own city as a victor. In *Antony and Cleopatra*, the Empire is embodied in the young Octavius, called in the text 'Caesar'. *Coriolanus* doesn't have a figure of this kind. This may be because the play is about a state that doesn't know whether it wants to have authority figures.

The enemy of authority

Brutus and Cassius in *Julius Caesar* and Antony in *Antony and Cleopatra* attack the power of the authority figure. Coriolanus is again a very interesting case. Coriolanus plays both roles. He's the authority figure against whom the Tribunes fight and the destroyer figure who almost brings Rome down.

The defender figure

When the enemy has attacked the authority figure, a defender or champion is needed to restore the state. The most fascinating figure here is Antony, who defends Rome, but who is then cast in the role of the enemy in *Antony and Cleopatra*. In *Coriolanus* the defender is Volumnia, the mother of Coriolanus. In persuading him not to attack Rome, she ensures its survival.

24.3 Roles in a changing state

▶ **'deed-achieving honour newly named'** (*Coriolanus*, 2.1.170)

Characters in search of roles

Because Shakespeare presents individuals living in states that are still being formed, there's a problem with roles. In a nation that's not yet achieved its identity, there aren't precisely defined parts for the leading citizens to play.

This is most clear in *Coriolanus*. His mother revels in his exploits on the battlefield, but problems are caused when they try to find another role for him. The business of showing wounds in public is a ritual this new state has fixed on, but the one to whom the nation looks after victory in battle is the very person who finds this embarrassing. He has won an honour and acquired a new name, but there's no role that he can play with integrity.

24.4 Morality and honour

▶ 'the honourable men' (*Julius Caesar*, 3.2.152)

Honour

Honour is a Roman virtue. When Antony speaks to the crowd he destroys Brutus's reputation through the ironic use of the word 'honourable'. By repeating the word and showing the people what the conspirators have done, he makes the people see that killing your friend is not honourable. This would not be effective in a state that, unlike Rome, had no place for such a quality.

No evil characters

Shakespeare shows that in the Roman tragedies:

● **there are no thoroughly evil characters.**

Nobody is like Iago or Goneril or Macbeth. The conspirators in *Julius Caesar* might be wrong and some might be worse men than others, but it would be wrong to call any of them evil. Similarly, in *Coriolanus* the Tribunes are not admirable and Aufidias is untrustworthy, but none of them would hand their fathers over to torture as Edmund does in *King Lear*.

The tragedies are social and political. What happens comes about because Rome is in a particular historical state.

24.5 The secular quality

▶ 'If Jupiter/Should from yon cloud speak divine things' (*Coriolanus*, 4.4.104)

The silent gods

The feeling in these plays is that Jupiter doesn't speak. The Roman tragedies don't give us much idea of the characters' religious outlooks or invite us to see the action in religious terms.

The 'secular' feel of these plays can't be put down to Shakespeare losing interest in religion. He's interested in questions of a religious kind if he can make drama out of them. He doesn't find such material in *Coriolanus*, but within a couple of years he's dramatising religion in the debate about art and nature in *The Winter's Tale*.

No absolutes

If there is an explanation of the absence of religious issues, it lies in Shakespeare's creation of the Roman world. The Roman world he presents us with is one that is not Christian. It doesn't deal with the absolutes of good and evil; this may be why there aren't evil characters.

In a world removed from Christianity, good and bad cease to be mysteries. This makes them less frightening and more open to reasoning. *Antony and Cleopatra* is sometimes excluded from the list of great tragedies. This may be due to the feeling that the tragedy is all too human in a way that *King Lear* isn't.

24.6 The code of suicide

▶ 'the high Roman fashion' (*Antony and Cleopatra*, 4.16.89)

Antony loses a battle, and he thinks Cleopatra has killed herself. He feels this as shame, so turns to his servant Eros:

> Thou art sworn, Eros,
> That when the exigent should come, which now
> Is come indeed – when I should see behind me
> Th'inevitable prosecution of
> Disgrace and horror – that on my command
> Thou then would'st kill me.

> (4.15.62–7)

He's not the only character in these plays that asks his servant to kill him. Cassius in *Julius Caesar* reminds Pindarus that he's bound to do all that his master asks.

- **Suicide is a part of the thinking of these characters.**

It's so central that Cleopatra sees death in Roman terms; the adoption of the 'high Roman fashion' is her way out of disgrace.

The duty (it almost amounts to that) of suicide is a further sign that this is not a Christian world. We might wonder whether Shakespeare sees something essentially self-destructive about the Roman state, that its values – honour, courage, military success – lead naturally to suicide, if characters fail to live up to them.

24.7 The importance of ideas

▶ 'a Roman thought' (*Antony and Cleopatra*, 1.2.77)

Philosophical ideas

Cleopatra is talking about Antony suddenly thinking of Rome. We can extend the word 'thought' and speak of the philosophical atmosphere of these plays. One of their features is the discussion of ideas.

The body politic

Coriolanus has as the centre-piece of the opening a long 'lecture' by Menenius about the image of the body politic (1.1. 87–161). It's a vivid tale and he tells it with wit, but the issues raised are politically important ones. The picture of the state is an organic one, each element has a place. It's also a hierarchical one; Menenius makes it clear that the belly, which he identifies as the Senators of Rome, should have priority when food is scarce.

The image of the body suggests that the state is unified. Nothing is further from the truth. Rome is split; it's not an organic society at all. The Tribunes don't behave as if they believed they were all members of one body; they look more like a faction competing for power. The picture that emerges is one of a society that's (inevitably?) divided against itself.

The issue of how societies work is one that several of the plays raise. What's significant about the Roman tragedies is that they present themselves in intellectual terms. We are shown events and are given the ideas in which they might be understood.

Exercises

24.1 How well and in what ways might the description 'soldiers, thinkers, lovers' be helpful in understanding the central characters of the Roman plays?

24.2 To what extent is it true to say that the dramatic interest of the Roman plays lies in the tension between the common people of Rome and a few outstanding individuals?

⎔25 Coriolanus

25.1 Mother and son

▶ 'he did it to please his mother' (1.1.36)

Coriolanus is about a family as well as a state. We hear within the first 10 lines that the plebeians (the common people of Rome) are against Martius (later called Coriolanus). Within the first 40 lines, his mother is held partly to blame for his behaviour. Shakespeare signals to us that what follows will be about the relationship between a mother and her son.

Son and husband

The mother appears in the third scene. Those who know something about Freud will find her opening words to her daughter-in-law shockingly revealing:

> I pray you, daughter, sing, or express yourself in a more comfortable sort. If my son were my husband, I should freelier rejoice in that absence wherein he won honour than in the embracements of his bed where he would show most love. (1.3.1–5)

She says that if her son were her husband, she'd be happier with the honour gained in war than in his love-making.

Whether we see this as compensation for an inadequate or dead husband doesn't matter. What's significant is that the powerful emotions of love and war are most intensely felt in Volumnia's feelings for her son. Later in the speech she talks with pride about how she sent him to war. This for her is a 'rite of passage':

> To cruel war I sent him, from whence he returned his brows bound with oak. I tell thee, daughter, I sprang not more in joy at first hearing he was a man-child than now in first seeing he had proved himself a man. (1.3.13–17)

Volumnia's imagery

Shakespeare shows the centrality of this disturbing mother/son relationship in Volumnia's imagery. When Coriolanus' wife is alarmed at Volumnia's imagined picture of 'his bloody brow' (1.3.36), the mother responds with this clumsy and ghastly image:

294   *THE ROMAN TRAGEDIES*

                    The breasts of Hecuba
         When she did suckle Hector looked not lovelier
         Than Hector's forehead when it spit forth blood

                         (1.3.42–4)

Blood is more beautiful than milk, a mutilated forehead lovelier than a mother's breast; Shakespeare knows this is crazy.

Sometimes, too much weight is placed upon a single image, but that mistake can't be made here. Volumnia later sees her son's valour as having been sucked from her:

         Thy valiantness was mine, thou sucked'st it from me

                         (3.2.129)

And we can't exclude the parallels; Volumnia sees herself as the mother of the greatest warrior of the ancient world. Because she's aware of a literary tradition behind what she says, we see that her response is also expressive of her culture. Rome, for all its military might, is looked upon as female:

             The country, our dear nurse

                         (5.3.111)

In Shakespeare's day a nurse was one who suckled a child; Rome is a woman whose breasts feed her citizens.

Boy

The word 'boy' is used to great effect in the last scene of the play, when Coriolanus argues with Aufidias:

Coriolanus: Hear'st thou Mars?
Aufidias: Name not the god, thou boy of tears.

                         (5.6.102–3)

Coriolanus might be a 'boy of tears' because he calls on the god of war like a small child crying for his mother or because he's a foolish child whose rash behaviour has caused tears. The text shows that he resents this:

             Cut me to pieces, Volsces. Men and lads,
             Stain all your edges on me. 'Boy'! False hound,
             If you have writ your annals true, 'tis there
             That, like an eagle in a dove-cote, I
             Fluttered your Volscians in Corioli.
             Alone I did it. 'Boy'!

                         (5.6.112–17)

This is his last big speech, his last claim that he should be seen as a hero. The style is high; there's an attempt at the epic manner in the reversal of standard word order in 'Alone I did it.'

He thinks that such a recital will rebut the accusation that he's a boy. But does it? The role can be played in such a way as to show that he's still the little boy trying to please his mother. This reading gives the play a symmetry. At the start he's accused of acting to please his mother; at the end he's accused of being a boy.

25.2 Coriolanus at war

▶ 'the Volsces are in arms' (1.1.224)

Coriolanus, along with *Henry V*, is Shakespeare's most sustained presentation of war.

The time of war

War comes when Rome is divided against itself. When news comes that 'the Volsces are in arms' (1.1.224), Martius's response is:

> I am glad on't. Then we shall ha' means to vent
> Our musty superfluity.
>
> (1.1.225–6)

The war is seen as an opportunity to 'vent' – sell or excrete – rotting left-overs. Martius is talking about the plebeians he's just been criticising.

It's one of the few moments when he shows acute (if grim) political insight, though, typically, he says it in the presence of those whom he's criticising.

War as combat

When war comes, Martius is excited; Aufidius is the ideal companion or foe:

> Were half to half the world by th' ears and he
> Upon my part, I'd revolt to make
> Only my wars with him. He is a lion
> That I am proud to hunt.
>
> (1.1.233–6)

Shakespeare is preparing us for the dramatic irony that Martius *will* make wars with Aufidias. He's also indicating that war is a kind of personal combat; the image is of hunter and hunted, and the prize makes the hunter proud.

Authority

There's a significant exchange immediately after Martius' words about Aufidias. A Senator reminds him that he promised to serve under Comminius. He replies:

> And I am constant.
>
> (1.1.238)

Shakespeare trusts his audience to see the significance of these words. They show that Martius is not an ambitious man. He may see war as a means of personal glory (his mother certainly does) but he doesn't seek positions of power, not even military power.

Fighting

In the battle for Corioli we see the best and worst of Martius. No production succeeds unless it make us see that he's a brave man. The audience needs to see him launching his attack on Corioli so they will be roused by the wonder of his heroic re-appearance, bespattered with blood, within the walls of Corioli. (See Illustration 7.)

Illustration 7   Coriolanus emerging from Corioli

But he remains the same scornful Martius when he rounds on troops that are not as valiant as he is (compare Comminius in Act 1, Scene 7). We all know this type – the good sportsman who bullies those who can't jump as high as he can. He seems to enjoy the fact that they are 'all hurt behind' (1.5.8).

Comradeship

The scene in which Martius and Comminius meet on the battlefield brims with intimate imagery, which expresses the comradeship of war. Emotionally speaking, it's the warmest in the play; Martius says:

> O, let me clip ye
> In arms as sound as when I wooed, in heart
> As merry as when our nuptial day was done,
> And tapers burnt to bedward!

(1.7.29–32)

Those who want to seek out psychological undertones might think sex and the battlefield are strangely linked, but perhaps Shakespeare's point is that there's an intimacy of the battlefield.

25.3 War and heroes

▶ 'this war's garland' (1.10.59)

● **Shakespeare knows that Rome is a society that makes heroes**.

The gestures of a hero

In Act 1, Scene 7 soldiers lift him high in a public acclamation:

> O' me alone, make you a sword of me?

(1.7.76)

This is the fulfilment of Martius; he's acclaimed while the battle is still in the balance, and soldiers flock to him. Lifting him high (one of the most stirring dramatic moments in Shakespeare) is a celebration of what he's done and an anticipation of victory.

The moment is symbolic; Coriolanus discovers the individuality – 'me alone' – which will cause the disasters of the middle and final scenes. He's a soldier of Rome; but he's more than that, and Rome can't cope with an individual nature that can't be fitted into the narrow requirements of public office. Symbolically, he's also Rome's sword; in a world in which Rome is threatened, her chief possession is the heroic fighter. Warrior societies produce warrior heroes.

The combat

Martius meets the 'lion' whom he's 'proud to hunt' (1.1.236) in Act 1, Scene 9. Martius's first words show that he's being more than a soldier; he's a hero who must fight with the opposing side's champion. Significantly, none of the soldiers who rallied to him in Act 1, Scene 7 are present. As in the taking of Corioli, Martius is alone, and he fights Aufidias alone:

> I'll fight with none but thee

> (1.9.1)

He proudly tells Aufidias of his heroic deeds:

> Alone I fought in Corioles' walls
> And made what work I pleased.

> (1.9.8–9)

Here are the beginnings of the tragic hero. Martius is celebrating himself, speaking of himself in the language of an epic, and bringing out that he 'alone' was responsible for the taking of the city. As an individual fighter he's a threat to the Volscians;

- **the irony is that he's also a threat to Rome and to himself.**

Rome has no way of dealing with such rampant individualism, and its inability to cope destroys him.

The creation of the hero

After the battle Comminius makes Martius a hero by anticipating the effect the story of his 'deeds' (1.10.2) will have on the people. Our understanding of the whole play depends upon how we read his reply:

> Pray now, no more. My mother
> Who has a charter to extol her blood,
> When she does praise me grieves me. I have done
> As you have done, that's what I can; induced
> As you have been, that's for my country.

> (1.10.13–17)

We might remember his scorn for cowardly soldiers (1.5.1–13) and think that he's posing here. But is he capable of such behaviour? Doesn't the play show that he can't act roles he doesn't believe in? If he could, he'd have successfully asked the people to consent to him being Consul.

- **Part of his tragedy is that there's only one role he can play – the hero soldier.**

If, then, he's genuine, we have to accept that public adulation (even that of his mother) is embarrassing. The truth is that he's content to do what he can for his country. It's not political cunning that makes him refuse special material rewards (1.10.36–40). The essence of the man is that he doesn't welcome 'acclamations hyperbolical' (1.10.50). Yet he is acclaimed with a new name; he becomes Coriolanus.

25.4 Heroes and politics

▶ **'I had rather be their servant'** (2.1.200)

Coriolanus is the tragedy of a man who's forced to play a role that he doesn't want and which doesn't suit him. Because the role is provided by Rome, the tragedy is hers also.

A warrior hero

Rome is threatened by her neighbours. The only way she can survive is through military success. As a consequence, the most important citizen is the one who brings that success. Shakespeare shows that if the currency of comedy is knowledge, the currency of Rome is soldiership: 'Yet welcome, warriors' (2.1.186).

Shakespeare realises that:

- **the soldier who has provided what Rome needs and is therefore the one who sums up the values of Rome is also a problem.**

What can the city *do* with such a figure?

When his mother implies he should be Consul, he says:

> I had rather be their servant in my way
> Than sway with them in theirs.

> (2.1.200–1)

He would rather serve Rome as a soldier than 'sway' with the Senate. 'Sway' is ambiguous; it can mean exercise power and bend. His view has been that, in the latter sense, the leaders of Rome have been swayed too much by the plebeians and their Tribunes. He's no taste for such swaying.

Rome, rewards and the consulship

But in Shakespeare's presentation

- **Rome is a young country with no way other than the consulship of rewarding her outstanding citizens.**

So Coriolanus is pressed by his mother and friends to seek an office he does not want.

And not only that. Shakespeare exposes the gap between the role the state wants him to perform and what has emerged on the battlefield – his character:

- **Coriolanus is an individual in a society which only really functions if people lay aside their individuality and serve the state.**

His individuality doesn't affect him on the battlefield but it does in politics.

- **What Rome can't see is that he's quite unsuited to a political role.**

The fiasco of showing his wounds and the ghastly scenes in which he's manipulated into speaking his mind show that he's no political sense at all. As Aufidias say later, he can't 'be other than one thing' (4.7.42).

The rejected man

Because Coriolanus is a soldier, there's nothing for him to do but show his outrage at his treatment in a soldier-like way. When he's expelled from the city he has saved, the code of the soldier binds him to the only other person he admires – Aufidias. Thus the one who was the defender of the state becomes the enemy of the state, because the state has no way of rewarding him other than making him into a politician.

25.5 The instability of power

▶ 'how soon confusion/May enter' (3.1.113–14)

Power

Coriolanus has no political sense but he does have political understanding. He thinks about what's going on, and he's uncomfortably aggressive about what he sees.

His view is very different from that voiced by Menenius. In the opening scene (see 24.17) he presents with wit and even charm the picture of the state as the body politic. The irony of the play is that neither the Tribunes nor Coriolanus agree. They see politics as a kind of war (class war?) in which if one side doesn't hold power, the other will:

> my soul aches
> To know, when two authorities are up,
> Neither supreme, how soon confusion
> May enter 'twixt the gap of both and take
> The one by th 'other.

> (3.1.111–15)

Does the play bear out what he says? My feeling is that it does. Shakespeare understands that in a society in which one group holds power, a single concession to the powerless group never satisfies them. He also knows that if society is so divided, those in conflict have no option other than to either defend their position or attempt to take over. Early Rome is a society in which there can be no 'middle way', no decent compromises.

25.6 Coriolanus and Aufidias

▶ 'Do they still fly to th' Roman?' (4.7.1)

The new hero

In Corioli Coriolanus has a different political status. He's the new kid on the block, the man who was admired as an enemy and who now stands with them. It's all a bit like a charismatic footballer, who moves from, say, Arsenal to Spurs. His status therefore depends upon his novelty, and that novelty hurts Aufidias.

A fragile popularity

Aufidias sees popularity as merely a matter of fashion. This leads to one of the toughest speeches of the play:

> So our virtues
> Lie in th' interpretation of the time,
> And power, unto itself most commendable,

Hath not a tomb so evident as a chair
T'extol what it hath done.

(4.7.49–53)

This has been described as cynical. Aufidias is waiting for the popularity Coriolanus has aroused to turn against him. Whatever is good about us is subject to the passing opinion ('interpretation') of the times. This might not be cynical but it's very close to relativism – the view that values are entirely made by society and change as society changes (see 13.6).

A tragic view

There is, however, another thought emerging in what he says. This is one much closer to tragedy:

- **power publicly celebrated by the one who has it leads to his destruction.**

The chair – a pulpit – is the place where power is celebrated, but that very act of celebration rebounds on the successful figure with destructive force.
    Perhaps there are two tragedies in *Coriolanus:*

- the tragedy of the man who embodies all the values of a society and yet is destroyed by that society's expectations of him
- the tragedy of the man who flamboyantly displays his power in such a way as to turn that power against himself.

25.7 Women and victory

▶ 'You have won a happy victory in Rome' (5.3.187)

Will he yield?

In Act 5, Scene 2, Shakespeare creates expectation at the start of the scene by making Coriolanus say that nothing will make him change his mind. No sooner has he said it than the women enter with his son. Their entry poses the question: will he yield? He knows that yielding is the natural thing:

All bond and privilege of nature break;
Let it be virtuous to be obstinate.

(5.2.25–6)

Yet another tragic possibility arises here. The irony is that if nature wins, then he'll be destroyed, because he'll have failed to help Aufidias take Rome. Yet the power of nature is strong. The image of the man who resists nature because he's 'author of himself' (5.2.36) shows that it is impossible to be unnatural. No man can be author of himself'. If we take that image seriously, we know he must yield.

Kneeling and yielding

Volumnia knows that what she's doing is also unnatural – she kneels. For a parent to kneel to a child (as Lear tries) is unthinkable (5.2.54–6). In the confusion that follows her kneeling, she says something of great significance: 'Thou art my warrior' (5.2.62). This is in keeping with the 'priority' of the play's relationship:

- **before he's a son of Rome, he's a son of Volumnia.**

That's the natural order. If she can establish that, then he might be led to see the rest.

If there is a crucial moment, it's their kneeling. She says they will 'shame him with their knees' (5.2.170). His reply implies that the sight of his kneeling mother has turned away his revenge:

> Behold, the heavens do ope,
> The gods look down, and this unnatural scene
> They laugh at.

> (5.2.184–6)

Those words suggest that he's suddenly seeing the world from a vantage point other than his own anger and hurt. In the eyes of the gods the 'unnatural' doings of frail mortals are comical. He knows, however, that the Volsces won't see it this way. He goes on to say in the epic mode of the third person:

> Most dangerously you have with him prevailed,
> If not most mortal to him.

> (5.2.189–90)

From that new vantage point he sees he's doomed. What follows is Aufidias's scheming and the violation of his body.

Our feelings

Coriolanus is not a favourite hero with many theatre-goers, but in the last scene he not only does the right thing but rises above his narrow resentments. Shakespeare is deeply suspicious of the cult of the hero, but he might have more time for someone who does what he sees as right, even though it will cost him his life.

Exercises

25.1 'We might not warm to Coriolanus but we are positively repelled by Volumnia.' Do you agree with this?

25.2 In *Coriolanus*, what is Shakespeare showing us about how a hero is created and how his existence creates problems for Rome?

---

26) Julius Caesar

26.1 Caesar, Brutus and tragedy

▶ 'O mighty Caesar! Dost thou lie so low?' (3.1.149)

Tragedy

The play has a clear tragic shape; it concerns the rise and fall of a mighty man. The opening scenes show the public response to a returning hero. Even those who plot against him use elevated language:

> And this man
> Is now become a god

(1.2.117–18)

Cassius loathes the public celebration of Caesar, but he recognises that Caesar is the focus of an adulation that has deified him.

And this figure falls; in Antony's words, he lies 'low', he's 'shrunk to this little measure' (3.1.151). The fall is not from riches to rags as in *Lear*, but from public acclamation to public rejection. He enters Rome as a hero and in his death he's branded by the conspirators as a man who's betrayed republican traditions.

Double movements

Julius Caesar is, however, more complex than the description above indicates. Without losing any of its classical features, the play doubles the movement of the plot, and it does this in two ways.

Falling and rising

Caesar falls and then rises. The movement is like a double wave. He enters Rome as a victor, and his reputation rises until he's struck down. But then through Antony and Octavius he rises and becomes the destroyer of the conspirators.

When he sees the dead bodies of Cassius and Titinius, Brutus says:

> O Julius Caesar, thou art mighty yet.
> Thy spirit walks abroad, and turns our swords
> In our own proper entrails.

(5.3.93–5)

In his death Caesar fell from the top to the bottom of the wheel of fortune; through Antony and Octavius he moves up to the top again.

Characters doubled

The second movement that's doubled is the paralleling of Caesar and Brutus. In the first half of the play, they are presented as doubles; they both grow in power, gathering support for their cause.

Caesar's fall corresponds to Brutus's rise. As Caesar lies in the dust, Brutus is applauded by the crowd; with horrible and quite unintended irony, one of the crowd says 'Let him be Caesar' (3.2.51).

Then as Brutus falls, Caesar rises. At the end, Caesar has won and Brutus, his tragic double, has lost.

26.2 Caesar: for and against

▶ 'the noble Caesar' (3.2.182)

Caesar is a much more significant character than productions and films often allow. He's often presented as old, fat and pompous. This won't do for two reasons.

- The first is that unless he's presented as a powerful figure, the conspirators appear to be head-cases rather than men who've legitimate fears about the future of the nation.
- The second is that he's a carefully drawn character, who provokes strong responses: the crowd love him; the Tribunes fear him.

The case for the prosecution

Caesar can be criticised in four ways. How strong are these criticisms?

(1) Ambition

The first criticism is that he's ambitious. This is to misunderstand what Shakespeare has done. Caesar's behaviour is ambiguous. The two Tribunes are 'put to silence' (1.2.286), but it doesn't follow that Caesar wants to be king.

(2) Weakness

The second criticism is the acccusations made against him by Cassius. These are that he wasn't very good at swimming in rough water and that he cried out when he had a fever. So?

(3) Superstition

The third criticism is that he's superstitious because he wants Antony, when running in the festive race, to touch his wife to cure her barrenness. But he's a rationalist when dealing with the soothsayer's warnings and Calpurnia's dreams.

(4) Arrogance

The fourth criticism is that he's arrogant. In the assassination scene he grandly talks of himself in the third person, as kings often do. But this is what we'd expect of a tragic figure; Caesar plays his role with dramatic force. Shakespeare uses direct self-explanation, so the audience can see what kind of a man he is.

The case for the defence

The following points can be made in support of Caesar being an impressive figure.

(1) Authority

He commands instant respect from Casca – 'Peace, ho! Caesar speaks' (1.2.2) – and Antony – 'When Caesar says 'Do this', it is performed' (1.1.12).

(2) Judgement

His judgement that Cassius is an envious man is sound.

(3) Gracious

When the conspirators meet at his house, he's welcoming and gracious.

(4) Sensitive

In his death, he's sharp enough to recognise the betrayal and even the tragedy of Brutus.

26.3 Cassius and the plot

▶ 'that spare Cassius' (1.2.202)

Cassius is probably the most interesting character to play. He's energetic, wily, intelligent and driven by intensely strong feelings.

He's responsible for the shape of the plot in the first half of the play. Were this play a comedy, he would be the chief practiser.

His envy

Yet in spite of his power, he remains a small man. The energy that drives him looks as if it comes from burning resentment and envy. This is what he says about the fever Caesar suffered in Spain:

> He had a fever when he was in Spain,
> And when the fit was on him, I did mark
> How he did shake. 'Tis true, this god did shake.
> His coward lips did from their colour fly

(1.2.121–4)

He says he 'did mark' as if this were a remarkably acute perception. But everyone with a fever shakes; that's what it means to have a fever. And why should he talk about his 'coward lips'; being ill isn't the same thing as being a coward at all. What we might see in all this is a hatred arising out of envy and inferiority. Although he doesn't mean it this way, he may be right when he calls himself 'a wretched creature' (1.2.118).

A malcontent

Cassius can be described as a malcontent. A malcontent is often a very interesting figure because he's a gifted man who has never prospered as he felt he should.

What we should feel is that the failure has turned him sour. The malcontent has poisoned himself with his own resentments and envy. This is why he's dangerous. Caesar is right:

> Such men as he be never at heart's ease
> Whiles they behold a greater than themselves
>
> (1.2.209–10)

His strengths

His greatest asset is his language; he can almost make a weak case convincing. Take, for instance, the scene in which he first talks to Brutus about the danger of Caesar (1.2.34–178).

He's alert to what Brutus says. When he rather carelessly says he fears the crowds have made Caesar king, Cassius seizes on the crucial word: 'Ay, do you fear it?' (1.2.82).

Without being smarmy, he lets Brutus know that he admires him. Brutus says he will listen without fear to Cassius, so Cassius, with the natural ease of someone saying what everybody knows, says: 'I know that virtue to be in you, Brutus' (1.2.92).

He plays on Brutus's pride; his crescendo of relentless run-on lines ends with an outburst that at one time there was a Brutus (an ancestor) who would have done anything to preserve his freedom (1.2.159–62).

His weaknesses

What's interesting about Cassius is that he's not successful. This is something to do with the fact that in the presence of Brutus, he's cowed. When there's a dispute, Cassius always gives way. When he's with Brutus, his will is frozen. He gives in over the issue of whether Antony should speak at Caesar's funeral and over the plan of the battle. Both these concessions are disastrous. Cassius's envy is the motivating force of the first half of the play; giving way to Brutus coincides with the decline in his and the conspirators' fortunes.

26.4 Difficulties with Brutus

▶ 'the noblest Roman of them all' (5.5.67)

Nobility

Brutus is a difficult character to think about. There's a general agreement that he's 'noble'. This is one of the important words in the Roman tragedies. It appears 32 times in *Julius Caesar*. It means upright, fair, honest and trustworthy. It also has the association of being elevated, above common aspirations and emotionally disciplined.

The conspirators want him on their side because his presence gives an integrity and authority to their plot. When Cinna, who doesn't know what Cassius has been up to, says:

> O, Cassius, if you could
> But win the noble Brutus to our party

(1.3.140–1)

you can hear in the longing of that 'O' what Brutus means to people – his presence validates any undertaking.

Self-estimation

The trouble with Brutus is that he *knows* he's noble. He's not a proud man but he's very self-assured. Perhaps it's this complete confidence in himself that makes Cassius submit to him.

As soon as he joins the conspiracy Brutus behaves, with natural authority, as the leader. When Casca suggest that Cicero, a citizen noted for his eloquence, should be approached, Brutus delivers his judgement with simple unforced confidence:

> O, name him not! Let us not break with him,
> For he will never follow anything
> That other men begin.

(2.1.149–51)

We've no idea whether this is a sound judgement on Cicero, but it's certainly a judgement that Brutus, by implication, is passing on himself. Unlike the egocentric Cicero, he presents himself as a man who'll follow what others have started. In criticising another, he becomes his own judge.

Judging himself

On occasions this habit of judging himself (always favourably) becomes insufferable. Listen to him before the battle, when Cassius has asked him whether he's content, if he loses, to go as a prisoner to Rome:

> No, Cassius, no.
> Think not, thou noble Roman,
> That ever Brutus will go bound to Rome.
> He bears too great a mind.

(5.2.110–13)

It may be true, but it's not Brutus's place to say that *his* mind is too great to allow him to go to Rome as a prisoner.

His tragic role

To say that he acts as his own judge is to draw attention to his awareness of his tragic status.

- **Brutus knows that he's a tragic hero.**

In his death he acts out the tragic role and comments upon his own performance. When he enters for what's to be his last scene he effectively poses with his friends in a tragic tableau:

Come, poor remains of friends, rest on this rock.

(5.5.1)

Once settled he speaks darkly of what is to come:

> Slaying is the word:
> It is the deed in fashion.

(5.5.4–5)

'Deed' shows that he's presenting himself as the epic hero and 'fashion' indicates his awareness of the role he's playing; part of what it is to be noble is to do things properly.

When he justifies his suicide, he does so according to the heroic code. He singles out for himself the role of the man who freely leaps into the pit before he's pushed; this he feels is more worthy than waiting to be pushed:

> It is more worthy to leap in ourselves
> Than tarry till they push us.

(5.5.24–5)

Again, he's being his own judge.

His last speech is the culmination of the tragic role:

> I shall have glory by this losing day,
> More than Octavius and Mark Antony
> By this vile conquest shall attain unto.
> So fare you well at once, for Brutus' tongue
> Hath almost ended his life's history.

(5.5.36–40)

We must be impressed by his assurance and his poise; there's nothing reckless about his actions. But he's his own judge. He decides he will have more glory than the victors, and he makes it clear that he's reciting, in the heroic third person, his own life story when he says his tongue has 'almost ended his life's history'.

26.5 Antony's change

▶ 'a masquer and a reveller' (5.1.62)

Antony

Those are the cutting words of Cassius on the eve of the battle; he's thinking of the Antony we met at the beginning of the play – the man who runs in public games, who loves plays (1.2.204) and who 'revels long a-nights' (2.2.116).

But the abuse is out of date; as Cassius has fallen, Antony has risen. The death of Caesar is the making of Antony. The actor playing Antony must show that when he enters (3.1.147) after the killing, he's a changed man. From then till the battle, he becomes what Cassius was in the first part of the play – the motivating force of the plot.

Meeting the assassins

Antony's entrance after Caesar's death is effectively the turning point of the play. Cassius is shrewd enough to see that he's an enemy. This must be based on his opening words:

> O mighty Caesar! Dost thou lie so low?
> Are all thy conquests, glories, triumphs, spoils
> Shrunk to this little measure.

(3.1.149–50)

Any one who speaks like that will be a dangerous orator at a political funeral. Already, he's casting Caesar in the role of the tragic hero – everything he achieved had been laid low and shrunk to 'this little measure'. Nothing we've seen before prepares us for such eloquence or such danger.

Antony's feelings

Antony's strategy is to play up his feelings. He appears entirely open, vulnerable, consumed with grief and, above all, politically naïve in that he acts out the role of Caesar's grieving friend without ambiguity:

> Shall it not grieve thee dearer than thy death
> To see thy Antony making his peace,
> Shaking the bloody fingers of thy foes –
> Most noble! – in the presence of thy corpse?

(3.1.197–200)

They think they know exactly where he stands. A clever man who keeps his true feelings concealed is someone to fear, but the man who doesn't hide what he feels is, in politics, a harmless eccentric. If Antony, by parading his raw feelings, can make the conspirators think that he's hiding nothing, then he's in a powerful position. The cleverest politician is the one who doesn't appear to be a politician at all; that's the role Antony plays.

Permission to speak

If they take him to be the man whose feelings are open to all, then they'll believe him when he says 'I am with you all' (3.1.222). A man who's so open can be believed even when what he says is quite unlikely. Having established that trust, he slips in his request to speak at the funeral as an after-thought:

> And am, moreover, suitor that I may
> Produce his body to the market-place,
> And in the pulpit, as becomes a friend,
> Speak in the order of the funeral.

(3.1.228–31)

That speech tries to smooth away any fears about him that might remain. 'Moreover' looks like a sudden thought rather than a piece of clever calculation; the phrase he slots in – 'as becomes a friend' – is hardly recognisable as ambiguous (whose friend?), and the request to 'speak in order' suggests that the order of the ceremony won't be disturbed.

Antony's soliloquy

Shakespeare allows the audience to know what they might have begun to suspect. Left to himself, Antony, in soliloquy, opens his heart. He talks of the 'butchers' (3.1.258) and says that Caesar's wounds will 'beg the voice and utterance of my tongue' (3.1.264). There follows a ghastly vision of 'domestic fury and fierce civil strife' (3.1.266) and he ends by saying Caesar's spirit will 'let slip the dogs of war' (3.1.276).

The funeral

By the time Antony stands in the pulpit, the crowd are not friendly. Brutus has convinced at least some of them that 'this Caesar was a tyrant' (3.2.69). Antony turns them round through the use of a number of strategies.

• The word 'honourable'

Very early on he produces the word that with increasing irony he uses against them. The repetition itself arouses suspicion: why is this word being used so frequently? He uses it after his declaration that he could stir them to mutiny. If he could, can it be that the men against whom the mutiny would be stirred are not honourable? When a member of the crowd shouts:

> They were traitors. Honourable men?
>
> (3.2.154)

We know that his message has got through.

• How to mourn

In the opening speech he asks why, since they loved him once, they don't now mourn for him. That's his way of saying that mourning is proper. What he's got to do is make them mourn as he wants them to. He does this by showing them how:

> Bear with me.
> My heart is in the coffin there with Caesar,
> And I must pause till it comes back to me.
>
> (3.2.106–8)

There is a devastating irony in this scene. Antony's heart doesn't come back to him, it remains with Caesar. The rise of Caesar, powered by Antony's heart, begins at this moment. Later, he says that were he an orator like Brutus he would 'put a tongue/In every wound of Caesar' (3.2).

• Caesar's body

Central to Antony's strategy is the actual body of Caesar. He does what he said he would in the previous scene – he puts his tongue into Caesar's wounds, so they speak loudly against the conspirators. Caesar's body is not approached directly; we only see it through his clothes. The cloak Caesar wore when he was killed conceals his body *and* reveals it in the horror of its mutilation. Nakedness can be shocking, and in erotic terms, none too exciting, but bodies clothed or partly clothed can excite:

Through this the well-beloved Brutus stabbed;
And as he plucked his cursed steel away,
Mark how the blood of Caesar followed it,

(3.2.174–6)

We see the vulnerable body of Caesar 'through' the garment that clothed him, and betrayal is evident in the warmth of 'well-beloved' and the intimacy of the blood following, as if in love, the 'cursed steel'.

● **Negative instructions**

Antony's method is to lead the crowd to to do what he tells them not to and to get him to do what he says he won't. He says he will *not* stir them to 'mutiny and rage' (3.2.123), that he will *not* read the will and inflame them, that he will *not* rouse them 'to such a sudden flood of mutiny' (93.2.206). All of these happen.

● **Appealing to the crowd**

The point of reading the will is that he appeals to their poverty and feelings of exclusion. They are the common people and as such don't have gardens to wander in. When they hear that Caesar had left them his (3.2.240–5), they've been given a privileged place in the nation. Antony presents Caesar as the people's Caesar. When people have lost someone whom they've been led to believe they love, the desire to take revenge is very strong.

● **Presenting the tragedy**

Antony gives the most vivid picture of Caesar's tragedy in the play:

Then burst his mighty heart,
And in his mantle muffling up his face,
Even at the base of Pompey's statue,
Which all the while ran blood, great Caesar fell.

(3.2.184–7)

The tragedy arises out of grief, and its enaction is theatrical. Caesar muffles his face and falls. The poetry is far more dramatic than that bare statement; the word 'fell' is held back by two clauses, which evoke the power of the event by placing the once-mighty Caesar at the foot of a statue, and making that statue appear to be bleeding.

26.6 Antony and the people

▶ **'Friends, Romans, countrymen' (3.2.74)**

The crowd – the people of Rome – are a feature of *Coriolanus* and *Julius Caesar*. What is to be made of them?

The popular voice

Shakespeare wants to make it clear that Caesar is popular, so he starts the play with a crowd rejoicing at his return from war. The crowd continues as supporters of Caesar in the scenes we hear about from Casca and, of course, at the funeral.

The consequence of this is to make a distinction between Caesar and Antony and the conspirators. Caesar and Antony might be described as populists, whereas, though Brutus has a high reputation, he's not a man of the people.

Their wit

The opening scene establishes them as representatives of that loveable English character – the witty working-class man. Alternative comedians still find it necessary to speak in Estuary English, no matter what their original social class is. The puns show members of the crowd to be more nimble than the serious Tribunes, and, importantly, their wit makes it impossible for us to dismiss them as dolts.

Their changeability

Because *Julius Caesar* is a political play, Shakespeare must find a way of dramatically presenting one of the elements in politics – changes in outlook. The crowd is his means of doing this. In them is embodied one of the facts of political life – the brevity and instability of reputation.

Their danger

The last crowd scene is one of the most chilling in Shakespeare. Cinna the poet is murdered in the street because he has the wrong name. The scene is both grim and farcical. Poor Cinna has been dreaming of Caesar when he meets a mob, which has to kill somebody. The savagery (even if it's comic) indicates the depth of hatred aroused by Antony.

26.7 The morality of assassination

▶ 'These many, then, shall die' (4.1.1)

Assassination

It's been said of *Julius Caesar* that it's the only play in English that deals with the morality of political assassination. Morality might be an odd word to apply to the scene, which begins with Antony saying that those on the list 'shall die'. A grisly bargaining begins in which friends and relatives are marked down to be eliminated. In less than 10 lines, Shakespeare establishes how coldly unscrupulous the new power in Rome is. Perhaps, Shakespeare prompts us to think, the conspirators, now fled from Rome, were not so bad. They were 'honourable' in a way the new boys aren't. And as soon as one of them, Lepidus, leaves the stage, Antony and Octavius start to plot against him, The conspirators stick together.

But before we condemn the triumvers, consider this from Brutus:

> And, gentle friends,
> Let's kill him boldly, but not wrathfully,
> Let's carve him as a dish fit for the gods,
> Not hew him as a carcase fit for hounds.

(2.1.171–4)

He's talking about killing his friend and he dresses it up as if it were some religious ritual! Which is worse: killing people in cold blood as a political necessity or pretending that killing your friend is really a sacrifice ('Let's be sacrificers, not butchers' – 2.1.166)?

That's the question the play poses.

Exercises

26.1 Do you agree that what gives *Julius Caesar* life as a play is the contrast between Brutus and Antony?

26.2 In what ways is it true to say that throughout the play Julius Caesar is the most important character?

Antony and Cleopatra

27.1 Action and reaction

▶ **'Here is my space'** (1.1.36)

Its domestic atmosphere

The play, for all its gorgeous poetry, is a very homely piece. Cleopatra regards Antony as a husband (she calls him that in her suicide speech – 5.2.282), and when they are together the atmosphere, with all the servants and attendants, is that of the house of a rich lord. Another feature is that although the play deals with world politics, the stage is rarely full; much of the action is private. Moreover, most of the scenes are indoors.

Reaction rather than action

We don't see the great battles; Shakespeare concentrates on the *effect* they have on Antony. So though the play presents the rises and falls of his fortunes, it does so in a distinctive way:

- *Antony and Cleopatra* **might be described as a psychological drama in that the rise and fall in Antony's fortunes are chiefly present to us in his moods.**

What we see and hear is a man distraught or exhilarated, and those states are present in the language and their accompanying gestures. Whatever has taken place, we see it in the 'space' of Antony's mind. What interests Shakespeare is not the thrill of battles but the despair or ecstasy they provoke in Antony.

27.2 Antony's status

▶ **'The demi-Atlas of this earth'** (1.5.23)

All the major and some of the minor characters talk about Antony.

The words above form one of Cleopatra's lyrical outbursts. Atlas was the figure who supported the earth. She gives her man that status. The image has appeared at the start; one of his followers has called him 'the triple pillar of the world' (1.1.12).

But that follower, Philo, speaks those words in a highly critical speech.

- **One of the features of the Roman plays is that they all begin with fierce criticism of the central character.**

Philo's point is that this once great man – one of the three leaders holding up the world – has degenerated into 'a strumpet's [prostitutes's] fool' (1.1.13). In the play

- **Antony is regarded as hero *and* fool.**

Two points about the play arise from this clash of opinion.

A play of conflicting judgements

Throughout the play characters judge each other. The play abounds in conflicting opinions about the leading figure. Philo regards Cleopatra as a prostitute, but the famous speech of Enobarbus celebrate her as human yet already the stuff of myth (2.2.197–247).

- **Shakespeare achieves this by a theatrical framing.**

This is one of the functions of the opening scene. The two followers, Philo and Demetrius, act as an audience awaiting the entrance of the players. Antony and Cleopatra enter and set a tone in their renaissance love-debate quite different from the criticism of the frame. When they exit, the criticism continues. This framing occurs throughout.

The ambiguity of Antony

Antony is ambiguous because he's praised by characters we'd expect to criticise him.
   Were this a simplistic play, Caesar would do nothing but criticise, but he's the one who's most full of praise for what Antony was. In a long speech he paints a picture of him as a superhuman hero, who endured the most appalling conditions:

> On the Alps
> It is reported thou didst eat strange flesh,
> Which some did die to look on; and all this –
> It wounds thy honour that I speak it now –
> Was borne so like a soldier that thy cheek
> So much as lanked not.

(1.4.66–71)

Antony is not present, so the intimate form of the second person singular (thee, thou) has particular force. This is admiration touched with wonder as well as the sadness that Antony is no longer a man of such honour.

27.3 Love and adultery

▶ **'new heaven, new earth' (1.1.17)**

The play is about adultery. Caesar speaks of 'th' adulterous Antony' (3.6.93). When it begins Antony is married to Fulvia; after her death, he marries Octavia. He's unfaithful to both of them with 'Egypt's widow' (2.1.37). Furthermore, although it's not adultery, Cleopatra feels so strongly that Antony is hers that his second marriage is felt as a betrayal.

Many of the possible topics associated with adultery are not dealt with in the play; for instance, there's no emphasis upon guilt or secrecy. Antony feels the pull of Rome, but doesn't feel guilty about deceiving his wives. What then is Shakespeare interested in bringing out?

Love and holiday

For the married or those who are getting old (Caesar calls him 'the old ruffian' – 4.1.4), it seems the only way to rediscover the exhilarating joy of love is adultery. In the comedies, love is out of the ordinary; it's talked about in terms of games, play and holiday.

Where can Antony find such a world? The answer is Egypt. Egypt is associated with play. In the first scene the lovers engage in a debate about love; in the second the women question a soothsayer; throughout there are mentions of feasting and drinking, and in Act 2, Scene 5 the Egyptian court talks of music, billiards and fishing.

Hence for the ageing Antony,

- **Cleopatra is a rediscovery of love's essentially youthful adventure.**

The following sounds more like a first term at university than the antics of a man and woman well past youth:

> I laughed him out of patience, and that night
> I laughed him into patience, and next morn,
> Ere the ninth hour, I drunk him to his bed –
> Then put my tires and mantles on him, whilst
> I wore his sword Philippan.

> (2.5.19–23)

Age and comedy

But as we've said, Antony isn't young any more. In the first line of the play, the word 'dotage' sums up the contrary judgements about his behaviour (see 1.15). Their love is magnificent – 'new heaven, new earth' – but there's also something comical or even embarrassing about such outlandish feelings in people who'd no longer go clubbing.

27.4 Love and war

▶ **'What Venus did with Mars' (1.5.18)**

Antony and Cleopatra is one of the most sustained presentations of love and war. Mardian says he thinks on the love-making of the goddess of love, Venus, with the god of war, Mars. Antony is presented as a soldier, and the court of Cleopatra is devoted, at least in terms of its conversation, to love.

The fate of Mars

In classical mythology, the love of Venus and Mars was adulterous. Her husband, Vulcan, once trapped them both in a net. Mars, in other words, was ensnared.

There was a view in Shakespeare's day that the love of Venus and Mars was a symbol of the taming of a war-like man by a woman. There is, therefore, an ominous note in Mardian's words. Antony might be entrapped and made harmless. When in the sea-battle Antony flees after Cleopatra, Scarrus says:

> The noble ruin of her magic, Antony,
> Claps on his sea-wing and, like a doting mallard,
> Leaving the fight in height, flies after her.
> I never saw an action of such shame –
> Experience, manhood, honour, ne'er before
> Did violate so itself.

> (3.10.18–23)

The destructiveness of love

It's easy to see *Antony and Cleopatra* as a play praising love at the expense of public duty. Egypt is warm, playful and romantic; it's a place of love and revelry. Rome is cold and hard; duty to the state is always more important than anything in our personal lives. If we view the play in those terms, opting for Egypt and love is natural. But love can be destructive, so we might want to escape from it.

Antony feels something like this in the early scenes when he tries to break away from Egypt. In the speech in which he laments the death of his wife, this resolution interrupts his thought:

> I must from this enchanting queen break off.

> (1.2.122)

'Enchanting' must be given its full force – he's under a spell, which for his own safety and sanity he must break. The play shows that he, Mars, is incapable of making this break. Venus is much stronger than Mars, but that makes her as terrible and dangerous as the god of war.

27.5 Rome

▶ 'Octavia is of a holy, cold, and still conversation' (2.6.121–2)

What Enobarbus says of Octavia might be said of Rome.

- **Rome is impressive but without warmth.**

Caesar

Caesar is not an unreasonable man; he just has a very clear set of priorities, which are quite different from those of Antony. He tells Lepidus:

> It is not Caesar's natural vice to hate
> Our great competitor.

> (1.4.2–3)

There's no reason why we shouldn't believe him; his difficulties with Antony are not personal, and he's a successful politician because he's not a man of naturally strong passions.

He can sum Antony up with cool but not unjust precision:

> You shall find there
> A man who is the abstract of all faults
> That all men follow.

> (1.4.8–10)

Perhaps the double use of 'all' is excessive; not everybody has the faults of Antony. But his point is a revealing one; he can't do business with Antony. The differences are so marked that conflict is inevitable.

The picture that emerges is of a man whose sole concern is the running of the country. He's a man of strong self-control, cool judgement and a clear sense of how other people affect his position. What we don't see in Act 1, Scene 4 is his calculating cruelty. Later, however, when he's giving orders for the battle, he's particular about the troops who've joined him, after having deserted Antony:

> Plant those that have revolted in the van,
> That Antony may seem to spend his fury
> Upon himself.

> (4.6.8–10)

This is not only a hard piece of thinking – it's a cruel way of attacking Antony by making him attack those who only recently followed him. It may also have in Caesar's mind a symbolic force; Antony, in his eyes, is someone who's destroying himself, so why not enact that on the field of battle.

Octavia

Octavia matters because of what characters make of her. To Caesar she is

> A sister ... whom no brother
> Did ever love so dearly.

> (2.2.157–8)

This could be mere politics, but the scene in which she returns to her brother is not without affection:

> Welcome to Rome;
> Nothing more dear to me.

> (3.6.85–6)

There might be reasons why in Act 2, Scene 2 he claimed to have feelings he doesn't actually have; but 3.6 is more private, and he's no political reason to say what he doesn't mean.

In the case of Antony, Octavia's importance is a plot one. If the play is about the excitement of adultery, then the wife needs to seem like a wife; that is, someone with whom the husband has been long familiar.

She has a second function in Antony's life; it's Antony who, in Act 2, Scene 2 seems keener on the alliance than Caesar. Furthermore, Antony sees it in political terms:

> from this hour
> The heart of brothers govern in our loves

> (2.2.155–6)

The brotherly love of Antony and Caesar is more prominent than any feelings he has for Octavia.

To Cleopatra, Octavia is a rival. With typically theatrical wit, she's happy to sum up the reports of Octavia by saying she's 'dull of tongue and dwarfish' (3.3.16). This brings us back to adultery. Cleopatra is playing two roles; she's the alluring mistress whom a husband prefers and the wife who's been betrayed.

27.6 Antony and failure

▶ 'near him thy angel/Becomes afeard' (2.3.19–20)

Shakespeare dramatises the moment when it becomes apparent that Antony will always give way to Caesar. The soothsayer from Egypt approaches him, and Antony asks 'whose fortunes shall rise higher: Caesar's or mine?' (2.3.15). The reply makes clear the mystery of one person being cowed in the presence of another:

> Caesar's. Therefore, O Antony, stay not by his side.
> Thy daemon, that thy spirit which keeps thee, is
> Noble, courageous, high, unmatchable,
> Where Caesar's is not. But near him thy angel
> Becomes afeard, as being overpowered. Therefore
> Make space enough between you. (2.3.16–21)

'Daemon' means spirit or self (in the ancient world, another word for it was 'genius'). Antony's 'daemon' has all the epic and heroic qualities, whereas Caesar's has none. When, however, they meet, it's as if Antony's spirit is overcome.

27.7 Cleopatra's roles

▶ 'Royal Egypt, Empress!' (4.16.74)

Her language

Cleopatra's language is not what we might expect. Shakespeare might have given an exotic and magical woman a language that was either mysterious or elevated or emotionally charged. Most of the time he doesn't:

> Courteous lord, one word.
> Sir, you and I must part; but that's not it.
> Sir, you and I have loved, but there's not it;
> That you know well. Something it is I would –
> O my oblivion is a very Antony,
> And I am all forgotten.

(1.3.87–92)

Most of the words are monosyllables; between 'courteous' and 'something' there are 27 words of one syllable. With the exception of 'oblivion', all the words are ones that might occur in everyday conversation. The language is neither mysterious nor exotic. The language is simple, direct and familiar.

But not entirely; at one point, she says:

> O my oblivion is a very Antony.

Many meanings are compressed here; she seems to be saying that she forgets everything because of him, that she is forgotten by him and her memory is leaving her as Antony is. Yet the words don't feel dense and thick with meaning. They are stylish and easy.

Her sense of drama

Cleopatra is a performer. Throughout the play she strikes pose after pose – the abandoned woman, the lover musing upon a beloved, the betrayed woman, the loving and faithful woman. It's not a case of trying to say that this or that scene reveals the 'real' Cleopatra; the real Cleopatra is someone who plays parts.

- **To play is natural to Cleopatra.**

Her playing of roles is in keeping with the nature of Egypt; in a land where they hop, play billiards and fish, the Queen performs.

Her changing feelings

An element in her 'infinite variety' is that we are aware that her feelings constantly change. Act 2, Scene 5 opens with her 'doing an Orsino' – demanding music:

> Give me some music – music, moody food
> Of us that trade in love.

> (2.5.1–2)

The words have a purring quality; she relishes brooding on 'music, moody food'. Hear the 'oo'! Then she says: 'Let it alone.'

The mood is transformed by the arrival of the messenger with the news that Antony has married. The stage direction and her language indicate the violence of her feelings:

> *She hales him up and down.*

> Thou shalt be whipped with wire and stewed in brine
> Smarting in ling'ring pickle.

> (2.5.64–5)

In spite of the unthinkably awful pain involved, we might note that there's a characteristic Cleopatra twinkle in 'pickle'.

By the end of the scene, she's playing the woman overcome with emotional fatigue. It's a good performance:

> I am paid for't now. Lead me hence.
> I faint. O Iras, Charmian – 'tis no matter.

> (2.5.110–11)

Cleopatra is engaging on stage because emotionally she's always alive.

Her sexuality

Because Cleopatra represents Venus to Antony's Mars, she must be seen as sexually desirable. This is done in a number of ways. For instance, virtually every man Enobarbus meets in Rome wants to hear about her.

What Shakespeare chooses not to do is show her alone with Antony. That might have been a way of bringing over her fascination, but he sticks instead to the language she uses. Like that of her court, it's often bawdy. Her reveries naturally turn to thoughts of sexual activity:

> Or does he walk? Or is he on his horse?
> O happy horse, to bear the weight of Antony!

> (1.5.20–1)

She pictures him walking and then riding, and then imaginatively substitutes herself for the horse as she bears his weight and he rides her.

What others say

One of the functions of Enobarbus is to give an account of this shimmering scene:

> The barge she sat in, like a burnished throne
> Burned on the water. The poop was beaten gold;
> Purple the sails, and so perfumed that
> The winds were love-sick with them.

> (2.2.198–201)

Our senses are stimulated; the glimmer of the gold, the watery reflection with its alluring illusion of fire, the rich colour of the sails and the evocative fragrance of the perfume form a heady and gorgeous revelation of a not quite earthly beauty.

27.8 Folly and suicide

▶ 'The long day's task is done' (4.15.35)

Suicide

Suicide is preferable to dishonour. In the Roman tragedies, there's hardly a place for a Lear kneeling to Cordelia. In particular, suicide is preferable to being led through Rome as a captive. The spectacle of a triumphant return to Rome with prisoners haunts the play. This is a shame that no Roman can face.

Antony's suicide is a flamboyant public gesture. This is in keeping with his behaviour throughout most of the latter part of the play. When he's roused by the assurance of Cleopatra's affection from the despair of his first defeat, he opts with an appealing romantic flourish and irresistible bravado for 'one more gaudy night' (3.13.184–5). He's lost but he daringly commits himself to another fight and prepares for it with revelry.

When he's finally defeated, he takes on the role of Hercules, the epic hero who became a god and whom his soldiers say he loved (4.3.14). In a bitter exchange with Cleopatra, he says:

The shirt of Nessus is upon me

(4.13.43)

Nessus had been wronged when Hercules committed adultery with his wife, so in revenge Nessus got his wife to give him a shirt poisoned with the blood of Nessus. This caused untold agony to the wearer, and when Hercules tried to take it off, lumps of his flesh pulled away. It looks as if Antony is casting himself in the role of Hercules and is blaming Cleopatra for playing the role of a revenging wronged woman.

The point about this is that Antony says it of himself.

- **He's casting himself in the role of the legendary hero, and in doing this is being his own judge.**

In short:

- **Antony knowingly plays out his death as a tragic hero.**

Antony's 'death'

When he comes to take his own life, he sees it as a spectacle; in the underworld, the two lovers will outshine all others:

> Where souls do couch on flowers we'll hand in hand,
> And with our sprightly port make the ghosts gaze.
> Dido and Aeneas shall want troops,
> And all the haunt be ours.

(4.15.51–4)

This is stirring stuff; audiences must be very hard-hearted not to be moved and awed by the bravado of a man imagining all the inhabitants of the underworld gazing at their youthful bounce.

Yet this is tragic hubris of the most blatant kind; he parades his doomed love before the dead as well as the living, and in so doing passes a judgement on himself that only others can make.

Shakespeare has a trick to play. No character has flaunted his epic and heroic qualities with such theatrical splendour.

- **Theatrical hubris brings about theatrical nemesis.**

When the genuinely noble Eros without display kills himself, the self-proclaimed hero and legendary lover falls on his own sword:

> But I will be
> A bridegroom in my death, and run into't
> As to a lover's bed. Come then and, Eros,
> Thy master dies thy scholar. To do thus
> I learned of thee.
>
> (*He stabs himself*)
> How, not dead? Not dead?
> The guard, ho! O, dispatch me!

(4.15.99–104)

We have the thrill of seeing him defiantly posing as the bridegroom running into the arms of death, the bride. We see the generosity (a word Enobarbus associates with him) of his praise of the noble Eros, and, before he stabs, the simple yet stirring words in which, as a true tragic hero, he calls attention to the actions he's performing.

And then – farce: the ludicrous statement that he's not dead (if he were, he couldn't say it!) and the humiliating business of summoning a guard to 'dispatch' (not an elevated word) him, turns the heroism into a grim and embarrassing piece of slap-stick.

27.9 The magnificence of Cleopatra

▶ 'Give me my robe' (5.2.275)

Shakespeare has a further surprise; if he makes Antony look a fool, he doesn't do the same with Cleopatra. She participates in his death scene, so is present when the absurdity is made clear. When he's being hoisted up to the monument, the onlookers say:

'A heavy sight.'

(4.16.42)

This thump of a remark comes just before his haunting falling cadences:

'I am dying Egypt, dying.

(4.16.43)

Shakespeare doesn't allow the scene to settle in either the farcical or the heroic mode.

But Cleopatra, who resolves to 'do it after the high Roman fashion' (4.16.89) is given an end which is dignified. She opts for a ritual which she performs with magnificent precision:

Give me my robe. Put on my crown. I have
Immortal longings in me. Now no more
The juice of Egypt's grape shall moist my lip.

(5.2.275–7)

Her language, particularly the first two sentences, is characteristically simple, and with equal simplicity (an art that's come to be entirely natural) she turns from the subject of her clothes to her inner life. Her immortal longings are for her own state after death as well as herself as a cultural icon of alluring splendour, yet the tone avoids bravado.

She does indulge in self-congratulatory praise when she says of Antony:

I see him rouse himself
To praise my noble act.

(5.2.279–80)

She knows that 'act' has a theatrical meaning. But the piercing honesty and real (sexual?) longing of

Husband I come.

(5.2.282)

sounds different from the showiness of Antony's, albeit stunning, romantic bluster.

Like Antony she sees death as a lover, but we get from her a clearer sense of what lovers do. All we see of Antony is the bridegroom running; we're in the bed with Cleopatra:

> If thou and nature can so gently part,
> The stroke of death is as a lover's pinch.

(5.2.289–90)

Don't we feel that even though she's presenting herself as a lover, we've grateful that she's honest enough to tell us (something) of what it's like?

Her death, poisoned by asps, is in that low-key style that makes almost every simple, everyday word brim full of significances; were the language higher and more strident we'd feel less was being achieved:

Cleopatra: Peace, peace.
  Dost thou not see my baby at my breast,
  That sucks the nurse asleep.
Charmian: O, break! O, break!
Cleopatra: As sweet as balm, as soft as air, as gentle.
  O Antony!

(She puts another asp to her arm)

    Nay, I will take thee too.

  What should I stay –

(5.2.303–8)

At her end she sees herself in the humble position of the nurse that suckles another's child. The word 'peace' is spoken to those who might wake the baby and who want to make the scene (as Charmian does) a piece of high drama. The words could be addressed to almost anyone; they float on the soft air, allowing us to understand them how we will. 'Take', for instance, could be said to the asp, to Antony, to Charmian or to us. In her death she does 'take' us in a way Antony never does in his, but Antony has a place: 'take', we know, has another meaning.

Exercises

27.1 'The most glorious and yet the most absurd hero in Shakespeare.' What do you think of this view of Antony?

27.2 Examine how Shakespeare creates two distinct and contrasting worlds in *Antony and Cleopatra*.

Part VII
The Histories

28 Shakespeare's English history

28.1 England in the history plays

▶ 'this realm, this England' (*Richard II*, 2.1.50)

Shakespeare wrote a set of plays that tell the history of England from Richard II to Richard III. This was an enormous undertaking; altogether, there are over two hundred characters.

England

The name occurs frequently: 17 times in *Richard II*, 11 times in *1 Henry IV* and 50 times in *Henry V.* On most occasions it refers to the land or to the king of the land; sometimes the monarch is actually called England. This touches on what it is to be a king:

- **the body of the king and the body of his country are closely identified.**

This identification leads to a further one: that between the people and their land.

Geography

One way in which Shakespeare gives his audience a sense of England is through the 'geography' of the plays. We hear about lots of towns, cities, streets and buildings: Basingstoke, Bridgnorth, Chester, Clement's Inn, Gad's Hill, Gloucestershire, Hinckley, Lombard Street, London, Mile End Green, Pauls (St Paul's), Pomfret (Pontefract), St Albans, Shrewsbury, Smithfield and York. Those are all mentioned in the naturalistic *2 Henry IV*, but the emblematic and ritualistic *Richard II* also refers to a lot of locations.

Society

One of the pleasures of watching the history plays is their rich picture of the people of England. Unlike the Roman Tragedies, the common people are present as individual characters; many of them more lively (and more loveable) than the lords who exercise power over them.

In *Richard II* there are gardeners (though they sound more like poetic political commentators), in the *Henry IV* plays we meet whores and thieves in taverns and some rustics being pressed into military service, and in *Henry V* we meet the common soldiers who, with their suspicions and a degree of cynicism, talk to the king about their needs and fears.

The Northerners

Among the many nobles we meet, there's one group which broods over the plays, particularly the *Henry IV* ones – the Northerners. In the period Shakespeare was writing about the north was almost another country. North of the River Trent, England was ruled by The Council of the North, which sat in York. Its President was almost like a monarch. Big families dominated; in Shakespeare's plays the Earls of Northumberland, the Percies, are always dangerous figures. The king in London had to maintain good relationships with the northern families, because they helped to keep back the Scots. But because of the freedoms they were allowed and their remoteness, they were frequently troublesome; the plots of both *Henry IV* plays are concerned with a series of rebellions, most stemming from the north.

A vision of England as a garden

The most insistent scene in which England is presented as a garden is in *Richard II*; two gardeners tend a garden while regretting that the garden of England has been left 'full of weeds' (3.4.45). Behind this scene lies the idea of England as Eden. Within the play, this image derives from the speech of the dying John of Gaunt:

> This royal throne of kings, this sceptered isle,
> This earth of majesty, this seat of Mars,
> This other Eden, demi-paradise,
> This fortress built by nature for herself
> Against infection and the hand of war,
> This happy breed of men, this little world,
> This precious stone set in a silver sea

(2.1.39–46)

England might only be a 'demi-paradise' (a half-way house to paradise) but it is 'this other Eden', a seat of the god of war (Mars) but protected from war's outrages.

This speech is often quoted (as here) in part. What it goes on to say is that this 'other Eden' is now

> leased out ...
> Like to a tenement or pelting farm.

(2.1.59–60)

The England that Gaunt actually sees is one that's no longer any of the things that it's been celebrated for. England is now leased out and bound by legal documents.

The English epic

The history plays can be read as Shakespeare's epic. An epic is a work written in an elevated style about heroes, and its theme is often the foundation of a state or nation.

England is a place where heroes such as those who fought at Agincourt may be found. It's also the place which is divided by ambitions and where the impulse to make life into holiday clashes with the responsibilities of governing the state. The plays, in other words, are both chronicles of past times and mirrors which reflect (though sometimes dimly) the present.

28.2 The past, the future and continuity

▶ 'there is a history in all men's lives' (*2 Henry IV*, 3.1.75)

The knowledge of history

It's never easy deciding what an audience would have known and even harder thinking about what the author would have assumed they would know. However, we are, I think, on safe grounds assuming that the audience knew that what they were seeing was in some sense history. They could read about these events in popular histories. There were probably some people in the audiences who'd read what Shakespeare had read – the chronicles of Hall and Hollinshed – and so could judge what he'd made of their books.

Continuity

One of the things Shakespeare must have presumed is a sense of the continuity of history. What the audiences saw on stage somehow led to the present. In other words, there was a life beyond the play. History was now and always.

This is important at the close of each play. A tragedy has a sense of finality; what rivets the mind is the thought that a life has come to an end. In the history plays, however, there's a sense that the future is already mapped out and known by some in the audience. This means that the ends of the plays can have three characteristics.

• Hope

Some plays end with an unstated hope. Throughout the *Henry IV* plays, the King has worried about his son, Hal. We know that he'll turn into our most successful warrior monarch.

• Irony

Sometimes the passage of history produces an ironical effect. For political reasons Henry IV has to regret the death of Richard at the end of *Richard II*, but we know the disasters that will come upon the new monarch in the form of civil wars waged by those who once helped him.

• Perspective

History sometimes lends a sobering double view to a play. *Henry V* ends with the King having conquered France and marrying the French Princess. The audience can hardly help knowing the French possessions so gloriously won will soon be lost. In fact, the Chorus tells us this.

Individuals and history

Our sense of the continuing history of the nation adjusts our feelings about the individual characters whom we see.

- **No matter how momentous an individual life is, the movement of history puts it in context.**

This explains why the history plays are not usually dominated by titanic figures in the way the tragedies are. We might become engrossed by Richard II or Richard III but with their deaths, we know the nation moved on. The constitutional principle of 'the King is dead, long live the King' has a dramatic counterpart in the way each play ends with the knowledge that a new reign is beginning.

The past

In history the chief actors inherit situations for which they were not responsible. Blood shed in the past stains the present. Hence, the past is often present in recitals of events, in particular the foundation event of the whole cycle of history plays – the murder of Richard II. The Archbishop of York's uprising in *2 Henry IV* is powered by

> The blood
> Of fair King Richard, scraped from Pomfret stones

> (1.2.204)

Some characters are haunting 'left-overs' from the past. The chorus of women in *Richard III* have all suffered from his knavery. Old Queen Margaret haunts the stage like a revenging spirit.

The future in the present

No matter how dreadful the suffering of an individual is, history rolls on. Nobody in the history plays suffers as Richard II does, and news of his death is greeted in a grave tone. Yet before the deposed King is dead, Henry has fresh worries – his 'unthrifty son' (5.3.1).

28.3 The pressures of power

▶ 'the image of his power' (*2 Henry IV*, 5.2.73)

The instability of power

The failure to achieve a state in which all strife ceases shows how unstable political power is.

The deposed king

Shakespeare wrote plays about every English king who'd been deposed: Richard II, Henry VI and Richard III. The fall of kings was a topic that thinkers brooded over, because it showed how changeable and subject to the rule of fortune life is.

It also looks as if Shakespeare saw in this a confirmation of what he saw in kings and heroes – their vulnerability.

Loyalty

One of the subjects of the history plays is the way power passes from one figure to another. The power of the king holds most of the characters in awe; its passing is a solemn and even fearful occasion.

Because power is unstable, loyalty is tested. One of the interests Shakespeare takes in the human side of history is the painful matter of transferring loyalty to a new ruler.

In *Richard II*, York is a potentially poignant figure. In him Shakespeare dramatises the plight of one who attempts to serve whoever is king while recognising the rights of others. When he first meets Bolingbroke after his return, York courageously insists on the etiquette of royalty while still being courteous to a man whom he thinks the king has wronged. Later in the play, this old man, the last surviving son of the Edward III, is divided against his wife and son over the new king. He tries to serve Bolingbroke, while his son, with an adolescent romanticism, plots against the new king.

Oaths

More attention should be paid in Shakespeare to the taking of oaths. They were the standard way of establishing loyalty. In an unstable world, oaths maintained the power of the king and gave power to factions. At the end of the 'deposition' (the coronation in reverse) scene in *Richard II*, Bolingbroke announces that his coronation will take place within a few days. He leaves the stage, and Aumerle asks

> is there no plot
> To rid the realm of this pernicious blot?

> (4.1.314–15)

The Abbot of Westminster immediately talks of the ceremony of oath-taking:

> My lord, Before I freely speak my mind herein
> You shall not only take the sacrament
> To bury mine intents, but also to effect
> Whatever I shall happen to devise.

> (4.1.316–19)

In a dangerous world the swearing of oaths had to be a solemn business. Once someone had taken the sacrament (the holy communion), they were bound to a cause by the power of religious devotion.

The language of power

The influence of Machiavelli can be seen in the gap between fine words and the exercise of power. If it's necessary to make promises that won't be kept, promises are made. Shakespeare is alive to the way politicians have to use elevated language in order to succeed.

An example is John of Lancaster in *2 Henry IV*. He's sent to deal with the rebels in the north, who are led by the Archbishop of York. He meets them and gives his word to look into their grievances. The promise is sealed by a drink. It's a trick. When the rebels have dismissed their troops, the leaders are arrested on a charge of high treason. The Archbishop asks if John is going to break his faith. He replies that he promised to look into their grievances; he didn't promise to overlook their rebellion. Shakespeare presents politicians who will use any high-sounding words to gain an advantage, which they know is actually backed up by force of arms.

Compromise

Because that's how language works in a political world, the audience see the characters as compromised and diminished. The fall that the characters in history plays suffer is one of seeming smaller and sometimes meaner.

John of Gaunt comes over in some scenes as a noble figure fighting for a vision of a free and proud England. But we also see a man compromised by his position. In a dialogue with the Duchess of Gloucester, he shows that he thinks Richard was responsible for the death of her husband, but because Richard is the king – 'God's substitute' (1.2.37) – there's nothing he can do. He's caught by the circumstances of history, and those compromise him.

Beyond politics

The attraction of living a good life apart from the intriguings of the court was one that many in the sixteenth and seventeenth centuries found attractive. The word usually used of it was 'retirement'. Shakespeare shows that it's an alluring dream; he's also aware that political figures, in particular kings, can't escape.

It's when Richard II is alone in Pomfret Castle that he invents for himself an imaginary world. But even there he can't escape the memory of the events that have taken him from the world of politics:

> Then crushing penury
> Persuades me I was better when a king.
> Then am I kinged again, and by and by
> Think I am unkinged by Bolingbroke

> (5.4.34–7)

It's dramatically appropriate that since the world of politics invades his thought, so it invades his place of retirement; within 60 lines the murderers have entered to do their business.

Messengers

We become aware of history and power through the messengers. Their appearance shows how unstable and unreliable the world is. They also help us to see the size of the country, the dangers of rumour and the need for certainty.

Messengers usually bring bad news. The opening of *2 Henry IV* shows us a world spiralling into horror as the reports gradually confirm the death of Hotspur. Northumberland tries to assess the weight of the evidence and hopes that the news is not grave. He considerately tries not to blame the bearer of bad news:

> The tongue offends not that reports his death

> (1.1.97)

In some plays the more frequent messengers are, the worse the news. As *Richard III* loses power, the messengers become more frequent.

28.4 The power of kings

▶ 'the mortal temples of a king' (*Richard II*, 3.2.157)

The power of a king

In stressing Shakespeare's presentation of the vulnerability of kings, we may have lost sight of their real power. One of the thrills of the history plays is seeing mortal men wielding power with what for most of us is unimaginable strength.

Kings exercise considerable power. The changeable (and even unstable) Richard banishes Mowbray and Bolingbroke, but then, in pity of Bolingbroke's father, the aged John of Gaunt, he cuts the sentence from ten to six years. Bolingbroke comments:

> How long a time lies in one little word!
> Four lagging winters and four wanton springs
> End in a word: such is the breath of kings.

> (1.3.206–8)

This plain, low-key acknowledgement is quietly impressive. The image of breath is usually one of mortality; here it gains its power through the contrast between the life of a mortal dependent upon each breath he draws and the God-like power of a king who apparently rules time and the seasons.

The Divine Right of Kings

The idea of the Divine Right of kings is that the monarch is chosen, approved and rules with the permission of God.

In the English coronation service, the monarch was not only crowned but anointed with oil. This latter ritual is of deep religious significance; all the Hebrew kings were anointed as a sign that God had chosen them. A king is one who has been chosen.

Divine Right provides a vocabulary for kingly splendour. *Richard II* is where this is most clearly seen. We hear: God's 'deputy anointed in his sight' (1.2.38), 'great King' (2.1.87), 'the deputy elected by the lord' (3.1.53), 'the King's name is forty thousand names' (3.1.81). Most powerful of all is the image of the sun; as the sun is King in the heavens, so Richard is King on earth. The image gave Shakespeare considerable scope. The king could seek out wrongdoing (3.1.32–49) when, like the sun on the horizon, he looks upon a darkened world. But suns also set; his decline is enacted when he descends from the walls of Flint Castle to the 'base court'.

The education of a king

One of the subjects that runs through the *Henry IV* plays is that of the education of the king. This has a double edge. The powerful Bolingbroke becomes a broken and despairing man when he assumes power; he's educated into seeing that the life of a usurper can never be easy.

One of his trials is his son, Prince Hal. The Prince seems in the eyes of his father to be unfit to succeed him. What Shakespeare allows the audience to see is that one of the most important themes of the two plays is the education of this young man. His apparent profligacy is an education in the politics of concealment. Unknown to his 'friends', he's no intention of being a wild and dissipated monarch; while he's drinking in the south bank taverns, he's learning the essential art of politics – concealing your intentions from those who are closest to you.

▶ 'all in England' (*1 Henry IV*, 5.1.54)

Characters from chronicles

A good test of any Shakespeare play is to ask what opportunities it gives to the players. If you were a player, which part would you want to play?

The answer is probably: not many. For actors there's Richard II, Falstaff, Hotspur, Henry V and Richard III. For actresses –?

The reason for this is the nature of history plays. These plays tend to pare down the characters to fit the plot of unfolding history. No matter how dramatic their fall, characters on the stage of history are replaced by others. In tragedies, we often feel that the texture of life has changed; in histories, time will continue to weave patterns similar to the ones we've already seen.

One of the things we have to accept about these plays is that many of the characters have a faded look; they peer out of the pages of dusty chronicles. Can we really remember how Worcester is different from Northumberland or what makes all those lords who gather round Henry V distinctive?

Families

As with many of his plays, Shakespeare presents his historical characters as members of families. The Percy family looms over the events of *Richard II* and the two *Henry IV* plays. This gives a double perspective to events. At the beginning of *2 Henry IV*, Northumberland appears as the head of the rebels *and* as a husband and father. He's suffering a double loss; the rebels lost the Battle of Shrewsbury, and he has lost a son. He parallels the king, who has problems with the nation and his son.

The history plays show that nobody can live with an absolute distinction between what's public and what's private. The two are different but they're not separable. Hal has a kind of private life with Falstaff and his tavern chums, but he knows that there are public duties awaiting him. Falstaff makes the mistake of thinking that once he's king, Hal will continue to be the lad he drank with. The rejection of Falstaff is the rejection of the separability of the public and the private.

Motives

In a world where people have to balance the private and the public and to exercise political power, motives are likely to be questionable. The characters whom we see have to live with dilemmas.

Hal is the most interesting example. Can he really be friends with Falstaff when he knows that he must abandon his prodigal way of life when he becomes king? The question can be taken further. Can he be held responsible for the mistakes others make about him? Is he responsible for the wild fantasies Falstaff entertains about England under Harry the fifth?

Heroes?

The hero is always a deeply ambiguous figure in Shakespeare. All too frequently, he shows that the hero is the product of a warrior culture that survives by hubristic self-assertion and bloodshed. Macbeth is the kind of hero that emerges in warrior cultures.

As a general rule, there are no heroes in the history plays. Shakespeare's understanding of history doesn't allow potential heroes to grow into the dangerous yet charismatic figures that dominate the tragedies.

The two interesting exceptions to this are Hotspur and Hal. Hotspur clearly thinks he's a hero, and Hal in some parts of *Henry V* is certainly presented as one. Hotspur is young and outlandish in his claims about honour (*1 Henry IV*, 1.3.199–206); Henry V knows how to present himself as a hero as he rallies his troops before a battle he's likely to lose.

Both have heroic features; both are flawed. What Shakespeare is interested in is the hero who has to live with the compromises and dangers of history. Hotspur might think he's in a grand epic; what he has to learn is that his power is dependent upon the politicians who are plotting against Henry – not a very heroic thing to do. Henry V has to reject Falstaff and be tough to his old 'friends' merely because he's king. It's difficult to be magnanimous in a history play.

28.6 What is a history play?

▶ 'on the French ground played a tragedy' (*Henry V*, 1.2.106)

Comedy or tragedy?

Sometimes these plays strike us as being like comedies and sometimes like tragedies. The horseplay of *1 Henry IV* has elements of the comic about it, while the fall of *Richard II* can only be called tragic.

Sources

All of Shakespeare's plots, with the exception of *The Tempest*, comes from his reading. Of that reading, some was what we would call fact and some fiction. His comedies are fiction; he went for diverting stories, often with a strong folklore element. Most of his tragedies and, of course, the history plays are based on accounts that Shakespeare would have regarded as factual. *Othello* is an exception.

What significance does this have? One answer is that the plots he found in history might have something in common with tragedies. This idea gets us somewhere with two of the five plays we're going to look at: *Richard II* and *Richard III* have the shape of the tragic fall. Strictly speaking, history doesn't have a plot; we have to find significances in the welter of things that happen. In the case of kings, their fall gives a clear shape to their lives.

Plots with tragic shapes are to be found in the lives of important but not central characters. Buckingham in *Richard III* rises as Richard rises, but when Richard begins to question his loyalty, Buckingham falls.

War

There's a scene in the early *3 Henry VI* in which two soldiers enter; one is a man who's killed his father and the other a father who's killed his son (2.5.79–122). War is tragic; it breeds hubris, divides families and has an inevitability about its terrible progress.

This is particularly the case in the wars we see in the history plays, because they are civil wars. What we see is a country at war with itself. As in a tragedy war is ambiguous. We gasp at the bravery and are appalled at the cruelty and the loss.

But still comic?

If we take all the histories together, they bring the nation's story up to the birth of Elizabeth I, who appears at the end of *All is True*. If Shakespeare, regarded the time in which he lived as one of happy peace, then, taken as a whole, history is comedy. Its many setbacks and tragedies don't prevent it from giving the inheritors of these events a land that's free.

Another link with comedy is the formal one of the design of the plots. Tragedies are plays about one (and occasionally two) outstanding figures. Comedies are about groups who compete for influence and power. Many of the histories are more like the latter kind of play than the former. Families and factions plot and practise against each other. Because what matters is the political end, it's rare for any of the characters to dominate a plot. The two Richard plays are the exceptions; but they are close to tragedy.

28.7 History and plots

▶ 'they do plot/Unlikely wonders' (*Richard II*, 5.5.18–19)

Shakespeare gives shape to the sprawling material of chronicle history in a number of ways.

Sequencing

Since one of the subjects of the history plays is the working out of power, it's not surprising that a sequence of scenes shows this process as it happens. Shakespeare shows us that all's politically lost with Richard II by placing the scene in which the Welsh desert his cause after the one in which York can only use words to resist Bolingbroke's forces and before the one in which some of Richard's other supporters – Bushy and Green – are condemned to death.

Linking

The movement of history on the stage sometimes reminds audiences of earlier scenes. In *2 Henry IV* there are two occasions when Falstaff is in Gloucestershire. The second makes us cast our minds back to the first. It's while Falstaff is in Gloucestershire for the second time that he hears that the old king is dead.

We might think back to the first time he was in Gloucestershire. Shallow reminisced about their wild youth, a youth that's long faded. But Falstaff, in spite of being amused, doesn't get the point. His days with Hal – a kind of late, youthful extravagance – are also over. At least, he should know that. As it is, he rushes to London for the biggest brush-off in literature.

Motifs in the plays

Some significant events occur in several of the plays. In both the first and the last plays in the cycle, the landing of an army upon the coast is the prelude to the fall of a monarch.

Sometimes motifs are effective because they don't quite echo each other. The tavern scenes in *2 Henry IV* don't have the sprightly feel of those in the first Henry play. Also in the second play the destruction of the rebels without a battle is a clear contrast to the battle of Shrewsbury in the first.

Sub-plot

In the *Henry IV* plays a sub-plot – Falstaff – enriches the drama. Here we have a figure so imaginatively engaging that he's in danger of stealing the show. Shakespeare must have known this. This dominance makes for success. *1 Henry IV* is frequently performed.

Exercises

28.1 In what ways are history plays like and unlike comedies and tragedies?

28.2 'Kings are only men.' Is this what Shakespeare shows us in the history plays?

28.3 'There are no heroes in history.' Is this what we see in Shakespeare?

Richard II

29.1 The start of the history cycle

▶ 'And future ages groan for this foul act' (4.1.129)

Richard II is a play that looks forward to the plays to come, and they look back to it. It's the foundation play of the English epic Shakespeare eventually created – the story of the disasters that came on England in the fifteenth century. The death of Richard in 1400 was the start of conflicts which did not cease until the Battle of Bosworth in 1485.

Three plays later in chronological terms, Henry V prays before the Battle of Agincourt in the hope that his father's sin in deposing Richard will not be held against him in his present enterprise:

> think not upon the fault
> My father made in compassing the crown
>
> (4.1.290–1)

29.2 Ritual and ceremony

▶ 'And formally, according to our law' (1.3.29)

A medieval picture

Richard II has a quite distinctive identity; it's ceremonious, ritualistic, courtly and rhetorical. Everyone speaks in verse. The language is highly wrought, the wordplay from Richard is inventive, and the imagery runs through the play like gold threads in a richly woven fabric. All this gives an impression of being medieval. The scenes look as if they come from an illuminated manuscript.

Ritual

In keeping with this atmosphere, we hear words about procedures. We see this in the opening of the play – a dispute between Mowbray and Bolingbroke over the murder of the Duke of Gloucester. In the first scene the King orders Bolingbroke and

Mowbray 'to our presence' (line 15), where 'face to face' and 'brow to brow' the accuser will speak to the accused. The King makes a 'vow' (line 118) that he will be impartial, even though one of the contestants is his cousin.

The rituals can be impressive on stage and they convey a good deal about the place of the King in the court and the country. It also forms a means of showing that Richard is a wayward monarch.

• **He's at home with the rituals of kingship but he doesn't keep to them.**

The first and third scene are conducted according to the laws of chivalry, but Richard twice breaks them. First, he gives a promise in the first scene that he won't favour Bolingbroke because he's a relative, but in the third scene he cuts his banishment by four years because he feels sorry for Gaunt. Second, when the fight is about to begin, he stops it.

More seriously, he's presiding over a dispute for which he's chiefly responsible; the second scene of the play (almost certainly reliably) tells us that Richard himself ordered the death of the Duke of Gloucester.

29.3 Richard's guilt

▶ **'he did plot the Duke of Gloucester's death' (1.1.100)**

The dispute between Bolingbroke and Mowbray is about something we've not seen. The chronicles show that Richard ordered that one of his uncles, Thomas, the Duke of Gloucester, be murdered in Calais. Mowbray executed the plan.

If the audience knew this, they'd see that the King is vulnerable to Bolingbroke's accusations, and that Bolingbroke, in accusing Mowbray, is really accusing the King.

We might say, then, that what begins in the opening scene is 'the case against Richard'. Shakespeare has to make it credible that people should want Richard removed. He does this by showing that he's unjust and devious.

Gloucester's death serves another purpose: it gives the play a shape. It opens with the memory of Gloucester's murder and closes with the murder of Richard. The play begins in blood, and the cycle of plays can be understood as the consequences of the murder of the King.

29.4 The wayward king

▶ **'Richard my life's counsel would not hear' (2.1.15)**

Richard dominates the play. If we leave Falstaff aside because he's usually played by an older actor, there's no other part in the history plays that offers such variety of emotion and tone. Coleridge said that of all the characters in Shakespeare, he's second only to Hamlet in interest.

What is it that makes him interesting? The usual answer is a good one

• **Richard's moods are constantly changing.**

It's sometimes said that the only constant thing about him is that he's never constant.

This changeability is important in the plot. He acts on impulse. The dying Gaunt complains that Richard won't listen to his 'counsel' and lists those things that captivate him – flattery, art, fashion – but Richard's problem is not so much that he listens to the wrong people as that no one can predict how he's going to react to anything.

His constant changes have an important dramatic impact. *Richard II* is a play with little action.

- **What Shakespeare depends upon to create interest are the ever-changing moods of Richard.**

29.5 Language in the play

▶ **'Look what I speak, my life shall prove it true' (1.1.87)**

Richard II is about language. The two central characters have quite distinct approaches to how words work.

Bolingbroke

Bolingbroke is not a man who says a lot. His father comments on this in the third scene; Gaunt wants to know why he's so little to say:

> O, to what purpose dost thou hoard thy words…?
>
> (1.3.242)

The opening of the play gives a kind of answer to this question. Bolingbroke talks about what he can achieve. Because he sees a link between the word and action, his speech is reserved for those things over which he has control.

This is the answer he gives to Richard's question about what he has against Mowbray:

> First – heaven be the record for my speech –
>
> (1.1.30)

When he turns to Mowbray he makes explicit his principle that words should be accompanied by deeds:

> Now, Thomas Mowbray, do I turn to thee;
> And mark my greeting well, for what I speak
> My body shall make good upon this earth,
> Or my divine soul answer it in heaven.
>
> (1.1.35–8)

The crispest summary of his position comes at the start of his next speech:

> Look what I speak, my life shall prove it true.
>
> (1.1.87)

The view of language here is one that sees it as instrumental; it must always be seen in relation to what is done, and what he does is the only possible confirmation of his words. Language for Bolingbroke is functional and purposeful. Actions prove that what he says is true.

Richard

Richard is not a man of action. (He knows he's not Henry V!) Increasingly, he treats language as an end in itself. What matters to him is the inherent interest of ideas and the art of expression, not what it leads to.

The turning point of the play comes when he returns from Ireland; in the first half the player-king is uppermost with his images of himself as the sun and Bolingbroke as a thief operating under cover of darkness. When he gives up hope that he can survive as king, the poet takes over completely. He turns to story-telling:

> For God's sake, let us sit upon the ground,
> And tell sad stories of the death of kings
>
> (3.1.151–2)

The sad story takes the form of a conceit; the idea is that within the king's crown, death's court is present:

> For within the hollow crown
> That rounds the mortal temples of a king
> Keeps death his court; and there the antic sits,
> Scoffing his state and grinning at his pomp,
> Allowing him a breath, a little scene,
> To monarchise, be feared, and kill with looks,
> Infusing him with self and vain conceit,
> As if this flesh which walls about our life
> Were brass impregnable
>
> (3.1.156–64)

What the conceit reveals is that the real power lies with death. The poet Richard blends the value of this insight with the intricacy and pleasure he has in forming the image. He can see that he suffered from 'self and vain conceit' and he surely enjoys the appropriateness of 'walls', tying in with other images of building and space; 'temples', for instance, can refer to churches as well as the head.

This desire to poetically elaborate ideas is seen most clearly in the deposition scene. When he's musing aloud about how his sorrow has destroyed his face, Bolingbroke adds:

> The shadow of your sorrow hath destroyed
> The shadow of your face.
>
> (4.1.282–3)

This unusually poetic contribution from Bolingbroke inspires Richard:

> Say that again:
> 'The shadow of my sorrow' – ha, let's see.
> 'Tis very true: my grief lies all within,
> And these external manner of laments
> Are merely shadows to the unseen grief
> That swells with silence in the tortured soul.
>
> (4.1.283–8)

We hear in those lines the excitement of the poet working out a fresh idea. He rhetorically asks Bolingbroke to repeat the words and does so himself. Then a thought strikes him – 'ha' – and he tells himself to do some thinking – 'let's see'. He indicates that he likes the idea with the decisive Tis very true' before spelling it out in detail, including the rhythmical flourish on 'that swells with silence in the tortured soul'.

There are two important features of Richard's poetic language.

- **There's an inverse equation between poetic expression and political power. As his power declines, his poetic eloquence increases.**

- **If we condemn Richard we have to condemn poetry.**

Shakespeare gives us two options; either we favour the politician who seeks power or the poet who takes us out of this world. In the first case, we must abandon poetry; in the second we choose to be politically ineffective. These incompatible alternatives make the play tragic.

Language in the play

Language is a subject in other areas of the play. The banishment of Mowbray for life is understood by him in terms of language:

> The language I have heard these forty years,
> My native English, must I now forgo
> And now my tongue's use is to me no more
> Than an unstrung viol or harp

> (1.3.153–6)

To leave England is to leave the language that he knows, calling it 'native' suggests that it's basic and natural; to lose it is to lose something of his nature. It's appropriate that without his native tongue, he dies (4.1.82–91).

Oaths are very important in the play. In a play that's aware of language, loyalty is thought of in verbal terms. When in the deposition scene Richard is asked to 'read/These accusations and grievous crimes' (4.1.212–13), Richard replies that if Northumberland's crimes 'were upon record' (4.1.220) he would find

> one heinous article
> Containing the deposing of a king
> And cracking the strong warrant of an oath,
> Marked with a blot, damned in the book of heaven.

> (4.1.223–6)

A third way in which language becomes a subject is the place of prophecy. In the crucial speech by the Bishop of Carlisle in the deposition scene, he takes on the role of a prophet as he graphically foresees bloodshed as the consequence of deposing Richard (4.1.105–40).

The most eloquent prophecy is Gaunt's vision of England. It starts:

> Methinks I am a prophet new-inspired
> And thus, expiring, do foretell of him.

> (2.1.31–2)

He plays upon 'inspire' and 'expire' with the ingenuity of his royal nephew. A prophet is inspired; the word also means to breathe in. When we are born we are 'new-inspired' because we breathe for the first time. Gaunt, however, is dying – expiring – that is, breathing out for the last time. In poetic and prophetic terms, expiring is the consequence of being inspired. The poet-prophet breathes in and breathes out the poetic prophecy.

29.6 Rebellion

▶ 'If then we shall shake off our slavish yoke' (2.1.293)

Bolingbroke's rise

The movement from the opening scenes of the play to the fall of Richard is swift and almost inevitable. It's Shakespeare's way of dramatising history. We're aware of the rapid succession of events.

No sooner is Gaunt dead than we hear that Bolingbroke has set sail for England. In the next scene we hear he's landed, and in the next scene, that he's marched into Gloucestershire. He claims that because his father's dead, he's come to claim the title that's due to him. But he's a bit shifty here; if that's all he's interested in, why does he keep on promising to reward his followers? (2.3.60–2).

The next scene shows the desertion of the Welsh troops, and in the following one Bolingbroke acts like a king by ordering the execution of Bushy and Green.

29.7 The fall of Richard

▶ 'No matter where' (3.2.140)

One of the features of *Richard II* is that there's a lot that Shakespeare never explains; Bolingbroke doesn't say that he wants the throne, and Richard doesn't ponder whether he should give it up.

For Richard the turning point comes when he learns that Bolingbroke has executed his followers. He sits and talks in a series of defeated, falling cadences:

> Of comfort no man speak.
> Let's talk of graves, of worms and epitaphs,
> Make dust our paper, and with rainy eyes
> Write sorrow on the bosom of the earth.
>
> (3.2.140–3)

It's typical of him that he puts defeat in terms of a change in conversation. He no longer wants to hear of comfort; instead he suggests that they talk of mortality, of graves, worms, and (of course!) epitaphs. The speech is itself a kind of epitaph.

Effects, not causes

In the big middle scenes of the play, Shakespeare is concerned with *how* Richard reacts rather than *why* he gives up. Shakespeare shifts the focus from cause to effect.

This is in keeping with one of the themes of the play:

• **Richard loses power and discovers himself.**

One of the features of the mercurial figure of the first half was an inability to take anything seriously; he was flippant and heedless. Now he confronts mortality and the common needs of humanity:

I live with bread, like you; feel want,
Taste grief, need friends.

(3.2.171–2)

In those simple monosyllables he discovers what it is to be human.

Ritual and action

The other theatrical option Shakespeare takes up is that of showing the difference between the two main figures through what they do on stage. Bolingbroke and Richard begin to look like figures in two different kinds of drama. Bolingbroke is the man of action; we see him marching, making promises to followers and ordering executions.

By contrast, Richard looks like a figure in a a pageant; his actions are formalised and ritualised. Whereas Bolingbroke is seen marching, Richard sits upon the ground to tell 'sad stories'. His makes a symbolic descent from the walls of the castle, and in the deposition scene he smashes the mirror.

Through what they do, we see them as types – the practical man with a hint of the machiavel and the poet who wants to reflect upon the nature of human life.

29.8 The deposition scene

▶ 'for I must nothing be' (4.1.191)

Exchanging roles

In Richard's long speech before he descends the castle walls (Illustration 8) he imagines himself changing the regalia of kingship for the simple life of a hermit:

I'll give my jewels for a set of beads,
My gorgeous palace for a hermitage,
My gay apparel for a beadsman's gown,
My figured goblet for a dish of wood

(3.4.146–9)

These words anticipate the deposition scene; in imagination Richard is already giving away the privileges of a king. The audience is invited to see another movement; as he loses his external riches, he's in a position to gain those spiritual riches that nothing can take away.

The descent and the garden scene

Shakespeare places these scenes in sequence. This invites us to see the links between them.

The symbolic force of the scenes is to underline the contrasts of rising and falling. Richard says to the kneeling Bolingbroke that his 'heart is up ... although your knee be low' (3.3.192–3). The gardener has a complicated image of scales; at one point he says that the support Bolingbroke has 'weighs King Richard down' (3.4.90).

Illustration 8   Richard II on the castle walls

In both scenes the high meets the base. Richard elaborates on the 'base court where kings grow base' (3.4.179), and from the mouths of a base gardener the Queen hears his 'harsh rude tongue sound this unpleasing news' (3.4.75).

The problems of kingship

One of the ironies of the play is that as soon as Bolingbroke becomes king, he has problems very similar to Richard's.

The deposition scene opens as the play did; Bolingbroke is trying to investigate Gloucester's death. The tone is different: Bolingbroke questions Bagot like a lawyer. But then the proceedings collapse into comedy; Aumerle throws his challenge down, Fitzwalter does the same, as do Percy and Surrey. Aumerle then picks one up and casts it down to represent Norfolk's challenge. In the opening scene there might have been the hint that Richard wasn't entirely in control, but the number of angry young men all striving to fight with each other is horribly comical. Bolingbroke seems far less in charge than Richard!

The point would appear to be that for all his political power, Bolingbroke is not the true king. His failure to quell these noisy disputes is evidence that Shakespeare is prepared to show that the practical man is more successful than the dreamer but that if his power is not legitimate he'll have very big problems.

Richard's scene

After the childish squabbling of the opening, Richard's entrance changes the character of the scene. Here is a man who's trying to come to terms with the momentous change in his life.

He knows, or rather can express, what a momentous event is taking place. Bolingbroke is largely silent; the terms in which the deposition is to be understood are supplied by Richard in, for instance, his image of the well and the buckets (4.1.173).

The scene is full of strange contradictions. The one who is weak is dramatically the most powerful, the one who loses dictates the terms of the other's gains, the one we feel for is the one who's squandered the wealth and the honour of the country.

The tragic role

Richard is at his most tragic in this scene because he's at his most theatrical and poetic. He plays out his downfall with a controlled passion and a superbly judged sense of how his audience will respond.

At his most eloquent and most moving he's also at his most self-regarding:

> Yet I well remember
> The favours of these men. Were they not mine?
> Did they not sometime cry 'All hail' to me?
> So Judas did to Christ. But He in twelve
> Found truth in all but one; I in twelve thousand none.

> (4.1.158–62)

Those lines have the painful ingredients of tragedy. The betrayal stirs our sympathies, and we feel for Richard in the lonely isolation of twelve thousand deserters. But what pride! He compares himself to Christ in such a way as to suggest that his betrayal was greater than that which the Son of God suffered. And what self-absorption; look at the number of times he uses words about himself – 'I', 'mine', 'me' and back to 'I'. Here is a man who wants *us* to be moved by *his* tragedy because *he* is.

29.9 Richard's final soliloquy

▶ **'Yet I'll hammer it out'** (5.5.5)

Richard hammers out his elaborate conceit of how the prison is like the world with the inventive relish we would expect of a poet.

Making a world

In the absence of a flurry of public events, Richard has to invent his own world through the elaborations of his soliloquy. He peoples his imagination with a world of thoughts. By making the brain the female to his soul, he becomes once more the father of the nation.

Time

He does something similar with time. With little to pace his life by, he has to make a world in which he can recognise and make sense of the passing of time. In this he's helped by music, one of the most perfect representations of the movement of time.

Confession

By thinking about time, he comes to the clearest statement of his failure. Typically it has a poetic neatness:

> I wasted time, and now doth time waste me.
>
> (5.5.49)

He can see the shape of his life and recognise a certain justice in what's happened to him.

His compassion

Richard is grateful for the music:

> Yet blessing on his heart that gives it me
> For 'tis a sign of love, and love to Richard
>
> (5.5.64–5)

That warmth and tenderness is new, at least as far as others are concerned. The Groom enters, and Richard is welcoming; he calls him 'gentle friend' (5.5.81). The compassion he has learnt through his suffering is real.

The last two impressions of Richard are this tenderness and the heroic fight he puts up against his murderers. It's a typical end in that he's contradictory to the last – he dies a man of action and a man of prayer, enacting the the basic movement of the play in reverse – a fall and a rise:

Mount, mount, my soul; thy seat is up on high,
While my gross flesh sinks downward, here to die.

(5.5.111–12)

Exercises

29.1 Do you agree that if we want to reject Richard we must reject all that makes the play exciting and memorable – poetry, spectacle and heart-felt feeling?

29.2 In what ways do John of Gaunt and York show us that power in the history plays compromises and diminishes those who wield it?

29.3 'It's not true that *Richard II* is a play without action, it's just that it's not located in the places we might expect it.' Where do we look for drama in *Richard II*?

㉚ 1 Henry IV

30.1 New king, old troubles

▶ 'So shaken as we are' (1.1.1)

The Holy Land

The Henry of the *Henry IV* plays is not the Bolingbroke of *Richard II*. Bolingbroke is not an attractive figure but he does have purposefulness and a youthful force.

Shakespeare strikes a very different note at the opening of the play:

> So shaken as we are, so wan with care,
> Find we a time for frighted peace to pant
> And breathe short winded accents of new broils
> To be commenced in strands remote.
>
> (1.1.1–5)

In this exhausted state, he pants out thoughts about new wars in different places. What he has in mind is a crusade to the Holy Land. It's a common political ploy; when the nation is divided, a war is likely to bring it together.

30.2 Falstaff and the Henry IV plays

▶ 'little better than one of the wicked' (1.2.94)

Falstaff

This filmy start gives way to the character that gives the play life and colour – Falstaff.

A lot about Falstaff is given to us in Hal's first speech. This is the answer he gives to Falstaff's question about the time of day:

Thou art so fat-witted with drinking of old sack, and unbuttoning thee after supper, and sleeping upon benches after noon, that thou has forgotten to demand that which thou wouldst truly know. What a devil hast thou to do with the time of the day? Unless hours were cups of sack, and minutes capons, and clocks the tongues of bawds, and dials the signs of leaping-houses, and the blessed sun himself a hot fat wench in flame-coloured taffeta, I see no reason why thou shouldst be so superfluous to demand the time of day. (1.2.3–12)

To put it simply, the basics are there: Falstaff is fat, a heavy drinker, a glutton, sometimes slothful and a womaniser. Elsewhere in both the *Henry IV* plays we learn that he's a thief, a swindler and owes considerable sums of money. The common vices – drinking, eating, sex – while they might be pleasurable (for a time) to the participants, are not very interesting to anyone else.

Falstaff, however, has exercised a powerful hold over audiences' imaginations.

- **What, then, makes Falstaff so interesting?**

Playing

Falstaff is a knowing character; he's fully aware that his life is series of poses. The accounts he gives of himself are blatantly preposterous fabrications. He knows that others know that he's making up unlikely tales about himself.

Take, for example, his pose that he was a good man before he met Hal:

Thou hast done much harm upon me, Hal, God forgive thee for it. Before I knew thee, Hal, I knew nothing; and now am I, if a man should speak truly, little better than one of the wicked. (1.2.91–4)

If we didn't suspect that he knows that Hal knows it's a lie, we might think this is a mature reflection of a sinner who generously forgives the one who's led him astray.

The religious man

This leads on to one of his most used poses – the religious man. Some of the things he says have a biblical ring. When Hal reveals that he robbed Falstaff at Gad's Hill, Falstaff, pleased that they have the money, says:

Watch tonight, pray tomorrow (2.5.279)

That's a clever variation on a passage in the New Testament, where Jesus says: 'Watch and pray that ye enter not into temptation' (St Matthew 26: 41). He gives both 'watch' and 'pray' a riotous meaning, so 'watch' means both to keep a religious vigil and spend the night in revelry, while 'pray' works by way of a pun to mean talk to God and prey on people.

The young man

One of his most ludicrous poses is that he's young. In the ordinary sense of the word, he knows he's not; he says to Bardolph 'I am withered like an old apple-john' (3.3.4), that is, an apple that though edible is shrivelled. In *2 Henry IV* the Lord Chief Justice rebukes him; Falstaff, who never loses his temper, tries to be understanding:

You that are old consider not the capacities of us that are young. You do measure the heat of our livers with the bitterness of your gall. (*2 Henry IV*, 1.3.174–6)

An unexpected truth

Shakespeare springs an unexpected irony upon us. We know that Falstaff is a fat, old knight and yet when we hear him talk something else is evident. It may sound absurd to say but, nevertheless,

- **Falstaff is young.**

His mischievous humour, his love of trickery, his expertise in talking himself out of tight corners, his love of vice and his criminality are all practised with a youthful zest.

Riot and revelry

Falstaff presents a problem, perhaps *the* problem, for the audience. He stands for those thing without which life becomes stale – merriment, good cheer, companionship and play. The question the play asks is:

- **what is the proper balance between duty and pleasure?**

We can only ask that question because in Falstaff we see the epitome of holiday, of a view of life that sees it as all pleasure and recreation, all games and sports. In the words of a pop song: sex, drugs and rock n' roll.

Falstaff's language

There's a lot that can be said against Falstaff, but he remains popular because of his language. As in so many of his plays, Shakespeare values (perhaps above everything) wit. If anything can make human life bearable, if anything can save us from our own miseries, it's wit.

When we first meet him, he's talking to Hal about stealing:

> Marry, then sweet wag, when thou art king, let us not that are squires of the night's be called thieves of the day's beauty. Let us be Diana's foresters, gentlemen of the shade, minions of the moon; and let men say we be men of good government, being governed, as the sea is, by our noble and chaste mistress the moon, under whose countenance we steal. (1.2.23–9)

The wit is present in parody and pun. Falstaff is suggesting that thieves who operate at night should be compared to the attendants of a royal person. 'Squires of the night's beauty' and 'gentlemen of the shade' might be compared to posts in the Tudor court such as Gentlemen of the Chamber. Falstaff, in other words, is producing a delightful parody of the court. 'Beauty' is a pun on 'booty' and 'steal' means both rob and move with stealth.

Added to the wit is the lyricism of the words. The phrase 'minions of the moon' has a light, glancing quality; the alliteration is delightfully unemphatic, the tongue easily skims over the consonants. The language is zestfully smooth.

30.3 The comic elements

▶ **'What trick, what device' (2.5.266)**

Comic practices

The tavern scenes are similar to comedies:

- **they contain practices and devices**.

One device grows out of another. Hal asks Falstaff where they plan to steal purses, and Poins tells them that pilgrims will be on Gad's Hill. Hal says he won't join them, but when Falstaff leaves, Poins proposes to Hal that they lie in wait and rob Falstaff and his mates after the attack on the pilgrims. It's almost a case of measure for measure.

In a wonderful scene, Falstaff is led to offer a hugely farcical account of the many men who robbed him; First he claims 'sixteen at least' (2.5.176), and inflation sets in:

> if I fought not with fifty of them, I am a bunch of radish. (2.5.186–7)

When he's told it was Hal and Poins, Falstaff is not the least bit ashamed; he claims simply that he 'knew ye as well as he that made ye' (2.5.270).

30.4 Hal's soliloquy

▶ **'I'll so offend to make offence a skill' (1.2.213)**

Hal's soliloquy at the end of Act 1, Scene 2 is one of the most important speeches in both the *Henry IV* plays. What he says is shared only with the audience, so we know what he's up to, when none of the other characters do.

What it tackles is what we might call the Falstaff problem:

- **what is the place of holiday, recreation and revelry in the pattern of life?**

Hal is quite clear about this:

> If all the year were playing holidays,
> To sport would be as tedious as to work
>
> (1.2.200–1)

That's true enough; if every day were a holiday, no day would be a holiday because there'd be nothing to contrast holidaying with.

What's more important is the rest of the speech and the significance it has in the context of the play.

Relative viewpoints

The speech draws attention to the relativity of viewpoint. Because each character only represents his or her point of view, the audience can see how situations look different, depending upon who's viewing them. Think how differently Falstaff views his friendship with Hal: the merry-making of the tavern and the thieving at Gad's Hill. He thinks this is what Hal is really like and will therefore continue to be like when he's king.

The moral issue

What is the moral status of what Hal's doing? It can be regarded as deception. He allows them to think that he's one of them when all the while he's putting on an act:

> I know you all, and will awhile uphold
> The unyoked humour of your idleness
>
> (1.1.192–3)

What kind of friendship is that? Falstaff is not a deceiver; he makes no secret of the kind of life he wants. Hal, however, leads his companions astray.

The pressures of kingship

The moral case against Hal can be accepted, and yet his behaviour can be understood if we remember what he remembers – that he's going to be king. Learning to play a double game is what a king has to do; he has to use the grand terms of morality and yet exercise naked power when it suits him. Shakespeare might be showing the education of a prince consists in learning this tough lesson. If he does, he also shows who it's tough on.

Expectation

This is one of the moments when Shakespeare works by expectation, only the expectation occurs over two plays. The rejection of Falstaff that closes *2 Henry IV* is present in this speech:

> So when this loose behaviour I throw off

> (1.2.205)

When he does throw it off, we see with painful clarity who's been fooled.

The rejection of holiday?

Falstaff wants all holiday; Hal apparently wants the balance that makes holiday what it is. But does he achieve it? The rejection of Falstaff, both here and at the close of *2 Henry IV* looks more like the rejection of holiday.

30.5 Hotspur and honour

▶ 'To pluck bright honour' (1.3.200)

Hotspur

Hotspur lends verve and zest to the rebellion. What appeals to Hotspur is the danger; when discussing the rebellion, he says:

> If he fall in, good night, or sink or swim.
> Send danger from the east unto the west,
> So honour cross it from the north to south

> (1.3.192–4)

There's something in him of three characters Shakespeare went on to create – Macbeth, Coriolanus and Hamlet. Macbeth because the image of something dangerous stirs him to action; Coriolanus because what matters to him is the love of the fight, and Hamlet because the prize is 'honour'. Hotspur is not political; what matters to him is not increase of power but his reputation. The final image of his speech makes it clear that what fires him is the thrill of war and personal glory.

Honour

Hotspur sees that the hope of honour makes even the most dangerous task attractive:

> By heaven, methinks it were an easy leap
> To pluck bright honour from the pale-faced moon,
> Or dive into the bottom of the deep,
> Where fathom-line could never touch the ground,
> And pluck up drowned honour by the locks,
> So he that doth redeem her hence might wear,
> Without corrival, all her dignities.

> (1.3.199–205)

Honour is like stylish dress; a man would do anything to be seen wearing it. The poetic hyperbole of flying up to the moon and diving down to the depths captures the adventure of the young man in search of public esteem. There's also an amorous element here; honour is female, so wearing her is like going out with the prettiest girl in town.

The ideal son

In the King's eyes he's the son the monarch should have had. But we can see otherwise; for all his apparent irresponsibility, Hal is a calculating politician, whereas Hotspur is an irresponsible romantic. The irony is that the King has the son he needs; it's poignant that he doesn't see this.

Imaginative and impractical

A further irony is that Hotspur is actually closer to Richard II than any other figure. Both are men of excessive imaginations in a world in which practical politicians succeed.

A tragedy

This makes Hotspur's life one of the minor tragedies of the history plays. He has his own very strong image of himself and his world and he lives according to that image in a blaze of self-generated adulation. In the final battle, his wish is that

> no man might draw short breath today
> But I and Harry Monmouth!

> (5.2.28–9)

The irony is that when it comes to the combat between them (something Shakespeare invented), Hotspur loses. His dying words show him still sticking to the glamorous code of personal honour:

> I better brook the loss of brittle life
> Than those proud titles thou hast won of me.

> (5.4.77–8)

There's something stirring yet dotty about the man who regrets losing his reputation more than his life. But, as always, a figure isn't tragic unless, at the end, he's seen to be wrong.

The married man

Hotspur is the one major figure of the play who has a wife. Her dramatic function is to provide romantic ardour and the sense of a personal life beyond politics.

30.6 Fathers and sons

▶ 'I'll play my father' (2.5.437)

1 Henry IV is about the old and the young and about fathers and sons. Prince Hal has a 'father' in each part of his life:

- **at court his father is Henry IV, in the taverns it's Falstaff.**

The comic scene in which Falstaff and Hal parody a conversation between the King and the Prince comes after news of the rebellion has reached the tavern. This reminds us of what Hal knows: there can't be a complete division between the private and the public in the life of a prince.

When Falstaff plays the King, he questions Hal about his life, and the subject of thieving emerges:

Shall the son of England prove a thief and take purses? (2.5.413–14)

Here, of course, ironies of which Falstaff is unaware start to surface. He hopes the Prince will prove a thief, and England under him will be one long holiday. We know Hal has no intention of living his life that way; we also might see that if the issue is thieving, what has been stolen is Falstaff's innocent trust in Hal.

When the roles are reversed, and Hal plays the King, the anticipations of the eventual outcome are very strong. Hal rehearses the theme of rejecting evil influences, and though Falstaff pleads eloquently and slightly sentimentally, Hal as the King (and as the king that he will be) says curtly: 'I do; I will' (2.5.486).

30.7 The rebels

▶ 'our induction full of prosperous hope' (3.1.2)

Shakespeare takes the rebels less than seriously. When we see their ludicrous claims, their presumption and their bickering we know that the rebellion is bound to fail.

For a start, Hotspur plunges the scene into farce:

A plague upon it, I have forgot the map!

(3.1.5)

If the scene starts with this being lost, there seems little chance that the King will be defeated by this bunch.

Before they squabble over who's to have what, Glendower's manic outpourings (understandably?) anger Hotspur. Glendower is an appalling wind-bag; furthermore, he's conceited and superstitious.

Shakespeare shows that the rebels are an alliance of egotists, who find co-operation almost impossible. Through our laughter we see the inevitable defeat of such an ill-sorted alliance.

▶ 'We'll fight with him tonight' (4.3.1)

Kingly generosity

When the sun rises before the battle, Hal plays a clever game: he praises Hotspur, admits his own errors and offers single combat instead of war. The King follows this up with the offer of

> our grace,
> Both he and they and you, yea, every man
> Shall be my friend again, and I'll be his.

> (5.1.106–8)

Both father and son are behaving as men of royal blood; they appear generous and worthy of the people's loyalty.

Deception

The rebels, by contrast, are devious. The very first words of the next scene are:

> O no, my nephew must not know, Sir Richard,
> The liberal and kind offer of the King.

> (5.2.1–2)

It is, of course, another way of playing politics. The rebel leaders deceive each other in order to make war inevitable.

Parody

Throughout the preparations the figure of Falstaff marches, offering in what he says and does a parody of the high seriousness of war. In Act 4, Scene 2 he admits to letting his conscripts buy their freedom.

On the field of battle he falls in the fight in which Hotspur dies. His very presence punctures any sense of the heroic that Hotspur would like the scene to have. He hears the ambiguous tribute paid by Hal; the touching 'Poor Jack, farewell' balanced by 'I could have better spared a better man' (5.4.102–3). But the fat, old rascal rises up, stabs the dead Hotspur and carries him off as if he'd killed him.

Falstaff is Shakespeare's way of showing us that the play can be read both as epic adventure and burlesque.

Hal, Hotspur, Falstaff

In a kind of tableau Hal stands between the bodies of Hotspur and Falstaff. This symbolises the two choices that other characters (in particular the King) think lie before the Prince. Is Hal going to be a heroic figure who seeks honour above everything or is he going to be a wastrel who fritters his time away in idleness?

Hal is much too sensible and too calculating to become a charismatic warrior-hero, and we already know he's no intention of turning life into a long, uninterrupted holiday.

Victory

The plays end in a low-key, matter of fact way. Since what we are watching is history, there's the strong sense that events will unfold beyond the end of the play. There's something anti-climatic about the last couplet:

> And since this business so fair is done,
> Let us not leave till all our own be won.
>
> (5.544–5)

What we hear in those lines is a justification for *2 Henry IV*. What is gained is Henry's self-command. He hasn't made a pilgrimage, but though the rebels have shaken him, he hasn't fallen.

Exercises

30.1   How does Hal's soliloquy alter our entire view of the play?

30.2   'This is really Falstaff's play.' Is there anything more to be said?

2 Henry IV

31.1 Rumour in a changing world

▶ 'The sum of all Is that the King hath won' (1.1.131–2)

Rumour

The play opens with the figure of Rumour, who, with a grim though quite energetic relish, enjoys the power he exercises over a listening world. He prepares the audience for the agents of rumour, who ride to Northumberland's castle and who gradually reveal what Rumour has truthfully told us – that the King won the battle at Shrewsbury and that Hotspur is dead.

A changed world

The impression is of a changed world. This is felt in the language; Morton says that when the troops heard of Hotspur's death, they lost spirit:

> all the rest
> Turned on themselves, like dull and heavy lead;
> And as the thing that's heavy in itself
> Upon enforcement flies with greatest speed,
> So did our men

(1.1.117–21)

In 'dull', 'heavy lead' and 'heavy in itself' we hear the crushing effect of dreadful news.

31.2 The new rebels

▶ 'Let order die!' (1.1.154)

What is the effect of Northumberland's words:

> Let order die!

(1.1.154)

The Archbishop of York

Thirty lines after Northumberland's cry the uprising that will be one of the main strands of the play is first mentioned. It's instigator is the Archbishop of York, Richard Scrope, who

> Turns insurrection to religion.
>
> (1.1.200)

Great hope is placed in him, because he

> Derives from heaven his quarrel and his cause;
>
> (1.1.205)

It sounds grand, but the audience surely sees through this, even if the Archbishop doesn't. In the world of Henry's England what matters is power and holding on to it. Religious talk is just an attractive surface, which masks the real struggle.

The Archbishop is a puzzling figure. He's clearly sincere, but it's far from clear what he thinks he's up to. When we meet him, Shakespeare starts the scene in the middle of a debate:

> Thus have you heard our cause and known our means
>
> (1.3.1)

The difficulty is that we haven't heard his 'cause'; we simply don't know *why* he's taking to arms. The rebels debate the serious business of numbers. Lord Bardolph is quite open about why Hotspur failed:

> with great imagination
> Proper to madmen, led his powers to death,
> And winking leapt into destruction.
>
> (1.3.31–3)

'Winking' means with eyes closed, closed to the fact that his troops were few. Are the Archbishop's eyes open?

The climax of the rebellion plot leaves us little wiser; the nearest we get to a specific wrong is that they can't bring their complaints to the King:

> We are denied access unto his person
> Even by those men that most have done us wrong.
>
> (4.1.78–9)

That hardly justifies rebellion!

The conclusion that might be drawn from this fiasco is that rebellion is no longer a serious threat. In a land with such adept politicians as Prince John and such incompetent rebels as the Archbishop, no serious strife is possible.

31.3 Time and growing old

▶ **'We are time's subjects' (1.3.110)**

A feeling runs through the entire play that everyone is getting old.

Gloucestershire

It would be easy to pile up details concerning age, disease and weariness (Hal's first words are: 'Before God, I am exceeding weary.' – 2.2.1) and conclude that this is a dark and oppressive play. Yet this is to reckon without the Gloucestershire scenes; they are about age and the passing of time, but instead of being heavy they have a mellow, wistful and gently humorous quality.

Shakespeare knows how the old talk. They repeat themselves, they wander and they reminisce. Shallow's questions about Silence's family soon lead him to his memories – 'I was once of Clement's Inn' (3.2.12). With that the two old gents are back in the past – the recital of names, the happy memories of the women they've had, the tales of fights and the reflection that 'how many of my old acquaintance are dead' (3.2.33).

England

The speech of these old men has a touching (even plangent – heart-tugging) poetry. When Falstaff joins them, he also talks of the past. 'Jane Nightwork' is 'old, old', and when Shallow yearningly speaks of what 'this knight and I have seen', Falstaff delivers what's perhaps the most wistful line in the whole play:

We have heard the chimes at midnight, Master Shallow. (3.2.211)

In them we see another England, unconcerned with affairs of state and content with its memories.

Yet Shakespeare shows that these old men too are part of the nation captured in that slightly faded picture we call *2 Henry IV*. The opening of the last Gloucestershire scene has an appropriate setting:

> Nay, you shall see my orchard, where, in an
> arbour, we will eat a last year's pippin of
> mine own grafting, with a dish of caraways

(5.3.1–3)

How near and yet how far from the garden scene in *Richard II*. Shallow talks about his own grafting, but what we see, as in *Richard II*, is a picture of England as a garden. The fruit is last year's – that says it all; nothing much could have grown in the declining days of the usurper, Henry, and the audience, though not the characters, know that the old King is dead.

31.4 The troubled king

▶ 'Uneasy lies the head that wears the crown' (3.1.31)

When the King finally appears in Act 3, Scene 1 it's as if the victory at Shrewsbury has failed to hearten him.

Soliloquy

After a brief bit of state business, he lapses into a soliloquy about the King, his people and sleep. Its special tone is created by the fact that it's a series of questions, each one of which asks why every subject, no matter how uncomfortable the bed, can sleep while the King can't. His last line (quoted above) is as near as he gets to an answer; he can't sleep because he's the King.

The speech has another theme. The King's longing for sleep might also be a longing for the final sleep – death. The feeling runs through the play that nothing can help the nation, while Henry is King.

Disease

Even though we've seen the rebels are without hope of success, the King still broods on them; he says to Warwick:

> Then you perceive the body of our kingdom,
> How foul it is, what rank diseases grow,
> And with what danger near the heart of it.

> (3.1.37–9)

The image of the diseased body adds to the feeling of decline present in other parts of the play – Northumberland's crutch, the illness of Falstaff, last year's apples. Because the King's body is also the nation's body, the diseases he feel so acutely in the nation are actually his own diseases.

Thought

One of the features of the play is that there's quite a bit of thinking done in it. Life prompts characters to ask questions, so in soliloquy and dialogue the issues of time, public reputation and the nature of power emerge.

When he's with Warwick and Surrey, Henry has a long meditation about how, if we knew the outcome of events, we'd shut 'the book of fate' (3.1.44). He goes on to recall that Richard prophesied the disloyalty of Northumberland. It isn't just the King who mulls over these issues. Warwick has an alternative way of understanding Richard's role as prophet:

> There is a history in all men's lives
> Figuring the natures of the times deceased;
> The which observed, a man may prophesy

> (3.1.75–7)

This is a more historical (and even psychological and sociological) approach; we can see what made people act in the past, so on the basis of that we can make a good guess about the future.

31.5 Father, son and crown

▶ 'Why doth the crown lie there upon his pillow' (4.3.152)

The chief action happens within the family. The play is about power transferring from father to son, so the most fraught scenes are those in which the two attempt to come to some understanding.

The arrival of good news

When the news of the rebels' defeat arrives, the King is too sick to rejoice. He characteristically reflects on how opportunity and the ability to respond to it don't coincide. At the end of the speech he has what we might call a minor stroke – 'my brain is giddy' (4.3.110).

What's made him unable to rejoice is something which, again, we've seen before – Hal's behaviour. The irony is that in comfort Warwick speaks the truth:

> The Prince will in the perfectness of time
> Cast off his followers

> (4.3.74–5)

The crown

The King sleeps. This is what he's wanted, but when Hal sees him, he thinks this is the other sleep that the King's longing for repose was a symbol of. In sleep or death, the King becomes the vulnerable human being Shakespeare shows his monarchs to be.

Hal, believing him to be dead, takes the crown. This is one of those actions that reveals so much about the play. It shows that Hal is a king in the making and it shows how much the crown means to his usurping father. Henry's distress at waking and finding it gone is probably as great any he suffers in the two plays. There's a bitter irony that what caused him so much suffering is the very thing he now wants.

Father and son

Warwick's account of Hal's tears and Hal's expression of grief bring father and son together. The King's anger allows him to say what he's felt throughout – that Hal and his riotous companions will be the ruin of England. This allows Hal to speak of

> The noble change that I have purposed.

> (4.3.283)

Two features of this scene are very striking. The first is that Hal talks with the plain purposefulness of a Bolingbroke. The King feels that his unhappy reign is due to the circumstances in which he seized the crown. Hal reassures him:

> You won it, wore it, kept it, gave it me

> (4.3.351)

Functional language and political realism – we could be back in *Richard II*.

The second is in keeping with the first. The last piece of advice the father gives the son is that foreign wars can ease troubles at home; the new King should:

> busy giddy minds
> With foreign quarrels

> (4.3.342–3)

The next play shows Hal taking this advice. The King is taken to the chamber called Jerusalem to die.

31.6 The new king

▶ 'This new and gorgeous garment, majesty' (5.2.43)

When Hal enters as Henry V we should be aware that this is something we've been waiting for since the opening of *1 Henry IV*. Those on stage, in particular the Lord Chief Justice, think the thoughts that first surfaced in the earlier play:

> O God, I fear all will be overturned.
>
> (5.2.19)

Nevertheless, we feel differently. We know what Hal has said all along and we know what he's said to the King about his 'noble change' (4.2.283).

Justice

The new King deals justly with the Lord Chief Justice, who pleads that when he opposed the Prince he did so in the name of the King's justice. Justice is the basis of any society, but it's not a warm or comfortable virtue. Justice means you get what you deserve and nothing more or less. Its symbols are the scales and the sword. The new King's words confirm the Lord Chief Justice's position:

> Therefore still bear the balance and the sword
>
> (5.2.102)

But Hal goes beyond justice. Picking up one of the preoccupations of the play, he says:

> You shall be as a father to my youth
>
> (5.2.117)

We might wonder how much of this is deeply felt and how much is clever political manoeuvring, but as soon as we ask that question we should see how inappropriate it is; once Hal is King, all that matters is politics, so as long as it works, his sincerity is not at issue.

31.7 The rejection of Falstaff

▶ 'I know thee not, old man' (5.4.47)

As soon as Falstaff hears that the old king is dead, he rides for London. His self-confidence is pathetic; he tells the doddering Shallow 'choose what office thou wilt in the land' (5.3.123). Once there he has no doubts; he speaks with unquestioning assurance, addressing the King of England as 'my royal Hal!' and 'my sweet boy!' (5.5.41, 43). What he hears is the reply of the King. The drama works not only because of the disappointment of Falstaff as he crumples to his knees, but because on stage we see two characters who have diametrically opposed views and expectations of the situation.

What Hal makes clear is the public nature of his change. He's no longer 'the thing I was' (5.5.56):

God doth know, so shall the world perceive,
That I have turned away my former self

(5.5.57–8)

There's a Falstaffian play upon words here; the former self is the man whom Falstaff expected to find and Falstaff himself is the image of the disordered life the Prince led.

The saddest moment comes after the King has left. The wily Falstaff does, after all, know something of politics:

I shall be sent for in private to him.

(5.5.76)

He is sent for – but not in private. He's arrested for debt. The new reign has begun.

Exercises

31.1 'What is most distinctive about *2 Henry IV* is not the action but the atmosphere.' To what extent do you agree?

31.2 Do you agree that in *2 Henry IV* we are most aware of Shakespeare's approach to public affairs through the family?

---

32 Henry V

32.1 The Chorus and the stage

▶ 'Admit me chorus to this history' (Chorus, 32)

The Chorus

The Chorus is the most developed part of its kind in the whole of Shakespeare; he not only starts and ends the play but prepares us for the action with evocative pictures of new settings.

His manner is rhetorical and descriptive. His opening words are like a battle cry.

The Chorus and the stage

In one sense, he's theatrically modest; he tells us that the stage can't hope to do what's required:

> But pardon, gentles all,
> The flat unraised spirits that hath dared
> On this unworthy scaffold to bring forth
> So great an object.

(Chorus, 8–11)

This is something he insists on; in the speech at the beginning of Act 3 he tells the audience to keep up the necessary act of imagining – 'Suppose ... O do but think ... Suppose'.

The Chorus and judgement

The Chorus draws attention to the fact that

• the words of the play exceed what we see.

This might prompt us to ask whether this tells us something about the play as a whole. To the chorus, Henry is a hero:

> Then should the warlike Harry, like himself,
> Assume the port of Mars

(Chorus, 5–6)

The King appears like Mars, a mythical figure – the embodiment of warlike qualities. We have to ask whether we see him this way, and whether his warlike qualities are admirable ones.

32.2 The morality of making war

▶ 'May I with right and conscience make this claim?' (1.2.96)

This is the issue in first act: has the King the right to go to war with France?

Audiences and readers have a problem here. The first is that the argument as conducted by the Archbishop is exceptionally difficult to follow. The way to look at this is to remember that in the second scene the King, at first, says very little. All he does is ask the question above. Since that's all that concerns him, audiences might feel with justification that they shouldn't bother themselves further.

The issue of war

What Shakespeare does make clear is that Henry thinks hard before going to war. He may be acting on his father's advice (see 31.5) that a way of uniting the nation (one of the themes of the play) is to make war, but it can't just be that because he's aware of two things: the danger of Scotland and the human cost of war.

The second point is important:

> For never two such kingdoms did contend
> Without much fall of blood, whose guiltless drops
> Are every one a woe, a sore complaint
> 'Gainst him whose wrongs gives edge unto the swords
> That makes such waste in brief mortality.

(1.2.24–8)

This is what many commanders must feel but can never admit to their troops. If there's no good cause to fight, the leader is guilty of innocent blood. Henry is prepared to share that with his court but he can't say it on the eve of battle.

32.3 Treachery

▶ 'you would have sold your King to slaughter' (2.2.167)

War unites a nation, but rebellion doesn't immediately die out. The Chorus has to report treachery. France has found out

> A nest of hollow bosoms, which he fills
> With treacherous crowns

(2.1.21–2)

It may be that Shakespeare is playing with the tradition that the common people are always loyal, but the nobility can't be wholly relied on. (It may not be true but in the popular imagination, the would-be Nazi collaborators were toffs.)

The unmasking has a parabolic element. While the troops are embarking, the King suddenly announces that he will free the man who spoke out against him, putting his behaviour down to too much drink. The three whom the Chorus has told us are traitors suggest that the man must be severely punishment. They thereby seal their own fates. Henry emerges as both merciful and just.

32.4 Falstaff's death

▶ 'He's in Arthur's bosom' (2.3.9)

Falstaff's death

The placing of Falstaff's death after the unmasking of the traitors raises the question of who's betrayed whom. The traitors betray England and their King, but though it's excessive to call the King's treatment of Falstaff treachery, we can understand how desolate Falstaff must have felt. His death, however, seems to be without bitterness. The Hostess reports how his life ebbed away:

A' made a finer end, and went away an it had been any christom child. A parted ev'n just between twelve and one, ev'n at the turning o' th' tide – for after I saw him fumble with the sheets, and play with flowers, and smile upon his finger's end, I knew there was but one way. For his nose was as sharp as a pen, and a babbled of green fields. (2.3.10–17)

This is the death of a man in the extremes of second childishness. Yet it feels appropriate. For all his worldly corruption, there was a child-like trusting element in Falstaff. We might also feel that Shakespeare loved him, if not as a man, then certainly as a character. Evidence for this is that the speech is exquisitely worded – the details of the ebbing tide, the flowers he reaches for, his pinched nose and the delightful child-likeness of the word 'babbled' all show Shakespeare writing at full pressure.

32.5 The invasion of France

▶ 'Thus comes the English' (2.4.1)

Shakespeare presents a French view of the English. In some senses the French are a bit like audiences nowadays – they don't quite know what to make of King Harry. The Dauphin thinks that the spirit of Falstaff still rules:

No, with no more than if we heard that England
Were busied with a Whitsun morris dance.

(2.4.24–5)

King Charles, however, has a longer memory. He observes that he's 'bred out of that bloody strain' (2.4.51) that led battles against France in the past. Crécy is mentioned, and its victor, the Black Prince, is spoken of in awesome terms.

32.6 The siege of Harfleur

▶ 'Holding due course to Harfleur' (3.1.17)

Henry's speech

The King knows that war is a performance. His speech is about how the troops must play a fierce role:

> But when the blast of war blows in our ears,
> Then imitate the action of the tiger.
> Stiffen the sinews, conjure up the blood,
> Disguise fair nature with hard-favoured rage.

(3.1.5–8)

When summoned to war, men must 'imitate' the tiger, and through stiffening sinews and summoning up blood our natural expressions must be disguised by looks of rage. 'Imitate' and 'disguise' both have a place in acting. We are not naturally violent and bloody, but in war we must behave in that way.

His rallies his troops by appealing to the traditions of their fathers, who fought for England in France:

> On, on, you noblest English,
> Whose blood is fet from fathers of war-proof,
> Fathers like so many Alexanders
> Have in these parts from morn to even fought

(3.1.17–20)

The appeal is to their noble fathers (ancestors), who fought with the legendary heroism of Alexander the Great. The English troops must be worthy of their illustrious forebears.

The scoundrels

Shakespeare then shows some of the English troops – Nim, Bardolph, Pistol and the boy. All but the boy are scoundrels and cowards.

What Shakespeare achieves through the immediate juxtaposition of the heroic Henry and the cowards is a double perspective on war:

• **war can be heroic and it can be a grotesque farce.**

He achieves this by following a high style – Henry's ringing, epic verse – with a low style – a prose in which they sing scraps of songs and long for the ale-house.

The professionals

It's surely intended to be funny that when we see the 'real' soldiers – those who have time and again assaulted the breach at Harfleur ('once more' – 3.1.1) – they're not English!

They look like the cast for the Englishman, Irishman and Scotsman joke; the busy (but brave) Welshman, Fluellen, has already driven the English off-stage.

These professionals have a number of functions. They display the pride of the professional soldier with its jargon – 'you must come presently to the mines' (3.3.2) – and they speak of the code by which they fight – 'I know the disciplines of war' (3.3.82) (see 1.22).

Theatrically, they provide an opportunity for accents. We hear the distinctive timbre of three Celtic tongues – Irish, Scots and Welsh. We can't exclude the potential comedy of this. What it also gives us is that sense of a greater nation at war – Great Britain. This is a nation that doesn't yet exist (it didn't in Shakespeare's time) but it has a symbolic function. Even the Scots (talked of as troublesome at the end of 1.2) are 'on our side'. Indeed, the only ones who aren't are the cowardly English!

Comedy

Nim and Bardolph come near to burlesque. Henry says he sees his troops 'like grey-hounds in the slips/Straining upon the start' (3.1.31–2), but Nim's first words are: 'Pray thee corporal, stay' (3.2.3).

Fluellen provides something near the kind of comedy we find in other Shakespeare plays – a blend of oddity in character and involvement in practices. His distinctive speech is entertaining; he pronounces a 'p' in place of 'b' and insists to Gower that Alexander the Great was a Welshman (4.7.11–37). His involvement in the practices involving the King and Williams brings about a comic conclusion to what, had Henry been less generous, would have been a black scene for the soldier. His attack on Pistol is pure farce. As a comic counterpoint to the heroic tale of Henry's victory, he's vital to the design of the play. Most audiences like him.

Surrender

Henry's speech demanding the surrender of Harfleur is uncompromising; if the town doesn't surrender, they will see:

> The blind and bloody soldier with foul hand
> Defile the locks of your shrill-shrieking daughters;
> Your fathers taken by the silver beards,
> And their most reverend heads dashed to the walls;
> Your naked infants spitted upon spikes

(3.3.117–21)

The passage was thought too grim to be included in Olivier's war-time film.

Those who want to find Henry a tarnished character have ammunition in this speech. He threatens them with rape and murder. The defence is that he has to and that it works. Soldiers did pillage towns that resisted, and the custom was to show leniency if they capitulated. Henry conducts war according to those rules. As soon as they surrender, he says:

> Use mercy to them all.

(3.3.137)

▶ 'behold/The royal captain of this ruined band' (4.1.28–9)

Disguise

The scene in which Henry disguises himself and visits his troops is the best in the play. Using the conventions employed so successfully in the comedies, Shakespeare allows the King to hear and say what would have been impossible if the troops knew who he was. The troops can be themselves, and the reward to Williams in Act 4, Scene 7 for standing up to the King not only when he didn't know but when he did know who he was satisfies the audience's liking for the soldier and our sense of justice.

The likelihood of defeat

In order to understand both this scene and the battle, we have to pick up all the signs that indicate England is likely to lose. Henry didn't want to fight at Agincourt. He admits to Mountjoy, the French Herald, that his troops are sick, few in number and, if well, no better than the French (3.6.143–8). The English fear they will lose; the Chorus paints them as thin and even ghost-like in the light of the moon.

The hero and the brother

This is the hero of the Chorus – the captain who shares his people's plight. It's also consistent with the figure of the new King who modestly emerged at the end of *2 Henry IV*. There's no reason why we should regard the Chorus as more authoritative than any other character, but when we see what he says reflected in Henry, we can trust his interpretation of the King. The word 'brother' is used by the King, from the family intimacies of the opening dialogues of Act 4, Scene 1 to the promise to the troops before the battle that

> he today that sheds his blood with me
> Shall be my brother

> (4.3.61–2)

Pistol

Having borrowed Sir Thomas Erpingham's cloak, the King meets Pistol. Pistol is a man of swaggering words and very little else. His challenge is in French – hardly a sensible thing on the eve of a battle! He demands to know who the cloaked figure is, patronisingly asking:

> art thou officer,
> Or art thou base, common and popular?

> (4.1.38–9)

This must be a test of the King's self-control; 'base' can mean of low status and morally corrupt. Perhaps Henry sees the irony in 'common' and 'popular'; both are true of the King in senses not intended by Pistol.

Even worse is Pistol's insult, when he learns that this stranger is Welsh and, what's worse, a friend of Fluellen, he insults him:

The *fico* for thee then. (4.1.61)

'Fico' is Italian for fig. It has a number of bawdy meanings in Shakespeare and was a common insult, roughly equivalent to 'fuck off'.

Court, Bates and Williams

These three soldiers see the coming of the morning without hope. When the stranger says Sir Thomas Erpingham compares their situation to sailors beached on the sand, expecting to be washed away by the next tide, they want to know whether the King knows what this trusty soldier thinks. The speed with which Henry launches into his affirmation that the King is like an ordinary man rather suggests that this is something he desperately wants to say:

> I think the King is but a man as I am. The violet smells to him as it doth to me; the element shows to him as it doth to me. All his senses have but human conditions. (4.1.99–102)

This is the heart of the play and possibly the heart of all the history plays. Henry, in spite of power and position, is no different from the soldiers. It's important to remember that he's in disguise and has no intention of revealing who he is. Therefore, he can have no ulterior motive in declaring that he, like them, is a vulnerable human being. His declaration of humanity, therefore, can have no political motive; he says it solely because he wants to say what's true.

One of the themes of the battle scene – brotherhood – is raised by Bates, who wishes the King 'were here alone' (4.1.120). Because Henry's disguised, nothing prevents him telling the truth, so we can believe him when he says:

> I dare say you love him not so ill to wish him here alone (4.1.123–4)

Henry wants the companionship of those who before the battle he will describe as 'we band of brothers' (4.3.60).

The issue that takes up most of the scene is the one of responsibility. This, as we've seen, has concerned Henry from the very start (see 32.2). To the very real questions the soldiers ask about the King's guilt, he says:

> The King is not bound to answer the particular endings of his soldiers (4.1.154–5)
> Every subject's duty is the King's, but every subject's soul is his own. (4.1.175–6)

It's difficult to quarrel with the argument here. The King might be responsible for the death of a soldier's body but he can't be held accountable for the state of a man's soul.

Soliloquy and prayer

Henry is most like his father when he's left alone. He meditates darkly on sleep, responsibility and the differences between the King and his subjects. His speech to Gloucester at the beginning of the scene (4.1.1–12) shows that he thinks defeat is likely, and he's just heard Williams' moving account (like a medieval wall painting) of the Resurrection of soldiers who've died in battle (4.1.213–22).

But he gets one thing quite wrong; he imagines the common people sleeping easily when he's just met three common soldiers who are sick with sleepless anxiety about the coming battle. The irony is that he's even more of a brother to his soldiers than he thinks.

His prayer shows his real source of anxiety – his father's usurpation and the murder of Richard. Shakespeare gets very close to the medieval mind in the way he (pathetically?) points out to God (who knows it already!) that he's paid for 500 poor people to pray twice a day, so that the sin of Richard's death can be pardoned.

32.8 The battle of Agincourt

▶ **'Then call we this the field of Agincourt' (4.7.88)**

Those who get to know *Henry V* from Olivier's wonderful film are sometimes disappointed by what Shakespeare actually wrote about the battle. We don't get the spectacle of the battle and we get nasty scenes Olivier altered.

The French and the English

Is it going too far to say that Shakespeare stirs us against the French by presenting them as cruel to their horses?

> Mount them and make incisions in their hides,
> That their hot blood may spin in English eyes

(4.2.9–10)

It's difficult to like men who dig their spurs in horses for the purpose of making their blood spurt into the enemy's eyes.

Nor is it easy to like the smugness of the French. The Constable sounds a bit like Hotspur when he says 'our superfluous lackeys and our peasants' (4.2.26) could easily do the job.

Shakespeare presents the English as underdogs:

Warwick: Of fighting men they have full three thousand.
Exeter: There's five to one. Besides, they are all fresh.

(4.3.3–4)

No wonder Warwick wishes they had an extra thousand men with them.

St Crispin's day

Henry's speech before the battle tests audiences and readers; those who find it moving are prepared to forgive the King almost everything, while those who see it as a clever piece of play-acting withhold their approval and their sympathies.

The speech is both intimate and public. It starts in a low key as an interruption of the remark Warwick makes about the extra thousand. Soon, however, he's on to a familiar theme:

> But if it be a sin to covet honour,
> I am the most offending soul alive.

(4.3.28–9)

I think there's a difference between this and what Hotspur says in *1 Henry IV*, 1.3.199–206. Not only is Henry tentative about the morality of wanting honour, the honour he seeks is to be with his troops in battle. Hotspur said he'd do anything if he achieved honour by doing so. For Henry it's the other way round; he starts with the plight they're in and only seeks honour in that.

There is a passage about those who survive the battle showing their family and friends their wounds on each anniversary of the battle's eve. Clearly he's appealing to the idea of the heroic, but it's the heroic in a democratic and domestic form. All of those who fought will be heroes; furthermore, they'll become chroniclers of the scene:

> Then shall our names,
> Familiar in his mouth as household words –
> Harry the King, Bedford and Exeter,
> Warwick and Talbot, Salisbury and Gloucester –
> Be in their flowing cups remembered,
> We few, we happy few, we band of brothers.
>
> (4.3.55–60)

It's not entirely clear whether all who fought are included in the band of brothers; it could refer only to those who've been named, but another possible reading is that those who will remember the names will see them as brothers.

The Boy

The Boy is a victim of the war. We see him interpreting what Pistol's French prisoner says. Left alone he says of Pistol:

> I did never know so full a voice issue from so empty a heart. (4.4.63–4)

He's young but he's no fool. He says Nim and Bardolph had ten times more valour than Pistol, adding with the kind of hardness war breeds: 'and they are both hanged' (4.4.68). He then says what he must do:

> I must stay with the lackeys with the luggage of our camp. (4.4.69–70)

We never see him again. The French kill the boys, who are minding the luggage.

The French prisoners

The scene before Fluellen discovers that the French have killed all the boys guarding the luggage, Henry learns two things.

The first is that his brother, York, who asked to lead the vanguard (4.3.150–1) has died along with the Earl of Sussex. The second is that the French have renewed the attack. He gives orders:

> Then every soldier kill his prisoners.
>
> (4.6.37)

Grim comedy is brought to the scene when Pistol cries 'Coup la Gorge' (cut the throat) and suits the action to the words. It's costly business for him; in Act 4, Scene 4 his prisoner has promised him two hundred crowns!

God

When the Herald Mountjoy says to the King, 'The day is yours' (4.81), Henry replies:

> Praised be God and not our strength for it
>
> (4.4.82)

This is consistent with Henry's modesty and his concern that the campaign be morally justified.

After this the scene changes with the completion of the comic business set in action earlier in the play – Henry recognising the courage of Williams and Fluellen beating Pistol.

32.9 France, love and peace

▶ 'Our fertile France' (5.2.37)

Henry V deals with who's in and who's out. Henry unites the nation but finds there's always someone left out. Falstaff is left out when he sets the nation on its path to war. At the end of the play, Burgundy pleads that France won't be excluded:

> Why that the naked, poor, and mangled peace,
> Dear nurse of arts, plenties, and joyful births,
> Should not in this best garden of the world,
> Our fertile France, put up her lovely visage?

> (5.2.34–7)

The peace is sealed by the marriage with Catherine. He makes a pleasingly inept effort to become the lover, and though his professed affection is mixed up with legal arrangements, it's possible to play it as, if not quite a comic ending, then at least as a satisfactory one.

32.10 What do we make of Henry?

▶ 'This star of England' (Epilogue, 6)

Henry V is probably at the moment the most controversial of all Shakespeare's plays. The controversy is centred on the character of the King:

- **is he a noble hero or a calculating politician?**

The debate is intense. Can we admire someone who casts off Falstaff, threatens murder and rape at Harfleur, refuses to save Bardolph, tricks soldiers under disguise and who orders the deaths of the French prisoners?

One way round this is to say that the possibility of seeing Henry in two very different ways – hero and villain – is built into the design of the play. The drama, it can be said, works to give us the possibility of these two contradictory views.

I think when the issue of Henry's moral status is raised, we should remember that Shakespeare doesn't seem very convinced by heroes. *Henry V* might be his way of bringing home to us what a war hero has to do. He might be saying: have you the stomach to admire him?

Exercises

32.1 How does Shakespeare present the horrors and the glories of war in *Henry V*?

32.2 What is your judgement of Henry V?

---

33 Richard III

33.1 The dominance of Richard

▶ 'Famous Plantagenet' (3.7.100)

Many of the scenes in *Richard III* are difficult for audiences because they are long and are about events that took place before the play began. Sometimes it looks as if the characters are talking at unnecessary length about the scrag-ends of history.

And yet in spite of this, *Richard III* is usually a huge hit on stage as well as in the cinema. One reason for this is that it has a startlingly simple plot line – the rise and fall of Richard.

The centrality of Richard

But that alone doesn't make for successful theatre. What makes the play, in spite of all its shortcomings, marvellous to watch is the central character:

- **Richard may be a bad man but he's wonderful theatre**.

Whatever we may feel about his wickedness, we can't separate his depravity from the bubbling entertainment he provides. The play works when he's on the stage. The plot is directed by his purposeful energy, and scenes come memorably to life when he's on stage.

33.2 The fun of scheming

▶ 'Plots have I laid' (1.1.32)

The opening soliloquy

Richard buttonholes the audience with his outrageous honesty. It's hugely funny that someone who's so wicked is open with us; he tells us with a proud relish what he's up to:

> And therefore since I cannot prove a lover
> To entertain these fair well-spoken days,
> I am determined to prove a villain
> And hate the idle pleasures of these days.

(1.1.28–31)

His argument is absurdly comical; it no way follows that if you can't be a lover you have to be a villain, but Richard uses the language of logic – 'therefore since' – as if it's obviously true.

Fun

What comes over is the tremendous fun he's having. This isn't just evil plotting, it's plotting with a merry lilt and, so to speak, a light skip. The fun is there in his language. It has an irrepressibly merry quality. In his first soliloquy, he imagines the young man who's turned from war to love:

> He capers nimbly in a lady's chamber
> To the lascivious pleasing of a lute.

(1.1.12–13)

Though Richard goes on to draw a contrast between such a man and himself, the deft movements and the wit, all enacted in the light sounds of his sprightly verse, are expressive of Richard himself. His verse capers nimbly for us.

Richard and the audience

The effect is interesting and slightly disturbing:

- **the audience is on Richard's side, because he's taken us into his confidence in such an entertaining way.**

In making him so boldly and openly villainous, Shakespeare is asking the audience to respond to him more approvingly than those whom he dupes. We can only agree with him when he says those whom he dupes are 'simple gulls' (1.3.326).

Shakespeare is making two points:

- **those who know themselves are politically successful**

- **in a corrupt world, honesty and self-knowledge can be admired.**

33.3 Richard the role-player

▶ **'canst thou quake and change thy colour' (3.4.1)**

Richard the player

Richard puts this question to Buckingham. No one would ever dream of putting it to Richard; he's a very accomplished actor. At one point, Shakespeare makes him dress up for the part:

Enter Richard, Duke of Gloucester, and Buckingham,
in rotten armour, marvellously ill-favoured.

(3.5.1)

Richard is trying to appear to be a man in danger, so he puts on armour that no one would wear except in an emergency. This is an aspect of his adaptability and versatility:

- **he's successful because he can change from role to role.**

As in the seven ages of man speech from *As You Like It*, in his life he plays many parts.

And he plays them knowingly, always aware he's putting on an act. Because he manipulates the plot, he can be compared to the deputy dramatist figures who appear throughout the plays. The effect of this is both comic and pathetic:

- **most of the characters perform parts set down for them by Richard.**

He becomes a kind of puppet master controlling their movements. This is what makes them pathetic (we might say 'sad' now); they perform his play but they don't know what the outcome of the plot is.

The machiavel

The part he plays all the time is the machiavel – the unscrupulous politician who deceives others for his own ends. Whether he's cheering up his brother or wooing Anne, his aim is to advance himself. Sometimes he does this with an inventiveness that borders on the absurd or even the surreal. In Act 3, Scene 4, for instance, he enters in a very jolly mood, asking the Bishop of Ely to bring him some strawberries! He then exits with Buckingham to return, apparently with a withered arm, which he blames upon Hastings. The rest is one of the most memorable bits of English theatre:

> Thou art a traitor.
> Off with his head.

(3.4.75–6)

Hastings is taken out to the block, aware, too late, that Richard is not to be trusted.

The lover

Having said in his opening soliloquy that his deformity rules him out as a lover, he wins Anne in the second scene, while admitting that he killed her husband and her father. Again, there's a surreal element about the scene; he woos her in the presence of the body of Henry VI!

The wooing is a very agile performance. He flatters her in the manner of a Petrarchan lover, calling her 'divine perfection of a woman' (1.2.75); he's openly sexual in his declarations, claiming that the place that's fit for him is her 'bedchamber' (1.2.111); he claims that her beauty caused the deaths; she's given the chance of killing him and his wordplay is as nimble as Kate and Petruchio's.

The family man

Richard presents himself as brother and uncle.

In both roles he wins trust. Clarence goes off to prison with the promise that Richard will 'deliver' (1.1.116) him, and his son is equally deceived; he refers to Richard as 'my good uncle Gloucester' (2.2.20).

The misunderstood man

Perhaps his most outrageous role is that of the well-intentioned man against whom everyone is prejudiced. His entry in Act 1, Scene 3 is:

> They do me wrong, and I will not endure it!
> Who is it that complains unto the king
> That I, forsooth, am stern, and love them not.

> (1.3.42–5)

When Grey asks whom he's speaking about, he plays the wronged innocent:

> To thee, that hast nor honesty, nor grace.
> When have I injured thee?

> (1.3.55–6)

The role is so absurd, it seems pointless to disagree with him, but this only allows him to play the part of the misunderstood man with more relish.

The moralist

Not only does he play the innocent man, he blends this with that of the moralist.

When Hastings tells him that the King, his brother, is 'sickly, weak and melancholy' (1.1.137), Richard reflects upon the evil life the King has led:

> Now, by Saint John, that news is bad indeed!
> O, he hath kept an evil diet long
> And over-much consumed his royal person.

> (1.1.139–41)

The holy man

From the moralist, it's a short step to the holy man. He directly tells the audience that

> I clothe my naked villainy
> With odd old ends stolen forth of Holy Writ
> And seem a saint, when most I play the devil.

> (1.3.334–6)

The funniest performance of this role is when the people beg him to take the crown. Richard plays the part of the pious man who shuns the world of cares. He parades himself in an attitude of piety, appearing between two clergymen. He sustains the whole scene in this manner, protesting, at one point, that he's 'unfit for state and majesty' (3.7.195). Of course he is; it's double irony; he thinks he is fit yet the play shows he isn't.

33.4 Richard's enemies

▶ 'That foul defacer of God's handiwork' (4.4.51)

It's easy to let our enthusiasm for Richard blind us to what is said about him by some of the other characters. He's attacked in very colourful language:

Thou elvish marked, abortive, rooting hog

(1.3.225)

That bottled spider, that foul bunch-backed toad

(4.4.81)

In one sense, this is a compliment; Richard is so wicked that characters have to be inventive in order to make their condemnation adequate. They show a level of wit; Richard's heraldic symbol was a boar, hence the 'rooting hog'.

But there's a difficulty. Richard has said some of this before; furthermore, he's said it with his characteristic merriment:

> Cheated of feature by dissembling nature,
> Deformed, unfinished, sent before my time
> Into this breathing world scarce half made up –
> And that so lamely and unfashionable
> That dogs bark at me as I halt by them –

(1.1.19–23)

He can see that he looks a mess, yet he says so with jaunty liveliness; we get the feeling he quite enjoys the dogs barking.

Furthermore, he knows he's evil.

33.5 Movement and inactivity

▶ 'Set down, set down' (1.2.1)

Anne says this to the men who are carrying the body of Henry VI. It's a fatal move. They are about to move off again, when Richard appears. By the end of the scene she's promised to marry him.

The placing of this scene so near the beginning of the play helps to give it a symbolic function:

• **those who sit, hesitate or fail to act become victims.**

Richard, by contrast, is always active; part of what it means to call him a villain is the recognition of just how unsettling his energy and vitality are. Before the battle, he says to his troops: 'Come, bustle, bustle' (5.6.19).

33.6 The princes in the Tower

▶ 'The tyrannous and bloody act' (4.1.1)

One way of trying to control a character who's in danger of taking over the play is to make him or her do something exceptionally wicked. That usually restrains audience's interest and sympathy.

The story of Richard that Shakespeare used tells how he murdered the princes in the Tower. Shakespeare builds up to this abomination by showing Buckingham reluctant to do it. The man who is willing is Tyrrell. His brief answer suggests he's a professional:

I will dispatch it straight.

(4.2.83)

When, however, he returns, Shakespeare shows that even this hardened man is shocked:

> Dighton and Forrest, whom I did suborn
> To do this ruthless piece of butchery,
> Albeit they were fleshed villains, bloody dogs,
> Melted with tenderness and mild compassion,
> Wept like two children in their death's sad story.

(4.3.4–8)

The murderers become children like those whom they murder.

The next move Shakespeare makes is that of showing Richard's perverse eagerness to hear the details:

> Come to me, Tyrrell, soon, at after-supper,
> When thou shalt tell the process of their death.

(4.3.31–2)

We have the picture of Richard delaying his supper so he can eat while he hears about the murders. There's something particularly repellent about eating – the way to nourish life – taking place while one hears an account of the unnatural end of a life.

Nevertheless, it's worth noting that the murder of the Princes is reported, not seen. Is he unwilling to hand over his theatrical hero entirely to the moralists?

33.7 Evil and suffering

▶ 'And turns the sun to shade' (1.3.264)

Richard and punishment

The image of the sun is appropriate to royalty. It also suggest inevitability – we can't stop the sun. There's something of this in Richard's place in the history of the Wars of the Roses:

- **he's the punishment for all the evils people have committed.**

This is one of the purposes of the ritual laments in Act 4, Scene 4.

> I had an Edward till a Richard killed him;
> I had a husband, till a Richard killed him

(4.4.40–1)

The formal way of speaking (*anaphora*) reduces the personal note and makes the events referred to part of the unfolding pattern of history; part, that is, of the shadow Richard casts.

Margaret's curses

Richard, in spite of his dazzling ingenuity, can't escape history either. His evil catches up with him.

It's customary to see the play in terms of a pattern of sin and retribution; that's to say, if we do wrong we'll be punished.

Margaret has a part to play in this pattern. She takes on the role of a prophetess in 1.3.185–230. She curses Queen Elizabeth, Rivers, Dorset, Hastings and finally Richard. All her curses come true.

Nightmares

Before the battle, Richard is visited by the ghosts of those he's murdered. His sins are finding him out; he's done wrong and now he's suffering. The pattern of sin and retribution becomes dramatically clear. He's punished England for its sins, and now in the visible form of ghosts his sins return to haunt him. The language is tough; most of them say: 'despair and die' (5.5.81). Despair was the worst spiritual state anyone could fall into, because the one who despairs can no longer believe that he or she will saved.

The audience

We still have to ask a question:

- **what difference does this make to us?**

This is something each person must decide. In coming to a decision, answers to the following two questions are required:

- **How important is the pattern of sin and retribution to the drama?**

- **To what extent does the character of Richard step out of his confining history and appeal to us on the strength of his vitality?**

33.8 England reconciled

▶ **'We will unite the white rose and the red' (5.8.19)**

Richmond's closing speech is made as King:

> England hath long been mad, and scarred herself
>
> (5.8.23)

The purpose of this speech is to wrap up history and with the uniting of the Houses of Lancaster (red) and York (white) look forward to 'smiling plenty' (5.8.34). It's the speech of a politician.

It's not at all like Richard. When he rallied his troops he appealed to their private fears and desires; 'fight these French or they'll have your wives' is a simple summary. What Richmond gave his troops was a diatribe against the one whom he calls 'God's enemy' (5.5.206) and a promise that they'll do well out of the victory. In other words, in their speeches to the troops, Richmond is the politician and Richard isn't.

This is important:

- *Richard III* **isn't an essentially political play.**

Like Macbeth, Richard has no political programme, no understanding of the kind of nation he wants and no vision of the future. Those productions and films that present him as a Hitler figure or another political tyrant are quite wrong. What interests Shakespeare is the deception, the trickery and the relish for evil, not the business of political theory.

33.9 Richard and the stage

▶ 'The bloody dog is dead' (5.8.2)

That is Richmond's verdict on Richard. Is it ours? It's certainly never been the verdict of the millions who've flocked to the theatre to see it. Richard is certainly bloody and he has the energy of a dog, but his wit, his self-knowledge, his enterprising inventiveness and his abounding vitality make him much more than the bad man dismissed by a character who might have turned into Shakespeare's most boring king.

Richard III was probably the fifth play he wrote. Its central character is one of the most powerful he ever created. His power is of two kinds – power in the state and sexual power. He seizes the throne and he seizes Anne. Very early in his career Shakespeare is showing the theatrical potential of his two great themes – love and war.

__ Exercises __

33.1 How helpful is it to interpret *Richard III* in terms of a pattern of sin leading to punishment?

33.2 Why do audiences always respond to Richard?

Glossary

Advantage   The gaining of power over another character or characters. Advantage often comes about through trickery and often consists in knowing more than the character who has been tricked. Characters in disguise are usually at an advantage because other characters don't know that the disguised character is concealing his or her identity. Thus in *The Taming of the Shrew* the disguised Tranio has an advantage over the other suitor, Gremio. (See **Disguise** and **Knowledge.**)

Allegory   A story in which the features – characters, events, settings – correspond directly to the elements in a philosophical, political or religious system. In Shakespeare we can use the term in two ways. Individual scenes can be said to be allegorical; for instance, the garden scene in *Richard II*, in which the gardeners compare their tending of the garden to the neglected garden of England. A play might be interpreted allegorically; for instance, *The Tempest* has been read as an allegory of the artist's imagination or of an ideal state.

Alliteration and assonance   See **Texture**.

Art   Art is whatever we have made, as opposed to nature – that which has come about without our influence. The relative importance of art and nature was debated a lot in Shakespeare's day. Shakespeare clearly enjoyed playing with the riddle of showing the beauty and superiority of nature by using art. The theme is central to *The Winter's Tale*.

Aside   The moment in a drama when a character turns and speaks to the audience. An aside is distinguished from a soliloquy by length (asides are usually short) and by the fact that they occur when other characters are on stage. They can establish a bond between speaker and audience, point out an irony, subvert another character or underline a theme. Asides always remind us of the theatricality of plays. They often occur in comedies but are also present in tragedies. (See **Soliloquy.**)

Attachment/Detachment   These words refer to the way an audience relates to the characters on the stage. Another way of putting it is to talk about emotional distance. Sometimes Shakespeare makes it possible for us to feel very close to a character, while at other times we feel more distant. Comedy tends to work by detaching us; when we feel at a distance, we can enjoy the twists and turns of the plot and the ridiculous things characters get up to. Tragedy usually demands that we feel much closer to what's going on.

Bawdy   Language concerned with sex. The term is usually used of humorous wordplay, but can refer to any sexual matters. Bawdy always refers to the words characters use. Usually, characters play upon double meanings and employ puns.

Blank verse   Unrhymed lines of 10 syllables in which the stress or emphasis falls on the even syllables. In technical terms, it's written in iambic pentameters. Most of Shakespeare is written in blank verse. In the earlier plays, the lines are regular, while in the later ones the verse is freer, paying more attention the rhythms of the speaking voice and the emotional requirements of the action.

Bravado   The self-conscious assurance and gusto with which a tragic figure plays out his or her downfall. There's an element of pride about the way the figure's fate is played out. Hamlet conducts his doomed attempt to revenge his father with an energetic relish that shows he's enjoying playing his role. (See **Hubris** and **Tragedy.**)

Burlesque   Art which treats a serious subject in a light, mocking and often degrading manner. Though they don't intend it, the play performed by the mechanicals in *A Midsummer Night's Dream* ridicules high tragedy. In the *Henry IV* plays, Falstaff's presence in the war scenes shows that the epic subject of warfare can be burlesqued to bring out its ludicrous aspects.

Cadence   The rise and fall of the voice as words move to a close, either at the end of a clause or a sentence. Rising cadences are often associated with hope and enterprise, whereas falling ones express puzzlement, sadness, distress and disappointment. Sometimes, as in Othello's language, the rhythmical rise and fall of the cadences produces an appealing and harmonious verbal 'music'.

Carpe Diem   In Latin this means 'seize the day'. It refers to literature (often poetry) that urges lovers to fulfil their desires, because their time is short. In the song 'It was a lover and his lass' from *As You Like It* there is the line:

And therefore take the present time

(5.1.33)

It can also be felt in the strong preoccupation with the passing of time that's present in *Twelfth Night*.

Character/characterisation   The figures in a drama. Most of Shakespeare's characters represent people, though there are Chorus figures and in *2 Henry IV* a character called Rumour. Sometimes his characters have a small number of distinguishing marks (the servants are often like this), but the usual practice of Shakespeare is to give each character his or her own distinctive ways of speaking. Characters, therefore, are created by their language. Characterisation is the way a character is created – the words, actions and gestures each is given.

Comedy   A play with a plot about the fulfilment of love in which the characters devise schemes (devices or practices) to outwit others (rival lovers or the older generation) and achieve their goal, usually marriage. The plots are often complex, and the audience is intrigued to know how the playwright will bring about a happy ending. Because it's better to define Shakespeare's comedies in plot terms, less emphasis should be placed on laughter. We often do laugh at comedies, but that's not their chief characteristic. (See **Practices.**)

Conceit   An elaborate comparison which is capable of being extended over several lines of verse or, less usually, prose. A conceit allows for a display of ingenuity, and there is pleasure in seeing how the comparison is 'hammered out' (see *Richard II*, 5.5.5). Conceits occur more often in the earlier plays (an example is *Romeo and Juliet*); later in his career, Shakespeare opted for concentrated images.

Convention   A kind of agreement or understanding between audience and playwright that certain pieces of action and stage business will be regarded in a particular way. It's a convention that the stage can represent a series of different places, that time can pass quickly, that characters speak to each other in verse, that characters in disguise are not recognised and that in soliloquies a character always speaks the truth. Conventions are established by custom and though they may be clearly rooted in the realities of everyday living they are not literally true. For instance, it's a convention that someone who's fallen in love at first sight is so distracted that it's difficult for anyone to get through to them. Love is devastating, but not everyone goes about unawares of everything.

Courtesy   The charm and consideration characters show to each other in their language. The term is often coupled with wit and is manifested in compliments, requests, respect for titles and wordplay. We can't enjoy *Much Ado About Nothing* without appreciating the polished and gracious nature of the dialogue.

Cultural icon   A figure (usually in literature) who comes to be recognised as representing in a full and complete way the qualities that he or she embodies and stands for. One of the features of the plays with a historical basis is that the characters sometimes think of themselves and what they do in terms of the cultural icons that they will later become. This is the case with the conspirators in *Julius Caesar* and the lovers in *Troilus and Cressida*.

Dances   Dances occur either as part of the play, as in *Romeo and Juliet* and *Much Ado About Nothing*, or are used to conclude the action of a comedy. When they occur at the end they usually express a renewed society in which the people have been reconciled with each other.

Deception   Leading a character or characters to believe something that is not true. In Shakespeare's plays, particularly the comedies, deception is always done to establish an advantage over another character. Deception often comes about through disguise and misinformation such as Cassius throwing messages through Brutus' window or Maria leaving the letter for Malvolio to find in *Twelfth Night*.

Deputy dramatist   This is a useful term for describing those characters who within a play organise events with the thoroughness and control of a dramatist. In *The Tempest*, Prospero controls each character through what he calls his 'art', and, like a playwright, brings all the plot elements to a fitting climax.

Device   See **Practice**.

Dialogue   The to and fro of conversation on the stage. Usually, characters in dialogue want to achieve something, so there is an emotional pressure in what they say.

Direct self-explanation   Speeches in which a character says something which the audience need to know but which it would not be altogether natural for him or her to say in the dramatic context. There's an element of this in the opening speech of Claudius in *Hamlet*. These speeches are sometimes called exposition.

Disguise   The act of concealing a character's true identity. This gives the disguised character an advantage over others. Usually, he or she can say and hear what would normally be impossible. On the eve of the battle of Agincourt, Henry V could not learn what his soldiers think were he not in disguise. (See **Impersonation**.)

Doubling   The word has two usages. One is when we see two characters sharing some essential characteristics. The opening of *Hamlet* doubles Hamlet and Fortinbras. The other kind of doubling is when the text of a play makes it possible for one player to play two parts. With a bit of clever stage manoeuvering, one actress can play both Hermione and Perdita in *The Winter's Tale*.

Entrance   A character coming on to the stage. In Shakespeare's theatre this would be through the two doors or the curtained – off inner stage or the balcony. Entrances sometimes establish differences; for instances, in the closing scenes of *Julius Caesar* the opposing armies would enter at separate doors.

Exclusion   The separation of a character (usually a central one) from the family or society. This occurs in both comedy and tragedy. Exclusion occurs when a character is deceived, betrayed, distracted by love, mad or the victim of mistaken identity. This usually occurs in the middle sections of the play; it can be described as an ordeal, trial or test. In comedy the exclusion ends with the character being re-admitted into his or her society; tragedy ends with the death of the excluded figure.

Exit   A character leaving the stage. At the end of a scene all those on stage exit. Sometimes, the manner of the exit is important, as in *Twelfth Night* when Malvolio strides off in revengeful anger.

Expectation   The way the audience is led to look forward to what is going to happen. In Shakespeare the audience almost always knows what will happen, though not exactly how it will come about. He only very rarely (*Cymbeline* and *The Winter's Tale*) works by surprise.

Farce Dramatic action that is boisterous and rumbustious. It usually involves characters being beaten. Because the audience is detached, they don't regard the activity in a moral light. Thus we can laugh at the various beatings in *The Taming of the Shrew*. It's sometimes said that in farce, bodies are regarded as machines rather than seen in personal terms.

Flaw One understanding of tragedy is that tragic figures fall because there is a fatal flaw in their make-up that inclines them to evil and brings about their destruction. Thus, it's been said that Hamlet's flaw is thinking too much. It's true that all Shakespeare's tragic figures have faults, but on many occasions the plays emphasise a character's own responsibility for his or her downfall.

Folk We use to word 'folk' to mean associated with or of the people. Folk art (for instance, folk tales) is traditional; they are often passed down through village communities. Folk stories tend to be rambling and, contain coincidences, improbabilities and wonders. *The Winter's Tale* has some features of a folk tale.

Gage An item (usually a glove) used as a challenge to a duel. The challenger casts the item down, and the one challenged indicates his acceptance by picking it up. *Richard II* opens with Bolingbroke challenging Mowbray in this way.

Heroes Usually the central and remarkable figure in a tragedy or history. Conventionally, heroes have qualities common people don't possess or they have qualities we all share but to an unusual degree. Thus a hero is usually courageous, physically brave, determined, trustworthy and enterprising. Other characters regard them with admiration and even with awe. The emphasis we see in Shakespeare is that heroes are still touchingly human; they can be distressed (Hamlet), fearful (Macbeth), foolish (Othello) or reckless (Antony). It looks as if Shakespeare is suspicious of the cult of the heroic. He always wants to show us that these outstanding figures are very like the rest of us. Interestingly, although his plays contain many strong and outstanding women, he never uses the word 'heroine'.

History The term is usually used of the plays Shakespeare wrote about English history, though it can also be used of the Roman plays. History plays often have the following features: they are based on books, the plays give a picture of the nation, they often deal with the troubles of the king or leader, they are concerned with foreign or civil wars, the characters are less impressive than in tragedies and they end not with a sense of finality but with the feeling that a new chapter in the nation's history is beginning.

Hubris The arrogance or pride a character (most often in a tragedy) displays when he or she does something that everyone knows to be wrong. In Shakespeare, hubris has a theatrical edge; those who kill kings (Macbeth) or seek revenge (Hamlet) do so in the knowledge that they are being seen by others (at some points, the others might be the audience), whom, the tragic figure hopes, will be awed and impressed by the audacity of what is being accomplished.

Hyperbole Speech which is linguistically in excess of the subject matter. The word comes from the Greek, where it literally means: 'over the top'. It's used frequently of the high sounding language of lovers, who praise beloveds in outlandish terms. When they are under the influence of the love juice poured into their eyes, the lovers in *A Midsummer Night's Dream* use hyperbolic language in their extravagant praise of their beloved.

Image/imagery Any usage of language that imaginatively appeals to the senses. In Shakespeare's case, the images are usually figurative; that's to say, they involve blending meanings from different contexts. Sometimes these are similes (comparisons made explicit with the use of 'as' or 'like') as in

> And then the moon, like to a silver bow
>
> New bent in heaven
>
> (*A Midsummer Night's Dream*, 1.1.9–10)

or metaphors (speaking of one thing as if it were another):

> to see the sails conceive
>
> And grow big-bellied with the wanton wind
>
> (*A Midsummer Night's Dream*, 2.1.128–9)

A feature of Shakespeare's plays is that the themes and moods of each one are expressed in families of related images; in *Hamlet*, for instance, there are a number of images of disease and sickness.

Impersonation   Impersonation differs from disguise in that whereas disguise seeks to conceal identity, in impersonation one character pretends to be another. In *The Taming of the Shrew*, the Pedant impersonates Vincentio. (See **Disguise**.)

Irony   The gap in meaning between words and the significance of what is being said. Audiences are always aware of ironies, but usually the characters against which the irony works are not. It's often the case in drama that the irony emerges only later in the play; this is commonly called dramatic irony. In *Macbeth*, Duncan's praise of the beautiful situation of Glamis Castle is ironic because the audience can see that what looks so pleasant to him contains a host with a murderous intent. When in her sleepwalking, Lady Macbeth obsessively washes her hands, the audience recognises the dramatic irony of a character who earlier confidently asserted that a little water would clear them of 'this deed'.

Knowledge   The aim of scheming in many of the plays is that characters know more than those against whom they are struggling. This is particularly the case in comedies. Characters who know more than others have more power. Usually at the end of a play, knowledge is shared, when each character recounts what has happened to him or her. (See **Advantage**.)

Masque   An elaborate entertainment, usually consisting of intricately written lyrical verse, songs and dances. They were often gorgeously costumed and the stage effects, made possible by complex machinery, were spectacular. There was little interest in characterisation. The subject matter was often drawn from Greek and Roman myths, and the stories were frequently allegorical and performed to enforce a moral. Prospero's masque in *The Tempest* is presented to the newly betrothed lovers as a lesson in the control of their passions.

Morality play   A type of play popular in the fifteenth and sixteenth centuries in which the plot is simple and the characters represent moral qualities. When characters in Shakespeare approach being the representative embodiment of certain values, we might see in the action a shadow of this older form of drama. For instance, Falstaff is similar to the figure of Riot.

Mythology   Stories of heroes and sometimes gods and goddesses which reveal something about the nature of human experience. Shakespeare used many of the myths found in the Latin poet Ovid's work *Metamorphoses*.

Nature   See **Art**.

Overhearing   The act by which one character hears something (usually advantageous) when the speaker is unaware that he or she is being listened to. At the start of *The Taming of the Shrew*, Lucentio overhears a conversation in which he learns that schoolmasters are the only people who will be allowed to meet the woman he has just fallen in love with. In that knowledge, he adopts the disguise of a schoolmaster.

Parody   A form of humour in which the style of a piece of art is ridiculed by exaggerating its features. When Petruchio woos Kate he parodies conventional petrarchan language. (See **Burlesque** and **Petrarchanism**.)

Passions   The passions are strong feelings such as anger, lust and jealousy. Several of the tragedies (*Othello*, for instance) show characters controlled by these feelings. Hamlet struggles hard against being taken over by the passions.

Pastoral   A genre in which characters are usually shepherds and shepherdesses, who live in an ideal rural landscape in which they woo, sing, dance and look after their flocks. Both *As You Like It* and *The Winter's Tale* develop elements from the pastoral tradition.

Petrarchanism   The most popular picture of what it is like to be in love was derived from the poetry of the fourteenth-century Italian poet, Petrarch. He presented men as falling in love at first sight, praising their beloveds in very elevated terms (the language often had a religious ring), feeling melancholy, looking pale, liking music, writing poetry and lying languidly in the shade of trees. The beloveds were often blonde, had white skin with ruby red lips and rosy cheeks and spoke and moved with the grace of angels. They could be cool and cruel to their ardent admirers. Quite often Shakespeare's young men start to behave in this way when they fall in love. There's often more than a hint that they do this quite deliberately.

Plot   The order of events in which the playwright chooses to relate them to the audience. What matters about plot is the audience's knowledge and awareness of events. The plot can shape what they think and feel. For instance, the second scene of *Richard II* makes us revise our opinion of the King, because in it we learn that he was responsible for the death of the Duke of Gloucester.

Practice   A scheme, ruse, trick, device or ploy implemented by one character or characters in order to gain an advantage. Disguise and over-hearing are both examples. Comic plots are built round practices, but they also appear in tragedies such as *Othello*. One who implements such schemes is called a practiser.

Prose   Prose is language which is not formally written in lines of a given length. Shakespeare gives the common people prose (an example is the crowd in *Julius Caesar*). When characters go mad (Ophelia, for example) they speak in prose even though they normally speak in verse.

Reconciliation   The uniting of people who had been divided. In the late comedies, quarrels, ambitions and irrational feelings divide characters, who through the actions of their children are brought together in forgiveness and acceptance. Thus in *The Winter's Tale* the love of Perdita and Florizel heals the division between the King of Sicilia and the King of Bohemia.

Renewal   The word is useful when describing the hopeful feelings with which comedies end. Renewal comes about through the reconciliation of characters, the marriage of the young and the explanations each character offers about the confusing events he or she has lived through. *As You Like* begins with brothers in opposition; renewal comes about when their friendships are restored.

Rhetoric   The deliberate use of language to impress an audience. In Shakespeare's day, all educated gentlemen were expected to talk rhetorically by changing the standard word orders of sentences, linking words in formal patterns and using repetition. Rhetoric shows a delight in the resources of language. A character such as Richard II delights in patterning his language; his elaborate speeches reveal the poetic aspects of his character.

Rhythm   Most of Shakespeare's verse is written in blank verse (unrhymed iambic pentameters), so the rhythm of his verse is a movement from an unstressed syllable to a stressed one and back again. This is the rhythm that a lot of conversation approximates to, so although his characters don't talk as people ordinarily do, there is a link between everyday speech and the verse his characters speak. When characters are emotionally stirred and intellectually excited, their language becomes convincingly uneven.

Role   The word has at least two uses. It can simply mean a part in a play; we might speak of the role of Juliet. It can also mean the part a character knowingly or unknowingly plays in the plot. For instance, Richard III knowingly plays a number of roles: the lover, the good uncle, the holy man and so on. In *Twelfth Night* Sir Andrew, unknown to him, plays the role of the gull, when he's deceived by Sir Toby.

Romance   The late comedies are often spoken of as romances. Usually a romance plot consists of a series of incidents that are loosely linked. The incidents are sometimes extraordinary (gods often intervene), and the plot often depends upon surprising coincidences. *The Winter's Tale* is close to the conventions of romance.

Soliloquy   A monologue in which one character either addresses the audience directly (a public soliloquy) or speaks to him or herself (private soliloquy). The effect of soliloquy is that the audience is drawn to the characters, either because we are taken into their confidence or we look into their minds. This can be disturbing if, as in the case of Iago, the speaker is evil. The character is usually alone but does not have to be; Macbeth's soliloquy in Act 1, Scene 3 is delivered when other characters are talking amongst themselves.

Stage   The platform upon which a play is performed. Shakespeare's stage was very large, was entered by two doors (and possibly a trap-door), probably had an inner stage and almost certainly an upper balcony. The stage itself thrust into the audience, so although the theatres were large, the players were close to the audience.

Story   The technical meaning is the order of events in which they actually happened (see **Plot**). More loosely, the word can be applied to the original tales that Shakespeare used as the basis of his plays and the incidents characters recount to each other, such as the the long tale Prospero tells Miranda in the second scene of *The Tempest*.

Subversion   The undermining of a character or a convention. It can be used of what one character does to another or of what Shakespeare does when he experiments with conventions. For instance, the problem plays might be seen as subverting the conventions of comedy.

Texture   Texture can be used to talk about the effects of the material aspects of language – their sounds and rhythms. Alliteration (repetition of consonants) and assonance repetition of vowels) create the sound values, which help to form texture. Certain characters (and even whole plays) have distinctive linguistic textures. The textures of *Antony and Cleopatra* are rich and elaborate, whereas *The Tempest* is light and transparent.

Theatricality   The nature of actions performed in a theatre. Quite often Shakespeare draws attention the theatrical aspect of what he is doing. This is done by characters talking about performances in a theatre. When they have killed Caesar, the conspirators imagine their action being performed in a theatre. The effect of this depends upon the theatricality of the moment – it is being performed in a theatre. When art calls attention to itself it is sometimes called reflexive.

Theme   What a play is about. The word is used of the meanings or significances that emerge in the action of the play. Usually, an individual play can be understood as having a group of themes. Themes are present in words (often repeated ones), in images, in actions and in the movement of the plot.

Tragedy   A play which deals with the fall, suffering and death of an outstanding figure. The fall can be presented in social or personal terms. In Shakespeare, a tragic figure falls because he or she knowingly chooses to do wrong and enjoys acting out the downfall in a manner best described as theatrical. (See **Bravado**, **Hero** and **Hubris**.)

Unrequited love   The technical name for love that is not returned. The unrequited lover is often a figure of fun. We smile at Orsino's attempts to play out the role of the man who has little hope of securing the love of Olivia.

Verse   Verse is language organised into lines of a fixed length. Often the lines move with an approximately regular rhythm (see **Rhythm**). Shakespeare used verse for important and high-ranking figures. Its emotional flexibility and potentiality for grand effects makes it suitable for tragic figures and scenes of high tension. Othello speaks in verse most of the time; an exception is when he collapses in a trance. (See **Prose**.)

Vice   A figure from Morality plays who embodied evil. The Vice figure can be seen behind a character such as *Richard III*.

Wit   In Shakespeare the word has two common uses. It can mean the mind or intelligence. It can also mean cleverness with words. Verbal ingenuity is evident in wordplay.

Wooing   The technical name for courtship. It was expected that a young man should woo a young woman, but where this becomes impossible (as in the case of the tongue-tied Orlando in *As You Like It*), the young woman, often through disguise, has to take the lead.

Wordplay   The way in which meanings are generated by the associations of words. In passages of wordplay (such as the wooing scenes in the comedies), the course of the dialogue is shaped more by the associations of the words the characters have used than what we would normally call the 'content'.

Worlds   The word is usually used to refer to the distinctive locations and periods in which the plays are set. Each play has a special atmosphere that is evident in the actions and language of the characters. *Julius Caesar* creates a world in which Rome is moving from being a proud republic to an empire ruled by a single figure. Everything in *The Merchant of Venice* is coloured by commercial pressures and the hostility between Christians and Jews.

Further reading

The texts that I have found useful are: *The Arden Shakespeare* (originally Methuen, now Routledge), Cambridge, Oxford, Penguin and Signet.

The classics of Shakespearean criticism are Dr Johnson (available in Penguin), Coleridge (Everyman) and Hazlitt. A very useful collection of late eighteenth- and early nineteenth century criticism is *The Romantics on Shakespeare*, edited by Jonathan Bate (Penguin). If you want to explore Johnson (still our most stimulating reader of Shakespeare) G. F. Parker's *Johnson on Shakespeare* is rewarding.

Two good books on Shakespeare's stage are Andrew Gurr's *The Shakespearean Stage* and J. L. Styan's *Shakespeare's Stagecraft* (both Cambridge).

The best book on Shakespearean comedy is Northrop Frye's *A Natural Perspective* (Colunbia, available through OUP). In the very good Text and Performance series (Macmillan) Roger Warren's book on *A Midsummer Night's Dream* is stimulating.

A. C. Bradley is still the best on tragedy (*Shakespearean Tragedy* – Macmillan). The best book on Hamlet is *Poison, Play and Duel* by Nigel Alexander/Routledge. *The Lost Garden* by John Wilders (Macmillan) is very good on the histories. The best book on an individual history is Gary Wells's edition of *Henry V* in the Oxford Shakespeare series.

The following are interesting and thought-provoking studies: Graham Bradshaw's *Shakespeare's Scepticism* (Harvester) and *Misrepresentations* (Cornell); Juliet Dusinberre's *Shakespeare and the Nature of Women* (Macmillan); Howard Mills' *Working with Shakespeare* (Harvester) and A. D. Nuttall's *A New Mimesis* (Methuen).

Not all of these books are in print, so a visit to a library might be necessary!

Index of plays

General index

absolutes 291
acting, style of 84
action 66–8, 168, 262, 315, 342, 346, 355
actors, actresses 66–8, 281, 336
acts and scenes 50
adultery 18, 77, 316–19
advantage 97, 99, 101–2, 385
ambiguity 17, 22, 246, 273, 316
ambition 23, 67, 187, 261, 269, 279–80, 305
anaphora 76–7, 382
anticipation 56–7, 230
appetite 168–9
Aristotle 110–11, 225
Arsenal 301
art 82, 187–8, 190–1, 206, 222–3, 243, 342, 385
art and nature 61, 65, 135–9, 197–9, 200, 230, 244, 389
aside 81, 385
assassination 48, 310, 313–14
atmosphere 59–62, 274–5
audience 17, 18, 38, 42, 48–9, 54–6, 64–6, 70–1, 81, 95, 101–2, 129, 140, 142, 221–5, 240, 244, 248–9, 323, 348, 378, 383
authority figures 290, 306

balance 82, 172, 230
balcony 83
bar and impediment 92–3, 97, 107–8, 144, 154
battle 19, 56, 75, 276, 298, 315, 340, 372–6
Battle of the Somme 19
Battle of Waterloo 19
bawdy 79, 125, 170, 230, 372–3, 385
bed-trick 96, 162, 178–9
beginning 51–2, 56, 90–1, 164, 235, 316, 340
beloved, the 34–5, 134, 229–30
Bible, The 134, 177, 352
Blake, William 185
blank verse 69–70, 115–16, 385
blinding, blindness 57, 265
blood 277, 280
boasting soldier 41
bowls 112–13
Bradley, A. C. 252
bravado 219–20, 323, 386

brothers 5, 32, 187, 265–7, 372–2, 375
burlesque 358, 386

cadence 16, 44, 72, 137, 139, 257, 284, 386
catastrophe 56
categories 159, 213
catharsis 225
change 5, 53, 68–9, 90, 111, 121–2, 146, 156, 302, 309–12, 360
changeability 313, 321, 341–2
character 25–44, 133–5, 142–4, 150, 153–4, 164–6, 173–5, 175–6, 193–4, 202–3, 205–6, 222, 261, 290, 299–300, 305–13, 315–16, 336–9, 369, 377–84, 386
  stock 39–41, 43, 90, 102, 108
characterisation 38, 133–4, 386
children 32–3
chorus figures 30, 65–6, 80, 83, 331, 367–8
Christ 269, 348
Christian theology 269
Church of England 129
Church of Rome 129
Cinderella 32
class 26, 70, 152
classical 200, 304
clever servants 39
clown 40
coincidence 184
Coleridge, Samuel 252, 341
colonialism 201–2
comedy 8–9, 38, 49, 54–5, 58–9, 61–2, 70, 89–106, 107–14, 115–22, 123–31, 132–40, 141–7, 148–56, 159–79, 183–9, 190–9, 200–10, 214, 223–4, 227, 237–8, 245, 317, 337–8, 353–4, 371, 375, 386
comic release 102
compression 74–5
compromise 333–4
comradeship 19, 298
conceit 73, 125, 343, 386
confidence 143–4
conflict 23, 33
confusion 90, 100
continuity 81–2, 190–1, 331

identity 53, 98–100, 102, 110, 150, 167
illegitimacy 57, 267
imagery 52, 57, 73–5, 77, 119, 136, 173, 186–7,
    263, 269–70, 280, 283, 194–5, 315, 335, 388
imagination 65–6, 119–21, 270, 277–8, 282, 356
impediment *see* bar
impersonation 96–7, 389
inclusion and exclusion 54, 104, 387
Induction 110
inevitability 223–4
ingenious priest 39
ingratitude 4, 261–2
intelligence 173
interpretation 200, 202
irony 30, 99, 240, 259, 299, 331, 348, 373, 389
    dramatic 56, 296
isolation 102, 223–4, 348

jealous, jealousy 256
Jeeves and Wooster 39
Johnson, Samuel 105, 213, 217–18
journeys 90–1, 112, 184
judgement 55, 367–8
judging oneself 220, 258–9, 308–9

killing the king 29, 43, 274–80, 286
kings 5, 19, 27–9, 33, 59, 329–39, 340–50, 351–9,
    360–6, 367–84
kneeling 302–3
knowledge 48, 55, 101–2, 107–8, 238, 249–50, 389
Kundera, Milan, *The Book of Laughter and
    Forgetting* 241

language 37, 43–4, 63–82, 144–5, 153–4, 167,
    176, 187, 190, 194–5, 198–9, 203, 228–9,
    263–4, 266, 275–6, 279, 304, 307, 310–13,
    320–1, 333, 340, 342–4, 353, 370
language, figurative 73, 257
laughter 13, 98–9, 118–19, 121, 257–8, 357
law 92, 173–4
Leavis, F. R. 258
legitimacy 57, 348
limits 214, 268
linking, links 190–1, 262, 338
Lord and Lady of Misrule 95
lost, finding the 5, 54, 103, 186
love 6–16, 43, 46, 52, 57, 90–4, 103–4, 109–11,
    118–19, 123–5, 132, 139, 142–6, 151–2, 160–1,
    167, 190, 227, 229–34, 256–7, 263–4, 267,
    171–2, 317–18, 376, 391
    at first sight 8, 9, 13
lover, bashful 32, 92, 98
lovers 5, 10–13, 26, 33–5, 39, 64, 18–9, 266–7, 379
loyalty 57, 264, 332–3

machiavel 30–1, 40, 379
Machiavelli, N. 30, 266, 333
madness 51, 54, 71, 151–2, 184, 191–2, 242, 265
Madonna 121
malapropism 136
malcontent 40, 307
marriage 15, 33, 38, 55, 90, 103, 109, 114, 116,
    120, 131, 135–6, 176, 178–9, 192

Mars 317–18, 380
masque 206–7, 389
meaning 66, 72, 76–7, 214
measurement 271–2
men 13, 35, 91, 95, 118
metaphor 9, 73
middle scenes 52–3
mirroring 56–7, 63
misinformation 65
mistaken identity 99–100
mistress 34–5
misunderstood man 380
mood 67, 139–40, 160–1
moon 17, 356
morality 218, 236, 275–6, 291, 368, 374–5
    play 389
mothers 5
    and sons 18, 31–2, 42, 61, 244–5
motifs 339
motive 252, 336
movement 381
music 11, 149
myth, mythology 117, 148, 187, 289, 389

narrators 80
nation 7, 27, 185, 215
nature 5, 185–7, 197–8, 215, 267–70
nemesis 219, 323–4
newcomers 148
nightmares 217, 383
non-conformist churches 151
North, the, Northerners 330

oaths 333
old and young, the xviii, 23, 90, 93, 197, 244
old age 14–15, 155, 185–6, 317, 361–2
Olivier, Laurence 371, 374
opposition 221
order 215–16
overhearing 100, 250, 389
overlooking 64–5, 100, 166–7
Ovid: *The Art to Love, Metamorphoses* 111, 389

pace 27
parody 121, 358, 389
parting 17–18, 166, 232
passing of time 154–6
passion 226–7, 230–1
passions, the 169, 225, 292–4, 390
passivity 224, 248–9
pastoral 141, 390
personification 73
Petrarch, Petrarchanism 10–11, 34–5, 229–30,
    390
philosophy 119, 187, 292–3
pity 224–5, 278
pivot 51, 53
players 64, 67, 237, 378–9
plot 9, 31, 42, 45–59, 89–104, 107–11, 115–17,
    119–20, 126, 129–31, 135–7, 148–9, 177,
    184–5, 190–2, 237–8, 242, 262, 264–5, 274,
    306–7, 338–9, 377
poetry 277, 315, 344

variety 25, 70, 72–3, 81–2, 146, 262, 341
vast 213–14
Venice 9, 125
verse 69–73, 391
vice 391
viewpoint 18, 120
villain 64, 127, 221
vulnerability 25–8

waking up 119
wall paintings 373
war 6–7, 16–23, 79, 139, 160, 164–71, 227, 296–99, 317–18, 330, 337–8, 351, 358–9, 367–76

warrior culture 276–7, 300, 336
Western thought 204
wilfulness 261, 268
wit 135–6, 143, 153–4, 193, 313, 392
women 13, 35, 91, 95, 134–5, 142, 193
wonder 11, 55, 203, 207, 253–4, 257, 316
wooing 94, 126, 135–7, 379, 392
wordplay 62, 77–9, 108, 119, 136, 340, 392
worlds 51, 59–62, 183–9, 392

young in love, the 8, 90
youthfulness 93, 174, 226–7, 234